Any thing you Dont be Go to librara HAVE them Google it,

How Reasonable Americans Could Support Trump

Also by Brian Rees

Heal Your Self, Heal Your World:
Turn Illness and Suffering into Health and Peace
through Scientifically Proven Methods.
(1997. Available from amazon.com)

Terrorism, Retaliation, and Victory:
Awaken the Soul of America to
Defeat Terrorism without Casualties
(2003. Available from Xlibris.com)

Detained:
Emails and Musings from a Spiritual
Journey through Abu Ghraib, Kandahar,
and other Garden Spots.
(2015. Available from amazon.com)

How Reasonable Americans Could Support Trump

Helping liberals understand

the MAGAverse,

and whatever comes next

Brian Rees

Manu Publishing

eBook: ISBN 978-09652319-0-9
hardcover: ISBN 978-09652319-1-6
paperback: ISBN 978-09652319-2-3

Printed in the United States of America

Manu Publishing
1890 Diablo Drive
San Luis Obispo, California 93405

Cover photo from Shutterstock
Cover designed with Canva and Amazon Cover Creator

To Jay and Dave,
reasonable men,
best of friends,
with legacies of righteousness

TABLE OF CONTENTS

Introduction — Why This Book

We had fed the heart on fantasies,
    The heart's grown brutal from the fare,
More substance in our enmities
    Than in our love....

- - From *Meditations in Time of Civil War*
William Butler Yeats

Thanksgiving dinner, 2015

There was still more than a year left in the Obama administration. We were chewing deliberately enough that a brief silence had fallen over the table. In either an attempt to investigate the thoughts of my family members, or in an utter lapse in judgment, I paused over my mashed potatoes and said one syllable: "Trump."

Wow.

I had no idea that feelings were already strong. I didn't have any particular feelings about him then, I hadn't given him much thought. I knew he was a New York billionaire playboy, mostly liberal real estate mogul, friendly with the Clintons, now running for president as a Republican. I was vaguely curious, as a great fuss seemed to be developing.

My siblings had strong ideas, some for, some against. Maybe it would have happened anyway, but over the six years since then, our emails to each other have been full of Trump, and attendance at family holiday gatherings has been spotty.

Do you remember the first time you interacted like this with a friend or relative on the opposite side of the Trump divide? I have tried to engage, then sometimes had to ignore people who have been close friends for years, then unfollow, then unfriend, then block because of toxic comments they've made and insults they've directed toward me. I'm sure I'm not alone in this. My family and friends are not exempt from the forces tearing at the fabric of our nation.

But sometimes, I have been able to find common ground and build on it. I believe anyone can.

Why should anyone want to read this book?

In our personal lives, we bump up against friends and family with very different ideas. It would help if we had tools and practices we could employ to connect or reconnect with them.

In our public/political lives, most of us want to find a way forward that gets our nation moving on the right track. We see that our country is in trouble and we wish we could have some influence in providing real solutions.

If you're a never-Trumper, maybe you'd like to understand better your Trump-supporting relative at Thanksgiving dinner. Over 74 million of your fellow Americans voted for Trump in 2020. Despite all the things about him that make you crazy, they decided, 'that's my guy,' and filled in the dot or pulled the lever. Why did they? How could they? Is there any way to bridge the gap between you and them?

And if you're a Trump supporter, you might be tired of having "friends" beat you up by calling you a racist idiot; you could give them this book to help explain that there's more to the story. You might even begin to understand better what it was about Trump that you liked, and that some of those things may even be of interest to your liberal friends and relatives.

In either case, maybe this book can start a conversation that might just heal some of the rifts between us.

When I started to write this book, the impeachment trial (the first one) had recently ended and the pandemic was killing tens of thousands of Americans. As I wrote, the campaigns got underway and Trump was admitted to Walter Reed with COVID-19. The November 2020 elections finally happened and were called out as being fraudulent. One Wednesday, some people stormed the US Capitol, and some people died; the next Wednesday, impeachment; and the next Wednesday, a new President.

Trump lost, and there are some unhappy campers in this country.

As I'm finishing this book, Trump and many of his supporters still believe he won, and that the election was stolen from him. That's worth repeating: millions of Americans believe that our American democracy doesn't work, that the election was stolen, that the events of January 6th were justified and that usurpers are in power in the United States of America in 2021. Many of them believe that unless they take steps to make sure the next election isn't stolen, they'll lose the country forever.

Many liberals see the events of January 6th as a training exercise for the next coup attempt. They see that state legislatures are empowering themselves to overturn election results, regard those steps as precursors to the successful theft of the next election, and fear that liberal democracy will be lost to our country forever.

We are deeply divided, and both camps believe that the very existence of our nation is at stake.

If you lived through the Trump Administration, and through its ending, you may be wondering: what has happened to my country? How did we come to this?

Despite the election results, despite our differences, despite how raw many Americans feel, despite all of the rancor and venom we see our countrymen directing at each other, we will continue to live together on this continent.

This book has three parts. The first explores our own natures, attributes with which we're born that inform much of our moral and political perspective, and how these are channeled. We'll see why a lot of what we tend to do to influence others is doomed to fail.

The second part examines why the things Trump said and did resonated so robustly with his supporters. It's not that hard to understand, and even if you're a never-Trumper you should be able to see Trumpism in a different light. We'll explore a number of issues and see if there might be common ground between the Trump and never-Trump viewpoints.

The third addresses what we can do, to improve ourselves, to enhance our relationships with friends and relatives with apparently polar opposite views, and even to impact our nation's political life.

Instead of our primary focus being on fighting each other, we will all be better off if we can understand, and perhaps even appreciate, each other. It's worth reading a book if it can help us re-create a United States where we hear and value our countrymen.

Part I Why We're This Way

Chapter 1

Trump Supporters

What's My Tribe?

These days, many people want to know someone's tribe before deciding whether to listen to anything he or she has to say. Fair enough, but I'm all over the place; somewhere in this book you might decide which team(s) I'm on.

I'm male, white, a little bit old (chronologically... young at heart); I own guns; I'm a regular church-goer (well, not in these pandemic days); I've been married, once, to the same woman for close to 38 years as of late 2021; and I stand for the flag and our anthem. Part of my childhood was spent in Bakersfield, musical home of Buck Owens and Merle Haggard. I lived in Louisiana for six years. For almost eleven years I worked in state prisons. All of that is enough for some to think that I'm in the tribe of knuckle-dragging barbarian deplorables.

On the other hand, I'm a physician, I have an MD and two Master's degrees, I'm from California and I meditate twice a day every day. I've published in peer-reviewed scientific journals, my wife drives a Prius and we have solar panels on our roof. I'm mostly vegetarian, I used to be a surfer dude and I'm writing my fourth book. That's enough to put me in the coastal elite libtard snowflake tribe.

I talk to my dog, a lot. That can go either way.

There's another tribe, one with which I do self-identify:

I'm a veteran. And that's another reason I wrote this book.

I loved the Army. I love soldiers. I retired after 38 years of commissioned service, active and reserve, eight years in command assignments, five deployments to Iraq and Afghanistan, so I saw the good, the bad and the ugly. The Army wasn't perfect, no. But still, I loved it, for many reasons. It was as close to the ideal American meritocracy as I've ever experienced. We weren't and aren't great because we were diverse, but because of our commonalities. I loved the Army because, despite our differences, as a general rule we shared certain values. The fact that we could share community and values despite our diversity told us that our values were righteous and transcended our varied and unique individualities. Our shared values cemented an unspoken bond, a recognition that our racial and religious and gender distinctions were trivial compared to the strength of those shared values, a willingness to work together toward common goals, and in its most extreme, a willingness to die for each other.

Here's some Truth for you: if you're one of my liberal friends, there are Trump supporters who would die for you. They would die to protect your children from harm. There are people who would have been Trump supporters had they lived long enough, but they never got the chance, because they put their lives on the line, and they gave their lives for you. I'm not going to tell you "So show some respect," but I will ask you just to sit with that recognition for a moment, and then you decide if such people are worthy of respect.

And for my Trump supporting friends, the same applies. There are liberals who would die for you and for your right to be free; I've known them, I've served with them, and I've prayed over them after they've fallen. I suggest that if/when you go on social media and bemoan that all leftist Demonrats are communist anarchists who hate their country and are trying to destroy America, you're not correct, and you're not helping. (Well you may be helping Putin divide us, but you're not helping America.) So, stop, please.

Americans don't seem to recognize, much less treasure, our shared values. We seem to hate each other, or at least all too commonly mistrust and disrespect each other. Even veterans can seem to be turning against each other, and that breaks my heart.

I believe there is evidence to support the following six points. Perhaps by the end of this book, you'll believe them too.

1. If you're a never-Trump liberal, you won't end Trumpism by disapproving of or fighting his supporters.

If it's possible to change the minds and behaviors of Trump supporters, it is not through refuting their claims, disregarding their opinions or 'winning' arguments with them, but rather by connecting with them. And if you work at connecting, you may find that your mind changes a little bit too. That may be a good thing.

2. Liberals have failed epically in relating to their fellow citizens who have supported Trump.

Democrats, liberals, progressives, and liberal media mostly regard Trump supporters as fundamentally flawed; sometimes stupid, sometimes racist, but always flawed. But the way to interpret the beliefs and positions of Trump supporters is to recognize that most conservatives are similar to you and share many of the same values.

3. Plenty of reasonable people voted for Trump.

I know it may not seem that way to my liberal friends. And I'll be more specific about my definition of "reasonable" in the first couple of chapters. When it comes to the role of our reason, we have a lot to talk about.

Over 74 million Americans voted for Trump in the 2020 election. They'd lived through nearly four years of the Trump administration, just as progressives had. They considered their options and contemplated their futures. And then they stepped into the booth and marked their ballots for Donald J. Trump.

Liberals see people screaming at school board meetings, or at Trump rallies with chants of 'Build the wall' and 'Lock her up' and 'Send them back,' and think, 'who in God's name *are* these people?' But those are rallies, with people who select themselves to go to rallies and meetings, with some mob behavior added on. I'm not even sure half the people chanting believe what they're chanting in their sober moments. But all that aside, yes, there are plenty of racists and misogynists in our country, and plenty of them support Trump. For that matter, there have been plenty of intolerant people with looney ideas who supported Obama and Clinton and Biden.

Liberals see people, including lots of men in camo with long guns, protesting about the election being stolen, calling into question the electoral process and the peaceful transition of power, see people storming the United States Capitol, and it seems like the gulf between Two Americas is beyond bridging.

But that's not most of us.

In May 2016 (before Trump's electoral victory), conservative radio host Charlie Sykes said "I've cautioned my fellow conservatives, you embrace Donald Trump, you embrace it all. You embrace every slur, every insult, every outrage, every falsehood. You're going to spend the next six months defending, rationalizing, evading all that. And afterwards, you come back to women, to minorities, to young people and say, that wasn't us. That's not what we're about. The reality is, if you support him to be president of the United States, that it is who you are, and you own it." (1) [Those tiny superscripts used to denote references are too darn small. I'll use full-size numerals in parentheses. You're welcome.]

But for reasons we will be exploring, many if not most Trump supporters do not share that opinion. Many Trump supporters have very specific and selective reasons for supporting him.

Rather than embracing all of Trump's excesses, I believe that:

4. Most of Trump's supporters are neither racists nor misogynists (nor homophobes nor Islamaphobes, etc.).

(Well, not significantly more than the rest of us. We're all kinda racist... more on that later.)

And they're not going to disappear.

If you're a liberal, the problems you see in the Trump presidency will not disappear either, just because Trump has lost the election and left the White House. Whatever his faults, Trump didn't create our divisions, and his removal from office doesn't resolve them.

After the 2020 election results, millions of Americans who voted for Trump feel awful, like their ideas have been disregarded, like the country is going to hell, just as a different set of people felt the day after the election in 2016.

Nobody feels good when your guy or gal loses an election. But our current polarization is unhealthy and unnecessary. After the campaign and after the election and after the inauguration, and after the impeachment trial and January 6th, our wounds are still raw and our differences stark. Each half of the country thinks the other has lost its mind.

It may or may not be that Trump has committed crimes; certainly investigations have not ended since he's left office. For all of us, 2021 and 2022 and beyond won't be a picnic. People will disagree: some will insist upon accountability, others will say prosecutions are divisive. If he is indicted, tried, or incarcerated, the risk of greater polarization grows. You can be sure that outraged cries of hypocrisy and tyranny will fall like rain. 'We chanted lock her up, but you are actually locking him up! You complained of the Barr Department of Justice being politicized, but are now cheering on the actual prosecutions of your political enemies!'

Even if Trump disappears from public view, someone will claim to be his heir, will want his voters and will do whatever is necessary to get them. That may well involve polarization and division.

But folks, we're stuck with each other. We will either make this work, or not. And if we make it work, we can do that well, or poorly.

It would be best if we respected and appreciated each other. At least, we should tolerate each other. And respect and tolerance are fed by understanding.

The promotion of understanding is the purpose of this book.

My secondary thesis then:

5. There were good reasons for people to vote for Trump, reasons that liberals should be able to understand and appreciate.

This time in our country is not unique in having polarization and division. They are forces that demagogues exploit, forces that malign foreign actors amplify, forces I believe we must resist.

Many Trump supporters share the same concerns as liberals about the tweets and the untruths. I believe liberals and Trumpists are more alike than different, that they believe in the same basic things and want many of the same healthy prosperous outcomes for the country. When we differ greatly on policy, that's OK, because arguments over policy are the meat and potatoes of politics. If we can just get past believing the other guy is out to ruin the country, so that we might even begin to make our way to policy arguments, we'll be in much better shape.

6. We can make this work.

But at the moment, we're stuck. We're stuck in a weird feedback loop of polarization. People, institutions, politicians, the media, all have become more polarized, and have adapted to that polarization by becoming even more polarized. There are reasons for all this polarization, and we can hope that the truth will set you free... if you want it to.

Here's some of what this book is and isn't about.

It is neither an attack upon, nor a defense of, Trump or his behavior (until the end maybe).

It's really not about Trump; it's about Americans.

It is not a defense of the most extreme characters who support Trump. This book's title is 'How reasonable Americans could support Trump;' that doesn't include unreasonable people. So, if you believe Democratic leadership is running satanic pedophile pizza parlors, if you're in QAnon waiting for JFK Jr. to reappear as Trump's running 2024 mate, if you're borderline delusional, or if you think it's a good idea to kidnap a governor to precipitate the 'boogaloo' civil war, sorry, I can't advocate for you.

Fortunately for all of us, despite the ability of a terrorist mob to get inside the Capitol and commit violence and mayhem, I don't believe there are *that* many on the fringe; and while those on the extreme may find comfort in Trump, most Trump supporters are not to be found on the extreme fringe. I hope I'm right about that.

This book is not a fact-check extravaganza. There may be some of that, but not much.

Often I'll write opposing points of view. It will get old if I keep saying "Progressives think this" or "Trump supporters think that", so often I'll just say the argument without qualification. That doesn't mean that I personally agree with it (...but it doesn't mean I don't, either).

I may shorten "Trump supporters" to "Trumpers" (or "Trumpists," and "Trumpism"). It's just so you'll know what I mean; I'm not trying to insult anyone. There is overlap among Trump supporters, Republicans, and conservatives, but they are not identical. (And politicians are a whole other bag.)

For purposes of this book, I'm going to assume that most 'liberals' and 'progressives' are never-Trumpers.

While I'm going to dive a bit into the policy ramifications of the reasons people support Trump, and while I may comment to some degree about whether or when the things Trump said were fulfilled by his actions, a full polemic is the job of someone else's book.

This book is about why reasonable people could hear Trump and say, 'Yeah, that's my guy.' If you're liberal you probably disagree, you may believe that 'Trump is a con man and nothing he's said has any value because he lies all the time', and 'How could anyone believe that?' and 'But then look what he did!'; hey, I get it. But that's not this book. This book is about how so many of your fellow Americans listened to Trump, and based upon their lived experience, they felt deep inside: 'He gets me. This is the best guy to advance my interests. I'm going to vote for him.'

They felt it in their gut, even long before their minds weighed in... more on that later.

I hope you're curious enough about that to try to discover why they felt that way.

If this book can give someone pause before jumping to the conclusion that people with differing political views must be idiots who hate America, I'll have hit my target.

Let's start by considering why we believe such things about each other.

Chapter 2

We are selfish, and we are "groupish"

There was a time when my place in my group was threatened, and deservedly so. I screwed up, twice, in rapid succession. These events took place almost 40 years ago, but my face is flushing with embarrassment as I write this!

After medical school, you go to a year-long internship which typically turns into a multiyear residency. I did my internship and residency in family medicine in the Army, three years, in Hawaii. After residency, you get sent somewhere to go do your job. I was assigned to Fort Polk Louisiana. From Hawaii to rural western Louisiana, yeah, that was a bucket of cold water... long story for another day. Buy me a beer and we'll talk.

So I showed up at the hospital at Fort Polk in 1982, not knowing a soul. Almost everybody in the army moves every two or three years, so showing up someplace new is the norm. When you're the FNG (the... new guy), the thing to do is put your best foot forward and keep it there. But, that's not what happened.

I worked in the family practice clinic and in the hospital. Fort Polk was the home of the 5th Infantry Division (Mechanized), lots of young soldiers, with lots of young wives. We delivered lots of babies. One afternoon I saw a young woman (who was not in labor) in our outpatient clinic for a routine prenatal visit late in her pregnancy. I discovered she was pre-eclamptic, blood pressure up a bit, spilling some protein in her urine, brisk reflexes; pre-eclampsia puts a woman at risk for seizures and means you get admitted to the hospital and put at bedrest and given medicine if needed. But, she felt fine, and she really wanted to go home to take care of things rather than go into the hospital. I was busy (and maybe a little work averse) and I had no authority to make her go into the hospital against her will, so I negotiated a promise from her that she would stay in bed, and I would see her back the next day, and unless she was as normal as could be she should expect that I would put her in the hospital. That's a little fast and loose, but I figured things would probably be OK. I was making her happy by letting her go home, and I'd see her tomorrow (and no one would know, so what the heck).

Well, she went home... and then went into labor. She came back to the hospital; one of my colleagues was on call and admitted her, noted she was pre-eclamptic, and saw in my note in her chart that I had seen her just hours before and had sent her home. That's a screw-up. I should have pushed harder and admitted her in the light of day, not leave a potentially dangerous loose end dangling out there for my colleague to have to clean up in the middle of the night. She ended up doing fine but that was just by the grace of God, not by my judgement.

There are not many secrets in a small medical department. I had some damage control to do and I applied myself to it, and had rehabilitated my reputation. Until....

We had four different call schedules: 1) the doctor on call for the family practice (FP) department (admitting sick people to, and responding to problems in, the hospital, and we covered for the obstetric department, delivering almost all the babies), 2) that person's back-up in case s/he got swamped, 3) the FP doctor back-up for the emergency room if the ER got swamped, and 4) that person's back-up, just in case. #1 was real, you stayed in the hospital and often were up all night; #2 was rarely called at night but helped #1 make rounds on inpatients on weekends; #3 was even more rarely called, maybe every couple months, and #4 was just a nuisance, maybe twice a year if things were crazy. Confusing? Damn right. The competing schedules were a mess, and before smart phones and Google calendar it was easy to lose track of all the potential obligations. I wanted to go out of town one weekend and asked a colleague to swap back-up call (#2) with me. At my previous assignment, if you swapped, you informed all stakeholders of the shift you were *assuming,* not the shift you were giving up, (to avoid person A declaring person B will be doing a shift), so I thought he would tell everyone. He thought I would. So, no one did. Oops.

Saturday morning I get a beep from the guy on #1 call, 'where are you?' We worked it out, I did all the work the next day, but the damage was done.

Medicine is similar to the military. You're supposed to be strong and reliable, not weak. The mission is most important; you must do the work until the job is done. And you must exercise good judgement; mistakes can get people killed. I had internalized all of that. I was a rock. I was solid, I did the work. My view of myself was in part a function of being seen as professional. But after these mistakes, every day I had to anticipate that my colleagues thought (with good reason... ouch!) that I was an unreliable screw-up, and for a young physician to have a reputation with his peers as an unreliable screw-up is a fate worse than death.

Reputation is important. More about that later.

We are programmed to thrive and survive in groups.

There was nothing to do but keep my head down and quadruple my efforts by working hard and being meticulous. Eventually we all got to know each other, and after some weeks/months when they started ribbing me about my earlier mistakes and disclosing what a jerk they thought I was 'back then,' I knew I'd gotten over the hump. But for a while there I felt I was exiled from My Group, and it was awful.

Former US Surgeon General Vivek Murthy wrote:

> From a biological perspective, we evolved to be social creatures. Long ago, our ability to build relationships of trust and cooperation helped increase our chances of having a stable food supply and more consistent protection from predators. Over thousands of years, the value of social connection has become baked into our nervous system such that the absence of such a protective force creates a stress state in the body. Loneliness causes stress, and long-term or chronic stress leads to more frequent elevations of a key stress hormone, cortisol. It is also linked to higher levels of inflammation in the body. This in turn damages blood vessels and other tissues, increasing the risk of heart disease, diabetes, joint disease, depression, obesity, and premature death. Chronic stress can also hijack your brain's prefrontal cortex, which governs decision making, planning, emotional regulation, analysis, and abstract thinking. (1)

We are selfish obviously, and we also are drawn to be in groups. As Jonathan Haidt, whom I'll cite a lot more in the next chapter (and who I believe coined the word "groupish"), observes, "We are not saints, but we are sometimes good team players." (2)

We evolved to exist in groups. If our group did well, we survived and thrived. If our group was defeated, we were at risk not just of death, but of annihilation, our children enslaved or killed, our women taken to contribute to the perpetuation of our enemy's DNA.

Even though I was not at risk of death, no wonder I felt disturbed by even the weak "exile" I described above. To be exiled from one's group can recapitulate that threat of annihilation.

We will favor and do work for our group (our tribe, our team), to win against others.

We understand the advantages of our group outcompeting another group. If it's a 'zero sum game,' that is, if there's a finite amount of water or food or land or potential mates, and if those other guys get it then we don't, then of course, I want my group to win, and there is a direct benefit to me if 'we' win.

But there's more to it than just the recognized *in-group bias*.

To hate like this is to be happy forever.
-- Will Blythe

We will oppose the other group even if it means our group suffers.

It goes beyond just being drawn to being in a group and being willing to help our group win. Winning is *positional*: we don't just want to win; we want the other group to lose. We want to be in a better *position* relative to the other group or person. We often promote our group's interests, in the face of competition with other groups, even at some expense to our group and even to our individual selves.

In 2006 Will Blythe wrote a book by that title above, *To Hate Like This Is to Be Happy Forever*. It was about basketball, specifically about the rivalry between the fans of the college basketball teams of Duke and the University of North Carolina. As one reader noted, the book explores how that rivalry had given shape and meaning to the author's life at moments when little else did. (3) Blythe wrote, "The living and dying through one's allegiance to either Duke or Carolina is no less real for being enacted through play and fandom."

That may seem silly. But sport is a microcosm of life; if you're a sports fan, you understand.

My team is the Los Angeles Lakers. As I write this in 2020, the pandemic rages, the NBA Finals are taking place in the Bubble in Orlando, and the Lakers are favored to win. Life is good, because it's great to be a Laker fan. It has been the best of times, and the worst of times.

Bear with me for a minute, there's a purpose to this story.

I've been a Laker fan since the 1960s. In the 60s, the Lakers had a great team, with two of the greatest players ever: Jerry West, and Elgin Baylor. They were consistently great, and consistently one of the best teams in the National Basketball Association (NBA), one of the best teams in the world! They made it to the NBA Finals almost every year (and have been to the Finals more than any other team). And in the 60s they were a great team yes, but consistently, eternally, excruciatingly, the second-best team on Earth, second to the Boston Celtics. The Celtics tortured me. As I grew into puberty and established some of my various identities, the Lakers each spring would fall just short of a championship.

Finally in 1968-69, the Lakers had acquired Wilt Chamberlain to counterbalance Bill Russell, again made it to the Finals and had the final and deciding game of the championship series on their home court. Against the Celtics. I don't have to tell you what happened. I remain scarred.

Don't feel too sorry for me. The Lakers had arguably the best team ever when they won their first Los Angeles championship in 1972. Many teams have never even made it to the Finals, much less won a championship. In contrast, I thrived through the eras of Magic and Kareem and Worthy, and Kobe and Shaq and Kobe and Pau; that's eleven championships in my life as a fan (I was alive but not a Laker fan when the franchise won five championships in Minneapolis before the team moved to L.A.), and working on number twelve now in October 2020. Yet I remain scarred, and occasional regular season losses to the Celtics (to anybody, but especially the Celtics) are still tough to take.

My two favorite teams are the Lakers, and whoever is playing the Boston Celtics. I trained my (now adult) children to adopt this posture as well.

The point of this story is a question: How is it that a reasonably intelligent independent thinking man can be so enmeshed with the performance of a sports team? And not only *with* my team, but *against* another team?

The social scientist Henri Tajfel was a Polish Jew studying in France at the outbreak of World War II. He joined the French army, was captured and spent five years in German POW camps. He did not disclose his Polish ancestry; being identified as a Polish Jew, rather than a French Jew, would have been fatal. (4)

Perhaps understandably, he gained an interest in, and decided to investigate, the phenomenon of "Us versus Them." He first wanted to establish a baseline, determining what kind of cues are so light that no one would consider that he or she was in one group as opposed to another. Imagine being on a city bus when someone gets on declaring everyone on the right side is on Team A and everyone on the left side is Team B. Well, no; I don't really identify by which side of the bus I'm on; maybe I'm sitting across from my children, and I'm certainly not inclined to be on a team with strangers opposed to my children. Tajfel designed an experiment that would be below the threshold for people identifying as being in a group, and then he planned to add cues and variables until he began to find behavior that discriminated between the two groups.

In the first experiment Tajfel brought 64 boys aged 14 and 15 into his laboratory. The boys knew each other; they were from the same school. They were initially deceived into believing they were being tested on estimating the numbers of dots on a screen (that was bogus). Then they were told that while they were there, they would be divided to go into a different test by how many dots they'd estimated (again bogus; they were actually split randomly), so into a different test, one in which some of the boys would be given money, not to keep, but to hand out the money to some of the other boys. The experimenters would then see whether the boys would favor those whom they believed were in "their group." The expectation was that they would not show any favor; after all, remember, "their" group was baseless, supposedly due to counting dots on a screen, but was in reality, completely random.

Tajfel describes the surprising outcome: "A large majority of the subjects, in all groups in both conditions, gave more money to members of their own group than to members of the other group." (5).

Other study designs, other ways to create meaningless groups, generated similar results, favoring their group over the out-group.

The boys would give fairly when two recipients were both members of the givers' same group.

But researchers were surprised to find that when the choice was between a member in their group versus a member of the out-group, they would give more to the boy identified only as a member of their group; and critically they would do so, *even if it meant everyone overall got less in total.*

When they had the opportunity to give more to both groups overall, they *preferred to give less to their own group as long as they gave even less to the out-group.* Getting less was OK as long as there was a gap between what their group got versus what the out-group got.

When there was no intergroup competition, no scarcity, no zero-sum, they still would try to punish the out-group.

Tajfel concluded that the old idea that group conflict was due to zero sum competition for scarce resources was not correct. It wasn't the money, it wasn't just maximizing the benefit to their in-group (and again, these 'groups' were ridiculous, created on the weakest of bases). Rather, the discrimination was *positional*, they were motivated to maximize the difference between their in-group and the out-group. "Discriminatory intergroup behavior cannot be fully understood if it is considered solely in terms of objective conflict of interest.... *It is the winning that seems more important to them*" (italics added). (6)

As the Lakers are about to win their 17th championship this week, I am reminded that, after trailing the Boston Celtics in numbers of championships for all of my sentient life, my team will now be tied with them.

This victory will come largely due to the play of two great players, LeBron James, who first was a Cleveland Cavalier, then he was a Miami Heat (whom we are about to defeat... emphasis on "we"), then a Cavalier again; and Anthony Davis, who last season was a New Orleans Pelican. As it mattered not to Tajfel's boys, none of that matters to me: now LeBron and AD wear the purple and gold of the Lakers, and they are mine.

Winning is positional: the late Kobe Bryant and Shaquille O'Neal won three championships in a row in the early 2000s. They were both highly competitive, not just with other teams, but with each other. Eventually they had a falling out that disintegrated the team; Shaq left. Had they been able to figure out how to work together, they perhaps could have continued to dominate the league and win more championships; but their individual conflict and need to be seen as better than the other took precedence. When Kobe's Lakers (after Shaq had left) won the championship in 2010, he was asked about the significance of winning his fifth, to which he replied, "one more than Shaq." That is positional.

Our political identity used to be a fairly stand-alone phenomenon, but now it includes many identities.

On Election Day 1960, I rode with my parents to the polling place and waited for them to vote. My father was a Republican, my mother a

Democrat. That was not abnormal at the time -- while Americans have become more accepting of interracial marriage in the 21st century, we have backtracked on interparty marriage. As we were about to drive away, my father said, "Well, I voted for Kennedy," and my pleasantly surprised mother shook his hand, which I found very peculiar as I don't think I had ever seen her do that before (or ever again). My six year old self was impressed; voting was a serious responsibility, a rare activity done in private with only one's conscience, and after it was done, you shook hands, lived with the results and as much as was appropriate, and supported whoever won. I miss that.

Times have changed. In 1950, the top political scientists in the country published a paper bemoaning the fact that *we weren't polarized enough*, that our political parties were too heterogeneous, that voters couldn't tell the differences between parties. As Ezra Klein commented regarding that paper, "It is difficult, watching the party-line votes and contempt for compromise that defines Congress today, to read sentences like 'the parties have done little to build up the kind of unity within the congressional party that is now so widely desired' and hear the logic behind them. Summarized today, the report can sound like a call for fewer puppies and more skin fungus." (7).

Finding wisdom in strange places, then vice president Richard Nixon said in 1959 that "It would be a great tragedy if we had our two major political parties divide on what we would call a conservative-liberal line." It was a good thing that "we have avoided generally violent swings in Administration from one extreme to the other. And the reason we have avoided that is that in both parties there has been room for a broad spectrum of opinion." (8) And a political scientist called in to consult with the Republican Party in 1959 argued against what we have now. "With both parties including liberals and conservatives within their ranks, those differences which would otherwise be the main campaign issues are settled by compromise within each party.... Our national unity would be weakened if the theoretical differences were sharpened." (9)

If you want real confusion as to my tribe, try this. I ran for Congress as a Natural Law Party candidate, twice, in the 1990s. While the party no longer exists, our platform was ahead of its time and generally has held up well: we were utterly pro-science, basing decisions and policy proposals on the best available information. Part of our platform was critical of the two party duopoly, as we felt that money in politics and the Swamp had led to there being only barely recognizable differences between the two major parties. We didn't want polarization just for the sake of polarization, we wanted a choice away from the ubiquity of the uber-wealthy buying influence. In the "Be-careful-what-you-wish-for" Department, we wanted a real choice, real differences between the parties.

Well now the parties are different alright, and voters have adapted to the polarization by polarizing further. Conversations like the one between my parents are unlikely these days. People used to split their tickets, that is, vote for one party's candidate for president, and the other party's candidates in down-ballot races. Political scientists have documented that this has changed. "Looking at districts with contested House races, they found that between 1972 and 1980, the correlation between the Democratic share of the House vote and the Democratic share of the presidential vote was 54%. Between 1982 and 1990, that rose to 65%. By 2018, it had reached 97%! [A correlation of 100% means that two things essentially are identical.] In forty years, support for the Democratic presidential candidate went from being a helpful, but far from reliable, predictor of support for a party's House candidate to being an almost perfect guide." (10)

It would seem then that we Americans have fallen in love with our particular political party; but no. Paradoxically, over the last forty years people have become less identified with their own party; around 80% of voters in 1964 identified as either Republican or Democrat. That percentage had dropped from 80 to 63 by 2012, the lowest ever measured. (11) Also, researchers measure how warm and fuzzy people feel about political parties, and quantify the phenomenon on a "feelings thermometer" scale of 1 (yuck) to 100 (yay!). And of those who have remained in their parties, their feelings about *their own* party have not become hyper-supportive, no; they have even deteriorated some, from a score of 72 in 1980 down to 65 in 2016. (In the glass half full department, if you're a liberal and you can't stand those damn Republicans, you may have something in common with Trumpers: they often can't stand the Republican Party either.)

> Ninety eight percent of the adults in this country are decent, hard-working, honest Americans. It's the other lousy two percent that get all the publicity. But then - we elected them.
>
> - - Lily Tomlin

How can this be, that there are smaller percentages of people in each party, and those who remain feel worse about their own party, and yet people (including independents by the way) increasingly vote strictly along party lines?

This positional nature of winning finds expression in "negative partisanship." While people don't feel as good about their own party as they used to, they *really* don't like the other guys. Over the last forty years, the scores people give the *other* party have markedly declined, from a lukewarm score of 45 in 1980, to 40 in 1990, to 38 in 1998, to 29 in 2016. Ezra Klein puts a bow on this as follows: "So here, then, is the last fifty years of American politics summarized: we have become more consistent in the party we vote for not because we came to like our party more – indeed, we've come to like the parties we vote for *less* – but because we came to dislike the opposing party more. Even as hope and change sputter, fear and loathing proceed." (12)

Identity politics versus issues

Something has changed. We all have a host of aspects to our personalities and identities that didn't used to be particularly associated with our political leanings. But now, they are. I'm going to list some. See if you can decide which characteristic, versus the other, is more likely to be associated with being liberal versus conservative, which person is a Trump supporter or a never-Trumper:

Gay	straight
Rural	urban
Coastal	heartland
Evangelical	agnostic
Soccer	football
Immigrant	native born
White	non-white
Southern	Yankee
Whole Foods	Cracker Barrel
Meat	vegetarian
Prius	pick-up
Diesel	solar
Hollywood	Dallas
Piercing	tattoo
College	high school
Denny's	Starbucks

How easy was that?

All of these have some overlap (there are plenty of pierced Trumpers, and lots of tattooed and white liberal football fans, etc.). These characteristics really have almost nothing to do with tax policy, or size of government, or foreign policy, yet it was easy to broadly categorize the politics of each group versus the other.

Ezra Klein recalls how these differences can be exploited:

> In 2004, the Club for Growth, a conservative interest group that advocates for lower taxes and deregulation, ran a famous ad against then presidential candidate Howard Dean. In the ad, an older white couple is stopped outside a shop with patriotic bunting and asked about Dean's plan to raise taxes.
>
> "What do I think?" the man replies. "Well, I think Howard Dean should take his tax-hiking, government-expanding, latte-drinking, sushi-eating, Volvo-driving, *New York Times*-reading –" Then his wife cuts in: "Body-piercing, Hollywood-loving, left-wing freak show back to Vermont, where it belongs." And that my friends is pure, uncut mega-identity politics. (13)

Which comes first, the chicken or the egg? Klein elaborates: "...political elites are polarizing more and faster than the public at large, but as the public tunes in, it becomes more polarized too. And since politicians are most responsive to the part of the public that is most polarized, we're all living in a hyper-polarized system and being faced with polarized choices, whatever our personal level of polarization." (14)

Klein discusses at length the distinctions between sorting and polarization, and between polarization and extremism. These differences are subtle but important and make for an informative read. But for our purposes, suffice to say that:

> Issue-based polarization leads to political identity polarization: if there's more intense disagreement about [cannabis policy, for example], people will want their political representatives to fight for their beliefs, which will push the parties to polarize around the issue as well.... (15)
>
> When you vote for a candidate, you're not just voting for him or her.... You're voting for your side to beat the other side. You're voting to express your identity. You're voting for your

> members of Congress to be able to pass bills. You're voting for the judges your side would appoint. You're voting so those smug jerks you fight with in the comments section don't win, so that aunt or uncle you argue with at Thanksgiving can't lord it over you. You're voting to say your group is right and worthy and the other group is wrong and unworthy. (16)

Welcome to the United States of Schadenfreude.

In their 2015 paper "Red and Blue States of Mind," Patrick Miller and Pamela Johnson Conover reported their findings after having evaluated tons of data, polling, demographics, etc., to see how all that affected the likelihood of partisans getting angry and amped during an election. It's not nearly as much about issues as it is about identity:

> The behavior of partisans resembles that of sports team members acting to preserve the status of their teams rather than thoughtful citizens participating in the political process for the broader good.... Elections accentuate the team mentality of party identifiers, pushing them repeatedly to make 'us – them' comparisons between Democrats and Republicans that draw attention to what will be lost – status – if the election is not won. This results in both rivalry and anger. (17)

But what really gets people fired up is not just their identification with their team, but their desire to see the other guys lose. Polling data (18) demonstrates that the more engaged people are in politics (and if you're reading this book, that may well describe you) the more they're driven by their, uh, 'unfavorable' view of the other party. As one might expect, giving money (and voting) is increased among those who have a very favorable view of their own party. But what really increases contributing money is having a very *unfavorable* view of the other party. In a predictably vicious cycle, politicians try to get people angry with their opponents, and then listen harder to those who are more strongly engaged, because they contribute and they vote (and politicians listen harder still to those with lots of money).

Exit polls revealed that in 2016 Clinton won among voters who were motivated by support for their favored candidate; of those who voted for Trump, more people voted because they were against Hillary than voted because they were actually 'for' Trump. (19)

This antipathy toward the other side, negative partisanship, is an indicator of engagement and enthusiasm, because it is related to the person's view of himself. Johnston, Federico and Lavine in their book *Open versus Closed* found that the least engaged voters tend to look at how politics will affect their material interests, how will this tax or healthcare policy affect my budget and well-being; but the most engaged look at how a given policy position reflects on his or her identity as a person. We saw this playing out starting in the summer of 2020 in the strangest manner regarding a serious issue, the mitigation of the spread of the COVID-19 pandemic by wearing masks. It has become an index of red versus blue, no matter how irrational such a division may be. But we have seen this before, in Tajfel's experiments with the school boys. So it's not so much an objection to wearing a mask because it's uncomfortable or makes it hard to breathe, but because wearing a mask means you're one of the sheeple who have been seduced by the quivering fear-mongering snowflake politically correct WHO-supporting coastal elites.

But here's perhaps the weirdest thing. It's not just that issue-based polarization leads to political identity polarization, or even that the *identity* polarization becomes more important than was the *issue* polarization that started it. Identity can completely trump issues, and make policy differences insignificant. This can be quantified.

Political scientist Lilliana Mason in her 2018 book *Uncivil Agreement: How Politics Became Our Identity*, reports using the 'feelings thermometer' (remember? Score of 1 is yuck, 100 is yay), but she looked at self-identified Democrats who had conservative policy views that should have made them Republicans; they gave the Democratic Party a score of @ 70 and the GOP a score of @ 40. Republicans whose liberal policy views should have made them Democrats gave the Republican Party a score of @ 65 and the Democratic Party a score of @ 40.

You can find Jay Leno on YouTube interviewing Obama supporters on the street in 2008, asking them how much they support certain positions of Obama that were actually positions of John McCain. I imagine there was some selective editing for entertainment purposes, but those people readily agreed that these positions (actually of McCain) were brilliant and that's why they were voting for Obama. Similarly, YouTube has videos of Jordan Klepper of the Today Show interviewing Trump supporters who express support for the positions of Hillary Clinton and Joe Biden.

If you watch the videos, you may think they aren't representative because those folks just aren't the sharpest pencils in the box. But a study of college students back in 2003 found this same sort of phenomenon. (20) College psychology students who identified as having strong ideological views on welfare were given an article to read about two (unknown to them, fictional) welfare proposals, one lavish, one very spartan, and each supported (fictionally) by either House Democrats or House Republicans. Those students who identified as conservative would support the lavish proposal if it was supported by House Republicans, and liberals supported the harsh program if it was supported by House Democrats. Identity trumps policy.

It turns out that many people support parties that don't share their policy views, or more accurately, they oppose parties that do share their policy views.

This is in part because **many people don't care and don't know that much about policy; but they care a great deal and they know all about their identity**.

And even though the college students did know a lot, as Mason noted, "This is the American identity crisis. Not that we have partisan identities, we've always had those. The crisis emerges when partisan identities fall into alignment with other social identities, stoking our intolerance of each other to levels that are unsupported by our degree of political disagreement." (21)

It is simple enough to acknowledge, even if only subconsciously, that I might really not know or care much about what corporate tax rates should be, or how a particular piece of legislation is going to affect the supply chains for automobile manufacturers. If I did know, I'm sure I would have a great idea and make a great decision. But since I have neither the time nor the inclination to find out, and someone else is going to make that decision, I want that someone else to be just like me.

Because for too many of us:
if you're not like me, I don't like you. (22)

One of the darker aspects of this polarization is the use of political identity as a cover to make some forms of hate acceptable in society. If you hate gays, or blacks, or white southerners, that's rude and largely still somewhat socially unacceptable. But since more gays and blacks are Democrats than Republicans, you can just hate Democrats and you've got it covered. Similarly, if you hate white southerners or gun owners but don't want to be seen as hating people just because of their accents, if you hate Republicans, you've got a lot of gun-owning folks with southern accents covered. Stanford University's Shanto Iyengar commented, "Political identity is fair game for hatred. Racial identity is not. Gender identity is not. You cannot express negative sentiments about social groups in this day and age. But political identities are not protected by these constraints. A Republican is someone who chooses to be Republican, so I can say whatever I want about them." (23)

When and why did this happen? How did so many of our cultural differences, our geographic locations, religious beliefs, racial and ethnic characteristics, become so sorted, so stacked one atop the other, and so closely identified with our politics?

The reason for these changes is as American as apple pie: race.

Our political parties used to be heterogeneous. There were liberal Republicans, like Nelson Rockefeller co-existing with Barry Goldwater; and conservative, even reactionary white supremacist Democrats. There have been some ongoing tendencies, Republicans toward limited government and favoring free unfettered enterprise (with notable exceptions like trust-busting Teddy Roosevelt) and rugged individualism, and Democrats leaning toward labor rather than management, looking to redistribute wealth and balance the scales toward the poor and working people to redress the inherent strengths of Capital; but they were just tendencies, and both parties were fairly inclusive. Anybody could be anything. There was no such thing as a RINO (Republican In Name Only). As one Republican senator commented back in 1923, "Anyone who can carry a Republican primary, is a Republican." (24)

A Brief History of American Political Parties

The Republican Party was the party of Lincoln. (Yes, Lincoln was a Republican. A lot of people don't know that.... Sorry.) There were Democrats in the North during the Civil War, but both during and after the war, the GOP was recognized as having executed the war that defeated the Confederacy. Not all Democrats were southern and white, but if you were southern and white, or if you were a white supremacist, you were a Democrat.

This is not to say that all southern whites were racists (even if we had clearly defined that term and could look into the hearts of all white people in the South in the century following the Civil War), but if you were a white southerner and you weren't racist or just didn't support racist policies, if you wanted to be a Republican, or if you wanted the southern Democratic Party to lighten up on black people, you were fighting an uphill battle. Elected offices in the south were at times 95% held by Democrats. They controlled offices, they controlled the election process, and they controlled who got to vote. And by both legal means and extra-legal means such as violence and terror, black vote was suppressed.

When I first arrived in New Orleans in 1975 to start medical school, I had never been to the Deep South before. I walked around the city to familiarize myself, and New Orleans is a great, interesting, diverse, exciting city. But looking up at one prominent monument (it may have been the White League Monument at the end of Canal Street), I paused to read the inscription. As I recall it extolled the virtues of those who had fought for the South (OK, I get it), and how the Cause would not be lost forever as the South would rise again (hey, hope springs eternal, but good luck with that) and how it recognized white supremacy in the south. What. The. Hell? Yes, quote, "white supremacy," unquote. As I got to know some of my local classmates, I asked them about it, as in, what the hell? My more liberal white classmates commiserated, yes, it's awful; more conservative chums seemed oblivious to it, like it was old leather they'd gotten used to and didn't see any harm in an old monument; my black classmates were largely resigned. 'Brian, you're in Louisiana now.'

In the immediate post-Civil War period, @ 90% of blacks in the old Confederate states were registered to vote. (25) After the racist Andrew Johnson succeeded Lincoln and began to scuttle Reconstruction, black voting fell precipitously and remained low. By World War II, black voter registration in the South had fallen to 5%. For virtually a century, black voter registration was suppressed from 90% down to 5%! In the Black Belt of Alabama, where blacks outnumbered whites, black voter registration was 1.3% in 1944. (26) And those blacks who managed to register to vote still often were voiceless, facing beatings or lynching if they dared actually to try to vote. In his senatorial re-election campaign in 1946, Democrat Theodore Bilbo declared: "You and I know the best way to keep the [N-word] from voting. You do it the night before the election. I don't have to tell you any more than that. Red-blooded men know what I mean." (If you're wondering, yes, he won re-election.)

I love my country. But there's no point in sticking our heads in the sand. This white supremacist racial suppression is a shameful part of the history of our country. And while the history is long, it is not ancient.

The "Solid South" was Democratic, the "Dixiecrats." After the Civil War, the party as a whole was a mixed bag, but a vote for a liberal Democratic congressman from the West or North was a vote that put Democrats, including white supremacists, in charge of congressional committees; and for a long time. Democrats were not challenged in the South, so members of Congress remained there forever, became chairmen of committees (because that was based upon seniority), and never gave up power. They really were Democrats; aside from race, there was a confluence of interests. Often they were populists. The South was poor, the North was rich, and so redistribution of wealth seemed a good idea to Southern Democrats; unless the redistribution was directed toward blacks.

Southern Democrats were not marginal, they made up a huge chunk of the Democratic Party. From the late 19th century through the first half of the 20th century, they were almost always above 40% and usually closer to two thirds, of the House Democratic caucus. Nothing happened if they didn't want it to happen. The Republicans typically could not get something done without some Democratic support, and the Democrats couldn't do anything without the participation of the Dixiecrats.

(We see a similar persistent dynamic in contemporary times. When Republicans had the majority in the House after 2010 during the Obama administration, they couldn't do anything without the even smaller modern analogs of the Dixiecrats, the Tea Party. And so not much got done. That was a demonstration that government was a dysfunctional mess, so it's a waste to pay taxes, which should be cut; and cutting taxes is the one consistent message of the modern GOP.)

While our hero FDR got the New Deal passed and rescued our nation from the Great Depression, he did not support anti-lynching legislation. All of the achievements of our nation from the 1870s up into the 1960s, all that required bipartisan Congressional action anyway, were purchased at a high price: we could get things done, but only if we as a nation remained silent and complicit in the suppression of the rights of black people in the South. In fairness, before the internet and cable television, southern blacks were out of sight, out of mind. It was no doubt easy for white America to watch "Gone With the Wind," fantasize about the happy rustic lives of the dark people of the South, and live lives oblivious to the utterly un-democratic and un-American refutation of our supposed values taking place every day in our nation.

As the Rev Martin Luther King Jr. paraphrased Theodore Parker: "The moral arc of the universe is long, but it bends towards justice." In any case, it bends when people like Dr. King bend it. Harry Truman had desegregated the military (in 1948, by executive order, bypassing the Dixiecrats), the civil rights movement had gained traction, people from California to Vermont could see dogs attacking and firehoses directed at our black fellow countrymen on their television sets, and the stage was set for Lyndon Johnson to champion the Civil Rights Act. LBJ had won an overwhelming mandate in the 1964 election and he used his political capital to pass this landmark legislation.

There had previously been only modest sorting in our two major political parties. Geographically, white southerners were Democrats, and religiously, Protestants leaned Republican. But other than that, whatever demographic category you can think of, just about as many Catholics, or whites, or Californians, or vegetarians, whatever, were Republicans as were Democrats. (27) But the night before signing the Civil Rights Act, Johnson told Bill Moyers, "I think we just delivered the South to the Republican Party for a long time to come." (28) And he was right.

There was nothing to keep southern conservatives (and white supremacists) in the Democratic Party. Remember Tajfel's boys, giving less to their group as long as it meant giving even less to the other group? The populism of Dixiecrats, shifting wealth from North to South, was no good to them if it meant the economic upliftment of blacks: white supremacy was of, well, supreme importance. They left *en masse*, swallowed the ancient history of the Party of Lincoln and the War of Northern Aggression, and became Republicans.

> An identity is questioned only when it is menaced, as when the mighty begin to fall, or the wretched begin to rise, or when a stranger enters the gates, never, thereafter, to be a stranger: the stranger's presence making *you* the stranger, less to the stranger than to yourself.
>
> -- James Baldwin

This is not to say that the GOP became the party of white supremacists, that if you scratch a Republican any time after 1970 you will necessarily have found a white supremacist, no. As I said in my introduction, I do not believe most Republicans or even most Trump supporters are racists. (Or nasty racists anyway; I know I haven't defined that yet... stand by.) But if you are a white supremacist, you will find more of a home, be able to find more like-minded persons, in the Republican Party than in the Democratic Party, perhaps more so today in the party of Trump even than in the period following Nixon's Southern Strategy in the late 1960s.

Soon there was no Dixiecrat presence to dissuade previously Republican racially liberal northerners and westerners from joining the Democratic Party.

A Great Sorting had begun. Bill Bishop describes this phenomenon in detail in his 2008 book *The Big Sort*. There are always exceptions, and plenty of people (including me, for decades) were independents, but generally speaking:

Racially, blacks and other non-white minorities became Democrats or Democratic leaning.

Religiously, evangelicals and single issue (abortion) Catholics became Republicans or Republican leaning. The largest religious denomination among Democrats is 'none of the above.'

Ideologically, conservatives became Republicans, and liberals became Democrats; as a result, the Democratic Party became more liberal, kind of, and the Republican Party, with an influx of southern conservatives, became more conservative, and stronger. I say Democrats became 'kind of' more liberal, because the Democratic Party, while being more homogeneously liberal, is not (at least, not yet) really more liberal. It has adapted to the strength of the Republican Party by adopting previously Republican ideas, such as the individual mandate in Obamacare, or increasing deportations under Obama. The GOP has moved much further to the right. Positions held by Nixon and even Saint Reagan are far too liberal to get anywhere in today's GOP.

Geographically, obviously the white south mostly became Republican. But we have also sorted ourselves into rural versus urban. There are certain characteristics (that may be innate, more on that in the next chapter) liberals tend to have, such as a preference for new experiences, diversity and higher density of population that would have them tend to live in a city where they can walk to their market and see an ethnically diverse variety of people and a dozen coffee shops serving skim decaf chai lattes along the way. Conservatives tend to prefer order, tradition, and security, which translate into less dense and less diverse living.

Those geographical preferences reinforce themselves. A conservative friend of mine told me he likes a lot about California but wouldn't want to live there 'because of the politics.' In the 1950s, that wouldn't have mattered, because the politics in California were so mixed up you would have been hard pressed to find a conservative or liberal enclave, at least as compared to today (and because we were all less polarized back then). Now, he has sorted himself to live with other like-minded conservative people. (There still are millions of Republicans in California, but to some degree perception is reality. Due to the Electoral College, California Republicans' votes mostly don't count, at least not for presidential elections.)

As recently as 1976, only about a quarter of Americans lived in counties that voted for a particular presidential candidate by a landslide. By 2020, 58% of us live in such landslide counties. We have sorted ourselves.

Our politics, which used to be fairly independent of a wide variety of our identities, now is tightly associated with a bunch of them. And as it is with our identities, it is easy to be passionate in our advocacy for our guys and in opposition to the Other.

People who see a threat coming, are afraid. And the heretofore dominant group of white Americans sees change coming.

> Republicans know that their coalition is endangered, buffeted by demographic headwinds and an aging base. And that has injected an almost manic urgency into their strategy. Behind the GOP's tactical extremism lurks an apocalyptic sense of political stakes. It feels to many that if they lose, they may never win again -- and perhaps, with their current coalition, there's a kernel of truth in that. (29)

The mixed results of the 2020 election may indicate that the demographic headwinds have quite a way to go before blowing away the Republican Party. But the dynamics remain; demographic and cultural changes are still threats; many white Americans and Trump supporters still feel besieged.

On 17 Feb 2016, former Democratic Labor Secretary Robert Reich posted this epitaph: (30)

I'm writing to you today to announce the death of the Republican Party.
It is no longer a living, vital, animate organization.
It died in 2016. RIP.
It has been replaced by 6 warring tribes:
Evangelicals opposed to abortion, gay marriage, and science.
Libertarians opposed to any government constraint on private behavior.
Market fundamentalists convinced the "free market" can do no wrong.
Corporate and Wall Street titans seeking bailouts, subsidies, special tax loopholes, and other forms of crony capitalism.
Billionaires craving even more of the nation's wealth than they already own.
And white working-class Trumpoids who love Donald. and are becoming convinced the greatest threats to their wellbeing are Muslims, blacks, and Mexicans.
Each of these tribes has its own separate political organization, its own distinct sources of campaign funding, its own unique ideology – and its own candidate.
What's left is a lifeless shell called the Republican Party. But the Grand Old Party inside the shell is no more.
I, for one, regret its passing. Our nation needs political parties to connect up different groups of Americans, sift through prospective candidates, deliberate over priorities, identify common principles, and forge a platform.
The Republican Party used to do these things. Sometimes it did them easily, as when it came together behind William McKinley and Teddy Roosevelt in 1900, Calvin Coolidge in 1924, and Ronald Reagan in 1980.
Sometimes it did them with difficulty, as when it strained to choose Abraham Lincoln in 1860, Barry Goldwater in 1964, and Mitt Romney in 2012.
But there was always enough of a Republican Party to do these important tasks – to span the divides, give force and expression to a set of core beliefs, and come up with a candidate around whom Party regulars could enthusiastically rally.
No longer. And that's a huge problem for the rest of us.
Without a Republican Party, nothing stands between us and a veritable Star Wars barroom of self-proclaimed wanna-be's.
Without a Party, anyone runs who's able to raise (or already possesses) the requisite money – even if he happens to be a pathological nar-

> cissist who has never before held public office, even if he's a knave detested by all his Republican colleagues.
> Without a Republican Party, it's just us and them. And one of them could even become the next President of the United States.

Not to be rude about this prediction, but while it was in some ways prescient, in others it didn't age well. He certainly did a bang-up job describing the divisions within the Republican Party and his warning about who could indeed become president, but he didn't seem to account for the fact that in a binary choice like our presidential elections, identity with one's tribe (the GOP), or more importantly, identity against one's vilified opponent (Hillary Clinton, or Democrats in general), could overcome all divisions and could lead to victory for the GOP's candidate, even if he were Lucifer himself.

At this point it may seem that I've said Trump supporters are drones driven to support their team just because of fear and/or racism, with no perspicacity or moral tether at all. Certainly some are driven by fear; fear of Democrats, fear of minorities, fear of the future, fear a loss of status and a loss of control, fear of a loss of the country as they have known it, fear of economic disadvantage, fear of the changes immigrants will bring, fear of change in general. But it would be wrong to say all support for Trump is so motivated. The psychological dynamics of supporting Trump are complex. Some support has its basis elsewhere.

We will explore the things Trump said in Part II, but simply put, he told a story, an interpretation of the world around us, that resonated with many people. Some parts of the narrative are straightforward, realistic, consistent with lived experience, and objectively correct, as we'll discuss.

But other parts are not objectively correct, indeed some are utterly fantastical, and yet still appear to be accepted. I am not aware of research that has quantified how much the following perspectives influence people, but there are a number of outlooks worth noting.

We'll explore these issues more in later chapters, but the wilder conspiracy theories can make people feel they have information that most people don't have, information that explains why things aren't as they should be, and having this knowledge allows the holder to feel imbued with previously absent power and superiority.

Sometimes, after one has invested time and energy in a belief and social capital in espousing the belief and advocating for others who hold the belief, it can be very, very difficult to give up such a belief and admit one was wrong.

And sometimes, Trump supporters will say they believe something just because they know it will make liberals frantic ("owning the libs").

> I am just a poor boy.
> Though my story's seldom told,
> I have squandered my resistance
> For a pocketful of mumbles,
> Such are promises
> All lies and jest
> Still, a man hears what he wants to hear
> And disregards the rest.
>
> - - Paul Simon, *The Boxer*

Erroneous information can be accepted and espoused by otherwise reasonable people because it has come in association with or subsequent to other more credible material. Once a source of information has become trusted, it is easier to accept further information without scrutiny. But that gives a lot of credit to our reason, credit that may not be deserved.

In the next chapter we'll examine two other fundamental dynamics that are at play:

First, usually it is *not* our reason that is running the show.

Second, despite the fact that many liberals regard Trump supporters and Republicans at large as behaving unethically if not being morally bankrupt, there is reason to believe that conservatives in general may be even more strongly guided by moral concerns than are others.

Chapter 3

It's Really the Way We Are

If you're a liberal and you haven't been living under a rock since 2016, you know you've asked yourself, "How can Trump supporters believe the junk he says? So much of it makes no sense!" And "You can't talk sense to these people, they're impervious to reason. It's infuriating!" Right?

Well, yes and no, some Trump supporters are reasonable, and some unreasonable, but that's not the point of this chapter. The first point is, for all of us:

We are guided first and foremost by our emotions, then by our reason.

This is an old topic. Heavy hitter philosophers like Plato held reason above passion; in one of his dialogues he indicates that "...a man who masters his emotions will live a life of reason and justice, and will be reborn into a celestial heaven of eternal happiness. A man who is mastered by his passions, however, will be reincarnated as a woman." Ouch.

The opposite perspective was captured by David Hume in 1739 when he wrote: "...reason is, and ought to be the slave of the passions, and can never pretend to any other office than to serve and obey them." (1)

If you're like me, your first impression will be, I don't buy Hume's perspective. I mean, who was the coolest guy in the original *Star Trek*? It was Spock: no emotions, just logic. There was always a rational basis for what he did. Dr. McCoy was the emotional one. He was likeable too, but he readily went off half-cocked due to some emotional incontinence. And who was coolest in *The Next Generation*? It was Data, the android, again, incapable of emotions. (Plus, both Spock and Data were bad-ass in a fight, stronger than humans or even Klingons.)

When I was an adolescent, I wanted to be like Spock. As an adult, I thought the world would be a much better place if we all reasoned like Data.

But guess what: I was wrong, and David Hume was right.

Try this thought experiment. Suppose you're out walking your dog, and someone walks up to you and says "Hi there! I have a knife here I'd be glad to lend to you... why don't you kill your dog, and we could eat him?" My first reaction would be emotional, and I'd likely inform him that if he asks me another question like that he's going to lose some teeth.

If someone else came along a minute later and observed to me, "That sounded like a 'no' in response to that fellow's question... Why exactly did you answer that way?" well, I could come up with some perfectly sound reasons as to why I don't want to kill and eat my dog: I'm not hungry and I have other sources of food; I would be deprived of his companionship; I'm vegetarian; People would think ill of me for doing so; I love my dog; In my county it's illegal to kill and butcher one's dog; My wife and children and friends would become estranged from me; and so forth. But the real reason is: What the hell is wrong with you? Of course I'm not going to kill my dog, and you're a twisted piece of crap for suggesting it.

So, my emotions, my passion came first; the reasons I listed are just post hoc rationalizations for the emotional decision I had already made.

And by the way, Spock and Data did the same thing. One reason Spock was a fan favorite: he was unshakably guided by a moral center; he didn't lie or have any vices, and was reliably righteous. Similarly, Data's software included an "ethical program" that did the same thing as our emotions: filtered and evaluated courses of action presented by events, and if there was an ethical dimension, precluded most inappropriate possible solutions before any rational decision-making process had gotten its socks on.

This sequence has been studied and validated by psychologists and social scientists. In his book *The Righteous Mind: Why Good People Are Divided by Religion and Politics*, the social psychologist Jonathan Haidt recounts a number of experiments designed to discern the roles of emotions and reason in ethical decision making. (He eventually makes a subtle distinction between 'emotions' or 'passions,' and 'intuition,' and settles on intuition as the operative precursor to reason: "Intuitions come first, strategic reasoning second. That's a six-word summary of the social intuitionist model." (2) But for our discussions I'll often just say 'emotions.')

These studies involved getting the reactions of experimental subjects to various scenarios and then asking them to describe the reasoning for their reaction. His perspectives had been informed by having cross-cultural experiences, such as having lived in India for some time studying social and ethical constructs. He chose subjects from a variety of backgrounds so as to figure out which decisions were actually about issues of morality, which mostly depended on whether or not anyone was harmed, and which were just convention. For instance, Americans (around Philadelphia) distinguish between a moral violation, like a boy pushing a girl off a swing, and a conventional violation, like a boy refusing to wear a school uniform. But working class Brazilians felt that the rebellious uniform-refusing kid was committing a moral violation, not just breaking with convention. I highly recommend his book as it's an interesting and illuminating read, but these fascinating differences between (and within) cultures are beyond the scope of this book. Suffice to say, he did a lot of science, and there is a good amount of data to support much of his work that I'll be presenting, and certain principles hold true across cultures. But for the moment, we're just concerned about the decision making of Americans.

Here are some paraphrased examples of their moral-decision-making questions. Assume that no one sees what goes on, and just ask yourself, is this wrong? And if so, why?

1. A man has no money and steals a drug his wife needs to live.
2. A man buys a chicken at the grocery store, but before cooking it for dinner, he has sex with it.
3. The experimenter offers subject(s) $2 to sign a piece of paper selling their soul, a paper he will immediately tear up.
4. The experimenter offers the subject(s) a sip of apple juice; then he dips a dead sterilized autoclaved cockroach into the apple juice and offers a sip again.

Most people found that #1 was OK, a dilemma, but OK, the harm done to the outfit that was stolen from was outweighed by the harm that the fellow's wife would have suffered had he not stolen the drug.

Haidt identifies a phenomenon he calls *moral dumbfounding*. Many people found that #2 was wrong, but had trouble explaining why. It was his chicken; the chicken was already dead; nobody was harmed by seeing him perform the act; but still, it was wrong. Similarly, subjects, especially those who were atheists, had trouble explaining why they wouldn't sell their souls. They didn't believe in souls, but still, they didn't want to do it.

A surprising number of subjects were willing to drink the cockroach-dipped juice. For the record, the experimenter actually stopped them before they could do so The subjects were college students, so maybe the explanation lies there.

The ventral medial prefrontal cortex (vmPFC) is a part of the brain that mediates your emotional responses. People in whom it gets injured don't experience all those emotions that Vulcans suppress and Data couldn't experience. But instead of being cool sober rational efficient well put-together people, their lives are a mess. They are as intelligent as before, they know right from wrong, but every event is unfiltered, every decision needs to be figured out, thought through. You and I have short cuts; I don't need to weigh pros and cons about killing my dog, but folks without the contribution of their vmPFC have no visceral reaction, no gut response. Imagine the mess if every decision you faced was like figuring out which cell phone plan to purchase. We need our passions and prejudices; without them, our rational mind is overburdened, gets all wrapped around the axle, and makes bad decisions. (3)

Haidt also adopts a metaphor for emotions and reason: emotions are like an elephant, and reason is the rider. (The weight loss app *Noom* uses an identical elephant and rider metaphor; I don't know if that is just coincidence or what.) The elephant is bigger and stronger. But once humans started talking to each other, the elephant needed a press agent or lawyer to represent itself to others; that's the rider (or at least, the first draft of the rider). (4) As Chris Rock noted, "When you meet somebody for the first time, you're not meeting them, you're meeting their representative." We all have a press secretary, rationalizing to others our decisions.

These dynamics lead not just to deception, but to self-deception. Consider this anecdote from Haidt:

> On February 3, 2007, shortly before lunch, I discovered that I was a chronic liar. I was at home, writing a review article on moral psychology, when my wife, Jayne, walked by my desk. In passing, she asked me not to leave dirty dishes on the counter where she prepared our baby's food. Her request was polite but its tone added a postscript: "As I have asked you a hundred times before."
>
> My mouth started moving before hers had stopped. Words came out. Those words linked themselves up to say something about the baby having woken up at the same time that our elderly dog barked to ask for a walk and I'm sorry but I just put

> my breakfast dishes down wherever I could. In my family, caring for a hungry baby and an incontinent dog is a surefire excuse, so I was acquitted.
>
> Jayne left the room and I continued working....
>
> So there I was at my desk, writing about how people automatically fabricate justifications of their gut feelings, when suddenly I realized that I had just done the same thing with my wife. I disliked being criticized, and I had felt a flash of negativity by the time Jayne had gotten to her third word ('*Can you not...*'). Even before I knew why she was criticizing me, I knew I disagreed with her (because intuitions come first). The instant I knew the content of the criticism ('*...leave the dirty dishes on the...*'), my inner lawyer went to work searching for an excuse (strategic reasoning second). It's true that I had eaten breakfast, given Max his first bottle, and let Andy out for his first walk, but these events all happened at separate times. Only when my wife criticized me did I merge them into a composite image of a harried father with too few hands, and I created this fabrication by the time she had completed her one-sentence criticism ('*...counter where I make baby food?*'). I then lied so quickly and convincingly that my wife and I both believed me. (5)

Do you do that? Of course you do! As do I. And when I do, and I recognize that I have, it is still difficult to acknowledge that I have.

I promise I'll bring all this back around to Trump and politics etc., just hang with me for a minute.

Our reason serves to support our passions: Must I believe this, or can I believe that?

We tend to suffer from confirmation bias. That is, when we believe something, we more readily see and appreciate information that supports our perspective than information that refutes it. And being smart isn't the solution. Research has shown that people with higher IQs are better at coming up with more "my-side" arguments, but no better than lower IQ persons at finding reasons for "other-side" arguments. And this research is regarding inconsequential topics (like beliefs in why sequences of numbers proceed as they do). So it shouldn't be a surprise when people hang on to discredited information or conspiracy theories. When our elephant, our passions are fully engaged, we're even more likely to exhibit confirmation bias. (6)

Reason serves passion; must I believe, or can I believe.

In his book *How We Know What Isn't So*, social scientist Tom Gilovich posits that when we *want* to believe something:

We (unconsciously) ask ourselves, **"Can I believe it?"**

If it's something we *don't want* to believe, we ask: **"Must I believe it?"**

If we can find any piece of 'evidence' to support our perspective, or any bit of evidence to counter a position we want to disbelieve, we can feel justified in stopping our search, stop any rational critique of ourselves, and bask in the warm bathwater of righteousness, or even better, righteous indignation.

And being in the 'Information Age' is not necessarily helpful. As Haidt says, "Whatever you want to believe about the causes of global warming or whether a fetus can feel pain, just Google your belief. You'll find partisan websites summarizing and sometimes distorting relevant scientific studies. Science is a smorgasbord, and Google will guide you to the study that's right for you." (7)

Since our reason serves our passions, since we tend to spin things in our favor based upon our emotions, it might help to look under the hood to better understand that which guides our elephant.

There are moral dimensions we value

If you're reading this book, you may be WEIRD. Cultural psychologists have observed (8) that the majority of research and writing about psychology has been done regarding people who come from cultures that are WEIRD, an acronym for **W**estern, **E**ducated, **I**ndustrialized, **R**ich, and **D**emocratic (that's small "d" democratic, not the political party).

One of the heaviest philosophical hitters in the 19th century wrote "The only purpose for which power can be rightfully exercised over any member of a civilized community, against his will, is to prevent harm to others." (9) This was echoed by the Isley brothers when they wrote, "It's your thing, do what you wanna do. I can't tell ya who to sock it to."

This establishes the "harm principle," and it is this 'harm principle' that guides the moral decision making of many if not most WEIRD people.

In a gross oversimplification, liberals tend to rely strongly, sometimes exclusively, on the harm principle. This axis has "care" on one end, and "harm" on the other. Liberals tend to process moral decisions (and by extension, policy decisions) in terms of harm versus care (and some other moral attributes, as we'll see).

Conservatives on the other hand, rely upon a greater number of moral axes.

Craig and Haidt (10) identify their Moral Foundations Theory, with six moral dimensions, scales with these pairs of attributes on opposite ends:

Care versus Harm
Liberty versus Oppression
Fairness versus Cheating
Loyalty versus Betrayal
Authority versus Subversion
Sanctity versus Degradation

Their data support the hypothesis that these six foundations (with their twelve counterbalancing attributes) exist across cultures and persist over time. It's beyond the scope of this book to describe all the support for these six axes (read chapters six through eight of Haidt's *The Righteous Mind* for that), but they are not arbitrary. Indeed, there is evidence that we are born with them, they are innate; not immutably, but pre-wired, that is, "organized in advance of experience" (11), in our genes.

If these are the moral axes we experience, there must be reasons for us to have evolved that way. We needed shortcuts so our elephant, our passions, could guide us in directions that would assure the perpetuation of our DNA. We evolved in groups, and our individual survival was tethered to the survival of our group, structuring these foundational traits.

There were certain events that were threatening, and others that were reassuring, and our elephants were selected to avoid reflexively the one and embrace the other.

Here is the short version of how and why that happened.

Care versus harm: unlike snakes or fish that produce lots of offspring who don't need to be raised and most of whom don't survive, we needed to protect and care for our children. We were distressed by the experience of our children (and eventually, any children and many adults) suffering or appearing needy. We feel empathy.

Liberty versus oppression: this counterbalance keeps the group healthy, as the group is not healthy if being (too) dominated by (too) selfish bullies. Groups had to internalize means to use the power of the group to overcome the influence of the few who would try to usurp power.

Fairness versus cheating: in a group, one has two-way relationships, and cooperation is mutually beneficial and favored. Cheating and lying benefit the cheater and liar in the short term but are toxic to the health of the group.

Loyalty versus betrayal: needed alliances within groups are threatened by disloyalty from within. That's why the law demands that prisoners of war be treated properly but treason typically is a capital crime. LeBron James was (and is again) the pride of Akron Ohio, but when he left the Cleveland Cavaliers for Miami (after "The Decision"), Cleveland fans burned his jersey and booed him whenever the Miami Heat came to play in Cleveland. (He did return to play for Cleveland four years later, bringing the sole NBA championship in the history of the franchise and regaining the love of Cavalier fans.)

Authority versus subversion: groups are not egalitarian, and need to adapt to the efficiencies of hierarchies, recognizing and legitimizing who is dominant, and who submits. Threats to legitimate authority threaten the viability of the group.

Sanctity versus degradation: contaminated food, water, and waste products in the environment were recognized threats, and codifying means to address them and related behaviors became essential, to the point of ritual and religion.

It's really, really, the way we are. We evolved from those who were successful at internalizing these foundations that are so important to surviving and thriving within groups.

Of course, people are different, with different preferences and tastes; that's why they make both chocolate and vanilla. The values listed are not evenly distributed among all the members of a group, much less all the members of a nation-state; so these values exist in tension and in competition. And they are generally unrecognized.

We can see today that those who hold to certain sets of values more than to others, often look at their opponents, those who hold other, different, moral values paramount, as being bereft of both values and morality. This is both a cause and a result of polarization.

The data underlying the Moral Foundations Theory indicates that typically, liberals tend to embrace the first three imperatives much more than the next three; conservatives tend to engage along all of the axes more or less equally. Of course there is some nuance. For instance, liberals tend to look at Fairness in terms of *equality*, while conservatives tend to look at Fairness as *proportionality*, as we'll see.

I'll italicize these foundations occasionally below; it might help you recall them.

The moral dimensions we value are in our genes.

Around 600 to 700 thousand years ago, something changed. *Homo heidelbergensis* demonstrated "shared intentionality" (12), which can be described thus: "our ancestors developed the ability to share mental representations of tasks that two or more of them were pursuing together." (13) They apparently cooperated with each other to hunt big game together and share the resulting food. (14) They must have developed some rules for living with and relating to one another in order to get this task accomplished. In other words, they must have developed some morality.

We tend to think that our moral attitudes are strictly cultural add-ons, rather than biological, and certainly nothing that has been subjected to natural selection. Indeed, many have held that evolution broadly has stopped or at least slowed down the more 'civilized' we've become, because selective pressures have become less. I'm sure you've heard this argument about why our society is in the sorry state it's in: we encourage and protect weak, stupid and non-productive people. Instead of letting nature weed them out, we allow them to reproduce and so we're just not as manly and tough and smart as our ancestors were a few generations ago, and those ancestors were wimpier than were the really tough guys centuries or millennia ago, etc.

But according to the Human Genome Project (15), biological evolution continues; indeed human genetic evolution has greatly accelerated over the last 50,000 years. The changes were faster 40 thousand years ago, faster still 20 thousand years ago, and peaked about 12 thousand years ago perhaps ongoing to current times. And according to anthropologists Pete Richerson and Rob Boyd, cultural and biological innovations evolve along with each other. (16) Haidt describes an example.

Generally our distant human ancestors (and other mammals as well) did not have the ability to digest milk after childhood; we didn't nurse anymore and we stopped producing lactase, the enzyme that breaks down lactose, the sugar naturally occurring in milk. (You or some of your acquaintances even today may not be able to consume comfortably more than just a tiny bit of cheese or ice cream or milk: that's "lactose intolerance.") But these days, the vast majority of people can eat ice cream and drink milk. What happened?

Around 10,500 years ago our ancestors first domesticated cattle. (17) All our current cows may have come from as few as 80 animals domesticated from wild ox in what is now Iran. With cows came milk. Starvation was a constant companion to our predecessors, and now there was a big new supply of calories. People with a mutation that allowed them to keep producing lactase after childhood had an advantage, so culture (keeping cows) drove biology (the mutation to continue coding for lactase for at least as long as it would take to procreate). And that biological change also drove culture: cooperation was selected for, so more people would help to maintain larger herds of cows, so more people were valuing and protecting good grazing land, and making cheese, sticking your pinkie out as you pair the right cheese with the right wine, etc.

Similarly, while research has not yet identified all the specific genes involved, the "tribal instincts hypothesis" (18) holds (not just regarding cows and milk, but more broadly) as follows: "Such environments favored the evolution of a suite of new social instincts suited to life in such groups, including a psychology which 'expects' life to be structured by moral norms and is designed to learn and internalize such norms; [and] new emotions such as shame and guilt, which increase the chance that the norms are followed...." (19)

Haidt elaborates:

> ...Once some groups developed the cultural innovation of prototribalism, they changed the environment within which genetic evolution took place....
>
> In such prototribal societies, individuals who found it harder to play along, to restrain their antisocial impulses, and to conform to the most important collective norms would not have been anyone's top choice when it came time to choose partners for hunting, foraging, or mating....
>
> This process has been described as 'self-domestication.' ...Our brains, bodies, and behavior show many of the same signs of domestication that are found in our domestic animals: smaller teeth, smaller body, reduced aggression, and greater playfulness, carried on even into adulthood. (20)

So here's the main idea of this section. **Biological evolution didn't change just our bodies and physiology.** We underwent striking social and cultural changes that affected our bodies, and our behaviors, and **required the development of codes of conduct, that is, morality.** Selective pressures for these moral frameworks were strong, and encoded them, or at least predispositions toward them, into our DNA.

A few words about religion

Human societies have always had to deal with a couple of ongoing problems: how to effect cooperation among people who are not related to each other, and what to do about 'free riders,' those who seek to benefit from the work of cooperation in society without doing any of the work. (21) The bottom line here is: religions help coherence, and decrease free riders.

First, let's acknowledge critics of religion such as Richard Dawkins who decried the "time-consuming, wealth-consuming, hostility-provoking rituals, the anti-factual, counterproductive fantasies of religion." (22) Freud called religion "a universal obsessional neurosis" and referred to mystical experience as "infantile helplessness... a regression to primary narcissism." (23) Many people look at religious dogma, from talking snakes to virgin births to walking on water and wonder how anyone can believe such things. A review of the history of religion, the Crusades, the Inquisition, al-Qaeda, ISIS, etc., can lead one reasonably to conclude that the world would be better off without religion. Despite all this, while people can and do change religions or abandon the organized religion into which they were born or they adopted, religion as a phenomenon has been remarkably resilient and persistent.

My dog Jake, an 80 pound rescue pit mix, is a good boy; he's a hunter, alert to every movement he senses. When he encounters any form of life that isn't a human (he loves all people... he's a good boy) or another dog (he's cool with almost all dogs, and never abuses small dogs; did I mention he's a good boy?), he perceives prey. When he figures out that the movement is just a leaf being blown by the wind, he relents and ignores it. Cats are more religious; every time the string wiggles, cats seem to believe there is agency behind that, and they attack the string as if it was a mouse. Our ancestors saw the wind, timely rains making the fields fertile, excessive rains causing floods and killing people, attributed these phenomena to the Will of the Divine, and constructed beliefs and ritual to align human activity with that Will.

In counterpoint to Dawkins and Sam Harris and others who argue we'd be better off without irrational fantastical religions, Haidt points out that religion is *more about* ***belonging*** *than beliefs*; trying to figure out the draw of religion by looking at dogma and beliefs is like trying to figure out why people are so passionate about their football team by exclusively watching the movements of the football during the game. And atrocities are in-group / out-group phenomena, which can take place independent of, with or without, religious pretexts.

In any case, religion, which we can perhaps understand as a special or expanded case of the *Sanctity/Degradation* moral foundation, has been around for a long time and seems to be here to stay. Society requires some degree of sacrifice, and sacrifice can be hard to sell without sacralizing it. (24) If your homeowner's association, or your city, wants your time or effort or tax dollars, or government wants you to wear a mask in a pandemic, they'd better be able to show how your sacrifice supports your self-interest. But your church can appeal to your belief that it is sacred, for example, consistent with the teachings of Jesus for you to sacrifice for the benefit of the poor or needy. Religion then can function as follows: "To invest social conventions with sanctity is to hide their arbitrariness in a cloak of seeming necessity" (25), at times mandating cooperation without kinship, and at other times asserting that the faithful must act in accord with the wishes of God (or the gods) whose unblinking eyes see all and is intolerant of cheating free riders.

Social scientists Robert Putnam and David Campbell found that religion helps, it works: "By many different measures religiously observant Americans are better neighbors and better citizens than secular Americans -- they are more generous with their time and money, especially in helping the needy, and they are more active in community life." (26) And those behaviors are not associated with their belief in particular dogma or participation in rituals. Rather, the enmeshment of people with their co-religionists is what enhances generosity and the beneficial aspects of religion. "It's the friendships and group activities, carried out within a moral matrix that emphasizes selflessness. That's what brings out the best in people." (27) And the direction of causality, whether religion causes people to be more generous, or whether generous people tend to select themselves to participate in their chosen religion, doesn't really seem to matter.

Religion may or may not have begun with hypersensitivity to agency detection; but incorporating religion and the sacred makes societies last.

"Religions exist primarily for people to achieve together what they cannot achieve on their own." (28)

I'm not trying to make the case for religion here. Whether a religion is beneficial, whether people achieving together what they can't on their own, or whether making a particular society last, are good things, depends. The strongest combination of belonging strongly to a group and being fervently religiously observant I've ever personally seen was among the Taliban, so that's not a great advertisement. In fairness, I don't believe the Taliban selected for or were attractive to generous and kind persons (although it was hard to know whether they were being very supportive to each other, within their group). They could have been misogynistic Luddites all on their own, without Islam. But it does seem that the invocation of the sacred has allowed them to remain a coherent group that has taken over a country, again, despite the fact that not that many people in that country actually like them or support their policies.

I have not accounted here for the possibility that religion(s) originated, and persists, with experience of the Divine. Persons with clear experience of the Nature of Reality may have directly cognized God, and in describing the experience to others, enlivened in them some latent spirituality that is inherent to us all. The faults we see in religion may not be due to intrinsic inconsistencies but rather due to the inability of fallible disciples to fully apprehend the nature and significance of the experiences so described by spiritual masters. This hypothesis is beyond the scope of this book. I've described it elsewhere. (29) I leave such an exploration up to you.

Setting aside that Divine scenario, writer Nicholas Wade puts a bow on the argument for religion as a function of evolution:

> People belonging to such a [religiously cohesive] society are more likely to survive and reproduce than those in less cohesive groups, who may be vanquished by their enemies or dissolve in discord. In the population as a whole, genes that promote religious behavior are likely to become more common in each generation as the less cohesive societies perish and the more united ones thrive. (30)

The First Amendment assures us that our country has freedom of (and freedom from) religion, but our secular national values also can serve to bind us together in cooperation without kinship. Some secular organizations, like the Army, are almost like religions or even cults. The Army Values are not religious, but they are sacred, to my mind. Some imperatives in the US Army, such as the subordination of the military to civilian control first demonstrated once and forever by George Washington, are as dearly and fervently held as any religious value.

And a word about evolution, just in case.

You may recall from high school the theory of Lamarck that you could get species of lizards to have short tails by just cutting off their tails each generation. But that doesn't work. This business of our moral values being inherited may seem Lamarckian, added on anew each generation, but it's not.

Let's say that it became a cultural value all over the world that women wanted to have sex only with men with hairless chests. As has already happened to some degree, men would shave their chests. But their offspring would not be affected, and just as many boy babies would be born destined to have hairy chests as were born before.

Now let's suppose that women decided they wanted to have sex only with men with hairy chests. (Of course Mankind would invent chest toupees, or pressure and pay Big Pharma to create something that would have all us guys' chests looking like Austin Powers', but let's assume that they couldn't. Or if they did, the side effect was sterility. Whatever. Work with me here.) Then promptly, men with hairless chests would not find partners willing to reproduce, and (assuming men's hairiness is not coded for exclusively on women's X chromosome... unlikely but I didn't bother to investigate) it wouldn't take too many generations for hairless chested guys to become very rare.

The point is: culture would promptly affect biology.

The way we are, including our genetic heritage, influences our moral values, which influence our politics.

It seems unlikely if not completely wacky to think that my position on tax policy or fossil fuel subsidies is genetically determined. Is there evidence that our genes determine our politics? The short answer is, yes, with caveats. Remember what we said about being born with certain moral values, that they are pre-wired, that is, "organized in advance of experience." They are not immutably fixed, but we are not born with blank pages; our genes do confer innate predispositions. Likewise, certain genes can express themselves in ways that predispose a person to have liberal or conservative views.

Let's pause for a 30,000-foot look at liberalism versus conservatism. Most broadly and almost by definition, liberals are characterized by being open to new stuff, they have a willingness to set aside the old ways and embrace new experiences, new tastes, new foods, new ways of doing things and thinking about things. Society needs that, needs innovation and exploration in order to adapt and thrive, so such behavior is rewarded. But society also needs someone to pump the brakes and declare that society must slow its roll, because there is value in the old ways.

A conservative is someone who
stands athwart history, yelling 'stop.' (31)
-- William F. Buckley

Traditions didn't arise just because people had nothing else to do, they worked; they provide structure and certainty, they reduce bewilderment, and they avoid or mitigate threats. There is a baby in the bathwater. Many new things can be dangerous; new foods can be poison; new ideas can be subversion; new behaviors can threaten the family and the established functional social order. An oversimplified example: the US Army adopted new, looser ways of training and readiness after World War II, especially in the Army occupying Japan. This liberal adaptation happened not to be functional, indeed it was disastrous, and we got our asses kicked at the onset of the Korean War. The US Marine Corps did not so liberalize and arguably kept us from getting pushed off the Korean peninsula in 1950. As much as it pains me being an Army guy, score one for the Corps (and its conservative values, better suited to that time and place).

You may have immediately been drawn to one or the other description in the previous paragraph. But note, each can be needed at different times. Diversity is an asset because selective pressures may require a conservative or a liberal approach, so a given society should have access to both in order to be able to adapt. As John Stuart Mill said, "A party of order and stability, and a party of progress or reform, are both necessary elements of a healthy state of political life." (32)

And there are apparent discrepancies we will need to account for. After all, if you're a never-Trumper who wants to stop logging and burning down the rainforests, that can be seen as conservative, even reactionary. It goes back to the prism through which you are seeing things: is it really the conservative in you looking to keep things as they are, the moral axis of avoiding *degradation* of the natural world, or is it your liberal tendency to avoid *harm* and to be *fair* to indigenous inhabitants (and to anybody else on Earth who breathes)? And if you want a disrupter like Trump to take over, that can be seen as a very liberal, even revolutionary stance. But again, is it really your inner revolutionary that doesn't care that much about *subversion of authority* (political correctness), or is it your conservative imperative for the don't-tread-on-me flavor of *liberty* and intolerance of *oppression* (even if that oppression is more perceived than real)?

Here's a possible contemporary example of these moral foundations in action:

In the Trump administration, undocumented persons came to our southern border (let's ignore for the time being international laws to which the US is party that make it legal for someone to seek asylum). Consistent with policy, children were separated from their families and put in cages.

A never-Trump liberal sees children being **harmed**, and poor people being treated **unfairly**, and is outraged.

A Trump supporter sees adults trying to circumvent the law (engaging in **subversion** of our sovereignty rather than recognizing our **authority**), believes that many of the children are being brought by coyotes, and concludes that, well, even if the family separation policy is bad, and they were brought by their parents, they asked for it.

A conservative sees the **sanctity** of the family being violated, but also sees the Trump law and order view of **authority**, and is conflicted.

There is nuance beyond what we've considered here, such as where libertarians fit in to this model. Their name helps: they value liberty above all. Briefly, libertarians and liberals started off as those folks who saw the old repressive order of royalty and the church as *oppressing* (the *liberty* of), *harming*, and *cheating* the common people (note, those are the three foundations favored by liberals). In the nineteenth century liberals bifurcated; some whom we now call liberals in the USA came to see the super-rich, the new robber barons of the industrial revolution, and corporations, as being the new aristocracy and they saw government, *a la* Teddy Roosevelt, as being the only entity strong enough to protect us all from runaway capitalism. The others, libertarians, retained their distrust of government *authority*. Libertarians are liberals when they resist government intrusion into our lives, so if we decide to smoke pot or get an abortion libertarians believe that's not the government's business. But they do not value the *care* foundation as much as *liberty*, so they're conservatives when it comes to government programs to care for the poor or deliver healthcare etc.; and the individual mandate, or government requiring an individual to purchase health insurance? No way. And forget about seatbelts or helmets for motorcyclists or collecting taxes for social security too.

In addition to libertarians, you could imagine a million permutations on these six moral axes. Consider a conservative who values *sanctity*, whose parents were public schoolteachers and he had some life experiences that impressed him so that he regards education as sacred, and votes Republican on all matters except he is an untiring advocate for our public schools.

For our purposes, the relationships and linkages between our morality and just this paradigm of liberal versus conservative, should be enough. Most importantly, while not gospel and of course subject to change, this paradigm is not just theoretical, it has a sound empirical basis.

But back to the idea of our genes dictating our politics: studies of twins indicate that we inherit around a third to a half of the variability we have in our political views. (A surprisingly large number of attributes we might have thought were completely acquired rather than inherited have significant genetic contributions, from the music we prefer to how spicy we like our foods to how likely we are to get divorced; it's pretty amazing, but beyond the scope of this book.) Multiple genes differ between liberals and conservatives. Our genes affect the way our neurotransmitters function, and that has a lot to do with how we respond to new sensations, whether we seek them out or regard them as threatening, an essential discriminator between liberalism and conservatism. (33)

Danger provokes stronger reactions from conservatives than from liberals, from sources as diverse as from loud noises to germs. (34) The love of liberals for new and sensational experiences (think, hippies, sex drugs and rock'n'roll) may be mediated by their metabolism of dopamine. (35) And we've seen that data indicate that conservatives and liberals favor different moral foundations.

So this is where we've arrived:

Environmental pressures lead to certain genes being selected, Biology 101.

Our biology and our culture interact.

The environment includes social contacts, and our moral codes are part of that.

Our morality is integral to our political stance.

Our nurture and experiences do affect the development of our personalities and preferences. But our genes affect and at least partially determine our native liberalism versus conservatism, and as we've seen, perhaps half of our politics.

And while not all the exact genes that might code for the way we favor specific moral foundations have been determined, and future evidence about our genetic endowment may inform adjustments in the moral foundations Haidt has expounded upon (36), it is reasonable to conclude that a significant proportion of our inner elephant is just as genetically determined as is our eye color.

So when we encounter someone who holds a polar opposite political view of ours, it should be no surprise that trying to convince them of how correct our view is meets with roughly the same success as convincing them that they really should enjoy Indian food like saag panir with garlic naan rather than that cheeseburger they're eating. It's built in; it just doesn't taste right to them.

We can employ reason to modify our reactions and beliefs; but we must want it... as if our reputation depended on it.

Unfortunately, the tendency to create arguments to support our point of view is not limited just to lawyers and press secretaries. As we've seen, it's part of us, it's a feature, not some bug that we naturally tend to eliminate from our Spock-like logic. Attempts by academics to develop ways of "de-biasing" their students have generally failed. If an academic environment ostensibly dedicated to finding Truth has stumbled, consider how less likely the self-serving rough and tumble of politics or even family arguments at Thanksgiving are to succeed.

It's really, really the way we are.

Are we destined then to live in a world of spin and dissembling? Is there no escape? I believe the answer is that we can escape mendacity. Some environments do produce truth. It has to do with our reputations.

Reputation

Haidt recalls Plato's *Republic*, wherein Plato's brother Glaucon challenges Socrates and makes the argument that people are more concerned with their reputations, that is, with the *appearance* that they are doing good, than they are concerned with the *reality* of *doing* good. Men act properly because they're afraid to get caught; if they knew they wouldn't get caught, then they're dogs: without consequences they'll behave abominably. Socrates disagrees, asserting that a truly happy person is just and harmonious on the inside. Haidt regards this as being an argument for reason to prevail, and that's not the way things work, as we've discussed. His conclusion is that Glaucon is "the guy who got it right -- the guy who realized that the most important principle for designing an ethical society is to *make sure that everyone's reputation is on the line all the time*, so that bad behavior will always bring bad consequences." (37)

We consider reputation in the last chapter.

If we want to change people's minds, we must appeal first to their emotions

Recall the moral foundations:

Care/harm -- this moral foundation is felt by everyone including conservatives but is most strongly felt by liberals.

Liberty/oppression -- all three (liberals, conservatives, and libertarians) are motivated by this imperative, but especially libertarians. Liberals' affinity for equality is largely a function of this foundation.

Fairness/cheating -- both liberals and conservatives tend to feel that people who do the work should get the rewards proportional to that work, and they dislike cheaters and free riders. (Liberals feel that the adult children of rich people are free riders, and conservatives tend to feel the same way about welfare recipients.) Since it is frequently the case that *most* people do indeed do the work, that is, working people do the work, liberals lean toward equality in distributing the benefits. Conservatives are more sensitive about free riders. Since it is not always the case that everyone does the work, conservatives intensely dislike the prospect of free riders getting the benefits of their labor. They are more insistent about *proportionality* in distributing benefits, and thus are more tolerant of inequality, more aspirational toward high achievement and high reward, and often more deferential to those who have demonstrated such achievement, that is, the wealthy.

Conservatives find resonance with these first three, and with the last three as well. Liberals favor the first three, and not so much the last three. Indeed, liberals can be downright antagonistic toward these last three.

Loyalty/betrayal -- Liberals often view loyalty as just a polite way of legitimizing racial discrimination and exclusion.

Authority/subversion -- To liberals, authority is too often abused. Especially if you've seen or been on the short end of the stick when state power is employed, you are less worried about offending authority, and see authority as oppression.

Sanctity/degradation -- And lastly, liberals can see sanctity as an excuse for organized religion to justify misogynistic repression of women, homophobia, racism, etc.

Of course the liberal disdain for these last three is not absolute. Liberals want Joe Manchin to be more *loyal* to the Democratic agenda, they wanted the Trump administration to recognize and submit to the *authority* of Congressional subpoenas, and to whatever degree progressives had ever found anything *sacred* about the Presidential Medal of Freedom, they felt it was *degraded* when it was awarded to Rush Limbaugh.

The liberal blind spot

Liberals' relative disregard of the last three moral foundations gives rise to what Haidt refers to as "blind spot on the left." This blind spot adversely affects the ability of liberals to govern, as they don't adequately value traditions and can attempt too much change too quickly, and that confers an advantage upon conservatism. (38) I'm reminded of the scene in the film version of Doctor Zhivago wherein the titular character is talking with his communist policeman half-brother; Zhivago admires the revolutionaries, comparing them to surgeons, saying 'You cut out the social injustices of life, it's marvelous.' His half-brother (played by Alec Guinness) asks, 'If you feel that way, then why not join the [communist] party?' to which Zhivago (Omar Sharif) replies 'That's a deep operation. Someone must keep life alive, by living.' Revolutions can kill a society.

It is a paradox: liberals are more open to new experiences, they seek out new life and new civilizations, but they can't seem to appreciate the moral imperatives that motivate millions of their countrymen. Conservative politicians tend to touch on all six foundations, touch the emotions and capture the affections of those who value all six, not just the first three; but liberals and liberal politicians tend to value loyalty less, respect authority less, and appreciate sanctity less, and thus they ignore if not overtly antagonize those who are passionate about those last three.

The relative openness of liberals to new information is part of the reason the subtitle of this book is 'Helping liberals understand, etc.' Can you imagine if I'd targeted the more conservative Trump supporters? I have no idea if anyone is going to read this book as it is, but if it had a subtitle like "Helping Trump supporters understand why liberals supported Hillary and Joe," I don't think I could give them away. I don't want to demonstrate the bigotry of low expectations, but conservatives tend to be content with what they already know and with viewpoints they already hold (we all do, but conservatives more so, almost by definition). As reasonable as I assert most of them are, I don't think a lot of Trump supporters give much of a damn about trying to understand or appreciate or learn anything from those they see as smug coastal liberal elites. Maybe I'm wrong.

I can hear my conservative and Trump-supporting friends protesting. 'How can you say that liberals are more open and accepting? Liberals are all about cancel culture and are judgmental and hypercritical.' And there is truth to that. A liberal theater critic for the *Village Voice* wrote in 2004: (39)

> Republicans don't believe in the imagination, partly because so few of them have one, but mostly because it gets in the way of their chosen work, which is to destroy the human race and the planet. Human beings, who have imaginations, can see a recipe for disaster in the making; Republicans, whose goal in life is to profit from disaster and who don't give a hoot about human beings, either can't or won't. Which is why I personally think they should be exterminated before they cause any more harm.

That sounds like it includes some deliberately provocative hyperbole, and certainly doesn't reflect the views of most liberals. But for conservatives, it sounds very familiar and confirms how they believe liberals feel about them: liberal haters gonna hate.

The liberal burden

It's the job of liberals to bridge the gap. Sorry, that's the way I see it. If you're a liberal, you're supposed to be more open and inclusive; so, be more open and inclusive. I'm trying to appeal to liberals' willingness to ingest something new, learn what makes Trump supporters tick, because even as traumatized as liberals were in 2016, if liberals could really understand Trumpists, they wouldn't want their Trump-supporting countrymen to come to *harm*. Liberals want to be *fair* (or at least to be seen as fair). And they may be more open to seeing their own limitations (witness Democratic hand-wringing as they try to legislate), they want to know more about themselves and why they do what they do. Also I'm trying to appeal to Trump supporters who feel they have not been treated *fairly*, who feel that their patriotism, their national *loyalty* is not appreciated, and are at least willing to give a book to their clueless liberal friends and relatives (and maybe even read it themselves). It may seem manipulative on my part, and it can be, but I submit that I'm not that clever; I'm just trying to communicate in a way that people will be willing to hear.

I hope that the preceding chapters have laid the groundwork for us better to understand each other, and better recognize why people with differing views believe and act as they do. And I believe that our understanding can actually enhance communication. But if we really want to have an exchange of ideas, really want to change someone else's mind, or, miracle of miracles, actually learn something that changes our own mind, we must connect with people, and not just wish to or try to control them.

More about that when we get to Part III and talk about how to fix all this, for ourselves, our families, our communities and beyond.

But first, we need some appreciation for how it is that so many Americans heard Trump, felt such emotional resonance with his person and his message, and concluded he was the right person to lead the nation.

Summary of Part I

We are programmed to thrive and survive in groups.

We will favor our group (our tribe, our team) to win against others.

But we will oppose the other group even if it means our group suffers.

Our identity has expanded to integrate a number of our identities.

These different identities have merged in such a way as to influence our politics.

People who see a threat coming, are afraid.

The heretofore dominant group of white Americans sees change coming.

We are guided first and foremost by our emotions, followed by our reason (which our press secretary explains to others).

Our reason serves to support our passions: Must I believe this, or can I believe that?

We are groupish, rather than only selfish.

There are moral dimensions we value.

They're in our genes. They bind us to certain perspectives, and blind us to the legitimacy of those with other perspectives.

The way we are, including our moral values, influences our politics.

We can employ reason to modify the way we react, what we believe, but we must want it... because it blinds.

If we want people to change their minds, we must appeal first to their emotions.

If we want someone to listen to us, really hear us, we must connect; control doesn't work.

For you, my liberal friends, to be willing to listen and try to understand conservatives and Trump supporters, you would need to have some insight into the thinking of those Trump supporters.

How did they come to believe what they believe about Trump?

For that, let's move on to Part II.

Part II

The Things Trump Said That Connect with Some People

I'm not going to quote Donald Trump; but I'll paraphrase what he told people, in the following "Trumpisms":

We have lost something, but we can get it back.

Politicians (many or most of them) are full of it and our politics needs disruption.

Politicians (many or most) don't listen to you, you, the forgotten people;

they don't hear you,

they don't value you,

they don't care about you,

they don't give a damn.

The whole system is too corrupt; the system is rigged.

As a result, you're getting ripped off.

Political correctness has (often) swung too far and can be out of control.

There is a lot of Fake information, Fake News, out there.

We need our country to be safe and secure.

We should all love our country.

Trump was correct about all those things,

and many people felt that he was correct.

His sell was:

The coastal elites have contempt for you and are ripping you off.

Since you're getting ripped off, you should be angry about it.

Political correctness is out of control and needs to be reined in.

Believe only me.

I, Trump, know The Swamp, and only I can fix it.

You need a Disruptor, to blow up the whole damn thing, and I'm your guy.

This section is not a complete chronicle of all of Trump's claims or their veracity, or all the arguments for and against his policies or behaviors. But clearly, he said things, he conveyed ideas, and he tapped into concerns that propelled him to the presidency. If liberals, if we all as a country, do not adequately address the legitimate concerns and even the perceived grievances experienced by Trump supporters, we leave in place the forces that led to his rise and we are asking for a repeat.

Liberals are worried that Trump's actions have been anti-democratic, that his ability to command the thinking of his base and to intimidate GOP politicians, and that his rhetoric and behavior both before and after the 2020 election, have been and continue to be threats to the foundations of our republic. With all his baggage, Trump was able to tweet "#OVERTURN," overtly calling for the dismissal of millions of votes in multiple states so he could retain power, and yet he managed to get the majority of House Republicans to sign on to his lawsuit to do so, managed to get members of both the House and Senate to object to the legitimacy of the electoral college vote, and managed to retain the support of media viewed by millions of Americans. If you're a liberal and that scares you, if you have been turned off by what you see as Trump's unacceptable character and behavior, then imagine if you will what life would be like if someone you see as a right wing demagogue came along who was just as skilled at inflaming grievance but who was even modestly articulate, who wasn't as crass, who didn't have the history of misogyny and sexual assaults, who didn't offend some potential supporters with obvious lies, and who could claim more working class authenticity.

If such a prospect chills your blood, then you cannot dismiss the concerns of over 74 million of your countrymen. You need to address them, and before you can, you need to understand them.

> If there is any one secret of success it lies in the ability to get the other person's point of view and see things from their angle as well as your own. (1)
>
> -- Henry Ford

Chapter 4

Make America Great Again

Trumpism: We have lost something, but we can get it back.

> In October 1962, President Kennedy sent former secretary of state Dean Acheson to Paris to inform French President Charles de Gaulle of the findings that had precipitated the Cuban missile crisis. Acheson described the situation and brought forth the intelligence photos documenting the presence of the Russian missiles. But de Gaulle declined to view the photos, saying "The word of the President of the United States is good enough for me." (1)

I'm not going to spend a lot of time quoting Donald Trump. Even his supporters recognize that he is not always the most articulate; he takes pride in not being a politician, and not being politically correct. He often says things that are completely contradictory to what he has previously said, often quite recently, sometimes in the same paragraph. I could trot out any number of malaprops, plenty of scrambled sentences that make no sense, and others that are just clearly untrue. But that would be missing the point.

Remember the lesson of the 2016 Republican primaries? Trump's critics and opponents and the media took him literally but not seriously, and Trump's supporters took him seriously but not literally.

To his supporters, it really doesn't matter exactly what Trump said. What matters is how they feel about what he's said and more importantly, how they feel about who he is, what they believe he means, and what they believe he feels about them.

His policies may not be consistent with his rhetoric, but that doesn't matter, it doesn't bother those who are angry with establishment politicians, coastal elites and the Deep State. (And, he's a reality TV star... many Americans just love those celebrities.)

If you're a liberal, a never-Trumper, you may be hesitant to entertain what Trump said, why people could be ***for*** Trump, supportive of Trump. There must be some minimal threshold of intelligence and character and common decency that someone must meet before even being considered for high office, and Trump doesn't come close to that minimum. You have a litany of items that you feel render Trump completely unsuited to the presidency, so to any reasonable person he should be disqualified before hearing a word he says about anything. You just don't get it: how anyone could ignore this stuff? Surely Trump will fade away and Trumpism will disappear along with him. His hold on a big chunk of the American electorate must not be real.

Well friend, it's real, and you'll need to deal with it. Never-Trumpers fear that the rest of the world sees us and can't quite figure out what's happened to America. Writing in *Foreign Affairs*, Jonathan Kirshner points out that with the election of President Joe Biden, America has largely returned to its customary policies both foreign and domestic. But it is not clear that this change is here to stay. We don't know, and the world cannot know, if the self-absorbed approach of "America first" might not reappear in 2024 or 2028.

> The 2020 election put to rest the comforting fable that Trump's election [in 2016] was a fluke. Trump is the United States—or at least a very large part of it. Many Americans will choke on that sentiment, but other countries don't have the luxury of clinging to some idealized version of the United States' national character. Trump presided over dozens of ethical scandals, egregious procedural lapses, and startling indiscretions, most of which would have ended the political career of any other national political figure of the past half century. But the trampling of norms barely registered with most of the American public. Nor did the sheer, horrifying incompetence of the administration's handling of the gravest public health crisis in a century chase Trump from the political scene in disgrace. (Imagine what would have happened to Jimmy Carter, a decent man dealt a difficult hand by an oil shock and the Iranian hostage crisis. Those events were enough to have his approval rating plummet into the 20s and soon send him packing after his landslide defeat in 1980.) ... Even so, 74 million people voted for [Trump]—nine million more than did in 2016 ... One cannot paint a picture of the American

> polity and the country's future foreign policy without including the significant possibility of a large role for Trumpism, with or without Trump himself in the Oval Office. (2)

Let me oversimplify some rationale for how this could become true.

First let's recognize that most Trump supporters, most Republicans, indeed most Democrats and most Americans, are "low information voters". That's not an insult, it just reflects the fact that most people are not political junkies, they don't have the time or inclination to dive deeply into politics, to fact-check the things politicians say, even to question their own assumptions. If you're reading this book, there's a fair chance that you are atypical, a high information voter.

Also, let's recognize that our history of party politics travels forward with us. Many if not most Americans value all six of the moral foundations we've discussed, and tend to lean conservative, lean Republican; and of those who are more politically active and vote more reliably, even more lean Republican. While the polarization surrounding Trump has lit a fire under all voters that is scrambling this dynamic, there traditionally has been a more baked-in preference for the GOP ("Democrats fall in love, Republicans fall in line"). So, for many people, their elephants are already predisposed to favor the Republican candidate(s), and will filter incoming information accordingly. Most people consume their information in broad strokes, and as we've seen, those who do educate themselves more completely are just better able to construct arguments to convince themselves they were correct from the get-go. There has been no lack of right wing media providing fuel to support any pro-Trump position, and to disregard any anti-Trump position.

If you're a liberal, the broad strokes below will be unacceptable to you; if you're a Trump supporter, they may not be perfect but some of them may make some sense. Remember two things: first, his supporters tend to take him seriously but not literally, so they can dismiss a lot of the behavior as just Trump being Trump, being outrageous and 'owning the libs'. And second, all the rationales for his words and deeds need only make enough sense to allow a supporter to answer to himself 'yes' to the question, "*Can* I believe this?" Here are some of the broad strokes:

All the braggadocio, the bluster, the insults, the unpresidential behavior, mocking of the disabled, fall into the bucket of, "he's a fighter."

Every misstep, every instance of confusion about this or that policy, the fact that apparently those who brief him must simplify the material they present to him, all are unimportant because "he's not a politician." Trump's marginalized supporters don't trust the airbrushed blow-dried slick talking compromising politicians, and his willingness to say the outrageous separates him from politicians (and it's entertaining!).

His jaw-dropping, liberal-distressing *faux pas* like 'look at my African-American here,' his assertion that there are 'very fine people' among tiki torch wielding white supremacists, his plan to 'ban all Muslims from entering the United States,' that 'Mexico is not sending their best... they're rapists etc.,' all that just proves that he speaks his unvarnished truth because "he's not politically correct."

His unnecessary provocations of our neighbors and allies are because "he's being tough"... on somebody.

His trade wars, tariffs, removal of the USA from international accords, those are not wrong, they're his reaction to the stupid deals of his predecessors: "he's a businessman" who just wants to put "America first." Those left behind by the global economy feel that America has become weak and poor, and they throw their lot in with Trump since he says he's a successful businessman who seems (seemed anyway) to win all the time. What liberals see as populist demagoguery is attractive to many whose factory job has moved overseas.

When he seems to favor the Russian position over that of his own intelligence community, when he embraces dictators and fails to object to cyber-attacks or literal attacks such as the murder of a journalist working for an American newspaper or bounties placed on the heads of American service personnel downrange, that's because he is intuitive, "he has a great mind," he operates from his gut.

All the Trump misogyny and philandering, multiple wives, bragging about sexual assault, "grab 'em by the p##sy" and "when you're a star they let you do it;" he's a man's man, a billionaire playboy, and that's just how such people behave.

All the anti-science lies, injecting bleach and 'COVID is just the flu;' all go into the 'I love the poorly educated' because 'you're the elite, not these highly educated coastal wimps' bucket.

It may seem beyond the pale that he can try to extort an investigation of a political opponent from the Ukrainian president, or call the Secretary of State of Georgia and tell him he needs 11,780 votes. If you're a low information Trump supporter, that's not credible, it's all just mainstream media noise. "It was a perfect phone call" is enough of a rebuttal. And if you're a high information voter or the attempt to subvert the election in Georgia doesn't seem to be completely kosher, well, "he's a negotiator." He was a New York real estate developer, playing hardball with some tough hombres, of course he's going to have some rough edges.

Likewise, his history of racist or ethically suspect behavior, Trump University, Trump charity, pardoning a man (Steve Bannon) who was indicted for embezzling money from Trump supporters, etc., all go into the 'hey nobody's perfect' bucket. After all, we all knew about most of that stuff years ago. And, unlike you and me, he's a billionaire, so he must have been doing something right, he knows how the system works, and he's going to put that to work for us, so get over it and get out of the way.

That's the etch-a-sketch of our elephant versus our rider:

Must I believe the bad things about him, or can I believe what I prefer to believe?

Perhaps you finally draw a line at "The Big Lie," Trump's ongoing claims that the election was stolen and his supporters are going to lose their country if they don't fight like hell. If it seems to you that his supporters aren't rationalizing or agreeing with him with a nod and a wink, that all too many of them took him both seriously *and literally*, you have a point. We may never know if Trump himself actually believed (or still believes) that he won the 2020 election and that it was stolen from him, but he certainly said he did, repeatedly, unequivocally, vigorously.

Remember the *authority* versus *subversion* moral foundation. Daniel Day Lewis as the title character in the film *Lincoln* declared that he as president was cloaked in great power and authority, and he commanded his subordinates to find him the votes needed to pass the 14th amendment. I thought he was marvelous and inspiring in that scene. Despite Johnson and the Tonkin Gulf, despite Nixon and Watergate, despite Bill and Monica, despite Bush and Saddam's nuclear program, the default of many Americans is still to trust what their president says, especially if he literally wraps himself in the flag. And particularly if he explicitly declares that those who oppose him have subverted our democracy by literally cheating in the election. Trump supporters trust in the authority that Trump personified, and their elephants were already leaning in the direction of *authority* over *subversion* before those values were evoked and amplified. A President's words are important; they carry weight, more so if they are a call to arms. In the second half of 2021, we don't yet know if there will be a reckoning on that account.

But back to being great again

Just about every American politician harkens back to the days when Real Men Strode the Earth, when we weren't wimpy self-indulgent milquetoasts, y'know, back before we Lost Our Greatness. In my lifetime just about every president has dipped into that well. And it always resonates. Most of us have some feeling that at some time in the past, we as a people were stronger, bolder, more respected in the world, sharper in our vision, clearer in our speech, more square of jaw, broader of shoulder and narrower of hip, harder working, more creative, more clever, more productive, better dressed, taller, more attractive and better smelling. There were good old days and we've somehow lost them.

Whether this is true or not, it somehow feels true, so for argument's sake let's assume it is. Further, let's ignore the fact that whenever we look into our glowing American past, things get complicated because the racism just keeps on coming. Professor of African-American studies at Emory University Carol Anderson notes "America is aspirational.... Marginalized people have used those aspirations to say, 'This is what you say you are, but this is what you do.' But what also happens is those aspirations get encoded as achievements. You get this longing for a mythical past." (3)

But let's set that aside; we'll talk about race later, in chapter 10.

So when was America "great"?

Short answer: the 1950s.

In the 40s we were in World War II, the 30s were the Depression, the 20s were roaring but a fall was coming so, no, not the 20s, 30s or 40s. Back before that we've got World War I, we weren't close to being a world power and the turn of the century just becomes a quaint Twilight Zone episode. Forward from the 50s doesn't work either. The 60s had the War in Vietnam and hippies; the 70s were Nixon and Watergate and onset of the hostage crisis; the 80s had economic growth and Reaganism but the cocaine and excesses were decadent and unhealthy; and the closer we get to the present the more clearly we can see the precursors to all our current flaws, so no, we couldn't have been great then.

So, the 1950s; Leave It To Beaver hoop dresses, lots of happy (white) people, victorious in War (the Korean War was way over there and not on TV, so, fuggedaboudit...), and a booming economy. One parent working a job got you into a house with a car and a television, wives were at home, two kids were in school and jobs were everywhere. In the early 1950s there were more automobiles in Los Angeles than there were in all of Asia. America was Great.

All our current problems were present, if not overtly then at least in seed form, back in the 1950s. But there were some real differences. Corporations were generally not as avaricious as they later became. In 1951 Frank Abrams, the chairman of Standard Oil of New Jersey, said that "The job of management is to maintain an equitable and working balance among the claims of the various directly affected interest groups... stock-holders, employees, customers, and the public at large. Business managers are gaining professional status partly because they see in their work the basic responsibilities [to the public] that other professional men have long recognized as theirs." (4)

JD Zellerbach, namesake and chairman of the board of the paper conglomerate Crown Zellerbach Corporation and later appointed United States Ambassador to Italy in 1957, was quoted in *Time* that "the majority of Americans support private enterprise, not as a God-given right but as the best practical means of conducting business in a free society.... They regard business management as a stewardship, and they expect it to operate the economy as a public trust for the benefit of all the people." (5) Such views of corporations seem quaint now.

Corporate ethics and responsibility were not the only differences. Taxes were more progressive. During the Eisenhower administration, the top marginal tax rate was 91%. (Under a Republican, 91%!) Even at the onset of the Reagan administration, the richest paid taxes at a 74% marginal federal tax rate, and CEOs made 30 times as much as their companies' lowest paid workers. Reagan cut the top rate to 28%, busted unions, and subsequently CEOs no longer made 30 times, but now make roughly *373 times* as much as their lowest paid workers.

Education at our great state universities was inexpensive. I started out at a junior college, and earned my first degree, an Associate of Arts, for about ten dollars a semester. A year at the University of California Berkeley cost me about $1500, and it was easy to find a student loan to cover that. Union membership was at its highest in the 1950s so labor enjoyed the benefits of collective bargaining. We spent more on Research and Development (R&D) in the 50s than did any other nation. Federal spending on R&D as a percentage of GDP peaked in the 1960s and was more than twice what we spend now. With all the problems I've listed earlier about our politics of the 1950s, politicians knew each other, worked across the aisle with each other, and (often) respected each other.

Lastly, we were great when we had heroes, when we had Great Men who were touched and ordained to Greatness by God. This perspective is understandably strong among Evangelical Christians in our country.

I don't know Donald Trump personally, so I don't know if he is religious; but if I were he, I'd be tempted to believe in the wisdom of Providence. Born into wealth, a salary of a quarter million bucks a year as a toddler, Teflon despite bankruptcies and divorces, and then raised up from The Apprentice to the Presidency. I might conclude: I am destined to be the most powerful man on earth because I must be the greatest man on earth, the wisest of the wise. Look at the response I get from people; they love me, they show up at my rallies by the thousands because they recognize my greatness. My judgement and expertise are greater than that of all others, generals, doctors, so-called experts, coastal elites. I think of things others don't, like hitting the body with a powerful light, or using bleach inside, like a cleaning. Nobody else thought of that, just me. And if you liberals scoff and think that's stupid, you might want to wake up and notice: I was (and should still be) President of the United States of America, and you're not, and you never will be.

There was not much if anything in Trump's comments about all the elements mentioned in this chapter that were so much better back when We Were Great, but the general theme came through. We were great and now we're not, and it's somebody's fault.

We were great before you started getting ripped off.

And you're getting ripped off.

Because the System is Rigged.

Chapter 5

The System is Rigged

Trumpisms:

Politicians don't listen to you, they don't hear you, they don't value you, they don't care about you, they don't give a damn. Politicians are full of it, and stupid.

As a result, you're getting ripped off. Since you're getting ripped off, you should be angry about it.

Our politics needs disruption. You need a Disruptor, and I'm your guy.

The whole system is too corrupt; the system is rigged. Only I, Trump, can fix it.

The Ferengis would approve of our current American economic situation.

The 35th Rule of Acquisition states that "Peace is good for business."

This is in contrast to the 34th Rule of Acquisition: "War is good for business."

If you're rich, no matter what happens, you not only land on your feet, you get richer. For example, you or your loved ones may have been hurt financially during the pandemic that started in earnest around March of 2020. But consider: Amazon has 860,000 employees.

If Jeff Bezos had given every one of them a bonus of $80,000 in the autumn of 2020, EVERY ONE OF THEM, he would still have had more money left over *than he had at the beginning of the pandemic.*

And he is not alone. During the pandemic, as happened during the great Recession of 2008-2009, inequality grew. That just means, the rich got richer, unlike many if not most of the rest of us. Progressives point to some simple numbers as illustrative. Not to pick on Jeff Bezos again, but his wealth in 2009 was $6.8 billion; in 2021 it was $188 billion. Mark Zuckerberg's 2009 wealth was $2 billion; and in 2021 it was $117 billion. Between 2009 and New Year's Day 2021, the federal minimum hourly wage went from $7.25, all the way up to: $7.25. No matter what you think the minimum should or should not be or whether there should be a minimum wage at all, there is an apparent contrast in the way the distribution of wealth seems to be structured in our country.

No wonder people who are not rich feel like the system is rigged, and they are willing to throw a grenade into the system just to blow the whole damn thing up. And if the grenade's name is Donald Trump, he becomes president.

> The day will come when our Republic will be an impossibility. It will be an impossibility because wealth will be concentrated in the hands of a few. A republic cannot stand upon bayonets, and when that day comes, when the wealth of the nation will be in the hands of a few, then we must rely upon the wisdom of the best elements in the country to readjust the laws of the nation to the changed conditions. (1)
>
> - - James Madison

My brother says I'm channeling the sentiment of the Symbionese Liberation Army with my rhetoric in these next two chapters. Maybe he's right. You judge.

With some exceptions, here's the cycle:

The first priority of most of our elected politicians is: re-election.

The mothers' milk of politics is money.

Corporations and the super-wealthy have lots of money.

Politicians are beholden to those who finance their election and re-election.

So, politicians preferentially represent the interests of the wealthy, of capital.

The wealthy continue to support financially those who legislate on their behalf.

Rinse, repeat.

The connective tissue of the rigging is economic. It's like The Force, it surrounds and enfolds all the moral imperatives and the political sequelae we've discussed so far. Capital amplifies, facilitates and manipulates the expression of our elephants. And while a castigation of the role of money in politics may seem in this polarized day and age to be part of some socialist agenda, **Trump identified this rigging as a problem and his supporters felt it and feel it still**. My bias is that capitalism is potentially the greatest engine for the promotion of wealth broadly in society. But paradoxically, the success of capital in rigging the system is the greatest threat to the continuation of capitalism.

Complaints about the misbehaviors and toxic influences of corporations are not new, they date back literally hundreds of years. Thomas Jefferson in 1816 advised that we should "crush in its birth the aristocracy of our monied corporations which dare already to challenge our government to a trial of strength, and bid defiance to the laws of our country."

James Madison warned in 1817: "There is an evil which ought to be guarded against in the indefinite accumulation of property from the capacity of holding it in perpetuity by ecclesiastical corporations. The power of all corporations ought to be limited in this respect. The growing wealth acquired by them never fails to be a source of abuses."

So what's the big deal with corporations? How is it that the Founders regarded them as such a threat to democracy?

Let's consider some obvious facts: a corporation is not you.

A corporation does not share your interests.

It is not looking out for you.

It doesn't care about you.

And it's bigger and stronger than you.

Per Senator Sheldon Whitehouse, there are six attributes of corporations, and these attributes exacerbate each other. (2)

First, they just want to make money.

While corporate laws vary from state to state, so it may or may not be a legal mandate that corporations maximize shareholder value, "the notion has been embraced by increasingly powerful activist hedge funds that profit from harassing boards into adopting strategies that raise share price in the short term, and by corporate executives driven by 'pay for performance' schemes that tie their compensation to each year's shareholder returns. ...It is activist hedge funds and modern executive compensation practices... that drive so many of today's public companies to myopically focus on short-term earnings; cut back on investment and innovation; mistreat their employees, customers and communities; and indulge in reckless, irresponsible and environmentally destructive behaviors." (3)

Second, "Corporations have no soul or conscience."(4) They "have no personal attributes;" (5) a corporation is "without either mental or moral powers," (6) it is "without power to think, speak, or act except as live sentient human beings may think, speak, and act for it." (7)

Third, corporations are not American patriots. They don't say the pledge of allegiance. Big corporations typically are multinational. As the CEO of Exxon said, "I'm not a US company and I don't make decisions based upon what is good for the US." (8)

Fourth, corporations don't die, retire, or take vacations. Of course they can become obsolete or be outcompeted by other corporations and dissolve, but other than that, they enjoy an "artificial life extending beyond the natural lives of the incorporators, directors, and officers" (that is, "perpetual succession"). (9)

Fifth, they can be as big, which means as rich, as they can be; there is no legal or moral or political limit. And if there is no legal constraint on the ability of a corporation to use its riches to buy political influence, then there is no reason why it won't. Indeed, given point number one, that its purpose is to make money, there is every reason *for* a corporation to use its money ("invest" some of its capital) to purchase policies that will further enrich the corporation. That's its job!

Teddy Roosevelt recognized the inevitable malignancy:

> Our government, National and State, must be freed from the sinister influence or control of special interests.... We must drive the special interests out of politics.... The citizens of the United States must effectively control the mighty commercial forces which they have called into being. There can be no effective control of corporations while their political activity remains.... (10)
>
> To put an end to it will be neither a short nor an easy task, but it can be done. (11)

Sixth, as Whitehouse notes, "there is no natural limit to their appetite. No corporation says, 'You know, I think I've made enough money,' and pushes back from the table. No corporate lobby says, 'You know, I think I've acquired enough political influence,' and goes out to play with the grandchildren." (12)

> Behind the ostensible government sits enthroned an invisible government owing no allegiance and acknowledging no responsibility to the people. To destroy this invisible government, to dissolve the unholy alliance between corrupt business and corrupt politics, is the first task of the statesmanship of the day. (13)
>
> - - Teddy Roosevelt

I'm not making the case that corporations are evil; they need not be. They behave largely as one would expect, given their articles of incorporation and the laws that govern them. But a corporation is relentless; it is pretty much as my distant relative Kyle Reese described *The Terminator*: it can't be bargained with; it can't be reasoned with; it doesn't feel pity, or remorse, or fear. And it absolutely will not stop, ever....

The Tragedy of the Commons

"The Tragedy of the Commons" (14) was the title of an essay written by the late Garrett Hardin, my old biology professor at UC Santa Barbara. Tragedy in this sense is not just that something bad happens, but it had to do with what he called 'the remorseless working of things.' Due to their circumstances, the star-crossed love of Romeo and Juliet is doomed, as are they. The example of the commons is similarly inexorably tragic.

His essay went something like this. There is a village, with a 'commons,' a common area owned collectively by the entire village. There are ten shepherds, and the commons can support a hundred sheep, ten sheep per shepherd. No other resource for grazing is available. But one day one shepherd realizes, I can get more wool, or lamb chops, or whatever, if I get another sheep or two or more and graze them on the commons. That will exceed the carrying capacity of the commons, *but the detrimental effect is spread among all of us, while the benefit all accrues to me.* The second shepherd sees the logic in the first shepherd's actions, and he does the same. Multiply that thinking by all the shepherds, and you have the ruin of the commons. You must have a law that limits each shepherd to ten sheep in order to preserve the benefit of the commons to each of the shepherds. Without that law, voluntary compliance with long-term collective interest is doomed.

Good fences make good neighbors.
--Robert Frost

Today, the oceans, the air, the water, the natural and human resources of poorer countries, and the climate of the entire planet, all are the commons. Irresponsible countries and multinational corporations are the voracious shepherds. Even if the executive leaves the boardroom where a morally suspect decision has just been made, and feels misgivings as he kisses his child goodnight, like the second shepherd, he and his company must keep pace with the competition in the Darwinian corporate world, or they will become extinct. Without proper international regulation we are creating problems for ourselves and our children for generations to come, political problems, environmental problems, problems resulting from the destabilizing influences of poverty and from the anti-American sentiment that grows in the soil fertilized by corporate greed. We also commit the people who run Big Business to courses that are sometimes immoral, and often in the best long-term interest of no one.

Whitehouse continues:

> Add to these characteristics the twentieth-century advertising and marketing skills corporations have developed to sell their products, which apply well to the task of manipulating human voters. Add on size sufficient to dwarf many sovereign nations, and the massive profit that political ventures can provide. Then add the twenty-first-century technologies of constant communication. Finally, add secrecy. The result is a power that could turn our popular democracy into high-tech corporate feudalism if we don't learn how to restrain it. (15)

Whitehouse notes that as early as 1839 (you can imagine what the Founders would have thought about our current 21st century relationship with corporations and financial institutions!) a Pennsylvania congressman gave a speech warning "that in government 'corporation power is now an overshadowing influence,' and called for the 'restoration of public supremacy,' without which, he said, 'banks are government, and the very worst government.'" (16)

Somehow, we have not taken the actions necessary to wrest back control of the country. Remember that, more so than liberals, conservatives intensely dislike the prospect of free riders getting the benefits of their labor, so they are more insistent upon *proportionality* in distributing benefits, and thus are more tolerant of inequality, more aspirational toward high achievement and high reward, and often more deferential to those who have demonstrated such achievement, that is, the wealthy.

That's only fair, right? Because the "Unseen Hand" of the Free Market dictates who gets how much. This is the logical cascade:

People get paid, or otherwise come to possess capital, pretty much in proportion to the value of what they supply to society.

And in American society particularly, the value of what you supply to society, which can be identified by how much money you have, is a fairly direct reflection of how much you are "worth" to society.

Further, how much you are "worth" in a mercantile sense is a manifestation of your virtue, because your wealth is a function of your industry, which is an intrinsic good, or pleasing to God, or both.

I find this cascade highly suspect.

It ain't no disgrace to be poor, but it might as well be.
-- Kin Hubbard, American humorist and journalist

In her final weeks as my mother was dying, she was semi-comatose. Even so, we knew she wouldn't want her sons bathing her, but my sister needed help with our mom's hygiene. Hospice sent to the house a young Mexican woman, not fluent in English, an immigrant, someone we'd never met. We had reservations about having a stranger care for our mom, and we were not inclined to tolerate any roughness or insensitivity. We needn't have worried; she was gentle and caring and just an angel. At that place and time, we had a great need, and the value to us of having that need fulfilled in that manner was enormous. We knew she was probably getting only minimum wage and we wanted to give her a big gratuity, but she declined it. She told us that she was doing this out of the love and respect she had had for her own deceased mother.

There is a Russian proverb that says "You can't pay someone to do what a mother will do for free." This young woman was not related to us; she was paid to do a job, but there appeared to me to be very little relationship between how highly we valued her service and how much she was paid, nor between how much she was "worth" to society and how much money she had. My suspicion was that we had just happened to have encountered someone who was in the top 1% of virtuous people on our planet. So the above conclusion about 'wealth varying directly with virtue' is commonly, utterly, incorrect.

The pandemic has brought this into stark relief with the identification of "essential workers." We are impacted greatly by those who do the heretofore unvalued back-breaking work of harvesting our food or collecting our trash. When the chips are down, we must have relatively low paid grocers and bus drivers and nurses' aides; multi-million dollar per year hedge fund managers, not so much.

But let's also challenge the initial assumption.

Is the "Free Market" really free?

A market must have rules. There are exchanges of goods and services for money, and something must protect both buyers and sellers from getting ripped off. We must trust that some dynamic in the market prevents someone from hitting me on the head and taking my money, or paying for my goods with something that turns out to be worthless. As contemptible as "regulations" have become in the minds of some, without them, there is no trust that the market will function.

Without rules, a market is just a mugging.

The keys are: what the rules are, and who makes them.

There is a sweet spot, a Goldilocks zone wherein the market functions best. It is free from regulations that burden and from incentives that distort. When the natural strength of capital is balanced by a "countervailing force," then the rules tend to be "fair". But most Trump supporters (and I suspect most progressives and those who voted for Obama and then voted for Trump) know in their bones that things are not fair.

Trump said the system is rigged, meaning distorted in ways that you don't know about but that work against you, the forgotten American man and woman -- and Trump was right.

When it comes to the market, there is what you can see, and what you can't.

You can see welfare and low apparently progressive tax rates and earned income credits, and it may seem that the system is bending over backwards to distribute money downward from the rich to help the poor. And to many Trump supporters it appears that those indolent free-riders, Cadillac-driving "welfare queens" are getting away with murder.

We'll come back to taxes, but first, what you *don't* see is the rigging, what former Clinton Labor Secretary Robert Reich calls the ***pre-***

distribution upward: "This upward redistribution is invisible. The main conduits for it are hidden within the rules of the market -- property, monopolization, contract, bankruptcy, and enforcement -- rules that have been shaped by those with substantial wealth and political clout. It is, in this sense, a *pre*distribution upward that occurs inside the market mechanism itself, a small portion of which government later redistributes downward to the poor through taxes and transfer payments." (17)

It's beyond the scope of this book to detail all the specifics of how "property, monopolization, contract, bankruptcy, and enforcement" effect the predistribution, but certainly we non-billionaires have all experienced being on the short end of the stick. How many lawyers and lobbyists do you have pushing for your interests when members of congress are defining the rules of the market, marking up some bill in the dark of night? We're all American citizens competing in the same global market; but consider a few examples.

Property: If you're a corporation with intellectual property, or real property located overseas, your government will wrestle mightily with China or other countries to protect your property. But if you don't have huge financial assets or intellectual property, if all you have is a job, you're on your own; or worse than on your own, you're at the mercy of the corporation that owns the factory within which you work, the corporation that may send that factory overseas in a heartbeat. In opposition to a bill that would have prevented sending American jobs overseas, the US Chamber of Commerce wrote to the US Senate in 2010, "Replacing a job that is based in another country with a domestic job does not stimulate economic growth or enhance the competitiveness of American worldwide companies." (18) Thanks a lot.

Monopolization: The rules allow the big boys to squeeze out small competition. Remember diapers.com? Amazon didn't like the idea of competition from this upstart, so they undercut the price. Amazon can sell diapers at below cost until Rapture and not break a sweat, but if you're the new kid on the block, you can't afford that. Such anti-competitive practices (not just in diapers, but cable, broadband, financial systems, digital platforms, social media, etc.) are supposed to be against 'the rules', but that doesn't seem to matter. If you, Joe Citizen, want to open a hunting goods store like Cabela's, or a hardware store that would compete with Home Depot, do you believe you would have any success approaching state or local government for a subsidy or tax break or zoning waiver like the big boys get?

Contract: From credit cards to online purchases, you regularly sign agreements, with ink or digitally, that you do not read, and you do not know what you've signed. Trust me, the lawyers for the financial services companies know just what you've signed, and what you've signed away. Do you get paid for your identifying and purchasing data? If a big company is late on a loan payment, does their interest rate rocket up to 21%? Or do they get to 'restructure' the terms of the loan instead? From cell-phone plans to health care, you often sign away your rights, such as the right to sue if you've been wronged.

Bankruptcy: If you or I are faced with bankruptcy, we're up the creek. We lose almost all the assets we'd managed to grow, and our credit rating has a shadow on it for years to come. Homeowners can't reorganize their mortgages; former students can't reorganize their student loan debt. But large businesses use bankruptcy to get out of union contracts; dump their pension obligations on the federal Pension Benefit Guaranty Corporation (that's you, the taxpayer); fire people, then hire them back at half the wages; have the corporation's stock prices soar; and then give bonuses to the executives who oversaw the bankruptcy. Some of those who ran businesses into bankruptcy even run for high office.

Enforcement: You and I are justifiably afraid of breaking the law; both because we don't want to do the wrong thing, and because we know that if law enforcement is after us, we're in trouble. We don't want to be outlaws. But corporations don't care, they are not sentient, they don't have a conscience. And if you're an executive of a big enough corporation, you don't need to worry about it. Did you see the movie *Deepwater Horizon*? Large companies routinely lobby lawmakers to cut the funding and thus the staffing of agencies charged with inspecting and monitoring the companies' activities. As a result, government fails to uphold laws or to impose adequate penalties, and fails to hold executives accountable.

If you sell loose cigarettes, you risk getting choked to death. But crash the economy and you get a bailout and a bonus.

Government lawyers are often outgunned; large corporations have more assets than many entire countries, and can out-compete even the US Department of Justice. Walmart and fast food chains use often illegal tactics to defeat unionization; but as the budget for enforcement of laws and regulations regarding the rights of workers to organize has been cut, there is no penalty. Like most watchdog agencies, the National Labor

Relations Board has had its teeth pulled; there are long backlogs; and when a company is busted, the penalties are too weak to matter. If you can save $10 million by cutting corners and breaking the rules, and *if* you get caught it's only going to cost the company $1 million, it makes business sense to flout the law. And if you as an individual are functionally protected from personal liability by the corporate shield, you have no worries.

This phenomenon of "regulatory capture" is worth more discussion in the next chapter.

Our values can allow for rigging

Many conservatives and Trump supporters feel that the system is rigged, but don't rebel against the specifics of the rigging. Liberals protest: what is up with these people? Why do they keep voting against their own interests? You can understand your Trump-supporting countrymen thus:

First, remember that we are wired to favor our team over the other team, even if it means that I and my team get less than we could have gotten had I been more even-handed. Once the arguments have been understood within the frame of right versus left, or Trump versus never-Trump, or Republican versus Democrat, or all of the above, or whatever polarized perspective floats your boat, that's all most of us need or want to hear. Someone I like, someone I see as being like me, believes this is the way to go, so that's the way I'm going. Even if a deeper analysis would reveal that going that way is not good for me, we are groupish, we are tribal; and the chance for my team to gain a victory over the other side takes precedence.

But it's not only a matter of which jersey advocates are wearing. This behavior can be consistent with the core values favored more by conservatives than by liberals. Conservatives, as the name implies, tend to favor conserving that which already exists. Because even if the way things are isn't perfect, there is danger in changing too much too fast. So it is not self-deception for the following deeply held values to be operative:

If the wealthy can rig the game in their favor, they are at *liberty* at least to try to do so; and if they succeed, they have demonstrated an enviable mastery of the rough and tumble of the marketplace.

What goes around comes around: to invoke the regulatory powers of Big Government for redress of corporate abuses today would too greatly strengthen central government and would invite governmental *oppression* tomorrow.

There is a global sense of the system not being *fair*, of being *cheated*, but there is a respect for and deference to the wealthy who have rigged the system.

Those wealthy have presumably gotten wealthy because of the *proportionality* (a flavor of *fairness*) of the distribution of rewards in accordance with their brilliance and business savvy (or because of the *sanctity* of being selected by God to be born into a rich family).

And once these predistribution advantages have been codified into law, conservatives tend to defer further to the *authority* embodied in them, and regard liberals who rail against the *harm* being done as being *subversive*.

It may seem that combining such conservative values with a vote for a Disrupter to blow things up is a recipe for cognitive dissonance. But a talented demagogue can convince people he can thread the needle and only blow up the bad stuff that the bad guys on the other team have put in place.

The elephants of conservatives then can lean toward allowing misbehavior by corporations and the super-rich. There is a litany of assumptions (italicized below) regarding corporate excesses and abuses. Such rhetorical devices do not survive much scrutiny, but they typically don't get much scrutiny, and without much scrutiny, they survive just fine:

'Corporations and the wealthy deserve to be rewarded for taking risks.'

Typically, corporations don't pay for risk. Corporations are soulless beings as described earlier, so they don't care, and their CEOs often get paid no matter what (see below). Corporations and the big player private-equity manager types typically don't risk any of their own money. As exemplified by the financial institutions that created the derivatives schemes that crashed the world economy in 2008, they have the best kind of socialism: they risk other people's money; if the risk pays off they get the rewards, and if it doesn't pay off there are a myriad of tax breaks and 'special dividends' or straight up bailouts that essentially require the government (that is, you, the taxpayer) to subsidize the losses. (19)

'Times have changed since the days of relatively low CEO pay of the 60s and 70s; corporations need to pay CEOs more than they did back then in order to compete.'

No, there is no good evidence for that. One study demonstrated that the 150 companies with the highest paid CEOs returned less to their shareholders than did their peer companies. (20) Returns were lower in the higher CEO paying firms than the lower paying firms.

Corporations have become inequality producing worlds unto themselves. The super-rich seem to live in a universe different from the one the rest of us inhabit, a reality without consequences.

If you screw up at work, do you get a bonus? After CEOs screw up, they do, for example:

> On the list: Martin Sullivan, who got $47 million when he left AIG, even though the company's share price dropped by 98% on his watch and American taxpayers had to pony up $180 billion just to keep the company alive; Thomas E. Freston, who lasted just nine months as CEO of Viacom before being fired, and departed with a severance payment of $101 million; Michael Jeffries, CEO of Abercrombie & Fitch, whose company's stock dropped more than 70% in 2007, but who received $71.8 million in 2008, including a $6 million retention bonus; William D McGuire, who in 2006 was forced to resign as CEO of UnitedHealth over a stock-options scandal, and for his troubles got a pay package worth $286 million; Hank A. McKinnell, Jr., whose five year tenure as CEO of Pfizer was marked by a $140 billion drop in Pfizer's stock market value but who left with a payout of nearly $200 million, free lifetime medical coverage, and an annual pension of $6.5 million... Douglas Ivester of Coca-Cola who stepped down as CEO in 2000 after a period of stagnant growth and declining earnings, with an exit package worth $120 million.... (21)

The low wages of working poor, that's just the free market at work.

Nope. As we've seen, the free market isn't really free, and there has been a shift over the last forty years or so away from the strength of collective bargaining, and toward the movement of wealth upward to the already wealthy. With the evisceration of unions, with legislatures serving the wealthy and passing so-called 'right-to-work' laws, the force needed to counterbalance capital has waned.

Those savings on wages trickle down and are passed on to consumers.

No; in recent years, there has been an increasing shift of the cost of poverty on to taxpayers. One of many examples: in 2012, a study out of UC Berkeley and the University of Illinois at Urbana-Champaign found that over half of fast-food workers depended on some form of federal assistance (food stamps, welfare of some kind, etc.). That means the fast-food industry, which makes money hand over fist and pays good returns to those wealthy enough to be shareholders, pays its workers poverty wages, and you the taxpayer subsidize those low wages. (22)

I mentioned we'd get back to taxes.

Higher taxes slow growth. The savings from lower corporate and marginal tax rates trickle down and are passed on to consumers.

Again, no.

Historically, when we had marginal tax rates of 71% to 92%, growth was at 4%. When marginal rates were from 28% to 39%, growth was at 2.1%. Economic growth is complicated, and correlation is not causation, but this certainly doesn't support the idea that higher taxes mean slow growth.

You have no ability to reform the tax code. Corporations have great ability to make sure it is not reformed.

As Trump told you, heads they win, tails you lose.

If something was going to trickle down to you, it has had decades to do so, and it has not.

This 'trickle down' thing has failed to happen for a long time, yet zombie-like, it just won't die.

The Tax Cuts and Jobs Act of 2017 added $1.9 trillion to the deficits over a decade while reducing taxes, modestly for ordinary people, greatly for corporations. The idea was that corporations would be flush with money, would build new factories and hire new people and pay higher wages; but no, that didn't happen. Corporations mostly took that money and bought their own stock with it, raising prices (increasing the value of the stock) and further enriching the rich who already owned their stock. How much of that money was 're-invested' in purchasing the voting power of your representatives is difficult to discern, but from the corporations' soulless perspectives, that's money well spent, and the results have proven its worth.

In 1952 corporate share of federal revenue was 32%. (23)

In 2020, it was 7%. (24)

Was the middle class in the toilet in the 1950s? No, that was back when We Were Great. But since then, even though corporations have gotten much richer than average Americans, the proportion of revenue that comes from corporations has dropped and the proportion that comes from individuals has risen.

That same Congress in 2017 voted to spend lots and lots of money; so how do we pay for it? We tax, and/or we borrow.

If you don't like borrowing then we need to tax in order to pay. (There are theories about just printing more money, that debt and taxes are just illusory, but I'm not going to consider those.)

Nobody likes taxes, myself included, because it's an injury to have the government take my money. I get that. But, I want roads, and an army, etc., so I'm willing to pay.

So what's a 'fair share'? Who is injured more by taxes? I don't think it's class warfare to ask: who should pay more? The guy in the middle class who loses to taxes $10,000 of his 75 grand in income, or the rich guy who (sometimes, possibly) loses a higher percentage of his tens of millions of income but still has tens of millions left over? (Not to mention the fact that the middle-class guy is paying a higher percentage of his income in the regressive payroll tax, and likely has a higher *effective* income tax rate, as he can't afford the tax-avoidance strategies that the wealthy employ.)

I don't like borrowing to cut the taxes of corporations and those making millions. The corporations didn't hire more workers, they just bought back more stock and paid more to already rich executives. The rich have benefited greatly from being Americans, they didn't need the tax cut, so why did we borrow from tomorrow's middle class to make it happen?

Sometimes income and wealth inequality is due to the hard work and insight of those destined to become rich. Many life stories of self-made-men or women begin in humble surroundings and track the paths of long hours of persistence and perspiration.

But many of the beneficiaries of our current inequality are known as the 'non-working rich.' Elimination of estate taxes has allowed for untold wealth to be transferred via inheritance to those who did literally nothing, *nothing*, to earn it. Over 60% of the great wealth in America is inherited. Estate taxes are decried as 'death taxes' that are destroying the wealth of the middle class; that's nonsense. Those taxes don't even start until a couple has an estate of over 22 million dollars! They affect only around 2000 American families. We are growing an American wealthy class reminiscent of the aristocracies of old Europe. Investment of such wealth allows the non-working rich to benefit from capital gains tax rates that are lower than are the income tax rates paid by the middle class and the working poor.

In spring of 2021 as I am writing this, the news is filled with arguments about a proposed increase in corporate tax rates, from 21% to 28%. But here's the deal. You and I figure our taxes and we calculate or have software that tells us what we must pay, and we can see what our tax rate is; and it's for real, we pay our taxes or we're in trouble. And maybe our effective tax rate is in that neighborhood of 20-something-percent, and we may think, well, 21% or 28% corporate tax rate, I guess that's fair. But guess what; while the corporate tax rate may currently be 21%, corporations don't actually pay 21%.

Here's a simple way to look at it. Name three big corporations that you would figure would benefit greatly from people being locked up in their houses avoiding COVID-19. How about Netflix, Zoom, and Amazon? (And yes you're right, they have benefitted, mightily.)

Since the pandemic began, Netflix, Zoom, and Amazon have paid no taxes.

Indeed in 2020, fifty of the largest and most profitable corporations in the US paid no taxes.

Something is rotten.

The wealthiest individuals are in the same non-taxpaying boat.

If you're a more or less regular guy like me, and your wealth increased by $80,000 in a given year, that was probably because you worked for it, and you got paid, and what you got paid was *income*. And on that income, you paid, yep, income tax. Let's say you managed to take $20,000 in deductions, so your taxable income was $60,000. If you're single you paid around $9,000 in taxes, about 15% of your income.

For people who are doing fantastic, making taxable income over $518,400 per year, the top tax rate is 37%; so if your taxable income was, say, 600 grand, you'd pay $222,000 in taxes. That tax is a big hit, but you'd have $378,000 left over, not too shabby. And guess what, if you're taxable income was 600 grand, the common reality is that your total income before deductions was probably millions, and you spent some of that finding ways to shelter your millions. So you didn't pay 37% of your millions; your effective tax rate was much lower. Paying that $222,000 in taxes when your actual income was, what, two and half million, means your tax rate was really less than ten percent.

But if you're super-rich, all of this income tax stuff doesn't apply to you, it's like you're from another planet with different rules. Recent disclosures from ProPublica (25) revealed that between 2006 and 2018, Jeff Bezos' wealth increased by 120 billion dollars (yes, billion, with a "B"). For every hundred dollars his wealth increased, he paid a $1.09 in taxes, about one percent. That's not the way it works for middle class Americans. Elon Musk paid 3.27%. Michael Bloomberg paid 1.3%. Warren Buffet paid 0.10%. When asked about this, Warren Buffet said he doesn't have a tax planner, "I have 535 members of Congress." Here's one way this works.

Unlike you and me, when the super-rich increase their wealth they manage not to have income. Jeff Bezos' salary at Amazon is $80,000 per year just like our middle class example above. How do you build a half a billion dollar yacht (literally) on $80k per year? The richest people gain assets, more stock, more property, but they don't sell it; so they have 'unrealized' gains, they don't show income even in the form of long-term capital gains. And guess what, if you have billions of dollars in wealth, you don't need income. You can borrow against your assets. You can have a ten billion dollar line of credit. You can have your accountants and attorneys cook up legal schemes for mobilizing your wealth such that you can purchase any product or service or experience that the human mind can conceive, without actually having any "income" to pay for it, and even take the interest payments on your loans as deductions against your paltry income. If you don't have income, you don't pay income tax. And since we don't have a wealth tax, you just don't pay much tax at all.

Only the little people pay taxes.
- - Leona Helmsley

Somehow the natural logic that people should be rewarded for thrift and hard work, and that wise societies should not tear down their most successful and creative members, has transformed into the message that the super-rich beneficiaries of non-earned wealth are the engines of job creation, and if we as a society take any steps to restore balance to our systems of taxes and markets, we will break their hearts such that they'll no longer employ the rest of us dullards. There is no rational basis or economic data that support this contention. Warren Buffett and others have consistently acknowledged that they don't need all the tax breaks that get shoved at billionaires.

Something is very rotten.

In not so many words, **Trump's message that the common working man is being exploited and forgotten rings true** and is essentially the same as that of liberal Robert Reich: "The underlying problem, then, is not that average working Americans are worth 'less' than they had been, or that they have been living beyond their means. The problem is that they have steadily lost the bargaining power needed to receive as large a portion of the economy's gains as they commanded in the first three decades after World War II, and their means have not kept up with what the economy could otherwise provide them." (26) More about workers' bargaining power in a couple chapters.

Or as Al Capone is alleged to have said, "You're at the table or on the menu."

If you don't have armies of lawyers and lobbyists, then you are not at the table, and your interests are not protected when decisions are made in the halls of power. But those decisions and the policies that ensue are the domain of the highest of high information voters. Most people depend upon someone they see as being similar to them to interpret the world around them and to focus an appropriate response.

Trump told his supporters they're getting ripped off: the system is rigged against them. He was correct. The whole system, including the so-called "free market", is tilted in favor of The Swamp, in favor of those who get to create and control the rules of the market. Trump tapped into this truth and generated a free-floating outrage. The outrage was directed not at the specific market policies and compensation offences described above, but rather was available for direction at any number of targets.

If you're a never-Trumper, even though you voted for Obama and Biden, you may now feel a bit of sympathy and understanding toward your Trump-supporting countrymen. And that's good even despite the fact that your identities may not match up well with white conservative Trump supporting rural folk.

If identities are a problem for you, consider this: there is a significant block of people who voted for Obama, and then voted for Trump. Over 13% of Trump voters in 2016 had voted for Obama in 2012. (27) They heard Obama's message of hope and change and pulled the lever for him. Apparently they didn't believe in birtherism or the socialist evils of Obama in 2012; and then over eight million Obama voters voted for Trump.

There is evidence that as early as before 2005 the white working class Republican base was "quite okay with raising the minimum wage, and raising taxes on the wealthy, they were upset about globalization, and skeptical if not hostile... to free trade." (28) As you read these chapters, if it helps, you can recall that a lot of people were just like you in 2008 or 2012, voting for Obama, but then they heard something that convinced them that Trump was the right guy.

Chapter 6

Drain the Swamp

Trumpisms:

Politicians don't give a damn. Politicians are full of it and our politics needs disruption. You need a Disruptor, and I'm your guy.

The whole system is corrupt; I, Trump, know The Swamp, and only I can fix it.

As a result of all this corruption, you're getting ripped off. Since you're getting ripped off, you should be angry about it.

The CIA was reported to have concluded, as did just about everyone else, that the Crown Prince of Saudi Arabia, Mohammed bin Salman (MBS), had ordered the murder in 2017 of the US resident, Washington DC-based journalist for the *Washington Post* and vocal critic of the Saudi royal family, Jamal Khashoggi.

Late in 2020, Treasury Secretary Steven Mnuchin was visiting a host of Arab Gulf nations. As it turns out, these nations have what are called 'sovereign funds', investment funds that are owned and managed by their national governments. It's not unusual for the US Treasury Secretary to visit Middle Eastern nations, the US has important interests there. And the existence of the sovereign funds may just be a coincidence.

In 2020, President Trump waived a number of ethics rules that would have precluded a cabinet secretary such as Mnuchin from benefitting personally from his official dealings with a foreign government. Perhaps that also was a coincidence, and while no particular rationale was put forth for waiving those ethics standards, perhaps there were some reasons.

Then in January of 2021, Mnuchin again visited the same Gulf states. Indeed, that's where he was on 6 January when insurrectionists were storming the US Capitol. And while it's difficult to imagine what pressing US government concerns could have required the Secretary to visit the Middle East so late in the lame duck period of the administration, who knows, maybe there were.

The other shoe fell six weeks later on 24 February 2021. Mnuchin announced that he, as a private citizen, was forming an investment group with the sovereign funds of Saudi Arabia, Qatar, and Kuwait. (1)

That, ladies and gentlemen, is The Swamp.

> Which shall rule, wealth or man; which shall lead, money or intellect; who shall fill public stations, educated and patriotic men, or the feudal serfs of corporate capital?
>
> -- Edward G Ryan, Chief Justice of the Supreme Court of Wisconsin, 1873

I don't mean to pick on Steve Mnuchin, or President Trump (who may not even have known what Mnuchin was up to), or suggest that only Republicans are swampy. I just happen to be writing this part of this book on the 25th of February 2021. The story broke yesterday, and certainly is topical.

It may be that Mnuchin did nothing illegal. He may not even have violated the spirit of ethical guidelines (especially since those guidelines had been waived). And what's the big deal anyway, airfare and accommodations and security for him on his trip, just so he can feather his nest after he leaves office; maybe it's a million dollars or so of your taxes, still that's chump change in the big picture. But we don't know and we may never know: what American interests was he bargaining away to get whatever sweetheart deal he got?

This story is an illustration of The Swamp. Even if his actions weren't illegal, they should have been. There oughta be a law. And if it turns out that there's not a law, that's even more evidence of The Swamp: the rich and powerful making sure that the rules don't get in the way of the rich and powerful getting more rich and more powerful, while the regular working men and women in this country struggle just to make ends meet.

The Swamp is the culture that allows for the System to be Rigged. We vote for people to represent our interests, but somehow they end up voting for, and advocating for, and assuring the success of, the interests of the rich and powerful, and becoming more rich and powerful themselves.

Whenever a man has cast a longing eye on offices,
a rottenness begins in his conduct. (2)
-- Thomas Jefferson

The revolving door

Have you ever wondered what your representative does after he or she leaves office? They get a good retirement, but often, they don't retire. Some pursue careers of integrity, in business or in academia, or in other forms of service. But many jump into The Swamp with both feet.

There is no distinctly native American criminal class except Congress.
-- Mark Twain

Just like swamps in nature, The Swamp comprises an entire eco-system. In both parties and all branches of government, there are literally thousands of people who cycle in and out of government, and in and out of the private sector. Some of this is legitimate. These people live in the DC area. If you're a congressman and you need someone knowledgeable about defense contracting or environmental regulations or whatever, it makes sense to hire someone with experience in that area. If your party just got elected, you may well find a job in government. It gets a little dicey when one leaves office or government service. Our system allows for just about anyone to lobby for the interest of a given business (including foreign businesses). Private companies are glad to hire someone who just left the White House, or a congressional office, or more likely, an agency, and who still has contacts and friends in those places. This has become a way of life.

There is something rotten about the prospect of being a congress-man or a senior staffer, or just an operative working with or on a commit-tee or in a regulatory agency that oversees a given sector of society, and know that just over your government service horizon lays the likelihood of a six or seven or eight figure salary with a company in the sector you are currently regulating. Your potential future employer comes to you seeking your influence regarding this regulation or that legislation. Whose inter-ests would you serve?

Ninety percent of the politicians give the
other ten percent a bad reputation.
-- Henry Kissinger

There doesn't need to be an explicit *quid pro quo*, an overt agreement that 'I'll write language in this bill the way you want it' or 'I'll vote this way if you give me a well-paying job when I leave this government gig'. If it happened infrequently it may not be a sure thing. But if it happens thousands of times, year after year after year, it's so ubiquitous that it can just be understood to be a reliable career path. And this is no secret. Go to https://www.opensecrets.org/revolving/index.php and you can see chapter and verse about who is shuffling in and out of government in this manner. It is so routine that no one seems to care.

When Trump tells his followers that we must "Drain the Swamp", he's right.

Remember the cycle of the rigging of the system from the last chapter:

The first priority of our elected politicians is: re-election.
The mothers' milk of politics is money.
Corporations and the super-wealthy have lots of money.
Politicians are beholden to those who finance their election and re-election.
Consequently, politicians preferentially represent the interests of the wealthy, of capital.
The wealthy continue to support financially those who legislate on their behalf.
Rinse, repeat.

And here is just some of the waste water connectivity that keeps the Swamp swampy:

The interests of the rich and powerful are not the same as your interests.
Moneyed interests influence government much more than you do.
Politicians pick their voters more than their voters pick them.

The interests of the rich and powerful are not the same as your interests.

I have nothing against rich people. I would like to be one of them some day. You probably would too. I know some wonderful, kind-hearted, generous rich people who do wonderful, kind-hearted, generous things with their wealth (as do a lot of rich people I don't know). But like the rest of us, many rich people have issues.

> They were careless people, Tom and Daisy - they smashed up things and creatures and then retreated back into their money or their vast carelessness or whatever it was that kept them together, and let other people clean up the mess they had made.
>
> - - F. Scott Fitzgerald, *The Great Gatsby*

There is an anecdote of the middle-class man commenting to the rich man,

"I believe I have something that you may never have,"

to which the rich man retorts,

"No way. What could that possibly be?"

The man of modest means replies:

"Enough."

So we must recognize that, on the whole, taken as a class of people, it is just true that the bell shaped curve of interests of the rich may often not align with the interests of the rest of us. Many rich people get rich just by focusing on building a better mousetrap. Their attention is on providing a product or a service that has not been so provided in the past, and the world beats a path to their door. The riches are incidental to their mission. But not all rich people are that way. Some just really, really want to get rich, and the devil take the hindmost.

The process of getting super-rich selects, to whatever degree, for people who want to get super-rich, and once they've gotten super-rich, many want to get richer, even if others get hurt. This is not just the perspective of progressives and socialists. The most conservative politicians offer lip service at least to this idea that the rich, especially the super-rich, and corporations as we've discussed, benefit greatly at the expense of the middle and working classes. Kentucky's Republican Senator Rand Paul stated that the GOP "cannot be the party of fat cats, rich people, and Wall Street." Senator Ted Cruz of Texas observed that the "rich and powerful, those who walk the corridors of power [are] getting fat and happy." Republican David Brat beat GOP house majority leader Eric Cantor after accusing him of "crony capitalism" and excoriated American corporations as only wanting "cheap labor... that's going to lower wages for everybody else." (3)

Even Donald Trump skewered his GOP primary rivals for being puppets of the donor class when they sought the support of billionaires. (4)

Of course this is not new. Political corruption by wealth is as old as wealth. The Founders knew it, thus their warnings about corporate influence. Regarding the Gilded Age, historian George Thayer noted, "Never has the American political process been so corrupt. No office was too high to purchase, no man too pure to bribe, no principle too sacred to destroy, no law too fundamental to break." (5)

Corporations and the super-rich don't have as much need for government services as do the rest of us. If the roads are bad they can take their helicopter. They can hire their own security instead of relying upon the police. You don't need parks or playgrounds if the property surrounding your mansion is beautiful, and if you get tired of it, you can fly wherever you want in your private jet. High quality public schools are not much of a concern if you never send your kids to public schools. Clean air and water are not problems in our richest locales; pollution tends to differentially affect the poor, and communities of color.

In general, corporations and the rich don't want regulations, or taxes. Of course nobody likes being told you can't build something here or dump something there, but we recognize that without the regulation, somebody else will be a jerk and build something noisy next to my house or dump something poisonous that will flow into my backyard. Nobody wants to pay taxes, but we want teachers to teach and the police and firefighters to show up when we call. We can kvetch and moan, but we still obey and pay. But if you're the Koch brothers or their ilk, you can do more than just complain.

Here are a couple of sad truths:

The rich will fight for economic benefit of the rich,
even if it's unfair to the poor.

If you look inside deregulation, you find polluters and Wall Street.

Indeed, if you've got enough pull, not only can you avoid taxes, you can get the government to subsidize your business. Multinational oil companies, one of the most successful and mature industries in the history of planet Earth, have benefitted from the largesse of the American taxpayer for generations.

For corporations, "...the desire to exercise political power tends mostly to animate a few highly regulated sectors, particularly finance and fossil fuels, but also insurance, pharmaceuticals, chemical manufacturing, and, to a lesser degree, defense." (6) When the rich get more sway, working people have less of a voice. **When Trump says that The Swamp is**

taking away the wealth of forgotten common American working people, he's right, and many working people feel that he is right.

In addition to transferring the wealth of the middle and working classes upward to the rich, corporations and the super-rich have ways of making sure that their efforts to make money are not obstructed by the pesky little people who want to be safe in their homes, jobs, schools, neighborhoods, and purchases. In essence, this involves turning the assets we all share into assets they can exploit, such as in *The Tragedy of the Commons.*

They do this in part through what is called regulatory capture.

Regulatory capture

Like many regulatory agencies, the Office of Pipeline Safety had been captured. As you might discern by the name, they were supposed to assure the safety of pipelines, but the revolving door had emasculated the agency all the way down the line. The legislators who define or limit the regulations hadn't done an adequate job; the laws had been watered down. The agency itself "grants the industry it regulates significant power to influence the rule-making process, and... has stubbornly refused to take a more aggressive regulatory role" (7) and as a result it was weak in its "regulations, its inspections, its assets, its staffing and its spirit." (8)

But who cares? Do we really need such a regulatory agency? Isn't this just more bureaucracy, more government red tape that gets in the way of the energy of business, saps our productivity, stifles growth and contributes to job loss?

Let's back up. I practiced medicine for 35 years. I still do on a limited volunteer basis. It was axiomatic that there were two kinds of doctors, those who had been sued for malpractice, and those who were going to be sued for malpractice. This is for at least two reasons: because doctors make mistakes, and because patients have bad outcomes. (Also, our system is dysfunctional, our medical insurance system is broken, we don't have a rational way to take care of people who have disastrous medical outcomes so we resort to litigation... but that's too long a story.)

True confession: I wasn't perfect. I made mistakes; not a lot, but some. Dozens of patient encounters daily for 35 years equals plenty of opportunities to make mistakes. If one of my mistakes caused a bad outcome with injury, by definition, that's medical malpractice. As it turned out, though I've been sued, I never in fact got sued for actual malpractice. I made mistakes, and I had bad outcomes, but they just never linked up in a lawsuit, by the grace of God. I got away with my mistakes: either it wasn't a significant mistake and the patient did fine despite my error, or I or somebody else caught the mistake and cleaned it up before anything bad happened (thank you, dear colleagues), or the outcome wasn't very bad and the patient liked me and didn't want to sue (thank you, dear patients). As it turned out, the bad outcomes I did get sued for happened not to be the result of any mistake, they were inevitable, just bad luck.

The point here is that you can miss or ignore a lot of bad stuff and through good luck, get away with it. Regulatory agencies can get in the habit of missing and ignoring things, and nothing bad happens on a given day, or the next day, or the next week or month, and hey, we really don't need to regulate this industry: if we don't pay attention, it doesn't really matter, because usually nothing bad happens.

In June of 1999 two ten-year-old boys, Wade King and Stephen Tsiorvas, were playing in a field in Bellingham Washington near Whatcom Creek. An 18-year-old recent high school graduate named Liam Wood was fishing in the creek. Unfortunately for them, the Office of Pipeline Safety had not been doing its job. The Olympic Pipe Line Company had a gasoline pipe nearby. It was poorly maintained, and poorly inspected, and it ruptured, sending 200,000 gallons of gasoline into the creek. Liam Wood was overcome by the fumes, collapsed into the creek, and drowned. A spark ignited the gasoline, it exploded and burned, and Wade and Stephen were burned. They died the next day.

You can ignore inspections and regulations, and often, nothing bad happens... until it does.

You've probably never heard of this event at Whatcom Creek. It's just one of a countless number of such events that result from inadequate regulation due to regulatory capture. Some are globally catastrophic, like the 2008 Wall Street collapse that led to the Global Financial Crisis and the Great Recession. Others are more localized in their effects. The Sago Mine disaster, Deep Water Horizon, trains transporting crude oil derailing and exploding and burning... I could go on, and on, and on, and still on, but you get the idea. Preventing these disasters requires vigilance. It might seem that corporations would want to avoid the possibility of being sued for allowing deadly 'accidents' to occur; but such suits are a recognized cost of doing business. The corporations make more money ignoring the problems and paying some smaller amounts when disaster strikes than they would make if they spent what is required to correct the deficiencies that lead to the disasters. The business decision is in conflict with the well-being of the public. In order to protect the public, corporations must be forced to do so, by the only entity that can do the job: government. So, corporations take steps to emasculate government to avoid the costs of being forced to protect us.

> If the government is to tell big business men how to run their business, then don't you see that big business men have to get closer to the government even than they are now? Don't you see that they must capture the government, in order not to be restrained too much by it? (9)
>
> -- President Woodrow Wilson, 1913

The narrative that regulations are burdensome and anathema to freedom is relentlessly propagated by The Swamp. Shawn Otto in his book *The War on Science* points out that "[W]e accept limitations on our freedom in order to gain greater freedom," freedom "from the tyranny of others' stupid decisions." He notes that this freedom is delivered by "regulations that reduce smog, acid rain, ozone destruction, the use of DDT, backyard burning of garbage, driving while intoxicated, noise pollution – and more recently, exposure to secondhand smoke, injuries caused by not wearing seatbelts, and texting while driving." (10)

You may wonder, whatever happened after the kids in Washington died due to the capture of the Office of Pipeline Safety; surely that situation was fixed. Indeed, the whole agency was disintegrated, or at least, renamed, becoming the Pipeline and Hazardous Materials Safety Administration, or PHMSA.

As reported by Senator Whitehouse, "the last head of PHMSA was a former pipeline industry lawyer who had to recuse herself in a major oil spill inquiry because of conflict of interest." (11)

Senator Whitehouse further reports (12) that all witnesses at a senate committee hearing (13) led to bipartisan recognition of the following points:

First, agency capture is a real problem, and a threat to the integrity of government.

Second, the enormous stakes for regulated entities give them an incentive to gain influence over regulators.

Third, regulated entities usually have organizational and resource advantages in the regulatory process compared to public interest groups.

Fourth, regulatory procedures can be gamed by regulated entities in their quest for influence over regulation.

Fifth, regulatory capture by its nature happens in the dark, as invisibly as possible.

Sixth, the potential damage to the public from agency capture is enormous.

Moneyed interests influence government much more than you do.

> The true friend of property, the true conservative, is he who insists that property shall be the servant and not the master of the commonwealth.... The citizens of the United States must effectively control the mighty commercial forces which they themselves have called into being.... (14)
>
> All contributions by corporations to any political committee or for any political purpose should be forbidden by law.... (15)
>
> -- Teddy Roosevelt :

Through TR's leadership, over a century ago we had this much better figured out. Congress passed the Tillman Act, which precluded a lot of the shenanigans of money in politics. The Senate committee debating the measure found what we have accepted today to be so corrupting that they concluded as follows: "The evils of the use of money in connection with political elections are so generally recognized that the committee deems it unnecessary to make any argument in favor of the general purpose of this measure. It is in the interest of good government and calculated to promote purity in the selection of public officials." (16)

Through a series of legislative acts and judicial decisions, we have regressed awfully in this area:

"Although America is home to about 120 million families, nearly half of all the money contributed through the spring of 2016 in the 2016 presidential contest came from just 150 families, most of them with corporate connections, and most contributed secretly, through super PACS and 501(c)(4)s." (17)

Senator Chris Murphy (D-CT) gives a firsthand account of the effects of money in politics: "You spend a lot of time on the phone with people who work in the financial markets. And so you're hearing a lot about problems that bankers have and not a lot about problems that people who work at the mill in Thomaston, Connecticut, have." Senator Dick Durbin (D-IL) echoed his sentiments: "I think most Americans would be shocked — not surprised, but shocked — if they knew how much time a United States senator spends raising money. And how much time we spend talking about raising money, and thinking about raising money, and planning to raise money. And, you know, going off on little retreats and conjuring up new ideas on how to raise money." (18)

> Suppose you go to Washington and try to get at your government. You will always find that while you are politely listened to, the men really consulted are the men who have the biggest stake - the big bankers, the big manufacturers, the big masters of commerce.... The government of the United States at present is the foster child of special interests. (19)
>
> - - President Woodrow Wilson

If the US government was 'the foster child of special interests' over a century ago during the Wilson administration, it's worse now. The way we finance and run our elections is a mess. We have the influence of institutional donors, and the increasingly important grassroots donors and activists.

Political scientists Martin Gilens and Benjamin Page investigated which of these classes of donors actually hold sway with our government. The question was, do you and I and our (probably polarized) like-minded countrymen have much power in our system? This was in 2014, before the worst effects of *Citizens United* and before the political run of Donald Trump. They concluded: "The central point that emerges from our research is that economic elites and organized groups representing business interests have substantial independent impacts on US government policies, while mass-based interest groups and average citizens have little or no independent influence." (20)

Trump supporters did not need to read that research to feel in their bones that the conclusion is true. They felt left behind and still feel that now, and it makes common sense that "economic elites and organized groups representing business interests" are valued and heard while the common man is not. This was the thrust, the gist, the spirit of the Trump campaign; it was true, and it did not require a great deal of detail to ring true and to motivate voters.

In criticism Senator Sheldon Whitehouse, quoting *Politico*, points out that:

> ...of the thirteen men Donald Trump announced as his economic advisory council, "five are major donors whose families combined to give Trump's campaign and his joint fundraising account with the Republican Party more than $2 million." Trevor Potter noted of Trump this was "the path he has said was corrupt, raising large sums of money and then giving donors special access." The inevitable switcheroo pulled a fast one on Trump's primary voters, who were "an easy mark for a P.T. Barnum con man," said right-wing Iowa radio host Steve Deace. (21)

But such details generally did not come to the attention of Trump supporters; and if they had, they still could be dismissed as the hyperbole of Democratic politicians and never-Trumpers. Of course we have very little way of knowing what was in the hearts of those five of thirteen Trump economic advisors. They may have had a 'come-to-Jesus' moment and been inspired by Trump to leave behind their 'access for money' model and instead look out for the common man. Remember:

Must I believe that Trump is swimming in and further fouling the same Swamp that he has condemned, or:

Can I believe that he is just playing the game and when he gets in the White House he will indeed work for my best interests?

The campaigns of 2016 and since have taught us that some dynamics are changing. No longer do smoke filled rooms dominate. Rather, primaries rule, built to satisfy the most intensely partisan activists, with an added boost to Iowa and New Hampshire. This, and the internet, have weakened parties and strengthened anyone who can trend on twitter, leveled the playing field so that anyone can become president. Isn't that a good thing?

Raymond La Raja and Brian Schaffner in their book *Campaign Finance and Political Polarization: When Purists Prevail* found that campaign finance restrictions tend to lead to polarization. Ezra Klein summarizes:

> We've flipped from a system that selected candidates who were broadly appealing to party officials to a system that selects candidates who are adored by base voters. Put differently, neither Donald Trump nor Bernie Sanders would've had a prayer in the 1956 presidential primaries, but one of them won and the other nearly won the 2016 presidential primaries. (22)

Klein describes this phenomenon, differentiating between what he identifies as 'transactional,' that is, rich, institutional or corporate wealth driven; and 'polarizing,' the most passionate base voters:

> In my experience, transactional giving drives the bills no one has heard of, the provisions few people read, the regulatory processes the public and the media tend to ignore. But at the macro level -- the level of presidential politics and legislative fights that lead front pages day after day -- it's partisan dollars that dominate outcomes. If the business community could purchase its preference in all things, immigration reform and infrastructure investment would've passed long ago and Jeb Bush would be president. Once an issue becomes a red-blue collision, corporate cash often loses out to the zero-sum logic of partisanship or the fury of the base. But that isn't to dismiss the power of access-based money: we don't hear about most of what politicians do, leaving a truly vast space for the corruptions of transactional fund-raising to warp policy. And there are moments when the transactionalists and the polarizers settle into alliance with each other: that's often been the story of the Trump administration, which tweets about kneeling NFL players in the morning and passes corporate tax cuts in the evening....
>
> If individual donors give money as a form of identity expression, institutional donors give money as a form of investment. Individual donors are polarizing. Institutional donors are corrupting. American politics, thus, is responsive to two types of people: the polarized and the rich. (23)

Almost everyone hates The Swamp. Congress is exceedingly unpopular, in some polling less popular than toe fungus, hemorrhoids and cockroaches. One might conclude that the solution would be to throw the bums out, yet, they keep getting re-elected. How does this happen? Well, The Swamp keeps The Swamp in business.

Politicians pick their voters more than their voters pick them.

Gerrymandering: another way The Swamp feeds The Swamp.

The "gerrymander" dates back to Massachusetts in 1812, when the governor Elbridge Gerry needed to protect a state senate seat. He arranged for the district to be drawn in a bizarre shape that had nothing to do with natural features or community boundaries. On the map, it was not "compact," it looked like a salamander. Smush together his last name Gerry and the apparent salamander and presto, a portmanteau that has stuck: the gerrymander.

Here's the idea. In a fair representative democracy, ideally we'd want majority rule, with minority rights. Typically, state legislatures get to determine the size and shapes of districts, districts for state assembly houses and state senates, and congressional districts. But once a party gets into power, they want to stay in power. Remember, the first priority of any elected official usually is his or her re-election. There are few better ways to assure your re-election than to make sure that the people voting for you are of your party. Rather than have to change your message and your legislative priorities and ideas to serve the needs of your constituents, just choose your constituents to fit your priorities and ideas. Both parties do it, and here's how.

Let's say there are ten districts in your state with ten voters in each, so a hundred voters. And let's say there are 40 Democrats and 60 Republicans. (I know, that's a really small state... that doesn't seem to have any Independent voters; and the others all vote along party lines. It's an illustration. Stay with me.) In a fair representative democracy, in this example you'd probably end up with six districts having GOP representatives, and four with Democratic representatives.

Example 1: Proportional

District	A	B	C	D	E	F	G	H	I	J
# Dems	10	10	10	10	0	0	0	0	0	0
# Repubs	0	0	0	0	10	10	10	10	10	10
Results:	D	D	D	D	R	R	R	R	R	R
Representatives:	Four Democratic, six Republican									

There ya go, districts A, B, C, & D have Democratic representation, and the other six districts each have Republican representatives. That's majority rule, fair enough. The minority is represented, and if they can convince just one or two of their GOP colleagues of the greatness of an idea, it would carry the day.

[Of course nature doesn't organize things that way. As geographically polarized as we're becoming, we're still more mixed than that. Ideally, districts are fairly *compact*, including communities that share space and interests. Maybe it would look something like this, more mixed up, but still proportional and fair, four Democratic districts G though J, and six Republican districts A through F.

Example 2: Proportional, more realistic distribution

District	A	B	C	D	E	F	G	H	I	J
# Dems	1	2	3	3	3	3	6	6	6	7
# Repubs	9	8	7	7	7	7	4	4	4	3
Results:	R	R	R	R	R	R	D	D	D	D
Representatives:	Four Democratic, six Republican]									

If every district had the same proportion of Republicans and Democrats, it'd look like this:

Example 3: Majority on Steroids

District	A	B	C	D	E	F	G	H	I	J
# Dems	4	4	4	4	4	4	4	4	4	4
# Repubs	6	6	6	6	6	6	6	6	6	6
Results:	R	R	R	R	R	R	R	R	R	R
Representatives:	Zero Democratic, ten Republican									

Each district would have a Republican representative. It's fair in a way, because after all, each district does have a majority of Republicans, so they should be represented by a Republican, right? But it means that all ten representatives are Republicans, and that's not fair. It's majority rule, but the minority has no representation at all, no voice.

If you think that might not be fair, wait for the gerrymander.

The Democratic dominated statehouse draws the districts in such a way that the Republican voters are mostly located within, and have majorities only in, four districts A through D. The other six districts have Democratic majorities.

Example 4: The Gerrymander

District	A	B	C	D	E	F	G	H	I	J
# Dems	0	0	0	4	6	6	6	6	6	6
# Repubs	10	10	10	6	4	4	4	4	4	4
Results:	R	R	R	R	D	D	D	D	D	D
Representatives:	Six Democratic, four Republican									

So despite the fact that the majority of voters in your state are Republicans, the representation of your state has six Democrats and four Republicans. That is minority rule, and that's definitely not fair.

Unfortunately, this is too commonly the case. In recent years, Republicans are much more focused on it, and much better at it. The GOP spent over $30 million on REDMAP (the Redistricting Majority Project) and were successful in electing GOP majorities in swing states. For example, in Pennsylvania in 2012, 2.79 million voted for Democrats, and 2.71 million voted for Republicans. That's a narrow Democratic margin of 83,000 votes. (24) You'd think that Pennsylvania's Congressional delegation would be pretty close to 50/50, maybe a slight edge to Democrats. But no, they sent five Democrats and thirteen Republicans! They drew districts to lump the Democrats in supersaturated districts, and spread out Republicans to make slim majorities in the other districts.

This is gerrymandering in action. Also in 2012, Ohio voted statewide for Obama and Democrat Sherrod Brown for Senate, but sent only four Democrats compared to twelve Republicans to Congress. Wisconsin voted for Obama and Democrat Tammy Baldwin, but sent only three Democrats versus five Republicans to the House. Nationwide, 1.59 million more votes went to Democratic House candidates than for Republican candidates, yet Republicans won the House with a majority of thirty-three seats.

Those who engage in it are often quite unabashed. As one North Carolina Republican representative declared within the last decade: "I propose that we draw the maps to give a partisan advantage to 10 Republicans and three Democrats, because I do not believe it's possible to draw a map with 11 Republicans and two Democrats." (25)

A racial gerrymander is illegal, but the Supreme Court has found that outlawing a partisan gerrymander is just too doggone hard. In *Rucho vs Common Cause*, Chief Justice Roberts declared for the 5 to 4 majority that while the partisan gerrymander is unjust, "partisan gerrymandering claims present political questions beyond the reach of the federal courts." The minority opinion written by Justice Elena Kagan stated: "Of all times to abandon the Court's duty to declare the law, this was not the one. The practices challenged in these cases imperil our system of government. Part of the Court's role in that system is to defend its foundations. None is more important than free and fair elections. With respect but deep sadness, I dissent."

As a consequence of gerrymandering, the general election result is often pre-determined. In a deep red district or state, the Republican is going to beat the Democrat (and vice versa for deep blue districts or states... don't hold your breath for the next Republican senator from California). Rare exceptions to this occur. If you insist on running a candidate credibly accused of being a serial abuser of teenage girls as was Republican senatorial candidate Judge Roy Moore in Alabama, you can manage to lose to a Democrat (in Alabama!), as he did. But most of the time, it is the primary election of the party in power that determines who will win the seat.

In a battleground district that could go either way, the candidates must be somewhat moderate, as there's no point in winning the primary if you're just going to be too extreme to win the decisive swing voters in the general election. But primaries in deeply partisan areas (that is, gerrymandered areas) tend to result in extreme candidates. Turnouts are traditionally low for primaries. A partisan primary in a non-presidential election year... who cares? Those who are most active in the primaries tend to be the most dedicated and vociferous partisans. And if there is no adverse consequence for picking an extreme candidate because you know he's going to win the general no matter what, there is no incentive to choose someone who needs to be reasonable in order to win the general. As a result, you get a firebrand, a bomb thrower; you don't get someone who will compromise and work across the aisle to get things done.

Another component of politicians picking their voters has to do with who gets to vote. In addition to sequestering voters likely to oppose you in gerrymandered vote ghettoes, it'd help secure your re-election if you could be sure that a lot of voters likely to oppose you, no matter what district they're in, just could not vote.

The issues of voting rights, voter fraud, voter suppression and voter ID are caught up in a Niagara of disinformation, so we'll deal with them in the chapter on Fake News.

Trump presented himself as an outsider. He reveled in having never held any public office. He gleefully admitted he'd spent decades exploiting The Swamp to his benefit. To paraphrase, he said: 'Politicians are crooked and stupid, and I've given money to them and bought the advocacy of politicians of all stripes; but I'm rich, and I no longer need the benefits of The Swamp. But having exploited it, I know how it works, and so "Only I can fix it."' All of that rings true to his followers.

When Trump rails against The Swamp, he is calling on people to recognize the threat that The Swamp represents, a threat that most Americans feel deeply even if they cannot articulate Swampy details. Because Kagan was right: "these practices... imperil our system of government." People who don't feel represented, who feel that government is run by a minority that doesn't hear or see them or have their interests at heart, is a government that cannot be trusted and will not be valued. We can see that on both the right and the left, many Americans do not value our government, and all too often with good reason.

> We can have a democracy or we can have great wealth in the hands of a few, but we cannot have both. (26)
>
> - - Justice Louis Brandeis

Summary:

The Swamp includes a revolving door between moneyed interests and government.

The interests of the rich and powerful are not the same as your interests.

Many rich people fight for the economic benefit of the rich even though it's unfair to the poor; and they're better at that fight than you are.

If you look inside deregulation, you find polluters and Wall Street.

The Swamp keeps The Swamp swampy in part through regulatory capture.

American politics is responsive to two types of people: the polarized and the rich. Moneyed interests, the rich, influence government much more than you do.

In The Swamp, politicians pick their voters more than their voters pick them.

The Swamp is undermining our democracy and threatening our way of life.

Trump was correct when he told us we must "Drain The Swamp."

Chapter 7

Conservative Judges

Trumpisms:

The whole system is too corrupt; the system is rigged. I, Trump, know The Swamp, and only I can fix it.

As a result, you're getting ripped off. Since you're getting ripped off, you should be angry about it.

If there's one thing we can all agree on, it's that Trump delivered when it came to the appointment of nominally conservative judges. ("Nominally" in that they were actually quite activist, contrary to conservative, not at all 'strict constructionists,' as we'll see.) Whether you are a delighted supporter or a distressed detractor, you can have no doubt that he and Mitch McConnell formed a tag team that was relentlessly efficient in this endeavor.

My parents were schoolteachers. They were intelligent and involved, good citizens; they paid their taxes and they always voted. But when I was a kid, they didn't know or care anything about judges. I don't recall them ever talking about judges or Supreme Court justices. Judges were supposed to be like doctors, or at least our idealized perception of good doctors: dispassionate, not allowing biases to get in the way, just calling balls and strikes without rooting for one side or the other. Granted this was before cable news and the 24-hour news cycle, before the internet, before social media. But even with political campaigns and the news we had on our three network channels, judges, they just weren't a thing.

Now, they are very definitely a thing. For most people, it's pretty simple. If you're low information, you just go with your team: red team, you want 'conservative' judges; blue team, 'liberal' judges.

This reflects our values. Judges interpret the law, they tell us what our laws command, what is right, and what is wrong. They are an extension of our values, particularly the axis of *Sanctity* versus *Degradation*. (There also is an element of connection versus control that we'll talk about later.) In our secular society, police and prosecutors enforce the law, but judges are the final serene arbiters of justice. You may not know much about the law (hey, it's complicated), but if you're conservative, you know you want someone conservative to be that arbiter, defending the *Sacred* and preventing *Degradation*. If you're liberal, you can see *Sanctity* often as an excuse for the law (and religion) to justify continued repression of women and maintain the status quo of white supremacy and capitalist power, and you prefer liberal judges with compassion who do not allow the victims of bad laws and societal inequities to come to *Harm*. So most liberals and most conservatives favor the judges whom your team favors, and that's about all you need to know.

If those who are most excited about judges bother at all with specific issues, they are often single issues, such as abortion, or guns. If you're on the red team, it's 'no' on abortion, and 'yes' on guns; blue team, the opposite. We'll deal with these wedge issues in Chapter 12, because they do indeed command a great deal of our attention and have caused a great deal of mischief.

But wedge issues are mostly created issues, they aren't the real issues at all. They are a Trojan Horse, they are the magician's misdirection, enticing you to follow this shiny object while he pulls a quarter out of your ear.

The real action behind all of the media bluster, all of the noise and excitement surrounding judges, is part of The Swamp, the same Swamp that Trump railed against.

Remember in the last chapter we talked about how money has found its way into politics. While banning corporate political donations by passing the Tillman Act in 1906, the US Senate recognized that "The evils of the use of money in connection with political elections are so generally recognized" that they saw no need to discuss it. The Publicity Act of 1909 required candidates (who couldn't receive corporate donations) to disclose the identities of all the human beings who contributed to their campaigns.

We have regressed.

Senator Sheldon Whitehouse in his book *Captured* pointed out that "In 2010, five corporate-minded Supreme Court justices ruled that corporations had a constitutional right to spend unlimited amounts of money to influence elections, and that this would pose no possible threat of corruption. Such a dramatic change could not, and did not, happen by accident." (1)

How did we get here?

The 1960s were tough on the American business community. Long-haired hippies, anti-Vietnam War sentiment, riots, assassinations, civil rights, sex drugs and rock'n'roll; all were components of a zeitgeist hostile to "The Establishment". To the counterculture, business meant oil companies and pollution; it meant Dow Chemical which meant napalm burning Vietnamese children; "plastic" became a pejorative; the admonition 'don't trust anyone over 30' included commerce and the corporate world. Events such as the Cuyahoga River catching fire and Ralph Nader's book *Unsafe at Any Speed* were translating into regulations enforced by then new agencies such as the Department of Transportation, the Environmental Protection Agency, and others.

At the invitation of the besieged US Chamber of Commerce in 1971 a lawyer and soon-to-be Supreme Court Justice named Lewis Powell wrote a pro-business operations plan. Known as the "Powell Memo", it laid out a strategy for making business pre-eminent again. Some were straightforward steps such as better public relations, and others a little sleazy like getting pro-business faculty into universities and promoting changes in textbooks to portray business more favorably. (2)

Also, he advocated greater efforts in established channels, like more lobbyists; and business responded. In the decade mostly of the 1970s, the number of firms with registered lobbyists in Washington went from 175 up to almost 2500; corporate political action committees (PACs) went from fewer than 300 in 1976 to over 1200 in just four years. (3)

But among the more salient and novel components was a shift from lobbying exclusively the regulatory agencies and lawmakers, toward seeking influence in the courts. This included "impact litigation". Instead of the usual process of a client finding a lawyer, you assemble hotshot lawyers not primarily for the purpose of winning cases for their clients who hired them, but rather, changing the law itself, by selecting the case and the client. That is, they monitor and review legal cases all over the country, and when they find one that might advance the corporate agenda, they can swoop into a local county dispute with high-powered 'impact lawyers,' offer free top-shelf legal representation to the side they want to win, and sometimes bull their way to the Supreme Court (especially if the configuration of the Supreme Court has become favorable to your view). Also, your hotshot lawyers file amicus briefs with the Supreme Court regarding other cases you want decided a certain way.

In 1971 Powell was himself nominated to the Supreme Court, and in 1978 he wrote the death knell to the idea that the courts were a neutral place where the best and brightest legal minds impartially argued the finer points of law. Breaking with precedent and contrary to the law from back in Teddy Roosevelt's day, he delivered a decision asserting that the First Amendment protects corporate speech in politics. (4)

The conservative and business communities jumped on this horse and rode it. The Federalist Society, a legal organization that is zealously pro-corporate, established itself in law schools. It and other similar legal outfits became the de facto recruiting and screening arm of the Republican Party regarding the nomination of conservative judges. Those judges have for decades provided increasingly pro-corporate decisions. (5) Between 1986 and 2005, the Supreme Court (SCOTUS, Supreme Court of the United States) ruled in favor of the position of the GOP surrogate corporatist Chamber of Commerce 43% of the time. Between 1986 and 2005 that number was 56%; between 2006 and 2015 it had grown to 69%.

> The upshot... is that businesses are free to run their operations without fear of liability for the harm they cause to consumers, employees and people injured by their products. (6)
>
> - - Harvard law professor Arthur Miller

Senator Whitehouse details the history of this corporate takeover of the judiciary in great detail in his book *Captured*. This includes the diminution of our traditional ways of defining and recognizing corruption (7); corporate influence changing the Rules of Civil Procedure in ways that limit 'discovery' by plaintiffs, limit the ability of plaintiffs to get their case before a jury, and make it easier for corporations to have cases against them dismissed (8); boondoggle corporate funded retreats under the guise of 'continuing legal education' at golf and fishing resorts where judges hear from corporate 'experts' (who don't exactly tell them how to vote, but then again, they don't exactly *not* tell them either). All that is beyond the scope of this book. But there is one particularly malodorous case which typifies the takeover and is worth exploring here: *Citizens United*.

Citizens United v Federal Elections Commission

I'm not a lawyer, but I don't think one must be to understand *Citizens United.* If after reading this section you think I'm wrong, look it up and decide for yourself.

I think SCOTUS made a wrong decision. I don't know if the majority really believed what they wrote, if they were just clueless, or if they were deliberately corrupt. But there seemed to be some irregularities that just stink, stink like a Swamp.

Back in 1853, SCOTUS wrote: "to subject the state governments to the combined capital of wealthy corporations [would] produce universal corruption." That's obvious, isn't it? Well that was then, this is now.

In 2010, the Court contorted itself into a 180 degree opposite pro-corporate decision. They appear to have wanted to decide that corporations should be able to put as much money into politics as corporations want. (And they want to put in a lot, because it's a great, really great, investment, returning ten-fold or hundreds-fold what they put in.)

In order to do that, the Court had to decide that: corporations have the right of free speech, and that: money is speech.

In order to do that, they had to get around established law that held that the government has an interest in limiting free speech: you can't yell "fire" in a crowded theater, you aren't free to use your speech to offer someone a bribe or hire someone to commit murder, and you can't corrupt, *or even appear to corrupt*, elections. That was the law. It still is. They had to get around that.

There were other barriers to arriving at their apparent desired outcome. First, the *Citizens United* case as decided by lower courts wasn't really suitable. It was narrow, about a challenge to existing law that prohibited, in the 30 days before a primary election, the airing of an on-demand cable video critical of a candidate; narrow, and boring.

In the lead up to this case, as in every case that goes before the Supreme Court or any appellate court, the parties submit briefs that specify the "question presented", what the case is about, so everybody knows what issue the court is going to decide. The briefs present all the facts that have been presented to the lower court(s); and the appellate court(s), higher courts, rely upon those facts to decide what the law says. That's worth repeating: lower courts, with police and investigators gathering evidence and with their lawyers and juries, find the facts; courts of appeal don't.

Work-around number one: move the goal line.

After all the briefs were in, even after all the oral arguments were finished, SCOTUS came up with a new "question presented". As I understand it, that is just not to be done. The new question was no longer about the airing of a video within 30 days etc., it became a broad question about the power of government to regulate corporate spending on elections. Justice Stevens in his dissent observed: "five Justices were unhappy with the limited nature of the case before us, so they changed the case to give themselves an opportunity to change the law." If there is a definition of "activist judges" anathema to conservatism, contrary to *stare decisis* (Latin for "to stand by things decided," or follow precedent), not at all being a 'strict constructivist', that would be it. As right-wing Justice Alito said of *stare decisis*, "It is a Latin phrase. It means 'to leave things decided when it suits our purposes.'" (9)

By changing the question late in the proceedings, there was then no longer a factual record that addressed the "question presented", because they'd invented a new "question presented". Remember, appellate courts and SCOTUS deal with the law, they are not supposed to be finders of fact, that's done by the lower courts. Lower courts and juries listen to witnesses, examine exhibits, and find facts. Of course such a factual record exists in other cases, and could have been developed for this new 'question', but the briefs and arguments for this particular case were already done, finished. So the so-called 'conservative' majority on the Court was then free to come up with its own, alternative facts.

Work around number two: SCOTUS invents its own facts.

They declared as fact that "independent expenditures, including those made by corporations, do not give rise to corruption or the appearance of corruption." Say what? In the Army we used to call that pulling something out of a particular anatomical orifice. But these five Justices just invented a bald unsupported assertion and called it a fact.

Obviously, that is not true. The Founders, the courts, legislatures federal and state, the executive, have for literally hundreds of years warned of and found facts demonstrating the corrupting influence of corporate money. I've cited just a tiny bit of the historical record which recognizes and affirms that money in politics and corporate influence in politics are corrupting. You know it, I know it, **Trump said it, and Trump supporters feel it down to the soles of their shoes, that money in**

politics is corrupting, and we're all getting ripped off by the fat cats.

The Supreme Court didn't stop there.

You'll be glad to know that the *Citizens United* decision doesn't bother you, because "the appearance of influence or access, furthermore, will not cause the electorate to lose faith in our democracy." As a matter of fact, you love it. You love it so much that, corporations get to borrow your right to free speech, because otherwise you would be deprived of being inundated with corporate-sponsored political 'speech'. And life just wouldn't be free without all this corporate speech for us to wallow in. It's an absurd assertion, and while I'm sure it can be characterized differently by those who believe this kind of... stuff, I believe that's the essence of it.

Obviously, the idea that *Citizens United* has had no adverse effect upon the way we view our democracy is not true either. Polls have shown that 80% of Americans oppose *Citizens United.* Less than a third of Americans trust those ultimate arbiters of our laws, the Supreme Court. By a ratio of nine to one (nine to one!) we Americans believe that SCOTUS treats corporations more favorably than it treats the rest of us; even 80% of those who identify as conservative Republicans believe that. (10)

As Whitehouse points out, corporate money in politics:

> ...selectively amplifies the voices of a corporate CEO class, giving that class precedence over everyone else.... [it] can be used for bullying; it can be used for propagandizing falsehoods; it can be used to drown out other voices and deafen the electorate; it can used for buying political loyalty or punishing political disobedience; it can be the bait on a hook; it can be artillery; it can be blandishment; it can be a 'tsunami of slime.' (11)

Billionaire investor Warren Buffet put it succinctly: "They say it's free speech, but someone can speak 20 or 30 million times and my cleaning lady can't speak at all." (12)

And the pathetic thing is, the corporations don't even have to spend the money.

In 1757, the British Navy shot Admiral Byng for "failing to do his utmost" in a doomed effort to retake Port Mahon on the island of Minorca. He didn't have adequate forces to do the job, so he didn't. Politics were involved, and there was plenty of outrage and Fake News; it got out of hand and the agitation grew a life of its own, and he was executed on the deck of the *HMS Monarch*. The French loved it. Voltaire observed that the British like to shoot an admiral every so often, "to encourage the others."

The Mafia didn't actually burn down that many small businesses or murder that many citizens, at least not compared to the number of businesses or citizens from whom they extorted 'protection' money. Like the British Navy shooting Admiral Byng, the Mafia had established that arson and murder of some were not beyond them, so the others were encouraged to acquiesce. All Mafiosi had to do was walk into a business and say, 'nice place you got here, it'd be a shame if something were to happen to it,' or 'I saw your daughter getting dropped off at her school this morning, she's lovely.' Just the veiled threat is enough. (I can hear my liberal friends saying, 'you mean like "I want you to do me a favor though"?'. I hear you.)

The point is: if a corporation lets slip the notion that anyone who opposes position A or favors position B will find that his opponent in the next election will have the deepest imaginable pockets, that's enough. And we don't see it; it's not illegal; it isn't even 'dark money' because it never needs to be spent, and it never comes to the light of day. But as a result, many issues, many actions that would actually help real people, they just fade away because they ran afoul of corporations; and all too often nothing gets done and government appears to be worthless, because we allow it.

And that's why politicians don't seem to give a damn about the forgotten man.

Summary:

The Swamp extends to the judiciary.

The corporate takeover of the judiciary has been decades in the making.

The Swamp runs pro-corporate ball carriers down the field, often hidden behind the blockers of wedge issues such as guns and abortion.

"Conservative" judges may be conservative on social issues, but are not really conservative judicially.

"Conservative" judges often take extraordinary, activist steps to change the law in favor of The Swamp, such as *Citizens United*.

Trump warned against The Swamp, and he was right.

Chapter 8

Political Correctness

Trumpisms:

Political correctness is out of control and needs to be reined in.

The coastal elites have contempt for you and are ripping you off.

We should all love our country.

One the one hand, there was some truth to Trump's reaction to political correctness. Let me cite an example of political correctness gone awry.

If you haven't read Ayaan Hirsi Ali's books, you should. Her story is so incredible, her ability to lift herself from her upbringing through sheer willpower, her intelligence and strength and character are so clear, I think I'm in love. The narrative of her life is quintessentially American. She went from being a Somali refugee seeking asylum in Holland, to a member of the Dutch parliament, now a naturalized US citizen activist and writer. She has become labeled as 'anti-Muslim', and if you take her statements out of context sometimes that shoe can seem to fit. She has indicated that she supports the efforts of those who aim for a 'Muslim Reformation', though she expresses little hope that Islam can be redeemed. I hope she's wrong about that.

In 2014, she was invited to Brandeis University to receive an honorary degree and speak at some events surrounding their commencement; then she was disinvited, as she was accused of Islamophobia. I hope we have not reached such a state that anyone who can possibly take offense can wield veto power over someone else's speech. I wouldn't invite Nazis for an honorary degree, but Ayaan Hirsi Ali is so clearly academically legitimate, and her work for the rights of women and girls is so virtuous, that I am appalled that she was disinvited. Her stand that religion, specifically Islam, plays a role in the oppression of women, is controversial, but certainly worthy of discussion, (especially at an American university!) not censorship.

On the other hand, this canceling business is not just the left trying to cancel the right. From GOP assertions that corporations should stay out of politics and Major League Baseball shouldn't move their All-Star game out of Atlanta, to the *Epoch Times* not being credentialed by the House Press Gallery Executive Committee, some Trump supporters have gone a bit overboard about this. Many frame these issues as attacks on the First Amendment right to free speech.

No, it's not the First Amendment. There is no constitutional right to be invited to speak at a university, nor to be allowed to post on social media, nor to be on television, or in the House Press Gallery, whether you're telling the truth or spouting lies or racism.

On the third hand, there's something to be said about canceling certain people. Nazis, murderers who become celebrities, felons who get pardons, people who lie and people who get paid to lie and get rich for lying; as far as I'm concerned, cancel them. I have no plans to buy any of their books.

And on the fourth hand, there is often silliness regarding charges of political correctness. At a Rose Garden press conference during the height of the pandemic, a reporter wearing a mask asked President Trump a question. Trump asked him if he could remove his mask and he more loudly replied 'I'll just talk louder.' Trump dismissed him with "Oh OK you want to be politically correct." C'mon man. The reporter was following the then current Trump White House guidelines for the wearing of masks. Likewise, Dr. Suess books being banned, black Santa Claus and bisexual Superman, they are just the shiny objects (see wedge issues in Chapters 11 and 12) distracting us from real issues, and are not really worthy of discussion.

Finally, on the fifth hand, there must be something else to be said about being politically correct. What is it about 'political correctness' that so upsets people on the right, and Trump supporters particularly? Why do they get so damn angry about it?

A friend wrote to me: "I think a lot of conservatives are exhausted by the politically correct, social justice culture, and Trump is just a refreshing slap in the face against it." But there is something deeper than just that fatigue and mild resentment.

If you get your news from Fox or Newsmax or Breibart or OAN, you'll hear a common theme: Coastal elites have abandoned working people. You should be offended, because liberals control the media, and liberals have contempt for you, you Okies and Arkies, you hillbillies, bumpkins and hicks, they think your country music and culture is stupid and your love for guns and trucks and ridiculous cowboy hats and boots is adolescent. This theme is not new. And while it is hyperbolic and in service of Swamp agendas, it is not without some basis in reality.

I grew up in part (kindergarten through third grade) in Bakersfield, home of Buck Owens and Merle Haggard and the 'Bakersfield Sound' (as opposed to the 'Nashville Sound') of country music. (If you're a liberal who wants to better understand rural Americans, and be thoroughly entertained and educated at the same time, watch Ken Burns' documentary on Country Music.) I was called an "Okie" by white people more than once, as I was white and was going to a public grammar school on the poor side of town. At first I didn't know what it meant, but I could tell it was an epithet. When I learned its meaning, it didn't bother me much, as neither of my parents were from Oklahoma (some concrete thinking there on my part but hey, I was a kid); but it did leave an impression on me that I could be insulted just for the way I looked (I dressed usually in blue jeans and a white T-shirt, like a clueless slob, something I'm still working on) even before I opened my mouth (I have a pretty standard bland homogeneous American television talking head non-accent so I didn't feel self-conscious about that either).

If you're a liberal, think about it, and try to put yourself in the shoes of a conservative white southern or heartland dwelling American. If you want to connote someone who is upper crust, rich and sophisticated, you can adopt a British or an extinct 1930s Katherine Hepburn East Coast accent. And if you want to indicate ignorance or stupidity, you adopt an exaggerated white southern/country accent. Look in the mirror and ask yourself if you ever do that. The guy from Iowa or Nebraska doesn't even sound like that, but he feels that your liberal contempt extends to him.

A couple of generations ago, you might have used an Ebonics, Amos 'n' Andy accent. That was stupid then, and would be unacceptably racist now. But a white country accent to represent uneducated ignorance? As recently as the month of December 2020 I heard a host on MSNBC employ that trope. You can't tell a Polish joke or a racist or anti-Semitic joke in polite company today, and rightly so. But try this: "Q: How is a tornado like a divorce in Alabama? A: Somebody's losing a trailer." No problem... because it's easy to go along and pigeonhole the people down there as poor rednecks, ignorant and racist, they live in trailers and marry their sisters and a few insults are the least they deserve. When it comes to white country people, judging and insulting the entire group by a few stereotypes is fair game. It seems to be the case in mainstream media, and on college campuses. It shouldn't be a surprise that people who identify as conservative or country feel that most media and colleges have liberal biases and are out of touch with 'real' America.

Recently General Mark Milley the Chairman of the Joint Chiefs of Staff was on Capitol Hill being questioned about "Critical Race Theory" and other 'woke' stuff being taught at West Point. He replied that West Point is a university, where students learn a lot of things; that he had read Marx and Mao and Lenin and that didn't make him a communist. He said that he wanted to understand what has come to be known as "white rage", he wanted to understand why (mostly white) people had stormed the Capitol on January 6th, why Americans had wanted to stop governmental processes and overthrow the election results. Aside from economic insecurity, fear of demographic change and other issues, I believe that the cultural disrespect coming from their countrymen as described in the previous paragraph, whether perceived or real, intentional or inadvertent, is an understandable cornerstone of white rage.

If you're a liberal, it may seem that white people have been on top for so long that, as the privileged class, white people don't get to cry about being the butt of jokes. Your logic may tell you that it's hypocritical for those who rail against political correctness on one hand to then decry insults and look for a safe space on the other. But if you can put yourself in their place, it feels a little different.

Sixty years ago (before the 1960s and hippies etc.) in most colleges there were certain expectations for behavior, proper clothing, addressing professors with respect, etc. If white students dressed in blackface, black people didn't like it, but no one was listening to black people, so there were no repercussions. "What has changed is not the expectation that colleges define norms for civility, but rather the definition of civility." (1)

As Yale psychologist Jennifer Richeson describes, "I call it the democratization of discomfort. There were whole swaths of people uncomfortable all the time. Now we're democratizing it. Now more people across different races and religions feel uncomfortable." (2) This looks like progress, and I believe the intolerance of blackface and racist jokes indeed is progress.

But country/southern/rural whites really have been the butt of jokes and disregard, from white people, often urban, coastal, more highly educated white people, for generations, and that hasn't seemed to have improved much. It can be confusing, because caricatures of white country culture are mainstream *within* white country culture. Just look at old episodes of Hee-Haw on YouTube, or the self-deprecating humor of Minnie Pearl at the Grand Ole Opry; if hillbillies make fun of hillbillies, what's the complaining about? Again, one must see it from the recipients' perspective. Even if it's alright for Chris Rock to drop N-bombs in his comedy routines; it's not alright for you (if you're white) to repeat them. Similarly, if you're not of the culture of rural whites, rural whites reasonably find it rude and offensive for you to co-opt their humor.

As a result, if/when some white rural Americans find snobby self-righteous liberals all a-twitter about some politically incorrect statement from Trump, many really don't care if snowflakes are upset, and enjoy 'owning the libs'.

Summary:

Political correctness exists, and has real-world adverse consequences.

Trump identified and amplified grievance against political correctness.

Discrimination against white rural American culture exists, and is generally acceptable in mainstream culture.

Trump identified and amplified white grievance, generally.

Chapter 9

Stronger and Safer America

Trumpisms:

No More Stupid Wars.

Uncontrolled immigration is an invasion and threatens our security.

Mexico's not sending their best. They're rapists, etc.

Our national debt is a disaster.

We need our country to be safe and secure.

We should all love our country.

As with almost all of his activities, whether he did a great job or a poor job in this domain depends upon your elephant.

No more stupid wars

When he was running in 2016 he often declared that he had opposed the war in Iraq before it began, and that he had said so dozens of times. A search of the public record doesn't support that; indeed the only on-record account of him addressing the prospective invasion of Iraq (of March 2003) was in an interview with Howard Stern on September 11th 2002. Stern asked him if he supported going to war with Iraq, and Trump replied, "Yeah, I guess so." But that only matters if you're taking him literally.

Never-Trumpers on the left and the right will see his record in keeping America safe and secure as inadequate. If you're liberal, you couldn't stand his bombastic threats about 'fire and fury such as the world has never seen'. Even progressives typically opposed to our intelligence community found Trump's siding with Putin over our own intelligence services in Helsinki to be a bridge too far. Traditionally conservative national-security conscious Republicans were apoplectic about Trump criticizing our allies and weakening the trans-Atlantic alliance while cozying up to autocrats, 'falling in love' with Kim Jong-un and extorting Ukraine for dirt on Biden, not to mention failing to even pretend to hold the Saudi Crown Prince accountable for the murder and dismemberment of a reporter for the *Washington Post*. Many veterans found his abandonment of the Kurds to be dishonorable, and felt ashamed.

But Trump supporters saw the glass more than half full. They saw that Trump didn't weaken the trans-Atlantic alliance, he made those free-rider NATO nations 'pay their fair share'. He didn't kowtow to Putin, he gave the Ukrainians lethal weapons. A couple of strikes in Syria and the assassination of Soleimani proved that Trump was tough, and being unwilling to blow up relations with Saudi Arabia proved that he was prudent. Bottom line, he took on the world's troublemakers with both carrot and stick, held the line in the Middle East and the Korean peninsula, and didn't get us into any More Stupid Wars. If you're a never-Trumper and you find this paragraph to be exasperating, remember:

Must I believe this? Or can I believe that?

Immigration

Immigration is a wedge issue and so could belong entirely in chapter 11 (and we'll see it again there, worry not), but it is often wrapped in national security raiment, so here is a taste.

Immigration is low-hanging fruit when it comes to triggering reactions based upon deeply held values. Trump was and is masterful in generating rhetoric that can ignite red hot passions. Without naming (or even knowing about) any of them, and without saying anything particularly new, Trump plucked the chords of these values in ways that mobilized his supporters. Like any good politician on the right or left, he activated the first three foundational pairs that just about all people value, in ways that resonated deeply with Trump supporters.

Care versus harm: He couldn't be much clearer about you and your family being at risk of harm because of illegal immigration. "They're bringing drugs. They're bringing crime. They're rapists." Invading caravans are threats to our national security and cannot be allowed.

Liberty versus oppression: Democrats want illegal immigration, so they can give them free stuff, including amnesty, so they can make them Democrats and oppress native-born white Americans.

Fairness versus cheating: Illegal immigration is cheating. It's not fair to the people who wait in line and immigrate legally. Also, people jump the line to come here just so they can get free stuff.

But Trump also activated the three pairs of moral foundations below, more valued by conservatives, that are in play in ways that may not be appreciated by liberals.

Loyalty versus betrayal: Sanctuary cities. From the perspective of (some, many, or most) Trump supporters, sanctuary cities are the result of disloyal Americans betraying the rest of us 'real' Americans. They provide a space where criminals (since all 'illegal' immigrants are at least possibly by a certain definition, criminals) may congregate freely without having to answer for their crimes.

Authority versus subversion: The Wall. I have the right to build a wall on my property, as do we true Americans collectively. When I build a wall, I am affirming my authority to do so, and if you go over, under, around or through my wall (yes, that's familiar if you're old enough), you are subverting my authority, indeed the authority of our entire nation, and that cannot be allowed.

Sanctity versus degradation: "Illegal immigrants" (as if the people themselves rather than behaviors are illegal) are being allowed to infect our nation. Trump has referred to them as an infestation, as one's house is infested by vermin. Allowing illegal immigration is inviting impurity to be within us. Rhetoric that extols the virtues of immigrants from Norway while lamenting immigration from "sh**hole countries" has obvious racial implications and triggers alarm about exposure to waste and filth.

I can feel my liberal friends sputtering "But, but, but...." I understand, and we'll talk more about how to address the divide here in a couple of chapters. But for the moment, I believe liberals should realize that the arguments by Trump supporters regarding immigration (or any number of other issues) don't arise *de novo* with no basis, they have deeply held reasons. Liberal arguments about policy, appealing to the rational rider, are doomed if the elephant has been expertly activated by appeals to passion.

The king of debt

Liberals recall that Trump has not always been coherent in his approach to deficit spending and the national debt. In June 2016 on *CBS This Morning*: "I'm great with debt. Nobody knows debt more than me. I've made a fortune by using debt, and if things don't work out I renegotiate the debt. That's a smart thing, not a stupid thing.... I like debt for my company, but I don't like debt for the country.... We'll have to start chopping that debt down." Trump further indicated that we must "Reduce our $18 trillion in debt, because, believe me, we're in a bubble."

In a 2016 interview with Bob Woodward of the *Washington Post*, Trump said, "We've got to get rid of the $19 trillion in debt."

Woodward: "How long would that take?"

Trump: "I think I could do it fairly quickly, because of the fact the numbers —"

Woodward: "What's fairly quickly?"

Trump: "Well, I would say over a period of eight years."

Some economists noted that 'getting rid of' the national debt within eight years would not be possible even if all governmental functions were eliminated and all the nation's liquid assets sold to the highest bidder. Trump later walked back his statements.

In the debates in 2016, he seemed to conflate our trade deficit with our budget deficit. On September 26: "We have a trade deficit with all of the countries that we do business with, almost $800 billion a year. That means, who's negotiating these trade deals? We have people that are political hacks that are negotiating our trade deals." And on October 9th: "I will bring our energy companies back, they'll be able to compete, they'll make money, they'll pay off our national debt. They'll pay off our tremendous budget deficits, which are tremendous."

In February of 2015, Trump tweeted that if the national debt went above $21 trillion by the end of President Obama's term in office, "Obama will have effectively bankrupted our country."

Later in 2015 he tweeted "When you have $18-$19 trillion in debt, they need someone like me to straighten it out."

When Trump took office in January 2017, the national debt was $19.9 trillion. Two years into his term in Feb 2019 (long before the pandemic), it surpassed $22 trillion.

Never Trumpers further note that according to the Congressional Budget Office, Trump's and the GOP's major tax accomplishment, the Tax Cuts and Jobs Act of 2017, was projected to increase the national debt by about $1.5 trillion over a decade.

For all the reasons previously discussed, none of these details about what he said or didn't say about the national debt, matter. For his supporters, how he has made them feel about his capabilities and instincts is what matters. Nuanced considerations of trade policy and trade deficits are for pencil-necked pointy-headed nerds; Trump has his gut and his ability to smell out a deal and make it happen.

As we are already seeing in the run-up to the 2022 midterms, and as the next iteration of Trump or his successor is sure to play the debt and deficit card, it may be worthwhile to take a broad view of the topic.

But first let's set one topic aside. *Trade deficits* are not the same as our *budget deficits*, and trade deficits don't really seem to matter all that much. That is, trying to 'fix' trade deficits in isolation without fixing a lot of other more important stuff, is foolhardy. As we discussed regarding The Swamp, corporations and the influences they have had on our trade deals have tilted the field in the direction of helping corporations more than American working people, so **Trump's rhetoric about the common man getting left behind resonated, because it's true**. Doing a better job negotiating trade deals to help American workers would be a good thing, and then let the chips fall where they may regarding trade deficits. But trade deficits aren't the deficits anyone is talking about when they bemoan 'our deficit' or 'deficit spending'.

An amateur's guide to debt & deficit

For decades, politicians have pandered with declarations of not raising taxes, then pandered out of the other side of their mouths and promised not to cut services. Or, they find they can't cut the services they'd promised to cut, and still must pay for them. They make up the difference by borrowing. The deficit is how short we are each year; the deficit especially matters in that it adds to our debt. The debt is what results from adding up the yearly deficits. Unfortunately, both are fertile grounds for demagoguery.

Most of us have been in debt, and it can be scary. What happens if I get sick and can't work? I can't pay off my debt, I'll go bankrupt, and my kids will be on the street. The unscrupulous prey upon those fears to extend them to the nation as a whole. And of course there is always a kernel of truth: obviously borrowing and debt cannot be unlimited, we can't borrow too much and get into too much debt; intuitively we feel that would be unsustainable.

Suppose you're a regular guy, and someone offers to sell you a house for 10 million dollars. It's worth it, as it's a really really nice big house in a great location, but, you think, no way; I can't afford a 10 million dollar house. Can't you? It would depend on the terms, wouldn't it? Suppose the terms are, zero interest, $10 per year for a million years. That'd work, you could service that debt, easily.

What matters is not so much your total debt, but whether or not you can service your debt. And in this, you and I (and Greece, and Ireland, etc.) differ very significantly from the United States of America. The American dollar is the reserve currency for the world. People and governments the world over want to buy US Treasury bonds, they're the safest place on the planet to put your money and know it'll still be there when you want it. And these days the US doesn't have to pay hardly any interest; everyone wants to loan us their money just about for free, just so they know their money is secure. There is no other candidate for the reserve currency; not China with its as yet undemocratic institutions and a population that will someday be demanding its freedoms, not the Eurozone with its unresolved issues about integrating different nations' economies, just us. The only thing that can screw this up in the short term would be the self-inflicted wounds of deliberate default, not raising the debt ceiling, or not servicing our debt. If you *can't* service your debt, that's one thing, you're in a world of hurt. But if you *don't* service your debt when you can, you're just being shortsighted and stupid, in recent years for short-term political gain.

But this can't go forever, right? You can't just borrow forever. Well we can't overdo it, but yes, we can be in debt forever. I the individual don't want to be, I don't want to pass debt on to my children, so I want to pay off my credit cards and mortgages before I shuffle off the mortal coil. Here's the thing: the US isn't going to die like I am. Even so, aren't we just passing on the debt to our children? Not really, because unlike my biological children, the future USA won't have to pay off this debt either. Arrgh! That's crazy, a Ponzi scheme! No; as long as the amount of debt is manageable, and the US can service its debt, it can and will stay in some debt forever, without a problem. The key words about our debt are: manageable, and able to service it. And don't overdo it... whatever that means.

Blessed are the young, for they shall inherit the national debt.
-- Herbert Hoover

I'm no economist, but like non-lawyers understanding *Citizens United*, I don't think one needs to be an expert or an economist to have an adequate understanding of debt and deficit. As long as debt doesn't continuously grow more than both inflation and economic growth, we should be OK. If our deficits are too big, as people have been screaming for years, then there are warning signs; big deficits mean the US government is sucking up all the money available for loaning that's out there to be loaned. That makes money for loaning scarce, and if you've got money to loan, you're in the catbird's seat, because you can charge higher interest, and so can all other lenders, so interest rates go up. But, as of mid-2021, that hasn't happened... interest rates are still zippo.

Apparently there's still plenty of money to loan, in part because many people want to save rather than spend, and spending has taken a hit due to the pandemic. Oh no! What happens when people want to spend again?! Then the economy is recovering, and growing, we're moving toward full employment, tax revenues increase and we don't need to borrow, and that would indeed be an appropriate time for some fiscal austerity. (That would have been a good choice in 2018 and 2019.) That's what we want, economic growth and full employment. And to make it happen, we should be putting money into people's pockets and improving our infrastructure at the same time. (1) Consider; what would you do if you owned a business and you were faced with deferred maintenance or needed upgrades, and you had the opportunity to remedy them by using OPM (Other People's Money): if you were smart your business would borrow at the current lower than one percent interest rate and then reap the benefits of its improved competitive position. Much is said about burdening our progeny with our national debt, but we must also consider the opportunity costs of not addressing our crumbling infrastructure, or our underfunded educational systems. When more bridges (and roads and airports, etc.) are literally falling down, our offspring will not have the option of waiting to rebuild them, and may be faced with raising taxes or borrowing at much less favorable rates than we have available to us now.

But still, this huge debt, it's over 28 trillion dollars! Look at the graphs on the internet, the debt just goes up and up and up, it just can't be OK; how do we get rid of it? What matters more than the amount of debt is the ratio of debt to our Gross National Product (GNP). Economics Nobel laureate Paul Krugman addresses this in his book cited above. At the end of World War II the US had debt of $240 billion (ah, the good old days), that was 120% of GNP. How did we pay that off? We didn't... we grew the GNP instead, and presto-chango, the ratio of debt to GDP went down. So, in 1946 debt was 120% of GNP; but now we've got over $28 trillion in debt! But, our GNP is over $22 trillion also, so the ratio is a bit less than 128%, just a little higher than it was in 1946. Japan's ratio of debt to GNP is around 200%; people have been predicting the crash of Japan for decades, but it doesn't happen.

(If you want to flirt with anxiety, go to USDebtClock.org , and watch the numbers change in real time....)

Am I saying then that debt and deficit are no problem, we can just tax and borrow and spend and not worry about it? No, I'm not; debt and deficit must be addressed. I don't know how high that ratio of debt to GNP can go, and I don't want to find out the hard way; I'd like us to have more cushion in case of future emergencies. We now pay about 400 billion dollars annually to service our federal debt; that's about 2% of our GNP and around 11% of tax revenues. If the service on the debt grows too much, it sucks up our tax revenues and crowds out our options for other spending. Those concerned about debts and deficits are justified by that fact; those concerns are legitimate and deserve serious debate. I would like to see a multi-decade plan for stabilizing that ratio of debt to GNP at something less than it is now, and a further plan with contingencies for sustainably addressing the debt and deficit in all possible permutations.

Interest rates will not stay low forever. Someday we may not be the reserve currency of the world. Perhaps the population of China will be satisfied with economic growth without political freedoms, and China appears to be the next economic superpower; or the Eurozone if their issues all work out smoothly. I still think the US has the edge in investor confidence, but if we squander that by flirting with elective defaults, government shutdowns, and inability to work together to solve problems, we could give investors the impression that we have forgotten how to govern ourselves, and investors may then look elsewhere.

And a word about inflation; nobody likes the dislocations it causes. But if it rears its ugly head, that's one way of reducing the national debt. If a loaf of bread costs a trillion dollars, our national debt is only 28 loaves of bread.

But consider: in thirty or a hundred years, the national debt could be an astronomical $100 trillion; but if the GNP is $200 trillion, we're good. Our debt should be addressed rationally and coolly, we have time, we have not reached a tipping point; but it should be better addressed. My concern is that fear-mongering can provoke voters into frantic action, favoring paths that are counterproductive. It may seem a paradox that cutting spending in times of underemployment and recession or depression, reduces GNP and makes debt worse long-term. I wouldn't believe

Krugman and his ilk except that their previous predictions and track records have been so superior to those of their critics.

Even if my analysis is completely wrong, even if my source is mistaken despite his Nobel Prize in economics, we should still take certain steps to fix our problems, and the sooner the better. If we had an all-powerful monarch, managing our debt would be easy: sweeping tax reform, rational reform of entitlements, putting money toward investments that are cost-effective in growing the economy (especially when we can borrow for free), a reasonable approach to borrowing and deficits, and the deal is done. But, we don't have a monarch; that cure would be worse than the disease. We could however insist that our elected representatives stop partisan posturing and get work done.

The last of this chapter's introductory Trumpisms are political truisms -- no one running for office can go wrong uttering them. Of course we need our country to be safe and secure, and of course we should all love our country. But for some, Samuel Johnson's aphorism comes to mind:

> Patriotism is the last refuge of a scoundrel.

Never-Trumpers are disgusted by someone they regard as a draft-dodger molesting the flag in a display of *faux* devotion to America.

Trump supporters see in him someone undeterred by political correctness, unambiguous in his preference for all things American and unashamed about openly declaring his patriotism.

Chapter 10

Do Black Lives Really Matter?

Trumpisms:

We need our country to be safe and secure.

We should all love our country.

You're a racist.

How do you feel about that?

If you start a conversation by calling someone a racist, you have probably ended the conversation as well. Them's fightin' words. In today's society, there aren't many terms more pejorative than "racist". And after all of the racism in our nation's history perhaps that's as it should be. While some bigots have been emboldened and often are brazen in flying the colors of white supremacy, more typically, even racists claim not be racist (think of David Duke running for office, in a business suit rather than in a white hood) because they recognize that explicit racism is unacceptable.

Let me take some of the air out of the tire of the label of racism.

True confession time:

Depending upon the definition, I'm a racist.

If you define racist, as does Ibram X. Kendi in his book *How To Be An Antiracist*, as "someone who is supporting racist policies or expressing racist ideas," I am a racist. Not all the time perhaps, but I have believed and have repeated racist arguments; I have supported some racist policies and been oblivious to others; I have participated in and benefitted from systemic racism. I have done so in the past, I'm almost certainly doing so today, and I'm quite likely to do so tomorrow. Stick with me here, please.

Doesn't that mean I'm evil? I believe that racism is an evil. Aren't racists evil?

I don't think I'm evil. I think I'm a pretty good guy. How do I reconcile being racist but not being evil? If I'm a good guy and yet a racist, then it must be OK to be a racist, so, what's all the fuss about?

I grew up Catholic. There's a boatload of guilt to be mined in that history, but nominally at least the message was, 'love the sinner, hate the sin'. When I was a kid, we were forced to go to Confession and tell the priest our sins. We were absolved, but only if we performed a sincere Act of Contrition, which included the promise (to try) not to sin again. Everyone recognized that we would fall short (there's job security in hearing forced confessions). So there's no free lunch: you don't get to be a sinner and just wallow in it, you must do your best to leave sin behind.

I don't want to be a racist. (For simplicity, I'm not going to make the same arguments about a lot in our history, about discrimination against women, against ethnic or national or religious groups aside from race, against people who are anything other than cis-gender heterosexuals; I won't address The Chinese Exclusion Act, the Trail of Tears, internment of Japanese-Americans, etc. etc. But the same essential dynamics apply.) Indeed I aspire to be an anti-racist when I grow up. Like any programs for self-improvement from losing a few pounds to kicking a twenty-year heroin addiction, the first steps are recognizing you have a problem and being willing to try to do something about it. There are lots of things of which I am ignorant and to which I am somewhat blind, and my racism has been one of them. I don't think I (or you) should be condemned for it.

> Don't be in a hurry to condemn because he doesn't do what you do or think as you think or as fast. There was a time when you didn't know what you know today.
>
> -- Malcolm X

Maybe we can lower the temperature around the word racism by differentiating between bigots who embrace their bigotry, and the rest of us who fall short of perfection in our appreciation of the issues around race. Try the label on for size for a few minutes, don't get defensive, take a couple deep breaths, and give yourself credit for wanting to be a better person and not have racism in your heart. Talking about race, acknowledging the existence of racism and maybe even our unwitting participation in it, doesn't have to be divisive. Indeed, recognizing and speaking the truth can be a step toward healing, reconciliation, and unity.

You don't know me, you don't know how conservative or liberal I might be regarding a given issue. But if you are conservative or a Trump supporter, you may be skeptical, and think I have just drunk deeply the woke Kool-Aid of Critical Race Theory, have succumbed to the latest version of liberal bedwetting, looking to cancel white culture, clutching my pearls and virtue signaling by engaging in the public auto-flagellation of self-loathing white guilt. Fair enough, you could be right. I'll tell you a couple of stories, and let's see if the shoe fits.

I started medical school in 1975. I recall looking at the class pictures that lined many of the hallways. Looking back year by year the students were increasingly male and white. Going back just a decade to the mid-1960s, it was almost all white men, and for decades and generations earlier back to 1834, nothing but white men. My class (class of '79) was fairly diverse in both race and gender so I felt I was part of an enlightened reality looking boldly toward a future full of racial equity.

When I did my first tour of active duty as a medical student for 45 days in the summer of 1977, I learned that hospital command positions were restricted to medical officers, physicians. OK, that made sense to me; I had no interest at the time in rank or command or administration, I just wanted to learn my craft, so I didn't question the idea that the boss of a hospital would be a doctor. It was only much later that I even considered what this might look like to a person of color.

I have no reason to believe that the people who admitted students to medical school or who determined which military Areas of Concentration (like job descriptions) were eligible for which positions, were any more racist than I was. It was just the way the system worked. But the effects were blindingly obvious, if you weren't blind to them. Most of our professors were white men. Hospital commanders were almost all white men (some great guys, don't get me wrong! But almost all white men). They were at least a decade older than I was; they were doctors; they were the ones whose faces had adorned the hallways of medical schools all across the country. The workforce, the enlisted medics and lab techs and ancillary healthcare workers, the junior officers and nurses, were increasingly diverse, lots of minorities, lots of women. Let's put the shoe on the other foot for a moment. If you're a white conservative today, and you had a job working as part of the biggest bottom rung in your field, and saw lots of white co-workers, but all the bosses were black, what would you think?

Again, I don't think the command selection board members were evil, no; it was just the system. It selected doctors, which makes some sense, and the doctors were almost all white men, which was (and remains) an historical vestige, but the result was that black people and women didn't get those command positions. Those policies favored white over black; the System favored white over black, male over female. If a System favors one race over another, that is "systemic racism," or institutional discrimination. Simply and correctly and succinctly put, the problem is, policies: racist policies (or sexist policies, etc.). And if you point to the occasional extraordinarily talented and persistent woman or person of color who was selected for a hospital command as being evidence of the absence of systemic racism, no: the exception proves the rule. (Likewise, the existence of poor white people or incarcerated white people doesn't prove that there is no such thing as white privilege. It just demonstrates that the most potent privilege is: money.)

The army (and other branches) recognized to some degree the error of its ways and also figured out that there was plenty of command potential untapped in allied health fields (nursing, physical therapy, whatever), and changed the policies to open command positions to non-physicians. Still, I was a white male physician, and that didn't hurt (not necessarily because I was white and male, but because I was a physician, and physicians tended to be white and male). The army wanted to retain physicians and tended to be more accommodating to me, I believe.

As my career in the Army Reserve progressed, I wanted to stretch myself and I developed an interest in command. It was more work and not any more pay. Reserve physicians are usually busy with their civilian practices, so it was not too intensely competitive, I don't think. I went to Command and General Staff College, which physicians, unlike other officers, don't need in order to get promoted, even through the rank of colonel. I attended and graduated from the US Army War College, which is quite uncommon for physicians; and I served eight years in command positions. I was benefitting mightily from the system that favored white males, and that didn't bother me at all. I was clueless, fat, dumb and happy. I was on my way to being promoted to flag rank, a brigadier general (BG)... so I thought.

Then it seemed my white male privilege hit a wall. A female nurse former subordinate of mine was promoted to BG. I was passed over. And another non-physician black female junior to me (she was a Lieutenant Colonel, or LTC while I was a full colonel) was promoted into the command position above me and my hospital. Was this double whammy reverse discrimination against my white male self? I'll never know what went on in the selection boards, whether race or gender played any role. But the fact is... my former chief nurse who became a BG, back before I'd figured out I was interested in stretching myself, well she was all-in working her ass off for years while I was just showing up. And I always had a suspicion that the black female LTC was just savvier about the army than I was, she had a better concept of all the moving parts and about how to get things done.

There's a well-known cognitive bias known as *self-serving bias*, the belief that while my successes are my responsibility, due only to my own hard work, any falling short is due to outside forces: not my fault! It can be *very* tempting for me or anyone to put the blame (if there is any) elsewhere. So as much as I would be tempted to justify my relative stagnation at the rank of colonel as being a result of a mistimed birth that not just squandered my white maleness, but even penalized me for it, I think the army actually managed to choose the best candidates for those positions. C'est la vie. But I can understand those white guys who feel bitter about having this privilege dangling in front of them, only to perceive it being snatched away... especially if it materially impacts their livelihood, which was not the case for me. I had my civilian physician job and I was going to land on my feet no matter what. And I can also understand women and minorities who don't give a damn about the distress of those having their white male privilege ended and feeling like it's unfair. Here's their thought bubble: 'Boo-hoo, woe is you. Welcome to our world. Now get over yourself.'

Here's another clueless white guy anecdote.

I do not believe I have ever called anyone the N-word. The grammar school I attended was plurality black, next was a large minority Latinx, then smaller minority white; I see two other white boys and three or four white girls in my old school photos. This was kindergarten through 3rd grade for me, a time when we were mostly oblivious to race. Anyway, mostly my friends were black, and when I first heard the N-word in 2nd or 3rd grade, when it was spoken by whites it sounded like it was meant to be hurtful to my friends and I stayed away from it. My parents didn't say it, neither did my siblings, for which I am grateful. I remember decades later watching Mark Fuhrman on the hot seat during the OJ Simpson trial and thinking how mortifying it would be to have been documented to have been using that word. Soon thereafter, I saw the Chris Rock HBO special *Bring the Pain* wherein he described those to whom the N-word should apply. Chris Rock is brilliantly hilarious. To my mind, comedians are our society's version of court jesters, or prophets, and they get to say provocative things that would otherwise be inappropriate. Somehow I came into possession of his book which has his comedy routine verbatim. And I thought my wife would find it funny if I read it to her. She didn't. She gave me that look she gives me when I say or do something stupid, and then she moved on about her business.

So, I'm not Chris Rock. And a white man reading aloud his comedy routine just doesn't make it. Here I was, saying the N-word, and my wife giving me The Look. Parenthetically, at that point, I decided to eliminate that word from my vocabulary, so I would henceforth be able truthfully to assert that those syllables have not crossed my lips since the day I cluelessly read Chris Rock aloud in the mid-90s. Hurray for me... I deserve a cookie. This policy of excising the N-word from one's patois is one I have recommended to white soldiers under my command, captive audiences to my intermittent Equal Opportunity or Army Values briefings. (I don't know if anyone ever followed my advice.)

In his book, Ibram X. Kendi states that Chris Rock discontinued this line of comedy. Kendi goes on to point out that the content of the comedy was racist. For Chris Rock to attribute characteristics to a group of people, a subset of black people that he called the N-word, rather than to individuals, is racist. It is the essence of racism, to vilify people by race. (Whether or not it is appropriate for *comedians* to say racist things is a question beyond me. Sometimes people can swallow criticism if they can laugh first.) If some black people act inappropriately, they are individuals acting inappropriately, who happen to be black. Rather than draw conclusions about an entire race based upon the behaviors of individuals, it is important to identify the racist policies that lead to unwanted behaviors. Because if some black people are poor, or take drugs, or are incarcerated more than are white people, there are two explanations. One is that black people have something wrong with them, something that has led to a 'culture of failure' etc. The other is that racist policies have led to black people living in poverty, or being more susceptible to drug use or crime. The first explanation is racist; the second is not.

A word about reparations

To my liberal friends, if your argument is that African-Americans should be compensated by white Americans for having been enslaved in centuries past, that is a difficult argument. Those on the right will respond reasonably that all those people are long dead. Most current white Americans have no slave-owning ancestors. While black Americans were enslaved, my Irish ancestors were being exploited and abused by their English overlords. (And while my English and Welsh ancestors were not landowning aristocrats, I suppose they may have benefitted from that abuse of my Irish ancestors. It's complicated.) Given the history of rape of enslaved women, it is likely that modern African-Americans have more slave-owning ancestors than do most non-black Americans. Those on the New Age left can even assert that for all we know those enslaved persons have been reincarnated as white taxpayers who should not then be required to pay anything.

To my Trump-supporting friends, consider the possibility that the above argument is mostly a straw man, designed to lose so that the idea of reparations can be dismissed. Sure, giving the tax money of hard-working white people to the children of Lebron James just because their remote ancestors were enslaved makes little sense. The vast majority of Southerners, white and black, had no significant wealth that survived the Civil War, so compensation for antebellum labor from which white people theoretically currently benefit is only borderline logical. But I don't believe that is the real argument.

In 1921, "Black Wall Street", the Greenwood section of Tulsa Oklahoma was destroyed by a white mob. Hundreds of black people were killed, thousands were displaced. Their property was destroyed or appropriated (that is, stolen). Insurance companies failed to recognize their claims. Some few of those people are alive today. Most of the original inhabitants have long since died. Their accumulated wealth was lost, and was not passed down to their descendants. Those descendants were harmed by the massacre and its sequelae, and *they are alive today*.

We know how to remedy such injuries, we've done it before. Sometimes we financially compensate people who took a hit for all of us, like the families of those killed in the 9/11 attacks or the hostages imprisoned by the Ayatollah through 1980. Sometimes our society recognizes that we screwed up, such as by interning Japanese-Americans at the onset of our entry into World War II. The US subsequently paid $20,000 to each internee.

The Tulsa massacre is only one of around a *hundred such massacres of black communities* that took place in the late 19th and early 20th centuries (massacres about which I learned absolutely nothing in all of my formal education). And the massacres are only one extreme example of the death of a thousand cuts that black Americans have suffered at the hands of our System. Redlining in the mid-20th century precluded many black people from accessing credit we all occasionally need in order to advance economically. *Those people were injured, and are alive today.*

This is not just dusty old history. Even in 2021, black people will sometimes have white friends stand in for them when getting their properties appraised, because 'owning while black' can cut the value of your home in half. Anyone can have their *Fairness* versus *Cheating* moral foundation activated by such a scenario, because that's not *Fair. Those people were injured, and are alive today.*

What exactly reparations will look like, who will get how much based upon what set of facts, is beyond my expertise. In keeping consistent with the *Proportionality* sought by conservatives, the devil will be in the details. But the idea that the law should serve those who have been wronged, that people who can demonstrate to the satisfaction of the law (a law as yet unwritten) that they have been injured should have the ability to be made whole, is nothing new or outlandish. We've done the right thing before, and we should do the right thing again.

"The System is Rigged" includes race

Kendi further makes the case that racism is damaging to white people; not as damaging as it is to minorities, but still. While discrimination along national or religious or tribal lines is very, very old, he also points out that racism is old, but not that old. Beyond the scope of this book to explore, racism dates back essentially only some centuries, and is tethered to colonial exploitation and capitalism. In order to justify policies that took the property of indigenous peoples, a rationale had to be built that such peoples were essentially inferior. While created by God, they were inferior by their very nature, and it was the burden of white Europeans to bring them Christianity and civilize them (and by the way abuse them and take their stuff in the process).

This rationale exploited the fundamental values of *Sanctity* versus *Degradation*. European Christians were favored, blessed by God, holy, mandated by God to rule; black and brown non-European people were unholy and impure. This value informs the racist underpinning of enslaving Africans, and the meticulous accounting for how much 'black blood' a given mulatto or octoroon possessed, as well as the Aryan master race ideology of the Third Reich, current American white supremacy, etc.

In her book *The Sum of Us: What Racism Costs Everyone and How We Can Prosper Together*, Heather McGee recounts events subsequent to mandated desegregation, for instance, of swimming pools in the South. Rather than integrate swimming pools, local officials filled them with dirt and covered them with turf or asphalt.

Everyone lost.

Just as Tajfel's boys were willing to have their group have less as long as the out group had even less still, racism allows for the dominant group to discriminate against the out group even if the dominant group loses something in the process.

But aside from simple ignorance fueling racism, perhaps 'the System is Rigged' includes the reality that racist policies generate benefits for moneyed special interests.

> If you can convince the lowest white man he's better than the best colored man, he won't notice you're picking his pocket. Hell, give him somebody to look down on, and he'll empty his pockets for you.
>
> - - President Lyndon Baines Johnson

Samuel Martin, Publisher of the *Birmingham Times* noted, "There is no doubt that racism was at the heart of it. However; I would argue that President Johnson's revelation was more about 'classism,' and a way for those with money (the upper class) to control the lower working class without the actual system of aristocracy that existed in Great Britain. The colored man was a convenient pawn. And the upper class has continued to manipulate the lower working class by simply refining their strategies to divide and conquer." (1)

There is evidence that racial resentment triggers economic anxiety. Per political scientists John Sides, Michael Tessler, and Lynn Vavreck:

> Before Obama's presidency, how Americans felt about black people did not much affect their perceptions of the economy. After Obama this changed. In December 2007, racial resentment -- which captures whether Americans think deficiencies in black culture are the main reason for racial inequality -- was not related to whites' perceptions whether the economy was getting better or worse, after accounting for partisanship and ideology. But when these exact same people were re-interviewed

> in July 2012, racial resentment was a powerful predictor of economic perceptions: the greater someone's level of racial resentment, the worse they believe the economy was doing. (2)

This anxiety can adversely affect one's quality of life and probably one's health. Our media and politicians and The Swamp often fuel these anxieties by magnifying grievance and the sense that "Others" are doing better at the expense of one's team. One 2016 poll found that 57% of whites agreed that "discrimination against whites is as big a problem today as discrimination against blacks and other minorities." (3) The political scientists cited found that "Republicans in the highest income quintile, those making more than $100,000 per year, were actually slightly *less satisfied* than Democrats in the lowest income quintile, those making less than $20,000 per year." Many are triggered to activate their *Fairness* versus *Cheating* moral foundation and feel that they are justified in feeling aggrieved, despite objective reality (in this case, higher annual income) to the contrary.

This is an old American story. Very few Confederate soldiers in the Civil War were slave owners. It was in the interest of slave owners (especially large plantation owners, who were much wealthier than non-slave owners) to have slavery remain legal, and to do so it was in their interest that states newly admitted to the Union were open to slavery. White non-slave owning farmers and white workers did not benefit from slavery, far from it; they were essentially in competition with enslaved workers, a true race to the bottom in terms of wages for workers and price margins for farmers. Moneyed slave owners then employed divide and conquer, framed their resistance to abolition under the argument not only of black racial inferiority and the threat of Yankee supported race-mixing, but of states' rights, again, northern and eastern elites telling the South what it could or could not do, disregarding and insulting the chivalry, the values, the *liberty*, and way of life of those in the South. Non-slave owners were sold that bill of goods, led to feel that they were part of something noble *even though it was against their economic interest to do so.*

It is a very old story.

Paradoxically, this dynamic gives some support to the myth of the "Lost Cause", that the Civil War had little to nothing to do with slavery, it was all about states' rights. It is true that soldiers fight mostly for their comrades-in-arms who stand beside them. They fight also for home and hearth, for shared values, and against aggressors. Geopolitical ambitions, the Flag and apple pie are much less important, far distant motivators. So while historians are correct in pointing out that the Lost Cause myth is ahistorical, that "but for" slavery there would not have been a war, that the Confederate national/regional strategic goal of secession and war was the perpetuation of slavery as described above, slavery probably had not much to do with motivating *Confederate soldiers* at the tactical level.

While it is a virtual certainty that Rebel soldiers held racist views and supported racist policies (Union soldiers too), a white descendant of a Confederate can with justification claim today that his ancestor fought not for slavery, but for his rights, his home, his family and community, for his *sacred* honor, for *liberty* versus *oppression,* in opposition to northern aggression. A white, likely rural, quite possibly Trump-supporting southerner feels slandered if he's told his non-slave-owning, probably low-ranking Rebel ancestor was fighting for slavery.

If you're liberal Yankee, have you ever considered that someone's distant Rebel relative cared more about his hometown and his reputation than about slavery?

If you're a white southerner attached to the Lost Cause, have you considered the concept that the Civil War would not have happened "but for" the institution of slavery?

We have never come to a national consensus about this part of our national story. We have had trouble speaking about our racially charged history, trouble listening to each other, and it should come as no surprise that today we have trouble understanding and accepting each other.

Black Lives Matter

Here's a third anecdote, personally repeated over probably many decades, up into the early 21st century. Countless times, I've read or heard or seen news reports of police shootings. We all have. That's America. It's a ubiquitous part of American life, both fictional and real: cops and robbers, drug deals, felons of all types, young Wild West going out like Butch and Sundance, high speed chases ending in gunplay. As often as not it seems, the person shot by the police was black. That sad reality also is America.

The first time I remember paying attention to the phrase "Black Lives Matter" (BLM) was probably in 2015 or early 2016, during the Democratic presidential primary. Former governor of Maryland Martin O'Malley was asked about BLM, and embedded in his reply was the pious rejoinder, "All lives matter." Well of course they do, but... though I think he's a good guy and at the time I wouldn't have had anything smarter to say, somehow his reply seemed tone deaf. For my white friends, here's a tip about "All lives matter": don't say that. You just sound foolish. Of course all lives matter, that's a truism. But that's the point of BLM.

And by BLM, I mean the idea, the vision that motivated people of all races to demonstrate after the death of George Floyd; I'm not advocating for every outfit that has a website with *blacklivesmatter* in its name, or for the agenda of every person who has ever tried to raise money or carried a sign or worn a T-shirt with BLM on it. Linking every crime committed by anyone who has uttered "black lives matter" to the concept or movement of BLM is inappropriate guilt by association.

When I heard and read all those reports of police shootings, my default over the years was, well, it's the police. The guy (almost always a guy, with some exceptions) was probably doing something wrong. He had it coming. And he, they, these persons were disproportionately black. Young black men, shot and killed by police. I heard about it all the time. And it didn't bother me much, if at all. If they weren't gangbanging criminals, they wouldn't have gotten shot, right? I didn't know what I didn't know. So it didn't matter. I wouldn't have said it out loud or even agreed with the statement, but *de facto*, apparently to me at that time, their black lives *did not matter*.

Trying to put myself in someone else's shoes, if I were a person of color, and I heard a white person reply 'all lives matter,' I would want to know:

Why didn't black lives matter back when they were being lynched?

Aren't *black* lives part of *all* lives?

Why don't they matter when they're being shot or strangled by law enforcement?

The reality all too often in our history has been that black lives *don't* really matter. As someone said, racism (and the killing of black people) hasn't gotten worse, it's just gotten recorded.

Apparently black people have known about this for a long time, and have been raising hell about it, and some of us have not been paying very much attention. And for us white people now to admonish black people that "all lives matter," oy vey, better just to be quiet.

We've seen that racism affects employment and promotions, the generational accumulation of wealth, economic anxiety, and society's perception of the value of black lives. There is a case to be made that structural racism directly impacts political representation as well, in ways that can be subtle or overt. For instance, Andrew Gelman and Pierre-Antoine Kremp, a political scientist and statistician, and a businessman and professor, respectively, found that "per voter, whites have 16% more power than blacks once the Electoral College is taken into consideration, 28% more power than Latinos, and 57% more power than those who fall into the 'other' category." (4) I'll leave that for now, as I address voting and the Electoral College elsewhere.

Trump and race

Part of the purpose of this book is to help open our eyes to the perspectives of those with whom we disagree. I've avoided picking fights, as they're often counterproductive. But since we're a good way into this book, let's see if we can wrestle with a hot topic. So at the risk of being provocative, is Donald Trump a racist? Or more precisely, without having to gaze into his heart, has he repeated racist arguments and/or supported racist policies?

Please read the next two paragraphs, and just as a thought experiment, pretend you are a member of the opposite tribe. Ask yourself as you read: must I believe this (that I would usually believe)? Or can I believe that (argument from the other side)?

Never-Trumpers can make some robust arguments, with facts that are well-supported. Trump took illegal steps to avoid renting to black people in the 1970s (and was sued by Nixon's Justice Department for it); he called for the execution of black teens who were exonerated by DNA evidence; he said '...black guys counting my money. I hate it!' and 'the only kind of people I want counting my money are short guys that wear yarmulkes' and 'laziness is a trait in blacks... it's not anything they can control' (and in 1997 he said about the author who wrote those statements "the stuff [he] wrote about me is probably true"); he led the groundless charge that our only black president wasn't really an American; he characterized undocumented immigrants from Mexico as rapists bringing drugs and crime; he called for a total and complete ban of Muslims entering the country; he hired as his strategist a man who identified his publication as the 'platform for the alt-right', he said a federal judge born in Indiana can't judge him because he's Mexican; he said a large group of neo-Nazis who were chanting "Jews will not replace us" included 'many fine people;' and so forth. How can anyone argue that doing any one of those things, much less all of them, is not evidence of racism?

Trump supporters of course have a different take. (Again if you're not a Trump supporter, for a moment, pretend you are as you read this.) Most of the above arguments are old news, and either didn't really happen, or were just business decisions born of an allegiance to the well-being of a company that had been created by his father. As President, Trump oversaw the most sweeping reform in sentencing we have seen, reform that disproportionately helped black Americans. His actions have greatly benefitted Historically Black Colleges and Universities. Accusing him of being a Nazi-loving anti-Semite makes no sense: his grandchildren are Jewish! Each of these points is like an alibi. He was out of town with plenty of witnesses when the crime was committed, so one can dismiss whatever circumstantial arguments you make, as they fall flat in the face of what he has actually done as President.

Policing

I have known lots of cops. I like cops. I trust cops. When my kids were little, I would introduce them to police in uniform and explain to them how to recognize police; I taught them that if there's trouble or they're lost, they should seek out a policeman.

On 7 July 2016, a Black Lives Matter (BLM) demonstration took place in Dallas Texas to protest the police killings of two black men, Alton Sterling in Baton Rouge and Philando Castile outside St. Paul. There were about 800 protesters, and about 100 police officers were assigned to monitor the protest. A sniper, a black man and Army veteran named Micah Xavier Johnson opened fire, targeting white police. (After a shootout and standoff, he was killed by an explosive-bearing police robot, a newsworthy event.)

You can search YouTube and find videos of protesters describing the scene. Initially, as one would expect, there was tension (but no violence) between police and protesters. The protesters are protesting and are unhappy about the behavior of police, and of course police like any humans are not thrilled to have people yelling at them and protesting their behavior. In an instant, the dynamic shifted. Protesters are running from gunfire, and police are running toward it. Whatever their feelings may be about BLM, if there is an active shooter the attention of the police goes there and their training to protect civilians kicks into high gear. Protesters tearfully reported how police told them which way to go toward safety, and how the same police against whom they had been protesting put their police bodies between the civilian protesters and the shooter. The spontaneous recorded reaction of BLM protesters to the targeting of police was not celebration. There are phone videos made by protesters showing police lying in the street, one video with the protester voicing, "I hope those people are just hiding."

Unfortunately, many of them were not hiding or seeking cover. The sniper ambushed and murdered five police officers and wounded nine other police and two civilians.

In the aftermath of these horrific murders, the BLM organizers noted that they could never have imagined that their protest, designed to save lives by bringing to light the killing of unarmed black men (mostly men) by police, would be the setting for the deaths of police officers.

Is it possible to reconcile support for police, and recognition of valid concerns of BLM? Or are we destined to live in a world where we must choose between the perspectives of many police unions that seem to believe police can do no wrong, a view holding that BLM is a terrorist organization, versus those who believe we should not just support social services but Defund the Police until there are no more police?

> The test of a first rate intelligence is the ability to hold two opposed ideas in the mind at the same time and still retain the ability to function.
>
> -- F. Scott Fitzgerald

I believe the vast majority of police are good, decent public servants who put their lives on the line every day to protect the rest of us. Similarly, most BLM (and Antifa, and MAGA) protesters are peaceful; but some are not. Those who are violent or destructive should be arrested and held accountable. Likewise, most police behave properly most of the time. Despite the fact that implicit racism exists (type "implicit racism test" into your internet browser and take a test yourself, it's free and eye-opening), there are literally millions of instances every day in this country of black drivers who are *not* pulled over just because they're black. There are millions of interactions between police and people of color where nothing bad happens. But that may not be good enough.

Policing is important. Soldiering is important. Soldiers typically make mistakes with their guns only overseas and kill foreigners, which we find less objectionable than killing our own citizens. But police officers are on our streets, day in and day out. If we are going to give someone the authority to carry a gun on behalf of us all, and if necessary, use that gun to take someone's life, those persons must be tethered to fundamental moral values in addition to being well-trained and professional.

The evolution of commercial airline safety can be instructive. Inevitably, sometimes airplanes crash, and people are killed. But we as a society are intolerant of airline crashes. For decades, we have demanded only the highest standards of safety and professionalism. We have required that the industry, from soup to nuts, in recruiting and training pilots, in constructing and maintaining aircraft, in regulating airspace, everything, identify any deviation from perfection so it can be scrutinized and remedied. As a result, while air travel is not perfectly safe, it is pretty darn close to being perfectly safe.

So policing mostly is professional and appropriate. And while exceptions to that professionalism are relatively rare (relative to the entire population), there are too many exceptions, and those exceptions tend to skew in the direction of adversely impacting minorities. And on top of those mistakes and exceptions, there are systemic problems.

Policing in America has, at times and at places, been a mechanism of social control of minorities. I'd like to believe such policing is a geographic and temporal relic of Reconstruction and Jim Crow, but that belief is a luxury of being white. If you are a racist, and if you like to get in fights and beat and dominate and intimidate people, how can you do that? Aside from being a mixed martial arts fighter or a boxer, what career could you choose that could possibly combine those aspirations? Well, law enforcement. Police departments know that, that's why they take steps to do extensive psychological screening to weed out such applicants. But they're not perfect, indeed some departments sometimes just need warm bodies, and bad apples slip through.

But the even bigger problem is something more insidious. Fortunately, it's something that I think can be fixed.

One of my colleagues in the army (one of many) was a policeman in civilian life. He told the following story about how he and his fellow law enforcement officers (LEOs) looked at the world. He said, there were cops, and there were wolves; and it was the job of the cops to find the wolves and deal with them. But, some of us asked, 'what about regular citizens?' 'Citizens,' he said, 'everybody else, were just sheep.' Ostensibly, sheep are the reason for cops to chase the wolves, but mostly, sheep just get in the way. And sheep can be annoying and suspect, because they sometimes, either unwittingly or deliberately, hide the wolves who try to blend in among them.

In the movie *Fallen*, Denzel Washington's character is in a bar with two other cops (played by John Goodman and James Gandolfini... it's a really good scene in a great movie. You're welcome). Paraphrasing by memory, Gandolfini says to Denzel, 'what's up with you, you don't take cream?' (graft, payoffs, some mild corruption, unimportant to the plot). Short version, Denzel replies 'no I don't, but I don't judge, because whether a cop takes cream or not, 99% plus percent of the time, a cop is doing more good everyday than any lawyer or businessman or whatever. Cops are God's chosen people.'

I know, one's a personal anecdote, the other is fiction, but they both reveal a truth. Cops are a group, a tribe, and like other groups, you're either in or you're out. And nowhere is that more important than if/when the out-group is dangerous. I've never been a policeman, but I was in the army; those who wore an American flag on their shoulder were my group; the civilians on the battlefield were sheep (suspect sheep); and the Taliban or al-Qaeda were the wolves. And brother I knew whose side I was on.

Also, I worked in state prisons for eleven years. I wasn't a correctional officer (CO), I was one of the sheep, medical, free staff. The inmates were the wolves (or perceived as wolves, even though many if not most of them really weren't), and they had us outnumbered, in a big way. I identified heavily with the COs, because without them, I could be in big trouble; and if trouble arose, it would be the COs who would pull my fat out of the fire.

The vast majority of soldiers, and police officers, and correctional officers, are good people doing hard jobs. But they're not perfect, and some of them are a mess. I served at Abu Ghraib (the year after the scandal) and I never saw detainees abused. Similarly, I never saw a CO abuse an inmate in a California state prison. I'd like to think that if I had seen abuse or illegal behavior, I would have spoken up; but we'll never know. Because the pressure to support the members of one's group, whether they're right or wrong, is extremely powerful. I felt that way in the army, and I was a senior officer and a medical puke, barely *in* the army culturally. Similarly, being a medical type in the California state prison system, had I seen someone do something wrong and I'd have said something, I wouldn't be burning bridges as much as a CO would. Imagine the consequences of speaking up if you're a 20-something year old junior enlisted infantryman in a rifle company who saw a fellow soldier, perhaps even someone senior to him, doing something wrong. Fortunately, explicit in the army are values that affirm the duty of each soldier to maintain honor and integrity, and to speak up when necessary. Still, it takes tremendous moral certainty, strength of character and personal courage to speak up.

Like soldiers, police are powerfully invested in the *Loyalty/ betrayal* value foundation: the Thin Blue Line. For all the reasons discussed, it is imperative for police to be loyal to one another. Betraying a fellow officer is an unacceptable breach of a closely held moral value.

So now imagine a rookie policeman seeing his supervisor kneeling on the neck of someone. Is that someone a sheep, in which case this is wrong, or is he a wolf, in which case it's OK, because, what the hell, he's a bad guy, or probably a bad guy, so who cares. And if he's black, well, statistically, and anecdotally, it's more likely that he's a criminal, isn't it? And maybe his life doesn't really matter, at least, not as much.

As with any close-knit community, the insular "Us versus the World" perspective can lead to unhealthy, dangerous attitudes. One police social media post stated that "It's become acceptable in today's world for a cop to be murdered." That's not really true. But if you're a policeman who believes that the random motorist you just pulled over believes that murder of police is acceptable, what reason do you have to restrain your own worst impulses?

Of course, these scenarios are not OK, either way. But unless there's someone with a cell phone nearby, we never learn of such an incident. And if that rookie policeman sees that this is the way it is, that police misbehavior can be rationalized away (the guy we sat on really was a bad guy, he could have threatened our lives, we were in fear of our lives, the cop is a good cop he just had a bad day or made a mistake, etc.), that reports can be written in such a way as to make everyone inside the System happy that the incident goes unexamined; what is he to do? Channel his inner Al Pacino and become Serpico? Serpico was exiled by his group even while he was still in it and ended up getting shot in the face, so maybe that's not such a rewarding approach. Police unwilling or unable to police themselves is a very dangerous and potent dynamic.

As far as many persons of color are concerned, the *Loyalty* imperative is just a polite way of legitimizing racial discrimination and exclusion.

Patrick Skinner, a police officer in Savannah, GA and veteran of the CIA, the US Coast Guard and the U.S. Capitol Police, published this in the Washington Post:

> We police need to fight the destructive reaction we have resorted to before, saying that if we can't do our job the way we have always done our job, well then, we won't do our job at all. We might still collect a paycheck, but we will stop a lot of work because of an exaggerated fear of running afoul of the "new rules." Rules such as "Don't treat your neighbors like robots of compliance," "Don't escalate trivial matters into life-or-death matters," and "Treat your neighbors as if they were your neighbors." That anyone would consider these rules "new" is a problem in itself. Few police officers reading them aloud would take issue with such anodyne statements, but put accountability behind the statements and now they're an attack, not just on all police but the very foundation of American policing.

Police also are invested strongly in the *Authority/Subversion* moral foundation. When police encounter someone who may be a wolf, a policeman is intolerant of any hesitation or resistance to his *authority*. From the perspective of many minority citizens, this authority is too often abused. If you've been on the short end of the stick when state power is employed, you see authority as oppression.

So how do we get out of this situation? It falls on all of us, especially white people, to insist upon an evolution of culture within law enforcement.

But also we must get real about what we're requiring of police.

On the one hand, we train police to be able to deal with the most extreme situations. As a consumer of police services, whenever I'm pulled over, I assume that this guy's partner got shot during a traffic stop last night. I understand that traffic stops are dangerous, that police have a difficult and often thankless job. I turn on the inside light and put my hands at 10 and 2 on the wheel. I don't argue, I tell him where my license and registration are before I reach for them (unless I already got them out while waiting for him). It's easy for me, because almost always, he was right, I was wrong, I was speeding or whatever. I may feel different if I were black, and afraid, and especially if I were driving in a white neighborhood and hadn't done anything wrong and had been pulled over for no reason many times before. And if anyone thinks that doesn't happen, you are privileged, almost certainly white, and not to be rude, but in my opinion, somewhat clueless.

We must consider the burdens we place on police, and then recognize that our support for them is utterly inadequate. Ask police: what are the kinds of calls they dread? How are police supposed to solve the problems of mental health crises and family disputes, homelessness and substance abuse? How lazy can a society be that when a teenager is unruly in school or a child disobeys the rules in class or is too loud at a store or parking lot, we call the police to deal with it? We call someone who is authorized to use force to arrest people, we call the men and women with badges and Tasers and guns, and then we're shocked when they use them.

I believe that good police *want* to hold their compadres accountable, and again, that the vast majority of police are good police. Because after all, aside from those who are the victims of police misbehavior, it's the good police trying to do the right thing who bear the heaviest burden of the smaller number of misbehaving police. If almost everyone is Serpico, then it's easier to be Serpico. If for instance, mistreating detained persons is an outlying event, everyone learns coming up that this behavior is not tolerated, the people inclined to perpetrate it are marginalized, and it diminishes.

Summary:

Trump said "The System is Rigged;" and racist policies are a part of that rigging.

Racism is deeply woven into the history and culture of America.

Race and policing are often convenient wedge issues that can be exploited.

Racism exists, but it's not something that white people must feel guilty about; because you didn't know what you didn't know.

But if you didn't know, now you know.

Chapter 11

Wedge Issues and Bad Arguments: The "Other"

Trumpisms:

There is a lot of Fake information out there. Believe only me.
We should all love our country.
Mexico is not sending their best.
This American carnage stops now.

> Most of our so-called reasoning consists in finding arguments for going on believing as we already do.
> - - James Harvey Robinson

A wedge is one of the simplest tools. Stick the sharp narrow edge into a small space in some object, and push, or hammer it, deeper. The small space will get bigger; the object will be increasingly divided. Wedge issues do just that, they divide us.

Wedge issues serve The Swamp. Politicians and media outlets serve The Swamp; they distract you, command your attention by holding up the bright shiny object with one hand so you don't notice that with the other hand they are picking your pocket, pre-distributing wealth from working people and the middle class to the super-rich of The Swamp.

They typically are issues that have a high moral valence. Wedge issues are often manifestations of what has been characterized as the "culture wars," arguments that are clearly more related to values than policy. Even though we may not disagree that much about the substance of an issue, the issue feels important, and if the wedge can be driven into even a small perceived disagreement, it promptly can feel like a huge, insurmountable disagreement.

The unfortunate reality is that wedge issues and culture wars are effective, they work. As Jia Tolentino noted in her book *Trick Mirror: Reflections on Self-Delusion*, "Having a mutual enemy is a quick way to make a friend -- we learn this as early as elementary school -- and politically, it's much easier to organize people against something than it is to unite them in an affirmative vision. And, within the economy of attention, conflict always gets more people to look." (1) The political right was much earlier to recognize, attend to and exploit this phenomenon. For a time, a visitor from Mars could have been forgiven for thinking that we had no problems more important than whether or not athletes stand for the national anthem.

Traffic in wedge issues is not limited to politicians or formal news outlets or talk radio. The internet and social media may have begun as benign and quick ways to share information and cheerful collections of bake sales and affinity groups, but they have morphed into battlefields. Populated by trolls and bots and covert Russian operators and political activists of all stripes, these platforms amplify inflamed passions and evolve into *ad hominem* rants that turn us against each other.

A friend of mine I'll call Zach wrote to me the following: "Although some would say I'm a Trump supporter solely because I agree with some of the things he does, I also disagree with many of the things he does. When Obama was President, I was called racist by left-leaning, liberal Democrats because I disagreed with many of his policies; I deeply resent that. Because I support some of what Trump does I'm called racist by left-leaning, liberal Democrats. Because I oppose abortion I'm called sexist, misogynist, anti-women's-rights, or many other names by left-leaning, liberal Democrats. And numerous other examples of name-calling by left-leaning, liberal Democrats.

"Now, because I support liberty and individual freedom, I support decriminalization of marijuana, removal of government from the non-secular business of marriage, and a host of other issues, I get called names by right-leaning, conservative Republicans."

Occasionally one may have an argument wherein one person changes his or her mind. But that is the exception, and usually is a result of respect and connection rather than brilliant debate. And often it is not really changing one's mind as much as it is a recognition that on important aspects of the issue, such as the values that are being excited, the arguers actually don't disagree that much.

Facebook arguments and political sound bites typically share a plethora of logical flaws. That is a subject unto itself, and as passions rather than logic are more important, I'll mostly skirt that subject.

Logic is the art of going wrong with confidence.
- - Joseph Wood Krutch

Not to preach, but there are many unworthy mistakes that you (and I) probably unknowingly make, and, in my opinion it's worth our while to avoid them.

First, mistaking opinions for facts. It may be a fact that you hold a particular opinion, but that doesn't make the content of your opinion factual. So if you begin your post or conversation by stating "Trump (or Obama) was the worst president ever, that's just a fact," you stand a good chance of sounding ridiculous to most people. Stop, please.

Next is the straw man argument. For almost any argument you can make, there will be a kernel of truth in it. "The Democrats want to disband all police departments;" that suggests that anyone who is a Democrat wishes that. No doubt there is some small and finite number of Democrats who want that, but it is logically incorrect as well as disingenuous to indicate that all do. That's a "straw man," a fake argument you would choose to put in place just so you can knock it down by arguing against the weak and widely unacceptable idea (unacceptable even among Democrats) of abolishing police. Generally, Democrats want to weed out racism and unnecessary police brutality, want those who abuse their power to be held accountable, and want other social services to be adequately funded so the police don't have to respond to a homeless person urinating in public, a mental health crisis, or an unruly child.

There can be straw men on top of straw men. "Republicans say that Democrats want to release all prisoners." I'm sure some Republican somewhere has said that, but to characterize it as an accusation broadly espoused by 'Republicans', is a straw man. Its purpose is to make Republicans seem silly and untrustworthy because they make such an unsupportable accusation.

In general, any argument that starts with "they say" is likely to be nonsense.

> It is always better to say right out what you think without trying to prove anything much: for all our proofs are only variations of our opinions, and the contrary-minded listen neither to one nor the other.
> - - Johann Wolfgang von Goethe

Despite von Goethe, I'm optimistic enough to hope that you'll listen to an opinion other than your own. See if you have ever employed arguments such as these below. And if you have, try for a moment to consider if the rebuttal might possibly have any truth to it.

"Democrats want a war against traditional marriage, they are trying to take God out of our lives, and we are here to protect the natural order that we believe God has ordained."
Democrats reply that they want people of all sexual orientations to be able to love freely, no matter who they love.

"Republicans want a white Christian nation that excludes other religions and races."
Republicans reply that while racists and white supremacists want that, real true Republicans aren't racists or white supremacists. Republicans want people of all races and religions to be able to practice and worship freely.

"Democrats want to destroy our culture and rewrite history."
Democrats say they want to recognize the ugly parts of our past, recognize that most Confederate statues were part of the Jim Crow era, and hold that racists and traitors to the Union should not be celebrated.

"Democrats/Republicans hate America. They hate America."
C'mon man.

You get the idea. The purpose of this exercise is to stimulate some appreciation for logical flaws, and for each of us to identify the mote in our own eye before we start finding flaws with others. The discussions below are not designed to help you win arguments, unless you define winning as a better understanding of a hitherto unexplored point of view.

> Logic: an instrument used for bolstering a prejudice.
> -- Elbert Hubbard

Also, in this and the following chapter, you'll find plenty with which you will disagree, no matter where you stand, whether you're pro- or anti-Trump. If you have no interest in changing the way you feel about anything, no problem, look at this as an exercise in "Know Thine Enemy;" it's hard to fight what you don't understand. If you go into it with an open mind, you may understand more. It's possible that on some heretofore unexplored or less explored point, you might even change your mind.

Here are some examples of wedge issues. This chapter focuses upon "The Other", The Big Other, immigrants. Most arguments are loaded with terms like "invaders", or "illegals", terms that tend to frame the issue in such a way as to preclude communication. If you're a liberal, I'm asking you to look past that and try to look for some common ground. I'll present some of both pro-Trump conservative perspectives and never-Trump liberal perspectives. I'll throw in some opinions, some which may even be mine. See if you can agree with some of the other side's arguments. If you're feeling particularly bold, try on the other guy's shoes. Pretend you're an actor, getting a bunch of money to play a role foreign to you: if you're a Trump supporter, pretend you're a liberal BLM supporter, and vice versa, trying to find any possible reason to believe the arguments from that Other perspective. Maybe challenge your assumptions, challenge your beliefs. Don't worry, it won't hurt. You're all alone, reading this book, nobody knows, and you don't have to tell anyone.

Immigration, sanctuary cities, and the Wall

My liberal friends really should be able to understand the simplest of conservative arguments regarding immigration. *Illegal* immigration is *illegal.* (For the moment let's set aside asylum, and our history of racism. Trump advisors Steve Bannon and Stephen Miller indicated that *legal* immigration as well is really 'the beating heart' of the problem; but let's set all that aside.) Persons who break the law when they enter the country shouldn't benefit from their apparent disregard for *Authority*. There is a process for entering the country; everyone should wait his turn. You don't get to jump the line, that's *Cheating*, it's not *Fair*. Liberals may grant that in a vacuum, these arguments may seem sound, but assert that we don't live in a vacuum.

Early in my career I did some moonlighting at an urgent care clinic in Watsonville California, an agricultural area. Many of my patients were migrant farm workers, many of them undocumented. Over the course of taking their history or waiting for their lab results or sewing up their lacerations, we'd talk. Of course they knew about the long and difficult formal legal immigration process, and knew they had bypassed it. We Americans tend to see the law holding out its hand like the giant statues on the river that flowed into Gondor in *Lord of the Rings*, signaling, 'Stop! No further!'

But these farm workers saw the other hand, beckoning them into the country, as work was readily available. They're not stupid. From their perspective, if we North Americans were serious about this "Stop" business, we wouldn't allow them to be hired. 'You North Americans haven't figured out your immigration policy, you've got some work to do there, fine, good luck with that; but don't blame us for your incoherence. If there was no demand for our services, the supply would dry up. If you required all employees to have social security numbers, and when you found undocumented workers, instead of deporting them, you arrested and incarcerated their employers, illegal immigration would cease.' (That's an observation, not a recommendation.)

The fact is, America wants these workers, we need these workers. When they would get caught and deported, they knew their employer would hire them again as soon as they could make their way back into the US. Employers (and the rest of us) benefit greatly from having an underclass to exploit. Low wages, cash under the table, no social security tax, no benefits, no unemployment, no health insurance, no retirement, no nothing. I'm not asserting that all employers of the undocumented are evil slave drivers. But if these people are abused, ripped off, assaulted, raped, by anyone, what are they supposed to do? Go to the police?

None of those points change the conservative perspective that they shouldn't have come extra-legally, and any argument that is founded on the idea that it was OK for them to circumvent the legal process is fatally flawed at its inception, violating an inviolable principle, *subverting* authority. To the liberal, the *Harm* that comes to these immigrants at the hands of our unworkable schizophrenic American approach outweighs any legalistic consideration. To a conservative, the opposite is true. But perhaps we can understand these immigrants, and understand each other.

Of course not all undocumented persons are farm or domestic workers. What about all the criminals?

If the argument is that undocumented persons commit crimes at a higher rate than do native-born Americans, that is incorrect, as studies have shown. (2)

If the argument is that some undocumented persons commit crimes, including violent crimes, of course that is true; any group much larger than the roster of a football team is likely to include a criminal.

If the argument is that such a group should not be allowed to exist in our society because of the risk we face from the potential criminal actions of its members, one could make a stronger argument against the population of native-born white male Christians.

Obviously, the idea that 11 million undocumented persons in the US commit zero crime is a straw man; no one believes that or asserts that. Studies indicate that rates of crime among undocumented immigrants are lower than among native born. If you're walking down the street with a couple hundred people around, statistically, you're safer if those people are mostly immigrants rather than native born.

If the argument is that we should have zero tolerance for any crime at the hands of any undocumented person because they don't belong here in the first place, that we should deport all 11 million undocumented if that would prevent one crime, or some crime, well, that's an argument. It's a rather absolutist view of the *Authority* imperative. Liberals readily respond that the downsides, the disruption of communities, the scapegoating, the tearing apart of families, not to mention the detrimental economic effects, are not worth it.

"Democrats want open borders."

The border between Maryland and Virginia is an open border. The border between Mexico and California is not.

Democrats reply that they want asylum seekers to be given their chance to seek asylum, want to help people who are coming from unimaginable terror and poverty help to give them the chances we have, want to ensure children aren't separated from their parents and that nobody is kept in cages; but do want proper vetting.

Sanctuary cities

This topic also can inflame particularly the *authority* versus *subversion* moral foundation. I mean seriously, sanctuary? On the face of it, someone seeking sanctuary is wanted by the authorities for something, such as illegal immigration. It's a simple argument: once you find wrong-doers, you deal with them, and those who have entered the country illegally are wrong-doers. My liberal friends, put yourself in the shoes of someone who deeply believes in and values *authority*. Affording "illegals" 'sanctuary' is an insult to law abiding citizens everywhere. Two wrongs don't make a right. It's outrageous! How can anyone rationalize this self-destructive idiocy? How would you feel if your family member was a victim of crime by an "illegal"?

This posture often precipitates a cascade of beliefs and assertions that are incrementally credible, such as these six, collected from an assortment of social media posts:

Local jails do not communicate at all with Immigration and Customs Enforcement (ICE).

Local police are violating their oath by not helping ICE.

Sanctuary cities preclude transferring violent criminals to ICE.

Sanctuary cities are breaking federal law.

There are "countless occurrences" of citizens suffering violent acts from criminals protected by sanctuary laws.

Sanctuary cities protect murderers.

All of those assertions are incorrect, but they beg the larger question: why should we have sanctuary cities at all? What good are they?

Here's the argument: sanctuary cities limit cooperation with ICE in order to enhance public safety. If undocumented persons understand that <u>any</u> encounter with police may lead to disclosure of their immigration status to ICE and subsequent deportation, they avoid the police and they don't report crimes even when they have been victimized. Local police dislike requirements to cooperate with ICE as it makes it difficult for the locals to get undocumented witnesses of crimes to testify against criminals, and those criminals then remain on the streets. This isn't a baseless opinion, but an informed one, shared by chiefs of police. (3)

Regarding being a victim of crime by an undocumented person, how would someone feel if his family member was victimized by a criminal who could have previously been put away except the witness was undocumented and would not come forward out of fear of deportation? Fortunately, both scenarios are low probability, and are more fodder for fear-mongering than they are cautionary.

I don't want to leave you hanging, so as an example of going down rabbit holes, let me address the six anti-sanctuary city arguments made above. If you're liberal, you'll love it; but remember: first, typically you can't change someone's mind by refuting his arguments, and second, these rebuttals don't change the primary concern of conservatives that illegal immigration unacceptably *subverts authority*. If you're conservative, just ruminate on these facts. Understanding them doesn't mean that your values are wrong nor does it mean that you are a bigot for opposing sanctuary cities. They're just facts. Do with them as you will, but if you want to avoid self-deception, your rider should find different better post hoc arguments to support what your elephant has decided.

Local jails do not communicate at all with Immigration and Customs Enforcement (ICE).

Jails make fingerprints available to the FBI and to ICE. ICE is capable of knowing about arrests and if some 'criminal illegal' has been put in jail for a misdemeanor or non-violent crime and either serves his time or is not guilty and is subsequently released, there is nothing that keeps ICE from grabbing them up whenever they want.

ICE generates a Detainer Request if they want local jails to hold someone. ICE requests, they don't order, they don't demand, because the Constitution states and courts have affirmed that the federal government cannot require states to enforce federal law.

Local police are violating their oath by not helping ICE.

According to the Bill of Rights, the 10th amendment, the federal government cannot force states to enforce federal laws, so state and local police do not take any oath to enforce federal laws or cooperate with ICE. It is a paradox that on this topic, those who typically are strident defenders of states' rights change their stripes.

Sanctuary cities preclude transferring violent criminals to ICE.

"Sanctuary" laws (SB54 in California) do not preclude transferring violent criminals to ICE. Over a hundred such felonies are exceptions wherein cooperation with ICE is allowed. Violent criminals and felons generally are not released from jails in sanctuary cities because they go to state prisons. California state prisons routinely coordinate with ICE.

Sanctuary cities are breaking federal law.

The federal government cannot force states to enforce federal laws (except on Constitutional grounds).

If you get arrested for urinating in public, the police don't care if you're late on your federal taxes or haven't registered for the draft (unless their state or local law says so), and when they release you, you haven't escaped and no, they aren't accessories.

There are "countless occurrences" of citizens suffering violent acts from criminals protected by sanctuary laws.

"Countless occurrences" of citizens suffering violent acts from criminals protected by sanctuary laws are largely a fantasy, as we've seen data indicate that such immigrants are less likely to perpetrate crimes than are native born. Any statement that begins with 'countless' or 'untold' should raise your suspicions. Anyone could claim that there are 'countless numbers' of criminals who have been incarcerated thanks to undocumented persons willing to testify against them because of sanctuary protection, but that also would be anecdotal, and difficult to support with firm data.

Deportations have second and third order effects that may well be undesirable. It is essentially impossible to know which undocumented person in a sanctuary city did NOT pull a gun and kill a cop during a misdemeanor traffic stop because he knew that he would NOT be held for ICE, and deported, essentially given a life sentence away from his family here in the US if he allowed himself to be arrested; nor can anyone identify specific children who stayed healthy in an intact family rather than become criminals after their family fell apart due to deportation of a parent. But it is difficult to believe that it helps US born English speaking children to have parents deported after a misdemeanor arrest or a traffic stop.

Sanctuary cities protect murderers.

People who commit crimes in "sanctuary cities" are held accountable for those crimes regardless of their immigration status.

If you're conservative, ask yourself, do you see no rationale, no reason that a thoughtful person might think there's a possible argument in support of sanctuary cities? Are those police chiefs lying, insincere, stupid, what?

A perspective prevalent in our current culture reduces all disagreements to the *ad hominem*, so that all persons on the left side of the immigration debate are anti-American snowflake Marxists who don't have the best interests of our country in mind. That would be the same error that some close-minded liberal/progressives make when they suggest that all those who oppose sanctuary cities (and all Trump supporters in general) are heartless racists.

Maybe we can agree that we should have more coherent immigration policies. That end may be best served by respectful discussion that minimizes the hyperbolic scapegoating of a largely law-abiding and vulnerable population while recognizing the fundamental values that underlie very different perspectives.

Arguments, good and bad, efficient and effective, or not

You may see a pattern here. I seem to be saying a lot more about liberal positions while refuting conservative ones. One reason could be that I'm a liberal snowflake and I'm trying to turn you into one too.

But there's another possible explanation.

Arguments and positions from the right tend to be short and to the point. If you're a liberal and you just can't believe how conservatives can hold some of the positions they hold, review the arguments above. This is somewhat overbroad, but conservative positions tend to be pithy, and they tend to go straight for the feels, directly for core values we all hold like *Fairness* versus *Cheating* (more the *Proportionality* aspect of *Fairness*), but also values conservatives favor more such as *Liberty*, *Authority*, and *Sanctity*.

This may explain in part why conservatives and the Republican Party have such success. In very general terms, when particular liberal policies are specified but not identified as being liberal, not associated with liberal politicians' names, most Americans tend to support those policies. Yet when those same Americans declare their allegiance and when they vote, they tend disproportionately to vote Republican, an apparent tribute to GOP messaging.

At the risk of being redundant it may be prudent to frame again the purpose of fleshing out these arguments. It is not to take up ink trying clever ways to change someone's mind. Remember as Haidt pointed out:

> Moral reasons are the tail wagged by the intuitive dog.... You can't make a dog happy by forcibly wagging its tail. And you can't change people's minds by utterly refuting their arguments. (4)

So we're aiming at understanding. This book is about 'helping liberals understand'; it should be easier for liberals to understand the arguments of conservatives than the other way around in part because generally, conservative positions support maintaining the familiar *status quo* and are simpler and quicker to frame. Liberals often seem to be playing defense (that is, losing). Liberal responses tend to be nuanced, frequently wrapped around the axle of details, perhaps tedious, sometimes boring.

But in case any conservatives or Trump supporters are reading this book, I'm including a sampling of these admittedly long-winded liberal apologetics. They're geared not toward making Trump supporters change their minds, but rather toward helping conservatives understand liberals so as to allow for a more peaceful Thanksgiving dinner, and perhaps even to refine conservative arguments after recognizing that an occasional liberal point might make sense. Let's try another.

The Wall

Once again the Trump supporters' position is simple. Walls must work (like guns). Look at medieval castles. If walls didn't work, why are the houses of rich liberals surrounded by walls? It's our country, our border, we can build a wall if we want, and there is no need for discussion beyond that.

Liberals find this logic frustrating. They don't think the question is 'can a wall work, yes or no?' but rather, 'where can a wall work, and for what?'

Liberal responses can be peppered with details and rhetorical questions. Does a wall work in isolated areas where there is no one observing, where no one tries to cross, and if they did, they could defeat the wall by climbing over, tunneling under, or sawing through it? Does it work on a remote mountaintop or in impassable areas? The wall is marketed as being necessary because of immigrants bringing crime, drugs and terrorism. How does a wall interdict drugs when the vast majority of drugs that cross the southern border do so at ports of entry? Does a wall work for drugs mailed in from China, or overprescribed by US physicians? How does a wall work interdicting suspected terrorists when they are mostly home grown, when those who enter the US do so at airports or from Canada, and essentially none have entered the US from Mexico? Is a wall the best way to reduce the threat from crime when undocumented immigrants commit crimes at a lower rate than do native born Americans, and most undocumented immigrants are visa-overstays, who never crossed the southern border?

Does a wall work in Texas, where 95% of the land on the border is privately owned, and those landowners (and their mostly Republican representatives) don't want their land seized for a wall?

Away from cameras and sound bites, sober politicians on the right and left ask, are there places on the border where a barrier is necessary and would work better than technological or personnel fixes? How much of the border is in that category, that doesn't already have a barrier? Until that is specified, all the "Build The Wall" rhetoric (not to mention the idea that Mexico is going to pay for the wall) is just political theater. But theater is popular.

Voting rights, voter suppression and voter ID

Voting rights arguments from the conservative side have their roots in the *Authority* versus *Subversion* fundamental, and *Fairness/cheating*. The state has an interest in preventing cheaters from subverting authority by voting illegally. On the liberal side, it's all the first three: *Care/harm, Liberty/oppression,* and *Fairness/cheating*. Voting is a right that should not be infringed; the default should be to be able to vote unless there is some compelling reason to deny that right, and the readily disenfranchised should not be harmed and oppressed by cheating lawmakers.

Consider the following real back and forth on Facebook between two friends (old classmates, both upper middle class white males with postgraduate degrees, one recently deceased). This exchange again demonstrates fairly simple conservative points and detailed liberal responses. At times they test each other's patience and appear headed for the Insult Abyss, but miracle of miracles, this actually led to a modest change of mind of both persons, who managed to find a little patch of common ground. (This was before the recent flurry of laws passed by predominantly Republican-led state legislatures in early and mid-2021. Many of the same arguments are relevant.)

From the right:

Every voter ID law discussed or passed has made it absolutely simple and nearly effortless for a LEGAL voter to meet requirements to cast their vote. You and those like you embellish this nonsense that it targets minorities. You insinuate that minorities are too inept to get a legal ID. It is not complicated at all.

And the left:

That is just not correct. Federal courts have found voter ID laws that "target African Americans with almost surgical precision." (5) However easy and effortless it has been for you and me to have the type of ID required, for many people, disproportionately minorities, students and elderly, it's not effortless. You can argue that they should be more ambitious, and if they want to vote they should work for it, etc., but the data show that they are *de facto* deprived of their right to vote. And that's not right, IMHO [IMHO = In My Humble Opinion].

I'll trust that you're sincere in what you say. But with all due respect, you're just flat wrong. For most people, for you and me, white, well educated, financially well off, it is hard to imagine a difficulty with something as simple as an ID. But over 21 million adult Americans do not have a government issued photo ID. If you want to vote, and you're a student without a car and you're told your student ID is no good, or you're old and don't drive and it would take time and money to get a replacement ID, or in too many other circumstances [to detail here], (not to mention early voting being curtailed and polling places closed in largely Democratic areas), the EFFECT is that many hundreds of thousands if not millions of those marginalized people either say 'to hell with it, They don't want me to vote, the system is indeed rigged,' or they just can't negotiate the maze to get an acceptable ID. They have a RIGHT to vote, and this is effectively a poll tax that takes that right away from them, in an illegally discriminatory fashion. And without any need for it: I might be sympathetic to your point of view if there was any, ANY evidence of significant in-person voter fraud, but there is not. These voter ID laws are leash laws for unicorns, addressing a problem that essentially does not exist, admitted by Republicans that they are designed by Republicans to suppress Democratic votes. Disgusting, and un-American. (6)

You can drill down into the cited decisions for even more details, all you might want to know about different kinds of IDs in North Carolina, who tends to have what kind, what used to be OK and then wasn't, some expired, some that miss a letter compared to someone's birth certificate, etc., with examples of plaintiffs', real people's, experiences dealing with the 'simple, if not completely effortless' restrictions.

The various citations also support the court's finding that "The record is replete with evidence of instances since the 1980s in which the North Carolina legislature has attempted to suppress and dilute the voting rights of African Americans." (Of course this is only one court regarding one law in one state, there are others.)

If you really want to know, you can read the court's decision. (7)

Figuring that you have other things to do, see below the Cliff Notes version, excerpts from the court's decision describing how the legislature designed the voter suppression efforts disenfranchising minorities (spoiler alert: they looked for how blacks vote, then outlawed that):

> Upon receipt of the race data, the General Assembly enacted legislation that restricted voting and registration in five different ways, all of which disproportionately affected African Americans....
>
> In response to claims that intentional racial discrimination animated its action, the State offered only meager justifications. Although the new provisions **target African Americans with almost surgical precision** [bold added], they constitute inapt remedies for the problems assertedly justifying them and, in fact, impose cures for problems that did not exist.
>
> Thus the asserted justifications cannot and do not conceal the State's true motivation....
>
> In this one statute, the North Carolina legislature imposed a number of voting restrictions. The law required in-person voters to show certain photo IDs, beginning in 2016, which African Americans disproportionately lacked, and eliminated or reduced registration and voting access tools that African Americans disproportionately used. Moreover... the legislature requested and received racial data as to usage of the practices changed by the proposed law.
>
> This data showed that African Americans disproportionately lacked the most common kind of photo ID, those issued by the Department of Motor Vehicles (DMV). The pre-*Shelby County* version [*Shelby County v Holder*, the decision that struck down most of the Voting Rights Act] of SL 2013-381 [SL is "Session Law," of the North Carolina legislature] provided that all government-issued IDs, even many that had been expired, would satisfy the requirement as an alternative to DMV-issued photo IDs. After *Shelby County*, with race data in hand, the legislature amended the bill to exclude many of the alternative photo IDs used by African Americans. As amended, the bill retained only the kinds of IDs that white North Carolinians were more likely to possess.
>
> The district court found that, prior to enactment of SL 2013-381, legislators also requested data as to the racial breakdown of early voting usage. Early voting increases opportunities to vote for those who have difficulty getting to their polling place on Election Day. The racial data provided to the legislators revealed that African Americans... disproportionately used the first seven days of early voting.

After receipt of this racial data, the General Assembly amended the bill to eliminate the first week of early voting, shortening the total early voting period from seventeen to ten days. As a result, SL 2013-381 also eliminated one of two "souls-to-the-polls" Sundays in which African American churches provided transportation to voters.

The district court found that legislators similarly requested data as to the racial makeup of same-day registrants. Prior to SL 2013-381, same-day registration allowed eligible North Carolinians to register in person at an early voting site at the same time as casting their ballots.... Same-day registration also provided an easy avenue to re-register for those who moved frequently, and allowed those with low literacy skills or other difficulty completing a registration form to receive personal assistance from poll workers. The legislature's racial data demonstrated that, as the district court found, "it is indisputable that African American voters disproportionately used [same-day registration] when it was available." The district court further found that African American registration applications constituted a disproportionate percentage of the incomplete registration queue. And the court found that African Americans "are more likely to move between counties," and thus "are more likely to need to re-register." As evidenced by the types of errors that placed many African American applications in the incomplete queue, in-person assistance likely would disproportionately benefit African Americans. SL 2013-381 eliminated same-day registration.

Legislators additionally requested a racial breakdown of provisional voting, including out-of-precinct voting.... a voter who appeared at the wrong precinct, but in the correct county, for all of the ballot items for which the voter was eligible to vote. This provision assisted those who moved frequently, or who mistook a voting site as being in their correct precinct. The district court found that the racial data revealed that African Americans disproportionately voted provisionally. In fact, the General Assembly that had originally enacted the out-of-precinct voting legislation had specifically found that "of those registered voters who happened to vote provisional ballots outside their resident precincts" in 2004, "a disproportionately high percentage were African American." With SL 2013-381, the General Assembly altogether eliminated out-of-precinct voting.

African Americans also disproportionately used preregistration. Preregistration permitted 16- and 17-year-olds, when obtaining driver's licenses or attending mandatory high school registration drives, to iden-

> tify themselves and indicate their intent to vote. This allowed County Boards of Elections to verify eligibility and automatically register eligible citizens once they reached eighteen. Although preregistration increased turnout among young adult voters, SL 2013-381 eliminated it. The district court found that not only did SL 2013-381 eliminate or restrict these voting mechanisms used disproportionately by African Americans, and require IDs that African Americans disproportionately lacked, but also that African Americans were more likely to "experience socioeconomic factors that may hinder their political participation." This is so, the district court explained, because in North Carolina, African Americans are "disproportionately likely to move, be poor, less educated, have less access to transportation, and experience poor health...."
>
> The only clear factor linking these various "reforms" is their impact on African American voters. The record thus makes obvious that the "problem" the majority in the General Assembly sought to remedy was emerging support for the minority party. Identifying and restricting the ways African Americans vote was an easy and effective way to do so. We therefore must conclude that race constituted a but-for cause of SL 2013-381, in violation of the Constitutional and statutory prohibitions on intentional discrimination.

Lastly, imagining you've actually read this far, I found one last statement from the court that addresses the "but it *could* happen" arguments about possible but as yet undetected connections between voter registration fraud and in-person voter fraud, and the proposed justifications for voter suppression:

"The justification must be genuine, not hypothesized or invented *post hoc....*"

From the right:

Most Americans who are in favor of voter ID laws do not favor voter suppression.

From the left:

I agree with you that in principle most Americans who are in favor of voter ID laws are not nominally in favor of voter suppression. But if they are sincere, they have been sold a bill of goods by Republican leadership, and are either ignorant of the voter suppression effect of those laws and ignorant of the extremely low incidence of in-person voter fraud, and/or are willing to disregard their cognitive dissonance in order to continue to identify with their tribe and its dismissal of the rights of minorities and other potential Democratic voters. The demonstrable fact is: the effect of these laws is voter suppression, with no measurable effect on the almost immeasurably small phenomenon of in-person voter fraud. States do not mitigate the voter suppression effects (after all, that's why they passed the law!), they don't supply the IDs, they don't make it easy to get them, they don't 'go to' voters to get them the ID. So unless you're OK with voter suppression, you should oppose these laws as they are currently executed in the real world.

A number of key Americans, right wing politicians and activists, *are* in favor of voter ID laws *in order to suppress* the votes of minorities, of students, of the elderly, who tend to vote Democratic. State representative then house majority leader Republican Michael Turzai, (later Speaker of the Pennsylvania House of Representatives), said the quiet part out loud back in 2012 while bragging about the passage of voter ID laws: "Voter ID, which is going to allow Governor Romney to win the state of Pennsylvania -- done." (8) Republican activist Paul Weyrich (more from him later) said, "I don't want everybody to vote," way back in the autumn of 1980. "As a matter of fact, our leverage in the elections quite candidly goes up as the voting populace goes down." (9)

From the right:

The only people against voter ID are those that want illegal voting to occur.

From the left:

Do you believe that I am lying to you when I say that I do not want illegal voting to occur, but I oppose most voter ID laws as being suppressive? I know how tempting it is to become hyperbolic on Facebook, it is a temptation I must work to avoid. I'd like to think that we can agree to disagree without questioning each other's values or patriotism.

From the right:

Fraud is widespread. Per the state's director of elections, reported on Fox & Friends and tweeted by President Trump, in Texas alone between 1996 and 2018 over 58,000 non-citizens voted and 95,000 non-citizens are registered to vote.

From the left:

Nope. Not even the state of Texas believes that, they just said "oops."

According to the AP, "Officials with the Texas secretary of state's office began calling county election chiefs Tuesday to warn about problems with its recent report questioning the citizenship of tens of thousands of registered voters, the latest example of a state backpedaling after raising alarms about potential widespread election fraud.

"Local officials told The Associated Press that they received calls from Texas Secretary of State David Whitley's office indicating that some citizens had been included in the original data announced Friday."

Florida did a similar thing, compared databases of people who weren't citizens when they got driver licenses but were on lists of people who voted, without taking into account the fact that a lot of people became citizens after they got their license. They started off with over 180,000 illegal voter-frauding-republic-killing-foreigners! Then they started scrubbing the list, and 180,000 is down below 100, so far.

Since about 60,000 people become citizens in Texas each year, over a half million since the late 90s, these numbers (95,000, with 58,000 supposedly having voted illegally since 1996) will no doubt dwindle to nothing as they did in Florida. (10)

Nice try though.

Speaking of Texas, the current Texas ID laws didn't go into effect until Jan 2018 because the previous law which went into effect in 2013 was overturned, found by the court to have "had a discriminatory impact" and that the legislature in enacting it had demonstrated a "pattern of conduct unexplainable on grounds other than (the) race factor."

I can help you guess how the current law could suppress a legal vote. You're a legal voter of color without a driver license etc., and your and/or your relatives' experiences have led you to mistrust police and the legal system. But you want to vote, so you bring your utility bill. Then you see that, unlike the white guy next to you in line who has a gun permit, you must sign an affidavit that threatens, in bold print, a misdemeanor or second degree felony. No thanks, I'm out; vote suppressed. I appreciate that such an experience is alien to most middle-aged white males.

Plenty of other courts and studies have found that voter ID laws result in voter suppression and are discriminatory. The Democratic party (Democrat being the noun, not the adjective) and other groups do conduct many such operations to register voters, get them IDs, and otherwise mitigate the effect of voter suppression legislation. Indeed, I believe these voter suppression efforts, while effective in the short term and having contributed mightily to results in 2016, ultimately will be self-defeating:

they are so offensive to our democracy that they will result (they are resulting) in robust actions to enhance the participation of minority voters.

If a given form of ID is known to be more prevalently held by racial group A than by group B, and there is evidence that the legislature opted to require that particular ID in order to suppress the vote of people in group B, that's racist, using the ID as a surrogate in order to discriminate racially.

From the right:

What forms of proof of identity do you think are fair?

From the left:

That deserves an answer.

First though, do we need *any* ID to vote? There's no constitutional right to buy bread, and no requirement to show ID to do so; why should ID be required to exercise the RIGHT to vote? The state has an interest in preventing voter fraud, and to be sure that only eligible persons vote. States have application procedures in place in order to register as well as means to scrub and validate voter rolls; if there are problems in voter registration in your state, fix them. Voter ID laws do not address registration problems. The only reason to have voter ID laws (beyond suppression) is ostensibly to address in-person voter fraud, which essentially does not exist, as we've gone over ad nauseum. So first then, there is no demonstrated state interest in requiring any ID in order to vote, after one has already satisfied one's state's requirements to register to vote.

But for purposes of argument, assuming ID were to be required to vote, in my opinion to be fair they would need to be forms of ID such that upon implementation of the requirement, it could be demonstrated that there was zero adverse effect upon the voting participation of any group of eligible voters.

From the right:

So then you would agree with me that voter ID laws are OK, that requiring just about any form of ID would be acceptable, as long as there was no evidence that the requirement results in voter suppression?

From the left:

Yes I would. And you would agree with me that such requirements are not OK if there is evidence that they do result in voter suppression?

From the right:

We would have to find some agreement on the facts regarding voter suppression, whether or not it happens.

From the left:
I tend to trust court findings, but yes, we would.
From the right:
We have come to a form of agreement. Praise the Lord.

The "Tragedy of the Commons" we discussed back in chapter 5 can be instructive regarding the idea of in-person voter fraud being committed by undocumented aliens. You'll recall that the 'tragedy' is the remorseless tendency for people to take advantage of a situation when the benefit accrues all to them while the costs are distributed among many others. The prospect of such voter fraud turns that 'tragedy' on its head. Think about it: undocumented persons, who are afraid to raise their profile with the police even after they've been assaulted, robbed, or raped, are postulated to decide to vote illegally.

In that circumstance, the benefit of casting a vote would be spread over all of society, while the cost is all theirs: *the risk of discovery and deportation is their individual burden, all just to Cast. One. Single. Vote.*

We have difficulties even getting American citizens to get off their behinds and cast their legal votes, but 'millions of illegals' risk prison and deportation to vote illegally? Aside from being unsupported by data, it seems unlikely because it is contrary to human nature.

Chapter 12

Big Wedges: Guns, Welfare, and Abortion

Trumpisms:

There is a lot of Fake information out there. Believe only me.

We should all love our country.

Guns

Gun violence. School shootings. Jeez.

To my liberal friends:

I own guns. They're locked up, and you don't have to worry about me. After 38 years in the Army, I know a lot of guys (and gals) who own guns, sometimes lots of guns. My brother has about a hundred M1 Garands. (Evidently, he really likes M1 Garands.) These people are not the problem. They are no threat to you or me or anyone (except someone who breaks into their homes). A lot of them have concealed carry. They've been trained, they're responsible, and you're safer when they're around than when they're not. Whatever we do, if it takes guns away from these people, or disallows their owning guns, in my opinion, it's not going to work in our country, with our history and culture. For good or ill, we're not Australia. If progressives aim for no guns for anybody, both sides will just dig in, identify with their tribe and we risk continuing to get nowhere.

To my conservative friends:

The status quo isn't working. Too many people in our country get shot. We need to work the issue and not get caught up in the fear-mongering rhetoric of "They're coming for your guns! Be afraid!" If we adopt the NRA hardline and resist all change as being the slippery slope, we increase the risk of an irrational overreaction that could end up being a self-fulfilling prophecy: they actually *will* be coming for our guns, taking guns away from law-abiding gun owners, or at least passing restrictive laws, and it'll be our own damn fault.

So what can we do?

There must be a common ground.

"A well regulated Militia, being necessary to the security of a free State, the right of the people to keep and bear Arms, shall not be infringed."

In my opinion, our current interpretation of the second amendment above, championed by the NRA which emphasizes the last phrase and ignores the first, isn't working.

Who are "the people" the amendment's talking about? Certainly not everyone: not children, not felons, not people who post on Facebook 'I wanna be a school shooter.' The 'right to bear arms,' like the right to free speech, is not absolute. You can't yell 'Fire!' in a crowded theater, and you can't (easily) own an M2 .50 caliber machine gun or a tank or a nuclear bomb.

Let's see if we can all agree on a few facts:

Gun violence including homicides, suicides and accidents kills about 40,000 Americans a year. That's roughly the same as motor vehicle accidents, pancreatic cancer, a typical flu season, breast cancer and liver disease. It's a lot less than heart disease.

Mass shootings are horrific and command our attention, but (in a typical year like 2019) only about one of every 400 gun deaths in America was the result of a mass shooting. More than half of gun deaths, over 20,000 per year, are from suicides. And yes people can commit suicide with drugs or rope or a tall building, but the ready availability of a gun can turn a momentary crisis into a permanent tragedy more efficiently than other methods.

Correlation does not equal causality; but consider these facts: (1)

There's a direct relationship between the number of guns in a society, and the number of gun deaths.

All the other developed countries in the world have many fewer guns, and many fewer gun deaths.

U.S. states with fewer guns, like a lot of New England and the Northeast, Midwestern states like Iowa and Illinois (despite Chicago), and California, have fewer gun deaths.

When state or local governments have restricted gun access, deaths typically declined.

As Michael Siegel of Boston University's School of Public Health says, "The main lesson that comes out of this research is that we know which laws work." (2)

So, the data, research, reality, all tell us that a lot of gun deaths are preventable. We should all be able to agree on that. Our differences will come when we try to decide what to do about it, what price must we pay, and who must pay it.

Progressive arguments such as "If we can save a single human life it's worth doing whatever must be done", don't quite ring true. We could reduce the over 39,000 annual motor vehicle deaths to nearly zero with a universal 20 mile per hour speed limit, but we're not willing to do that. Responsible, safe drivers like you and me would have to pay the price for drunks and lousy drivers by unnecessarily having to crawl at 20 mph on big wide safe roadways. If you're an anti-gun liberal who wants no one to own a gun, please recognize that, similarly, responsible gun owners don't want to be unnecessarily and excessively burdened, and if you want them to pay the price for your desire for regulation, you will not find willing partners.

Let's wait on discussing what to do, and try to find some more common ground.

Let's see if we can agree on these few simple opinions:

People who shouldn't have guns, shouldn't have guns.

People who do have guns are responsible for them and should secure their guns so that they don't end up in the hands of people who shouldn't have guns.

Virtually none of the people who have shot up schools were 'well-regulated'. So let's consider two more opinions:

"The people" whose 'right... shall not be infringed', are people who are suitable to be members of a well-regulated militia.

The NRA has something right: we don't enforce the laws we have, and we should. But, while those laws do and will help they don't go far enough. Because the NRA is *partially* right about something else: people are more important than guns. And it's still too damn easy for just about anybody legally (and illegally) to get a gun.

When someone walks into a recruiting station to join the Army, they don't walk out with a gun. Prospective soldiers get evaluated, examined, tested, inducted, and trained. And once they are a member of the well-regulated Army, their weapon doesn't get stuck under their pillow or left on the shelf in the break room. It's a sensitive item. Like encrypted radios or protective masks, it is secured. So, in my opinion, we need to tighten up on who can possess a gun, especially guns that can easily be concealed and guns that can kill a lot of people in a hurry, and assure that gun owners secure their gun(s). (Guns inadequately secured lead to suicides, accidents, and thefts, like the Newtown shooter.)

So who can have a gun? Most Americans, including most gun owners, believe that prospective gun owners should undergo a background check. This includes all gun ownership, all sales, all transfers of possession, gun shows, etc. It's an inconvenience if you're buying your neighbor's or your brother's rifle, but we live with inconvenience, we take off our shoes and belts to get on an airplane, that's a price we are willing to pay. If you've been trained, if you have been a member of a well-regulated armed force, I believe that's who the Founders had in mind with the second amendment. So, veterans, police, current serving military (so no, I don't think being 18 or 19 necessarily precludes you from owning a gun), all have undergone a robust background check (which should be updated intermittently for their civilian gun possession). Everyone who wants a gun should undergo some scrutiny. Where the default sits as far as 'you should get a gun unless you screw up' versus 'you need to show you're not a wacko-doodle before you get a gun', is fodder for debate. I would think their background check should include potential disqualifiers like domestic violence, violent behavior, their social media utterances, etc., and questions about how they secure their weapon, which must be locked away when not in use. Prospective gun owners should be required to document some safety and proficiency training, with the NRA or elsewhere.

Resistance to background checks or anything that might slow the pace of gun sales is framed in second amendment terms, that we have a God-given right as Americans to own guns and that right was enshrined by the Founders in the Second Amendment. But the individual right to bear arms (still with limitations, as we've noted) is a new thing, dating only to 2008. And that case (*District of Columbia vs Heller*) was decided out of thin air; like Citizens United, it was without precedent. Cases about guns have generally been about militias. But, as always, The Swamp, and money: gun manufacturers and the NRA pushed the agenda of the individual right, but it wasn't taken seriously. As recently as 1991, retired Chief Justice of SCOTUS Warren Burger said that it was "one of the greatest pieces of fraud, I repeat fraud, on the American public by special interest groups that I have ever seen in my lifetime." (3)

In most/many states, if you apply for concealed carry, you get asked, 'why?' I don't think it's unreasonable that some reason for gun ownership should apply to all weapons ownership. And the type of gun matters too. If you want a single shot bolt action .22 rifle for your 12 year old to learn gun safety and target practice, that makes sense and the threshold for ownership need not be that high (it should still be the law that the weapon be safely secured). If you want a gun that will fit into your wife's hand for home protection when you're away, that's understandable.

If you want a semi-automatic rifle with or without a high capacity magazine, and maybe you're a weirdo, you're not a veteran in good mental shape or a cop, I'm sorry, but I don't want you owning that gun in the same town as my kids unless and until you've undergone damn near as much scrutiny as for a security clearance. If you feel I'm infringing on your rights, you'll get over it, my kids and I have rights too. If you're a legitimate collector or a hunter or just want to have a gun in your house for the Zombie Apocalypse, once you've undergone a background check and been cleared, it should be easy to continue collecting or hunting after that. In the process of that scrutiny, I think we'll find a lot of people who shouldn't have guns, and a lot who need further attention and help. There have already been millions of gun purchases that have *not* been completed because of people failing background checks. In 2020 alone there were over 300,000 people who tried to buy guns and flunked their background check. (4) We'll never know how many lives have been and will be saved by those people *not* possessing guns.

Red flag laws that allow people to report to law enforcement when someone is acting squirrelly so police can evaluate the situation and temporarily remove that person's guns until his fitness for ownership is adjudicated, have proven helpful.

I don't know of much data supporting 'gun free zones'; they are like a non-peeing part of the pool, impractical unless they cover the entire pool (nationwide), as people with guns can easily cross municipal or state borders.

The NRA retort that "the only thing that stops a bad guy with a gun is a good guy with a gun" seems very weak to me. I don't believe that the questionable and marginal benefit that might possibly come from having enough people walking around with guns to trade fire at an all too common but still relatively rare daily American mass shooting (much less the rare-as-hen's-teeth terrorist event), would be better than the unintended consequences of having so many more guns around, consequences such as suicides and homicides by intoxicated or unbalanced people. The prospect of numerous inadequately trained individuals pulling out their guns and blasting away in the general direction of a shooter in a crowded theater or mall is not reassuring. In 2016 toddlers killed more people in the United States than did Muslim terrorists. (5) From 4 to 4.6 million children in the US live in households with loaded and unlocked guns. In the first few months of 2021 alone this has resulted in dozens of deaths at the hands of children wielding guns. This speaks to the ubiquity of guns, our collective failure to secure them, and our apparent inability to prioritize dangers.

How much gun violence will we have after we enact all these measures, background checks, licensure, training & securing, red flag laws, etc.? Less, but still some, and maybe too much. There's only one way to find out. It would be a start that would actually help and would respect the rights of responsible gun owners.

But what do we do after the results are in? With our current polarization we may never get results, but let's assume some good faith bargaining for common sense solutions, we move forward, do good work, and then... what? Not all gun violence will be gone.

Professional criminals who don't intend to follow any laws will not get a license or be dissuaded by any of the above measures. But again, many suicides (or accidental homicides at the hands of a toddler) are simply a function of the ready availability of guns, and many crimes (like many mass shooting) are perpetrated by people with legally purchased guns who are not professional criminals; with the barriers I've listed above, available data indicates there will be fewer gun-related suicides, accidents and crimes (as we find in other countries with better laws than ours). Again, these mass shootings and suicides and accidents generally don't seem to be committed by career criminals.

For my gun-advocate friends, please don't float the old argument that this or that specific measure would not have prevented this or that specific shooting. We all know that; none of these measures are perfect. The same is true for seatbelt laws and laws against drunk driving. Just because some fool drinks and doesn't stop at stop signs doesn't mean that laws prohibiting those behaviors don't work and we should get rid of them.

Even after these measures, our country will remain awash in guns. No matter how much we restrict weapon sales and transfers and possession, there are literally *hundreds of millions* of privately owned guns in this country, and securing them all (much less eliminating them) just isn't going to happen in our lifetimes. After all is said and done, short of the liberal fantasy of going door to door and collecting all the guns, guns will remain, and some gun violence will persist. After all the currently recommended gun control legislation has been enacted, there will be a mass shooting somewhere, followed by someone calling for even more restrictive measures.

Gun ownership is often a surrogate for deeply held values. Liberals as always value the *Care* versus *Harm* foundation, and few things are as stark in *Care* versus *Harm* as having unarmed civilians, such as children in schools, murdered with guns. Republicans are libertarians on this issue, valuing *Liberty* and seeing government intervention in gun ownership as *Oppression*. Indeed, many conservatives have elevated the 2nd amendment to the status of religious certitude and find attempts to circumvent it as violations of the *Sacred, Degradation* versus *Sanctity*.

And for my liberal friends, please understand that this is what even responsible gun owners are afraid of: the Slippery Slope toward Oppression and Degradation. Short of becoming China or Japan where private gun ownership is essentially non-existent, where does it end? They fear that your liberal agenda includes taking all guns from all Americans.

Trump warned of The Swamp. And it's The Swamp again.

Both the right and the left have an interest in fueling this wedge issue. The left for the obvious reason of limiting access to guns by unbalanced persons in order to decrease shootings, as well as some who want to control others and are biased against gun owners, and some politicians who just want to have an issue on which to raise money; and the right also wants to keep the issue alive ("this American carnage", 'people living in hell, walk down the street and get shot', 'need to arm teachers' etc.) to raise money, and fuel the fear of lefties taking away guns in order to sell more guns.

Ultimately, The Swamp in this instance is more active on the right. Campaign donations of the National Rifle Association (almost exclusively to Republicans) influence the debate, the NRA is essentially an organ of gun manufacturers, and they will sell more guns with Obama or Biden or any Democrat in the White House than with any Republican. Gerrymandering and the Electoral College favor the GOP and thus gun manufacturers.

Also, one of the favorite tools of the GOP, the filibuster, is pro-gun. It inhibits legislative action and protects the status quo, and the status quo is guns and more guns, guns for everyone.

As always, follow the money. Stoking fear of the socialists coming to take your guns is the best way of increasing gun sales.

A century or three from now, I imagine we'll have addressed this problem. Just as internal combustion will become a relic and all new vehicle sales will be for electric cars, all new weapon sales will be for guns that are biometrically matched to their owners so that no one else's hand will be able to fire the weapon. That technology already exists. Legacy firearms will be the province of collectors and family heirlooms.

Between now and then, we'll do a better job if we stop demonizing each other, stop swallowing the propaganda of moneyed interests, stop using gun possession and the second amendment as litmus tests and cudgels with which to beat each other, stop trying to control each other and instead focus on doing everything we can to keep guns out of the hands of poorly regulated persons. Given our history and culture, for the foreseeable future we may have to assume some risk of some gun violence. But can't we all agree that the current level of gun violence in America is too damn much?

Socialism and welfare

We have all known lazy people, people who don't pull their weight, who don't do their share of the work. We've all had a co-worker with whom we dreaded to work, the colleague with whom we shared some responsibility who did such a lousy job that it was easier for you to do your own job, plus do *his* part of the job for him, than it was to try to get him to do his job.

Liberals and conservatives both value the moral principle of *Fairness* versus *Cheating*. All societies must deal with *free riders*. Nobody likes free riders, but conservatives particularly just can't stand them. Free riders are The Other team, and conservatives are more willing than are liberals to take a hit themselves, or limit legitimate assistance to the needy, if they can keep benefit from going to free riders whom they regard as cancer in society. Indeed, lazy welfare queen types are seen as *degrading* society, violating the *sanctity* of the virtue of hard work.

The *loyalty* versus *betrayal* fundamental also is in play, as free riders and thieves and con men and grifters and fraudsters, and even just the inconsiderate, betray the rest of us. In his book *Tribe*, Sebastian Junger writes: "In this sense, littering is an exceedingly petty version of claiming a billion-dollar bank bailout or fraudulently claiming disability payments.

When you throw trash on the ground, you apparently don't see yourself as truly belonging to the world that you're walking around in. And when you fraudulently claim money from the government, you are ultimately stealing from your friends, family and neighbors -- or somebody else's friends, family and neighbors. That diminishes you morally far more than it diminishes your country financially." (6)

My friend Carl lifted himself out of a bad situation; his lived experience in his extended family and neighborhood was that welfare caused indolence. He worked hard. He doesn't care much for free riders. I can't ignore his experience. He saw government intervention apparently screwing things up.

Liberal arguments that ignore the experience of people like Carl will not be persuasive. They lose to the elephant already swayed by the moral imperatives; and even on those occasions when someone's elephant is not leaning much and is willing to entertain a new idea, unless arguments are properly framed with good data they can lose to the undecided too.

Let's pause for a few definitions.

Socialism, as I grew up with the term, was bad. Socialism was communism. Strangely, communism was good if you were in an early Christian community where no one owned anything and everyone shared everything, but it was bad for modern America, and for good reason.

In socialism 'the workers', the 'people', that is, the government, owns most industries. Socialism is an economic system, not necessarily a political one. In theory, everybody shares more or less equally in the proceeds from the work that is done. But historically the economic system of socialism as it was implemented in the 20th century (in the Union of Soviet **Socialist** Republics for instance) was typically joined at the hip with authoritarian, totalitarian political systems. A single party or individual ruled. Personal freedoms were curtailed. Individualism and innovation were not rewarded. Socialism mostly sucked.

We have some socialism in the United States. It can be described as **corporate socialism** as I've outlined in describing the Rigged System and The Swamp. As defined by *Women for Justice,* most major industries are privately owned, but still receive substantial tax cuts, bailouts, and other benefits at the expense of the taxpayer. It is driven by corporations' ability to influence laws with money to pay for legislation (and regulatory capture, etc.) that favors corporations' ability to make even more money. The wealthy become wealthier at the expense of the lower classes. **As**

Trump said, it's a rigged system. *Distribution of wealth* is unequal and capitalistic as profits go to the top, while *distribution of risk* is socialized, losses are spread out among taxpayers. This is plutocracy, rule by the rich.

Democratic socialism is a hybrid. Individual and small businesses are privately owned (capitalism), as are most major industries, but they do not receive handouts from the government at taxpayer expense. The tax burden is shared equitably, with wealthy corporations and individuals paying their 'fair share' (whatever that means; we'll discuss later) to help fund public services like education, healthcare, law enforcement, firefighters, roads, libraries, etc. With this system, the middle class thrives and poverty decreases. This most closely aligns with democracy, rule by the people. This model exists in vestigial form in the United States; it is more robust in western and northern Europe, and some Asian countries.

Unfortunately, most discussions do not differentiate between these various forms of socialism. If a conversation is just about "socialism", frequently the two parties are talking about completely different things and the whole interchange becomes hopelessly muddled. This often is done on purpose, to drive a wedge between people.

The conservative case against amorphous socialism writ large is, once again, simple and straightforward. Socialism is taking something (money, resources) away from the productive people in society, and giving to the unproductive. It is an injury to productive people, and it is an injury to all of society: it reinforces indolence, and disincentivizes hard work. It is an invitation to free riders to do nothing and get something.

And, it is not good for the recipient. The too-ready availability of handouts leads the potential recipient into temptation, places him in a dilemma; as if "Stop" signs instead said, "Please stop" and were not enforced by law; you'd be a fool to stop all the time while others get to go whizzing through. By incentivizing unproductive behavior, it takes marginally poorly productive people, and turns them into full free riders who embrace their lassitude, and never become the productive and fulfilled persons they could be. They then pass, to whatever degree, this antipathy to hard work on to their progeny, fostering a dysfunctional subculture.

Since we have all experienced free riders, we all know that there is at least a kernel of truth in this perspective. The argument can include the caution that any socialism is a slippery slope, just a camel sticking its nose under the tent; let in a little socialism and the next thing you know, we'll be North Korea.

Muddling accusations about 'creeping socialism' are very old. Liberal push back against it also is old. As President Harry Truman noted in a stump speech on the back platform of a train in Syracuse New York on 10 Oct 1952:

> Socialism is a scare word they have hurled at every
> advance the people have made in the last 20 years.
> Socialism is what they called public power.
> Socialism is what they called social security.
> Socialism is what they called farm price supports.
> Socialism is what they called bank deposit insurance.
> Socialism is what they called the growth of free and
> independent labor organizations.
> Socialism is their name for almost anything that helps all
> the people.

While there are indeed small numbers of left-over communists and anarchists, liberals point out that virtually no one in the Democratic Party, not AOC, not Bernie Sanders, no one in a responsible position is advocating for a Marxist form of government in the US. We already have socialism here, every time we tax to build a road or hire police or teachers or provide healthcare for someone over 65. (As noted, we especially have socialism in tax breaks and subsidies for large corporate moneyed interests: they get the profits but the losses are socialized, distributed among taxpayers. We could have less of that. One never hears The Swamp complaining about that form of welfare). We have seen what Marxism and Leninism looked like in application behind the Iron Curtain: that was a dismal failure that no one seeks to repeat. But the forms of socialism in place in Scandinavia and Western Europe have not demonstrated any slippery sloping toward totalitarianism in the generations they have existed, so liberals are not worried about stopping movement toward what they envision as an American society that does a better job of educating and providing opportunity for the needy and disadvantaged.

Indeed many liberals like Elizabeth Warren call themselves capitalists and advocate for the wealth-producing potential of capitalism. They view the current multinational corporate expression of capitalism paradoxically as the greatest threat *to* capitalism, fueling justified discontent and inviting government overreach if not outright revolution. The moderate forms of socialism we already have could use some refining, and could balance and actually save capitalism from its excesses.

Government assistance or "welfare" is the particular policy manifestation of socialism that can disturb conservatives, for all the descriptors above regarding socialism. They point out that in addition to its essential flaws, it is indisputable that there is fraud, waste and abuse (FWA) in government programs. These cheaters are cheating; I work hard and they take my money, and it's just not right. As one conservative friend of mine put it: "You see, social security's original inception was to pay back to those that paid in. Now, it's handed out like crack to many as 'disabled.' These addicted crackheads then buy into the idea that they can't make it without their crack and forfeit their independence. This keeps them dependent on their crack dealer, the liberal politician. So, the addict keeps voting for their dealer and the dealer keeps promising more crack. I've been paying into Social Security since I was 18. I expect to begin drawing at 68 = 50 years paying in. If the Good Lord blessed me to age 80, I will have paid enough for me and several crack heads.... Desire and sacrifice are the keys, not excuses and handouts. There is no kid in this country that grew up poorer than me. Why is it that I've created a reasonable life but the lazy asses with three degrees or other resources that I could never have dreamed of having, still come up with excuse why they are 'disadvantaged' or 'left behind' or whatever other pseudonym for lack of effort is cliché for the day?"

[And the liberal Facebook reply was: "Your statement that we cannot sustain an economy by taking away from over-achievers and rewarding under-achievers is exactly correct. I think the under-achievers are those who encouraged the bundling of predatory loans into derivatives that ran the economy into the ditch, impoverishing many but certainly not the high-level executives who rigged the game and got rich, and then further rig the game to ensure that their heirs inherit wealth while doing no work. The over-achievers are guys like you who are not quite as smart as you so they cannot become healthcare professionals; all they can do is work harder for stagnant wages. We are creating classes of non-working rich and hard-working poor."]

Fraud exists. "Fraud" in 'welfare' includes cheating and 'improper filing', or mistakes, which together run about 10%. It runs about 1 to 2% in the federal 'welfare queen' program, food stamps. (7). That's a lot of money, going to thousands upon thousands upon tens of thousands of people who are cheating, and it's understandably infuriating to hard-working people; the question is, is it worth cutting off the 98% to prevent the 2% fraud? That depends somewhat on the 98%; are they loafing, living on the backs of real workers? It turns out that about three quarters of them are the working poor and their families; they just have jobs that pay too little for them to stop being poor. But still, the argument goes, we can't keep paying exorbitant amounts, we'll go broke. (Well... see my comments on debt and deficit in chapter 9.) It turns out the fraction of our GDP that went to welfare (food stamps, housing assistance) in 2020 was around 1% (roughly, depending on whether you include earned income tax credits and so forth; but still, in the ballpark). (8) Some reasonably argue that the lack of a living wage for full-time low income workers transfers the burden of supporting them from the wage-payer to the taxpayer, that it's not the working poor that are loafing, but rather their corporate employers.

It is perhaps due to human nature that polls show people don't want any cuts to this or that specific government program ("keep your government hands off my Medicare"), but still want the government somehow to shrink. We as a society have generally decided that it is unacceptable, for instance, to have children starving on our streets. (Perhaps I'm wrong about that societal consensus; if I am, then that seems to be a good place to start for public debate.) Integrating the reality of government intervention needed for the 'safety net', with the need to pay for it, requires a public discourse that seems beyond us.

When my wife and I were approaching retirement, we prepared, read, researched and consulted with advisors. Typically over the years we had prepared a number of budgets as part of our overall financial planning. I anticipated coming up with a new one to reflect our upcoming life changes. But when I asked, our advisor told me, 'make a budget if you want to, but I don't need it.' What? How can we plan without a new budget? His point was: he would help us make a plan (if it was possible) to husband and distribute our money in such a way as to make sure we always had enough money to live our lives, basically, as we had been. And he knew what we'd been spending. Just look at our tax return and look at the amount of income we have left after taxes; yes account for expenses you won't have anymore (like paying into savings accounts and retirement instruments), yes account for big expenses that will change in predictable ways (like a mortgage being paid off), but basically look at the income you've been living on. That's what you need to live on. That's what you spend; that's you; that's pretty much what you're going to want to continue to spend in the future.

We Americans, our federal government, Republican and Democratic administrations both, spend roughly the same amount year after year. And in recent years they both seem just as willing to borrow to pay for it. For all of the Republican rhetoric about shrinking government and reining in government spending, that doesn't happen. Yes, many liberal peace activists want us to spend less on the Pentagon. And conservative politicians always say they want to cut entitlements or other services, but when they have the power to do so, they don't do it, because those programs are popular and people want them. Deciding what services we are not willing to provide should include an assessment of the risks of not providing them. If we decide we can't afford it, if we decide (not just by default as we usually do) we're going to cut some people loose, then our society must live with consequences. But once we've decided to provide a service and have been doing so for years or decades under leadership of both parties, it's past time whining about paying for it.

A recent experiment in Stockton California has added data to these old arguments. The city provided a Universal Basic Income (UBI) to a number of people. The idea was to test hypotheses, the conservative idea that such unearned income would make people lazy, versus the liberal idea that those people would enjoy more income and would continue to seek work despite getting paid for doing nothing. In this case, those receiving UBI sought and found employment at a higher rate than those without UBI. (9)

So which is true? If we pay people to do nothing, will they just waste away spiritually and materially doing nothing? Or will they use that pay to jump start getting ahead in life?

No doubt both are true. The devil must be in the details. Some people will take what they can get and contribute nothing, period, that's how they roll. Others will find a way to be more productive, many conservatives would say despite UBI, many liberals would say because of UBI. And it's not just catching UBI, but pitching it as well. How UBI is structured, how much pay for how long, associated with what other educational or training or credit opportunities. There's likely a sweet spot in there somewhere, different for different people at different times in their lives. It's probably complicated. That's not a bad thing.

Abortion

Human life begins at conception. That is the core of the conservative argument for the "pro-life" position (opponents assert the terms "anti-abortion" or "anti-choice" are more accurate, but without taking sides, 'pro-life' is more commonly used and understood, so that's what I'll use). It is a difficult position to assail, as it cannot be disproved. Even the most liberal among us should be able to appreciate that if someone truly believes that human life begins at conception, then it logically follows that ending such a life is morally abhorrent. Indeed, for those who are pro-life, abortion checks all the boxes for the fundamental moral imperatives: abortion is *harmful, oppressive,* and *unfair* to the unborn, it *betrays* the *loyalty* a mother should have to her unborn, defies *authority*, previously of the state and currently of (most of) the church, and is unholy, *degrading* the *sanctity* of life. Many pro-life conservatives just cannot understand why liberals believe in killing babies and feel that they must hold the line to protect defenseless voiceless babies against this modern holocaust.

Of course those who are pro-choice disagree. The idea that we can all agree that a 23 chromosome sperm or egg is just a germ cell that can be wasted without moral threat, but the moment it joins with another 23 chromosome germ cell and becomes a 46 chromosome zygote, this unseen unknown microscopic entity is a fully human person; well, pro-choice liberals just don't buy that idea as fact. While the assertion that life begins at conception cannot be disproved, neither can it be proved. (Despite 'new science' about when the fetus has a detectable heartbeat and how much it moves, etc., ultimately the issue is: when does the essence of humanity, the soul if you will, invest in a zygote or embryo or fetus and make it a human life? Good luck determining that. I am confident that medical science will not crack that code any time soon.) That means it's just some people's belief, a religious belief that they are welcome to hold but that should not dictate the personal freedoms of persons who do not hold that belief.

Also, the consistency of the conservative determination of 'personhood upon conception' demands scrutiny: if a zygote is a person, is that when child support should begin? Is the zygote a US citizen, and thus immune from deportation, requiring that the uterus it now occupies not be deported even though it is in the body of an undocumented woman?

The pro-choice community holds that prohibiting a woman from making her own decisions regarding her own pregnancy is *harmful* and *unfair*; they agree with libertarians that government should stay out of the business of enforcing the religious beliefs of some upon others, that management of a pregnancy is a matter to be decided by the woman and her medical consultants (and spiritual advisors if she so chooses), and it is *oppressive* for government to interfere in these most intimate and personal choices. And for reasons previously discussed, they don't particularly care about conservatives, typically a bunch of dry old uptight white men, getting upset regarding *loyalty, authority* and *sanctity*.

I have never performed an abortion, an elective termination of pregnancy (ETOP). But I have performed the procedure of dilation and curettage (D&C) many times, mostly early in my career. The procedure is the same as is done for an abortion, the difference being that when I performed it, the embryo or fetus had already 'died' (like liver cells can die without the cells having been considered to be a person) and the woman was experiencing an *incomplete* or *inevitable* abortion, a miscarriage. It was my job to evacuate from the uterus the products of conception; if they are retained, they are dead tissue that serves as a source of infection, which can be fatal for the woman. It's not a happy procedure for anyone.

Often miscarriages happen early on in pregnancy, and not to be graphic but the tissue removed is an indeterminate bloody mess, just like a big clot. On one occasion though, the pregnancy had been further along than I had appreciated. While performing the curettage, I began to see identifiable fetal parts. While I knew the intrauterine fetal demise had occurred long before I'd become involved, it still was very disconcerting and I remember it clearly to this day. I had never seriously considered including ETOPs among the medical services I would provide later in my career, but I could tell by the hair standing up on the back of my neck that evening that I never could. Maybe it's my Catholic upbringing, but for me, performing an abortion would put my immortal soul (assuming I have one) in jeopardy. There's just no way I could do it. (At least so I believe now, not being faced with a woman who'd been raped and was desperate to end her pregnancy.) I guess that makes me pro-life. On the other hand, my gut told me this feeling of mine was specific to me, as personal as could be. I felt no impulse whatsoever to export this experience into the control of the behavior of others who have their own excruciatingly difficult personal decisions to make. So that makes me pro-choice. Go figure.

During one of my deployments to Afghanistan, I attended a religious studies group and had occasion to have a number of discussions with a Catholic priest. (Paradoxically, while there's lots of work to do in war zones, with no family responsibilities or TV or other entertainment, one often has such free time.) Of course he was strongly pro-life, and as I rarely learn anything by just agreeing with someone, I wanted to explore the nooks and crannies of that position, so I was respectfully contrarian. The conversation went something like this:

The priest (P): Abortion is wrong, should be illegal, and you should vote for pro-life candidates.

Me (M): But if someone, particularly a pregnant woman, doesn't share that belief, why should she be ruled by your belief?

P: I cannot be responsible for her mistaken belief. If I'm wrong, society ends up with another birth. If she's wrong, we have murdered an innocent soul.

M: Should abortion providers, should women who have abortions, be subjected to our penal system and incarcerated? Or executed for murder?

P: That's for the state to decide.

M: Hmmm.... If the people you want me to vote for are going to punish these people, or even execute them, I'm reluctant blindly to support that.

P: Fair enough; no, it's not the position of the Church, and I personally don't care to see them punished. Hate the sin, love the sinner. I want abortion to be illegal to discourage abortions.

M: But if abortions are illegal, history tells us that many pregnant women will seek illegal 'back alley' abortions, and many will die as a result. How can you reconcile a "pro-life" position with these avoidable maternal deaths?

P: That is theoretical, and the women have choices; the babies do not.

M: Theoretical perhaps but affirmed by experience. Would not the end of fewer abortions be better served by education (and birth control, but let's table that) and the greater availability of spiritual and family counseling rather than by the legal system? Isn't this just a weird paternalistic need of men to control women's sexuality?

P: Perhaps. But even if so, it is important for society to stand firm and be explicit in its condemnation of the killing of innocents.

M: 'Society standing firm' seems little comfort for a woman who doesn't share your beliefs to be compelled to carry to term an unwanted pregnancy. Should there be no consideration for women and girls who are the victims of rape or incest?

P: Those are tragic circumstances, but none of that is the baby's fault.

M: You assume that the embryo or fetus is a 'baby', a person.

P: Yes.

I did not and do not have any doubt about the sincerity of his beliefs and position. We agreed to disagree.

But many progressives have doubts about the sincerity or at least the consistency of many of the people who are most vociferous in their objections to abortion. Since ultimately the objections are religious ones, involving the *sanctity* of life, progressives feel justified in pointing out what they see as hypocrisy, the mouthing of pieties for political expediency. This is well encapsulated by a post by Dave Barnhart, a pastor in Birmingham Alabama:

> "The unborn" are a convenient group of people to advocate for. They never make demands of you; they are morally uncomplicated, unlike the incarcerated, addicted, or the chronically poor; they don't resent your condescension or complain that you are not politically correct; unlike widows, they don't ask you to question patriarchy; unlike orphans, they don't need money, education, or childcare; unlike aliens, they don't bring all that racial, cultural, and religious baggage that you dislike; they allow you to feel good about yourself without any work at creating or maintaining relationships; and when they are born, you can forget about them, because they cease to be unborn. It's almost as if, by being born, they have died to you. You can love the unborn and advocate for them without substantially challenging your own wealth, power, or privilege, without re-imagining social structures, apologizing, or making reparations to anyone. They are, in short, the perfect people to love if you want to claim you love Jesus but actually dislike people who breathe.
>
> Prisoners? Immigrants? The sick? The poor? Widows? Orphans? All the groups that are specifically mentioned in the Bible? They all get thrown under the bus for the unborn.

<u>How we got here</u>

My discussion with a Catholic priest should be no surprise. I grew up with this stuff: being against abortion has been a Catholic thing since forever. Now a lot of the pro-life energy in the United States comes from the evangelical religious right. How did that happen? When I was young, before and during high school in the 1960's, Protestants regarded the anti-abortion position as a strictly Roman Catholic obsession, as another one of those weird Papist aberrations, not based on the Bible, just another unsupportable manifestation of papal infallibility run amok.

And I'm not just entertaining the way I remember it, there is contemporaneous evidence. The evangelical magazine *Christian Life* had an issue in 1967 which said: "The Bible definitely pinpoints a difference in the value of a fetus and an adult. Thus, the Bible would appear to disagree with the official Catholic view that the tiniest fetus is as important as an adult human being."

A year later in 1968 another leading evangelical magazine *Christianity Today* published a joint statement representing "the conservative or evangelical position within Protestantism." They didn't accept the idea of life beginning at conception. Said the consensus statement: "From the moment of *birth*, the infant is a human being with all the rights which Scripture accords to all human beings" [*italics added*]. (10) An accompanying issue clarified that "God does not regard the fetus as a soul, no matter how far gestation has progressed. The Law plainly exacts: 'If a man kills any human life he will be put to death' (Lev. 24:17). But according to Exodus 21:22–24, the destruction of the fetus is not a capital offense... Clearly, then, in contrast to the mother, the fetus is not reckoned as a soul." (11)

In 1971, before Roe v Wade, the Southern Baptist Convention supported abortion laws being liberalized to include consideration of the emotional health of the mother. A former president of the Southern Baptist Convention, later in May of 1976 explained the reasoning: "Protestant theology generally takes Genesis 2:7 as a statement that the soul is formed at breath, not with conception." (12)

Yet Jerry Falwell in his 1980 book *Listen America!* wrote that "The Bible clearly states that life begins at conception," stating that abortion "is murder according to the Word of God." He cited Psalm 139:13, wherein God "knit me together in my mother's womb." Many evangelicals and biblical scholars assert that this verse demonstrates the omnipotence and omniscience of God rather than specifying when life begins. In his 1984 book *Abortion: Toward an Evangelical Consensus* Professor Paul Fowler wrote "The Bible shows life begins at conception.... In the Genesis narratives alone, the phrase 'conceived and bore' is found eleven times. The close pairing of the two words clearly emphasizes conception, not birth, as the starting point." Fair enough, that's his opinion; like so much in the Bible, it means whatever you believe it means. At the end of his book he is adamant that "Scripture is Clear!" that life begins at conception. (13)

Either way, biblical support or not, what happened? How did American evangelicals come to adopt in four short years in the late 1970s what had previously been a fairly exclusively Roman Catholic position?

For that we must reconsider Paul M. Weyrich (the fellow who said, "I don't want everybody to vote"), one of the founders of the Religious Right. Randall Balmer reports that Weyrich's conservative activism had dated at least as far back as the Barry Goldwater campaign in 1964; he had been "trying for years to energize evangelical voters over school prayer, abortion, or the proposed equal rights amendment to the Constitution. 'I was trying to get those people interested in those issues and I utterly failed,' he recalled in an interview in the early 1990s." At a conference in the 1990s "Weyrich tried to make a point to his Religious Right brethren (no women attended the conference, as I recall). Let's remember, he said animatedly, that the Religious Right did not come together in response to the Roe decision." (14)

So, how did this happen?

Once again, it's about race

To complete Weyrich's earlier quote: "I was trying to get those people interested in those issues and I utterly failed.... What changed their mind was Jimmy Carter's intervention against the Christian schools, trying to deny them tax-exempt status on the basis of so-called *de facto* segregation."

Balmer's first-hand account from that conference is illuminating; the Religious Right was not born due to *Roe*, but rather, due to race.

> No, Weyrich insisted, what got us going as a political movement was the attempt on the part of the Internal Revenue Service (IRS) to rescind the tax-exempt status of Bob Jones University because of its racially discriminatory policies.
>
> Bob Jones University was one target of a broader attempt by the federal government to enforce the provisions of the Civil Rights Act of 1964. Several agencies, including the Equal Employment Opportunity Commission, had sought to penalize schools for failure to abide by anti-segregation provisions. A court case in 1972, *Green v. Connally*, produced a ruling that any institution that practiced segregation was not, by definition, a charitable institution and, therefore, no longer qualified for tax-exempt standing.

The IRS sought to revoke the tax-exempt status of Bob Jones University in 1975 because the school's regulations forbade interracial dating; African Americans, in fact, had been denied admission altogether until 1971, and it took another four years before unmarried African Americans were allowed to enroll. The university filed suit to retain its tax-exempt status, although that suit would not reach the Supreme Court until 1983 (at which time, the Reagan administration argued in favor of Bob Jones University).

Initially, I found Weyrich's admission jarring. He declared, in effect, that the origins of the Religious Right lay in *Green v. Connally* rather than *Roe v. Wade*. I quickly concluded, however, that his story made a great deal of sense. When I was growing up within the evangelical subculture, there was an unmistakably defensive cast to evangelicalism. I recall many presidents of colleges or Bible institutes coming through our churches to recruit students and to raise money. One of their recurrent themes was, We don't accept federal money, so the government can't tell us how to run our shop—whom to hire or fire or what kind of rules to live by. The IRS attempt to deny tax-exempt status to segregated private schools, then, represented an assault on the evangelical subculture, something that raised an alarm among many evangelical leaders, who mobilized against it.

For his part, Weyrich saw the evangelical discontent over the Bob Jones case as the opening he was looking for to start a new conservative movement using evangelicals as foot soldiers. Although both the *Green* decision of 1972 and the IRS action against Bob Jones University in 1975 predated Jimmy Carter's presidency, Weyrich succeeded in blaming Carter for efforts to revoke the tax exempt status of segregated Christian schools. He recruited James Dobson and Jerry Falwell to the cause, the latter of whom complained, "In some states it's easier to open a massage parlor than to open a Christian school."

During the meeting in Washington, D.C., Weyrich went on to characterize the leaders of the Religious Right as reluctant to take up the abortion cause even close to a decade after the Roe ruling. "I had discussions with all the leading lights of the movement in the late 1970s and early 1980s, post–Roe v. Wade," he said, "and they were all arguing that that decision was one more reason why Christians had to isolate themselves from the rest of the world."

"What caused the movement to surface," Weyrich reiterated, "was the federal government's moves against Christian schools." The

> IRS threat against segregated schools, he said, "enraged the Christian community." That, not abortion, according to Weyrich, was what galvanized politically conservative evangelicals into the Religious Right and goaded them into action. "It was not the other things," he said.
>
> Ed Dobson, Falwell's erstwhile associate, corroborated Weyrich's account during the ensuing discussion. "The Religious New Right did not start because of a concern about abortion," Dobson said. "I sat in the non-smoke-filled back room with the Moral Majority, and I frankly do not remember abortion ever being mentioned as a reason why we ought to do something."
>
> During the following break in the conference proceedings, I cornered Weyrich to make sure I had heard him correctly. He was adamant that, yes, the 1975 action by the IRS against Bob Jones University was responsible for the genesis of the Religious Right in the late 1970s. What about abortion? After mobilizing to defend Bob Jones University and its racially discriminatory policies, Weyrich said, these evangelical leaders held a conference call to discuss strategy. He recalled that someone suggested that they had the makings of a broader political movement—something that Weyrich had been pushing for all along—and asked what other issues they might address. Several callers made suggestions, and then, according to Weyrich, a voice on the end of one of the lines said, "How about abortion?" And that is how abortion was cobbled into the political agenda of the Religious Right. (14)

Asking the broader evangelical community to become politically active in order to defend the segregationist policies at schools was not an effective approach. It appealed to the *liberty* versus *oppression* moral dynamic, freedom from government intervention in how we run our own darn schools. But when the specific liberty being oppressed was explicitly segregationist, the activists were to whatever degree swimming upstream against *care* versus *harm* and *fairness* versus *cheating*, and they found that evangelicals were not enthusiastic. Liberals would say that the lack of evangelical enthusiasm for explicit support of segregation was despite a significant pool of racism; evangelicals would say it is evidence of a lack of racism. In any case, the switch from racism to the pretext of abortion, while rather Machiavellian, was both inspired and effective. But it does raise the question of why we believe what we believe, not just about abortion, but about anything.

If you are a Trump supporter or an evangelical who believes in 2022 that abortion is wrong, neither the ease of advocating for a population that disappears upon birth nor the shenanigans of the 1970s political history above necessarily mean that you are not sincere. And just because the evangelical position on when life begins changed for the political reasons described above (15), it doesn't mean that you are wrong if you believe that life begins at conception (how would I know if you're right or wrong?). Maybe you know why you believe abortion is murder, and you have no doubt that you are correct. Maybe you're right (how would I know that either?).

What you believe is up to you.

And *why* you believe what you believe also is up to you.

There's no harm in looking in the mirror and asking yourself why you believe what you believe. If you're happy with the answer, God bless, and drive on. Socrates and the temple of Apollo at Delphi tell us "Know Thyself." If you think your answer is a bit fuzzy and deserves a little more scrutiny, bless you as well. Because sometimes, the way we feel about things is born of our own insecurities and desires to control other people. The low hanging fruit of examples would include issues such as abortion, or guns: if you're a conservative ask yourself if you would like to be able to wave a magic wand and control the sexual and reproductive behaviors of women; or if you're a liberal ask yourself if you would like to control whether or not civilians can own guns regardless of how responsible they are. It's often less about the particular issue, and more about the control of other people. More about that in Chapter 15.

As we've explored in earlier chapters at length, sometimes even our elephant hasn't begun to lean one way or the other and our inner lawyer doesn't know what to say, so we take a shortcut. We believe things just because our team believes them. This shortcut can be helpful.

There are leaders I have known in the Army and elsewhere in my upbringing whom I would follow anywhere. One of the explicit tasks of any subordinate is to interpret and execute the "commander's intent". The assumption is that the boss is older, more experienced, wiser, and has authority; you assume that your commander is correct, ethically as well as professionally, until proved otherwise. So as long as his or her orders are legal, you try your best to carry them out. Sometimes the orders aren't comprehensive, and you need to show initiative, so you try to figure out what the boss would want you to do if s/he were here. Sometimes the leader was someone I outranked, but I could tell he or she was wiser, more experienced, more attuned in a given area than I was. So it's natural to identify people you like, whom you respect, whom you believe share your interests, people who are on your team, and just support what they support, believe what they believe.

Taking the shortcut and believing what the leaders of your team believe, is quick and convenient; but it's a double-edged sword. It means surrendering to others to some degree your powers of intellectual discrimination and it can close avenues of growth and understanding. 'If you're not like me, I don't like you.' There are lots of people I've met who are not like me, but who have had some great ideas. I've learned a lot from such people; almost by definition, they have different perspectives than I, gleaned from their different life experiences. Had I just dismissed them because they're not like me, I would have missed out on their wisdom.

In any case, shortcuts happen, people take them. And when it comes to finding shortcuts and swallowing arguments whole without any chewing at all, Americans tend to find their sustenance in the News. And all too often, it's Fake News.

Chapter 13

Fake News and Social Media

Trumpisms:

There is a lot of Fake information out there.
We need our country to be safe and secure.
We should all love our country.

He was correct about all those things,
and many people felt that he was correct.

His sell included:
Believe only me.

Those who can make you believe absurdities,
can make you commit atrocities.
- - Voltaire

You may wonder about the point of this chapter. I just spent half this book talking about the second class status of reason and data. Our passions rule, and we tend to select and reflect information that supports the perspective our emotional elephant has already adopted. So why bother with discussing fake news, or real news, or any news?

Spoiler alert: I think the way out of our current dilemma includes a journey through the terrain of Truth and Reality... more about that in a couple of chapters.

You may recall that many people don't seem to give a damn about facts. "Facts" are in the domain of the rider, and function only to support the elephant which already leans in one direction or another. That's a tough nut to crack, and we'll address that reality more fully in subsequent chapters. But in our most sober moments, in the court of public opinion, ideally, facts should be important. Since nominally at least, *well-informed* opinions derive from facts, and lies are the opposite of facts, perhaps we can start by assuming that facts are indeed important, and that exposure to and digestion of factual information is better than the opposite.

Trump was correct when he said that Fake News is out there.

I'll lump and split the information we consume into three broad categories:

Facts: things that can be demonstrated to be true.
Opinions: commentary, or 'spin'.
Lies: deliberate misrepresentations of truth, or failure to correct previous 'errors.'

The *Truth* is. It stands on its own. The highest forms of human knowledge are true. While the reality that each of us experiences is a function of our individual wisdom and awareness, objective truth is not negotiable. Facts and evidence are objective enough realities that in common experience we should all be able to share them. Facts are facts; by definition, "alternative facts" are either facts, or they are not facts. Without truth, there is no freedom in this world, because without truth there is no basis for holding power to account.

Opinions are the prerogative of the individual. While ideally informed by facts, opinions are not facts and need not survive the same scrutiny. Everybody gets to have his own opinion. Some opinions are worthy, better supported by the facts than other opinions, more representative of wisdom and a discriminating intellect. But ultimately, which opinions are worthy, is a matter of... opinion.

Spin is a flavor of opinion. We all spin. Politicians and their staffs spin incessantly. They interpret what happens, like a given debate that just ended that we all saw, and tell us what they want us to believe we just saw. They emphasize that which is favorable to their point of view, and de-emphasize that which opposes. The less tethered the spin (or opinion) is to the facts, the more it approaches a lie.

Lies and liars are not worthy. Lies, deliberate fabrications and distortions of reality, are not worthy (with some exceptions that serve a greater good, such as lies told and lived by undercover law enforcement or delivering disinformation to enemy spies, etc.). Spin designed not just to show off the favorable but to induce listeners to infer things that are not true, becomes indistinguishable from a lie. Indeed, many liars (to be defined) are spinmeisters: when they spin they deliberately inject fear and vitriol into the veins of the body politic. Such hateful venom is poisonous; such spinning and lying is cancerous.

Virtually all of us have lied. Recall the story of Jonathan Haidt when admonished by his wife about leaving unwashed dishes where she prepares their baby's food. But calling all of us "liars" would rob the term of meaning. Mistakes are by definition, not deliberate, they are not lies. Spontaneous lies that arise from our elephant and are elaborated by our press agent or inner lawyer before our rider can moderate what we say (like Haidt and his dishes and dog and baby conflation) are lies, but they are so close to unconscious that they do not make us liars, they just mean we're human. After the fact, the more honest we are, the more we strive to correct misinformation our elephant provoked our lawyer into uttering.

Liars are different. Liars lie habitually and deliberately; essentially they cannot be trusted, ever (even though they occasionally tell the truth). They know what's true, they disregard what's true, and they deceive anyway. I met many inmates who lied apparently because they had been trained to lie, trained as children, training that apparently was reinforced as they grew older. Even when the truth would have served them better, they just seemed to be unable to keep from dissembling. Others lie on purpose, they just seem to enjoy it, enjoy the manipulation and deception. And some lie, deliberately, for more base reasons: money, or fame, or influence. These lies are an evil... in my opinion.

> Not necessity, not desire - no, the love of power is the demon of men. Let them have everything - health, food, a place to live, entertainment - they are and remain unhappy and low-spirited: for the demon waits and waits and will be satisfied.
>
> -- Friedrich Nietzsche

I'm not claiming that the liars who afflict our body politic are evil people; I do not have standing to do so. I cannot see into their hearts, and I don't know what roads they traveled in life to arrive at their apparent need to lie. But adult liars are adults, responsible for their words and deeds.

As noted in the finish to the last chapter, we often take shortcuts in what we believe. We tend to believe those who seem similar to us, trusting that they have done the work necessary to discern the truth, to the degree that we value the truth. We are loyal to people whom we believe deserve our loyalty; we often have a default about what we believe and we will defer to others whom we trust, just because they appear to be on Our Team. If we are incorrect about the character of the persons we trust, we can end up believing spin and lies.

Unfortunately, both Trump supporters and never-Trumpers believe that the Other Side is being lied to by professional liars. Each side believes the other side is wrong; the other has bad opinions, and the other is being fed bad, incorrect 'facts.' All too often, issues that should really be outside the political sphere, such as public health measures and vaccines, have become politicized and thus vicariously become (un)fair game in that political arena, subject to the leanings of our elephants.

If both sides believe the other is not based in reality, and is forming opinions that are not based on facts, then we are at an impasse, as we seem to be in American discourse today. Neither side believes the other's sources of information. We are the victims of a self-inflicted sucking head wound, a cultural anarchy of intellect. Without common trust in either sources of information or means of determining reality, we seem doomed.

Yet there is room for hope. We have, and do, accept some sources of Truth, or as close an approximation of Truth as we can expect from other humans. We can do this. We have done so in the past, and we can do so again. Here are some examples.

Consider the National Transportation and Safety Board (NTSB); after they've investigated a plane crash and concluded that it was due to whatever, pilot error, or a software problem, or that there was or was not a bomb on board, their conclusions are pretty much universally accepted. Everyone seems to agree that since most of us fly on planes now and then (especially pilots!), even though it could make some short-term sense to try to cover-up or distort the truth about a crash, it's such a bad idea that we all accept that "They" aren't doing that. The NTSB zealously guards its *reputation* and will not allow deliberate misrepresentations of reality.

In courtrooms across the country (with notable exceptions such as the all-white juries of the Jim Crow era, or jury tampering or biases in jury selection, etc.), the jury process is still trusted by most. To paraphrase a trusted source (Captain Jean-Luc Picard), a courtroom is a crucible; in it we burn away impurities and are left with a pure product, the truth (within the constraints of the rules of evidence). We've seen that even very partisan citizens have been able to leave their political leanings at the door, listen to the evidence presented, evaluate it in accordance with the instructions from the judge, and arrive at a verdict that may run completely contrary to what you might expect given some jurors' admitted political prejudice.

Telling the truth is a feature of true professionalism. Not all doctors are wonderful, but whatever gripes one may have with the profession at large, most people trust their personal physician to have their interests foremost in mind and give them medical advice based upon their individual needs. Failure to do so, *betrayal* of that trust, is a most significant factor leading to lawsuits. Medical professionals and scientists traditionally are held in high regard. The recent further degradation in public opinion of scientists and researchers is a sad aberration, the result not only of politics creeping into science during the pandemic, but of a many years' long campaign against professionalism, against 'the elites'.

So how did we get here? We have at least to some degree a tradition that recognizes the value of facts and truth. Science pursues truth. Our schools are supposed to educate our young in truth, and in the critical thinking needed to find it. The profession of journalism is committed to seek out and verify and then report truth, often truth that powerful people would like to conceal. While lousy journalism is virtually synonymous with Fake News, the aspiration of good, unfettered journalism is so important to the health of the nation that the Founders enshrined it in the First Amendment to the Constitution. How then did we arrive at such a crisis of Fake News and disinformation, a climate wherein the President of the United States of America could call journalists the "enemy of the people"?

Rise of the crackpots

We have had lies and vicious spin in politics since we have had politics. Variations of the phrase "I'll stop telling the truth about them if they'll stop telling lies about me" date back at least to the 19th century. Passions have in the past been just as inflamed as they are now if not more so (think, Civil War). But while these passions at times lined up politically they only rarely lined up with our identities as they have now (as we saw in Chapter 2). Remember, we used to have liberal Republicans and conservative Democrats, etc.

In decades past, there was not the 'siloing' of news and information as there is now. We now have the option of withdrawing into "echo systems," bubbles which allow us to consume only that which exacerbates our belief and confirmation biases.

Within parties and political ideologies (which were not so identical as now), there was quality control that disallowed fringe elements from gaining too much traction. Liberals and the Democratic Party have had plenty of fringe characters and bomb throwers on the Left through the generations. Even today you can find YouTube clips of leftist anarchist types chanting "What do we want? Dead cops. When do we want it? Now!" and "Pigs in a blanket, fry 'em like bacon." (1) But if any liberal politician or TV personality said such a thing, he or she would be excommunicated immediately. In recent decades the Left-wing has been way behind the Right in leveraging the energies such fire-breathers can inject into politics. For that reason, for the moment I'll ignore the Democrats and the Left. The story of the conservative movement in the US is instructive.

By the 1950s conservatism in the United States was moribund, bereft of both intellectual heft and influence. One contemporary critic wrote, "The conservative impulse and the reactionary impulse do not, with some isolated and some ecclesiastical exceptions, express themselves in ideas but only in action or in irritable mental gestures which seek to resemble ideas." (2) Even the conservative lion William F. Buckley had disregard for the state of conservatives, writing that "when they are not being suppressed or mutilated by Liberals, they are being ignored or humiliated by a great many of those on the well-fed Right, whose ignorance and amorality have never been exaggerated for the same reason that one cannot exaggerate infinity." (3)

There were crackpots and conspiracy theorists back then too, folks who believed that "Alaska is being prepared as a mammoth concentration camp for pro-McCarthyites." (4) William F. Buckley and others took a stand though, asserting that conservatism must "be wiped clean of the parasitic cant that defaces it, and repels so many of those who approach it inquiringly." (5) With his platform at the National Review, he managed to play a key role in getting the John Birch Society (an outfit lead by Robert Welch, who made crazy accusations such as claiming that Eisenhower had been a secret agent of the communists) booted out of mainstream conservatism. Barry Goldwater agreed, saying that "we cannot allow the emblem of irresponsibility to attach to the conservative banner." (5)

Crackpots receded but did not disappear. In the 1970s rose the "New Right" (as we mentioned in discussing abortion), unhappy with what they viewed as the still robust vestiges of liberalism remaining in the GOP. They were attracted to George Wallace, despite, as author Kirkpatrick Sale wrote, Wallace having "no real policies, plans or platforms, and no one expects them of him… it is sufficient that he is agin and gathers unto him others who are agin, agin the blacks, the intellectuals, the bureaucrats, the students, the journalists, the liberals, the outsiders, the Communists, the changers, above all, agin the Yankee establishment." (6) Conservative writer and radio host Charles Sykes tells what happened next: "Ultimately the idea of backing Wallace fizzled out, when some of the calmer heads realized that would have meant an alliance with an unsavory coterie of crackpots, including anti-Semites and Holocaust deniers. But the flirtation with Wallace served to expose a soft underbelly of conservatism." (7)

Tension between the New Right and establishment conservatism persisted but was suppressed by the strength and communication skills of the rising Ronald Reagan. He held them together, espousing his 11th Commandment: 'Thou shalt not criticize another Republican.' Also, there was no significant right-wing media up through the 1980s. But then a couple of related things changed, the "Fairness Doctrine", and the collegiality of Congress.

In 1949 the Federal Communications Commission (FCC) had introduced the Fairness Doctrine, a policy that required holders of broadcasting licenses to present issues of public importance and to do so in a way that was truly fair and balanced. Further, it was a check on editorials and other commentary that constituted personal attacks. This doctrine worked well for almost forty years. It established so sensible a norm that it was only rarely enforced, as broadcasters behaved responsibly and almost universally adhered to the spirit of the policy. In response to one challenge in 1969, SCOTUS found that the doctrine did *not* threaten freedom of speech. Defining principles that could apply to today's social media or television or any other form of broadcasting, Justice Byron White wrote for the court:

> A license permits broadcasting, but the licensee has no constitutional right to be the one who holds the license or to monopolize a radio frequency to the exclusion of his fellow citizens. There is nothing in the First Amendment which prevents the Government from requiring a licensee to share his frequency with others.... It is the right of the viewers and listeners, not the right of the broadcasters, which is paramount.

The Court "ruled unanimously in 1969 that the Fairness Doctrine was not only constitutional but essential to democracy. The public airwaves should not just express the opinions of those who can pay for air time; they must allow the electorate to be informed about all sides of controversial issues." (8)

However, during the Reagan administration in 1987, the four commissioners of FCC (all appointed by Republicans) decided to revoke the doctrine, stating that "The intrusion by government into the content of programming occasioned by the enforcement of [the Fairness Doctrine] restricts the journalistic freedom of broadcasters ... [and] actually inhibits the presentation of controversial issues of public importance to the detriment of the public and the degradation of the editorial prerogative of broadcast journalists..." (9) and "Today we reaffirm our faith in the American people. Our faith in their ability to distinguish between fact and fiction without any help from government." With perspective gained in recent years, I do not believe those positions have aged well.

The Right was (and continues to be) much more dynamic and effective than the Left in its efforts to exploit the opportunities for political consequence afforded by the revocation of the Fairness Doctrine. If you're a conservative or Trump supporter, this is great: it's a bit of a sneaky exercise of raw power but that's how the game is played, all's fair in love and war and politics; your team was on the ball and ahead of the game, and the liberals were not... too bad for them. If you're a progressive, this is corrupt, contrary to the basic value of *Fairness* and damaging to the public good.

By the next year (1988) Rush Limbaugh was signed to a contract that syndicated his previously local Sacramento California radio program. Even though the Fairness Doctrine corollary "personal attack" and "political editorial" rules remained in effect, at least nominally, until 2000, from the inception of his syndicated radio program, Limbaugh used incendiary rhetoric that would have gotten him thrown off the air prior to 1987. And thus conservative talk radio as we recognize it today, the precursor to Right wing cable news, was born. (And with the exception of some faint wisps, there has never been anything analogous on the Left, which, whether because of a deliberate high-mindedness or through apathy or inattention or both, has essentially surrendered this arena to the Right... or as we'll see, because there is no good market for it on the Left.)

Enter Newt Gingrich. He replaced as Speaker of the House the late Bob Michel, Republican of Illinois known as 'Mister Nice Guy' for his ability to work respectfully (and effectively) with anyone. Gingrich's *Contract with America* was not content free, and the content was not new; but the sophistication of his campaign of inflammation *was* new. He created a playbook for his fellow Republicans. A pamphlet entitled *Language: A Key Mechanism of Control* (10), was sent to Republican candidates in 1990 complete with lists of words such as "anti-child, anti-flag, betray, corruption, disgrace, greed, hypocrisy, pathetic, shame, sick, steal, traitors." You'll recognize these terms as commonplace today, but they were not typical fare in elections of my youth; certainly such terms had not previously come packaged in a pamphlet with directions to "Apply these to the opponent, his record, proposals and party." They integrated with a new intransigence, an ideological purity enforced by right wing media which translated into a demonization of one's opponents and an unwillingness to engage in the staple of American democracy: compromise.

The GOP found success in releasing the Kraken. It riled up the base and the base turned out to vote. (The base also donated millions to Political Action Committees, many of which turned out to be scams that essentially pocketed the money.) Candidates vilified Democrats and described the terrible apocalyptic world we would see if Republicans didn't get elected to get in there and stop the radical leftist agenda, by repealing Obamacare and outlawing abortion, and so forth.

In 1944 Austrian-born economist Friedrich Hayek identified the preconditions for demagogues (11), writing:

> It seems to be almost a law of human nature that it is easier for people to agree on a negative programme, on the hatred of an enemy, on the envy of those better off, than on any positive task. The contrast between the "we" and the "they," the common fight against those outside the group, seems to be an essential ingredient in any creed which will solidly knit together a group for common action. It is consequently always employed by those who seek, not merely support of a policy, but the unreserved allegiance of huge masses....
>
> The enemy, whether he be internal like the "Jew" or the "Kulak," or external, seems to be an indispensable requisite in the armoury of a totalitarian leader.

(The sharp-minded readers of this book will remember the idea that we are selfish, and we are groupish.)

To progressives all this is evidence of moral bankruptcy and the descent of the GOP. But even the most progressive liberal cannot deny how effective the Republican Party has been. It is a minority party that often has control. It gets fewer votes, but more seats in Congress. It has structural advantages in the US Senate, with sparsely populated rural more conservative more Republican states having proportionately greater representation than more populous blue states, an advantage that is expressed as well in the composition of the Electoral College. In the six presidential elections of the 21st century, Republicans have won three, despite winning the popular vote only once. But those structural advantages do not exist in state and local elections. Yes gerrymandering has tilted the field in the favor of the GOP, but you can't gerrymander if you don't win statehouses that control redistricting, and winning those statehouses has been a greater priority for Republicans than for Democrats. So conservatives can taunt their liberal brethren: you snooze, you lose.

But there is no such thing as a free lunch. Once you release the Kraken, you must live with the results. Republican politicians over-promised and under-delivered. They demanded and threatened, speechified and pontificated; they could grandstand with a government shutdown, but that rarely accomplished anything beyond Ted Cruz reading *Green Eggs and Ham*. They failed in their signature priorities, accomplishments they'd claimed were essential to avoid calamity, for example, failing to repeal Obamacare, balance the budget, build the Keystone XL Pipeline, or outlaw abortion (that may change). The base was angry with these failures, as angry if not angrier at their failed Republican heroes than they were angry at Democrats.

Reagan's eleventh commandment evaporated. Republican politicians got traction by calling out other Republicans as RINOs who had betrayed the base. We've already explored how gerrymandering selects for the more extreme candidates within a party, because the gerrymandered district is 'safe' for the favored party; if you win the primary, you're almost certain to win the general, so there's no need to be moderate, just light your hair on fire and swing for the fences. Media unbridled after the revocation of the Fairness Doctrine coupled with explicit calls for scorched Earth politics were the undoing of the screening-out process put in place by the generation of Buckley and Goldwater: it was a recipe for the ascendance of crackpots.

"Betrayed isn't even the word here," said Rush Limbaugh, specifically about a budget compromise, but the theme was pervasive. "What has happened here is worse than betrayal, and betrayal's pretty bad, but it's worse than that. This was out and out in our face lying. From the campaigns to individual statements made about the philosophical approach Republicans had to all this spending. There is no Republican Party. You know, we don't even need a Republican Party if they're going to do this. You know just elect Democrats, disband the Republican Party and let the Democrats run it because that's what's happening anyway." (12)

Add in the dark money that has flooded politics since the 2010 *Citizens United* decision and there is every incentive for crackpots in both media and politics to fan the flames of division and negativity. One study found that negative ads in the presidential race had jumped from 9 percent in 2008 to 70 percent in 2012. (13) Even former governor of Arkansas conservative Republican and Baptist minister Mike Huckabee complained that such dark money is "killing any sense of civility in politics because of the cheap shots that can be made from the trees by snipers that you can never identify." (14)

Drawing the thread through this progression from outlandish promises through a sense of betrayal to the candidacy of Trump: "And these same Republican leaders doing this can't for the life of them figure out why Donald Trump has all the support that he has?" continued Rush Limbaugh. "They really cannot figure this out? Repeated stabs in the back like this, that have been going on for years, combined with Obama's policy destruction of this country is what's given rise to Donald Trump. If Donald Trump didn't exist and the Republican Party actually does want to win someday, they'd have to invent him." (15)

Cable news, and The Swamp, again

Television has changed since my pre-school and early school years when I was my Dad's remote, glad to get up and do something that he wanted me to do that I was perfectly competent at doing: twist the knob to change the channel from 2 (CBS) to 4 (NBC) or to 7 (ABC). (Adjusting the rabbit ear antennas was beyond me.) Those were the options. In so many ways TV is infinitely better now; in other ways, not so much. We shared trusted messengers then. Walter Cronkite had the Voice of God and when he said, "that's the way it is," that's the way it was. Americans had a shared frame of reference, shared facts; and journalism, while certainly not perfect, did a decent job of comforting the afflicted and afflicting the comfortable while sorting through and delivering the world's events in one half hour, and local events in another half hour. There were a few special political Sunday morning programs and weekly *Meet the Press*, but if you wanted to know more you had to read something, like a magazine or a newspaper, or even go to the library and check out a book. And it was clear when they were talking straight news, and when they were commenting.

Today's cable television news media need attract eyeballs to 24/7 programming, and so often portray the most extreme supporters of any position doing the most extreme things. That's not 'Fake News,' that's just always been the nature of the beast of journalism: dog bites man is not news, man bites dog is; if it bleeds it leads, etc. Most of us don't have close encounters with loud people with wild ideas on a regular basis, so seeing them on the news is interesting, which is perhaps by definition, newsworthy. Whatever channel we prefer tends to support our confirmation bias so we feel warm and fuzzy inside.

The polarized news and cable news phenomenon we know now is fairly new. A 2017 study in the *Columbia Journalism Review* (CJR) noted that of the main pro-Trump sites "only the *New York Post* existed when Reagan was elected in 1980. By the election of Bill Clinton in 1992, only the *Washington Times*, Rush Limbaugh, and arguably Sean Hannity had joined the fray. Alex Jones of Infowars started his first outlet on the radio in 1996. Fox News was not founded until 1996. Breitbart was founded in 2007, and most of the other major nodes in the right-wing media system were created even later." (16)

And again The Swamp raises its head. We see that the super-rich control what we see and hear. When Trump warned that "What you're seeing and what you're reading is not what's happening," he was somewhat correct. The voices, the beliefs, the agendas of the super-rich are amplified far beyond yours or mine, unless, as too many of us have, we adopt their agendas, turning them into yours or mine. The Mercer family poured millions of dollars into Breitbart, and into other sources of right wing orthodoxy supporting the usual suspects, such as lower taxes on the rich and the virtues of fossil fuels. Australian born Rupert Murdoch created Fox News, and while there are and have been legitimate journalists like Chris Wallace and Shepard Smith there, most of the content is not actually 'news,' it's opinion, spin. And no one is going to spin for long if they consistently run afoul of the intent of those who pay their salaries (unless they can play the role of the less credible foil).

The Swamp wants to divide and conquer.

The CJR study noted that "the right wing media system [had been turned] into an internally coherent, relatively insulated knowledge community, reinforcing the shared worldview of readers and shielding them from journalism that challenged it." Commenting on what have become known as "intellectual ghettoes", one reporter observed that "What's big news in one world is ignored in another. Conspiracy theories sprout, anger abounds and the truth becomes ever more elusive." (17)

As a result, the more engaged in political media you are, the more likely you are to be misinformed, especially about those who think differently than you do. One 2018 study noted that while "majorities of both parties' supporters are white, middle class, and heterosexual, and both parties modal supporters are middle aged, nonevangelical Christians," that's not the way we see each other. Researchers asked people "to estimate the percentage of Democrats who are black, atheist or agnostic, union members, and gay, lesbian or bisexual, and the percentage of Republicans who are evangelical, 65 or older, Southern, and earn over $250,000 per year," basically caricatures with which we are all familiar.

Author and commentator Ezra Klein describes the results:

"Democrats believed 44% of Republicans earned over $250,000 a year; it's actually 2%. Republicans believed that 38% of Democrats were gay, lesbian or bisexual; the correct answer is about 6%. Democrats believed that more than four out of every ten Republicans are seniors; in truth, seniors make up about 20% of the GOP. Republicans believed that 46% of Democrats are black and 44% belong to a union; in reality, about 24% of Democrats are African American and less than 11% belong to a union.

"But what was telling about these results is that... the more political media they consumed, the more mistaken they were about the other party....

"This is a damning result: the more political media you consume, the more warped your perspective of the other side becomes." (18)

If you're reading this book, there's a fair chance that you are a high-information voter, and a robust consumer of political media. That puts you at some risk.

Because The Swamp wants to divide and conquer.

> Every great cause begins as a movement, becomes a business, and eventually degenerates into a racket.
>
> -- Eric Hoffer, American philosopher

The morphing of television news broadcasting into mostly opinion and commentary is not isolated to the Right. Chris Hayes, the liberal host of MSNBC's *All In With Chris Hayes*, said "We have very strong metrics we get every day about how many people are watching our show. It is our job to get people's attention and to keep it. And getting people's attention and keeping it can sometimes be in tension with giving them information. There's an amazing Will Ferrell line in Anchorman 2, in which he says, 'What if instead of telling people the things they need to know, we tell them what they want to know?' Which is like the creation story of cable news.

"...we're wedding DJs. And the wedding DJ's job is to get you on the floor." (19)

It may be prudent to consider why you consume the media you consume. What is your intent? Because it is likely that cable news is giving you what you want it to give you.

Ezra Klein noted that "The political media is biased, but not toward the Left or Right as much as toward the loud, outrageous, colorful, inspirational, confrontational. It is biased toward the political stories and figures who activate our identities, because it is biased toward and dependent on the fraction of the country with the most intense political identities.

"Oh, and funny thing. So, too, is everyone else in politics." (20)

If 'telling people what they want to know' looks like wedding DJs on the left, it has developed a more militant appearance on the right. As Caleb Howe, former editor of the conservative website RedState said, "The problem, obviously, is that the talk/radio/conservative publishing/Fox opinion show model isn't about conservative policy and ideas, or good governance, or increasing our liberty, or social conservative values, or even really about the Constitution.... To a great extent, it is essentially about getting the audience outraged. Outrage clicks on links. Outrage tunes in. Outrage buys books." (21)

For all of its 'liberal bias,' it was the mainstream media that poured lighter fluid on the faintly glowing embers of the Trump campaign in 2015 and 2016. When he first came down the golden escalator his campaign had to hire actors to populate the crowd. He received millions upon millions of dollars' worth of free coverage just because he was polarizing, as outrageous as any professional wrestling villain. Contemporaneously, the chairman of CBS admitted that "It may not be good for America, but it's damn good for CBS.... It's a terrible thing to say, but bring it on, Donald. Keep going." (22)

But there have grown to be significant differences between mainstream media (if you're a Trump supporter, that's 'lamestream' or liberal media) and unabashed Trump supporting media, Fox or One America Network (OAN) or Newsmax. While some of the commentary on MSNBC or CNN for instance is hyperbolic and biased, such rhetoric is rarely presented as verified stand-alone fact. Rather, most of it is a synopsis or rehashing of stories from print media, often with interviews of the original print journalists committed to the principles of responsible reporting, such as having multiple sources to corroborate a story. Trumpers would counter that such 'journalism' is not valid; in a word, 'fake.'

Harvard researchers concluded that in 2016: "The leading media on the right and left are rooted in different traditions and journalistic practices. On the conservative side, more attention was paid to pro-Trump, highly partisan media outlets. On the liberal side, by contrast, the center of gravity was made up largely of long-standing media organizations steeped in the traditions and practices of objective journalism." (23) We see that MSNBC (and other mainstream and even left leaning media) has populated itself with a number of Republicans, from *Morning Joe* to Nicole Wallace in *Deadline White House*, who value traditional journalism. Ezra Klein notes that in his experience, while mainstream reporters do indeed tend to be liberal on cultural issues (such as, pro-choice), they're mixed in their views on economy and foreign policy. "Mainstream newsrooms are built around incentives that are different from, and often contrary to, liberalism as a political movement. The New York Times and ABC News fear a liberal reputation -- they want to be understood as neutral arbiters of truth -- and reporting oppositionally and inconveniently on the Democratic Party is both part of the self-identity and the business model."

But as we've analyzed, the details of policy issues have receded in the hearts and minds of partisans; the cultural issues, and these days the singular issue of Trump support versus Trump criticism, are often supreme in triggering identities and values. Whether or not a journalistic outlet is rigorous in seeking facts has become irrelevant for many. As Rush Limbaugh framed it: "We live in two universes. One universe is a lie.... Everything run, dominated, and controlled by the left here and around the world is a lie. The other universe is where we are, and that's where reality reigns supreme and we deal with it. And seldom do these two universes ever overlap."

"Conservative media activists advanced an alternative way of knowing the world, one that attacked the legitimacy of objectivity and substituted for it ideological integrity," wrote historian Nicole Hemmer, then of the University of Virginia. "That attack was embodied in their notion of 'liberal media bias,' which disputed not just the content presented by mainstream journalists but the very claims they make about their objective practices." (24)

Liberals see this as evidence that right wing media have no interest in calling balls and strikes because they are strictly biased toward Trump and have abandoned altogether the tenets of real journalism. David Roberts, a writer at *Vox*, calls this "tribal epistemology", writing that "...information is evaluated based not on conformity to common standards of evidence or correspondence to a common understanding of the world, but on whether it supports the tribe's values and goals and is vouchsafed by tribal leaders." This gets complicated; in essence he calls for the unbiased institutions of traditional journalism to take an anti-Trump stand, captured by the subtitle of his article: *Donald Trump and the Rise of Tribal Epistemology: Journalism Cannot Be Neutral Toward a Threat to the Conditions That Make It Possible*. (25) Trump supporters see this just as evidence of the liberal media saying the quiet part out loud, revealing that the libs have Trump Derangement Syndrome and are in league with the Deep State.

Since they're human beings, even the most professional of journalists make errors. But errors are a far cry from 'fake news.' Glenn Kessler of the *Washington Post* wrote "People seem to confuse reporting mistakes by established news organizations with obviously fraudulent news produced by Macedonian teenagers." (26) That is, there is a difference between mistakes, and lies.

The right wing echo chamber (including Trump) didn't run from fake news, but embraced it. Conservative radio host and author Charlie Sykes commented that "Having delegitimized much of the mainstream media, the Right had effectively also delegitimized the notion of 'fake news.'" (27)

In addition to those two phenomena (the provocation of outrage and the delegitimization of traditional reportage), there is another that is fairly unique to right wing media. That is, gaslighting, or more simply put, telling overt lies. We'll talk about conspiracy theories in a minute, but sometimes, anchors and commentators are unabashed about just telling lies. Examples abound, but I don't think there is much point in slogging through many of them. But one is illustrative, because it went to court, where you don't get to lie with impunity.

Michael Cohen was Trump's lawyer; you may recall that he was sentenced to prison for campaign finance law violations for his role in the hush money payments in the run-up to the 2016 election to porn star Stormy Daniels and former Playboy model Karen McDougal to keep secret Trump's affairs with them. Trump signed the checks; Cohen indicated that Trump had fully participated in the crimes, and Cohen's plea deal, while not calling out Trump by name, identified the unindicted co-conspirator "Individual 1" as the owner of the "New York City based real estate company" Cohen worked for, so, yeah, that'd be Donald Trump. Fox commentator Tucker Carlson was looking to support Trump by discrediting Michael Cohen.

Carlson told his viewers on Fox, "Remember the facts of the story. These are undisputed." He went on, "Two women approach Donald Trump and threaten to ruin his career and humiliate his family if he doesn't give them money. Now that sounds like a classic case of extortion." Pictures of the two women then were displayed on screen.

But, that wasn't what had happened. Now you can say whatever opinion you want on TV, that's protected speech. And you can tell lies and the government won't stop you. But if you deliberately tell lies on TV about someone who is not a public figure, you're likely to get sued. What Carlson said was not a fact, it was a lie. The truth was that Karen McDougal had never approached Trump to threaten or extort him. So, she sued Tucker Carlson for slandering her. And here's where it gets interesting. If you are a Trump supporter, you must admit that it is reasonable for liberals to find the events described below to be objectionable.

Carlson's lawyers argued, and the judge (a Trump appointee) agreed, that the "'general tenor' of the show should then inform a viewer that [Carlson] is not 'stating actual facts' about the topics he discusses and is instead engaging in 'exaggeration' and 'non-literal commentary....'

"Fox persuasively argues, that given Mr. Carlson's reputation, any reasonable viewer 'arrive[s] with an appropriate amount of skepticism' about the statement he makes.... Whether the Court frames Mr. Carlson's statements as 'exaggeration,' 'non-literal commentary,' or simply bloviating for his audience, the conclusion remains the same — the statements are not actionable." (28)

Even if you are a rabid Fox viewer and Trump supporter, you could understand that liberals hear the court telling everyone that 'you can't successfully sue him for lying about you, because his lawyers stipulate that he is a liar and his viewers should know that he is a liar, so you shouldn't be injured by his lies because no reasonable person would believe him.' One would think that if your profession is to speak on television to inform your audience, and you get caught lying, and it's not just a one-off but it's revealed that telling tales "full of sound and fury, signifying nothing" is your *modus operandi*, your career would be over. But no, he's still on the air and he's making $6 million a year, a lot more than you or I do.

There was a flaw in the judge's reasoning, in my opinion. While it may be true that his viewers *should* be expected *not* believe him, many if not most of them *do* believe him, implicitly. They look to him and his ilk for news. If you are a Trump supporter who believes Tucker Carlson, his own lawyers are telling the world, truthfully as officers of the court (under threat of disbarment or other penalty if they are lying to the court), that you either shouldn't believe Tucker Carlson, or you are not reasonable, not a "reasonable viewer". Another explanation could be that maybe you are inherently reasonable and you don't really believe him in your heart of hearts; but he's on your Team and you just want to own the libs more than you are committed to acknowledging the truth, so 'to hell with it, I'm going to believe him, or at least say that I do, or support him anyway, and the admission that he was lying was just lying lawyers working the system which is broken and doesn't work for me anyway.'

No surprise, there is a confluence of interest with The Swamp. Senator Whitehouse includes quotes from prominent conservatives:

"...commentator and author Jamie Weinstein wrote... 'the conservative movement may be nothing more than a collection of magazine offices and think tanks in Manhattan and Washington DC.' This collection I would add, is funded, run, and controlled by big money, not by little voters, so pushing big-money corporate agenda is easy to do. (Another glimpse of candor came from Romney chief campaign strategist Stuart Stevens, about the role of 'angry rich media figures' such as Sean Hannity and Rush Limbaugh in selling nonsense to the Republican base: 'they have made fortunes peddling bile and prejudice'; even if they are wrong, there is a lot of money to be made denying reality.'" (29)

Social media

Social media are cool, providing instantaneous communication with lots of people. There's a downside of course. If you're on social media, people can tend to get a little full of themselves and say things that they generally wouldn't say to a friend or relative face to face because it would be rude. But get behind the apparent anonymity of a keyboard and add a little righteous indignation and snark can become irresistible. Mea culpa, been there done that. And if someone responds in kind, or we get trolled, oh brother, we're on! And after you've hit 'Enter,' or 'Send,' it's too late.

But the upside, it's very cool. Little old me, I can say whatever I want, and if I say what a lot of people want to hear, I can blow up and be huge. I don't need a publisher, and I don't even need to be correct. Sometimes this is good for society, providing opportunity for anyone to lay claim to their long-neglected beliefs, a chance to bring to light something important that has been ignored or suppressed. But as Ezra Klein points out, social media also is "a channel through which racist lies and xenophobic demagoguery can travel as easily as overdue truths." (30)

If you want to go down to the park or a corner and stand on a soap box and spout lies or crazy stuff, you are at liberty to do so. Many people feel that it is their right as Americans guaranteed freedom of speech to have their post on Twitter or Facebook available for all to see. But there is nothing in the Bill of Rights that says that a lie must be amplified by social media platforms. The use of algorithms that amplify extreme content is in pursuit of profit, it is a business decision. Placing limits on those algorithms may not eliminate but would at least decrease the spread of hoaxes, lies, conspiracy theories, hate speech and Russian disinformation without injuring free speech in the slightest.

> In 1997, 14-year-old Nathan Zohner used the science fair to alert his fellow citizens of a deadly, dangerous chemical.
> In his report *Dihydrogen Monoxide: The Unrecognized Killer*, Nathan outlined all the alarming characteristics of the colorless, odorless, tasteless compound — DHMO for short — which kills thousands of Americans each year:
> - DHMO can cause severe burns both while in gas and solid form.
> - It is a major component of acid rain and often found in removed tumors of cancer patients.
> - DHMO accelerates corrosion of both natural elements and many metals.
> - Ingesting too much DHMO leads to excessive sweating and urination.
> - For everyone with a dependency on DHMO, withdrawal leads to death.

> After giving his presentation, Nathan asked 50 fellow students what should be done. 43 — a staggering 86% — voted to ban DHMO from school grounds.
> There was only one problem: Dihydrogen monoxide is water. (31)

The term 'Zohnerism' was coined to refer to the use of factual information to deceive the gullible. This example may seem benign enough, even funny.

Unfortunately, it is extreme content that tends to get amplified; in their unblinking electronic pursuit of profit, that's how the algorithms work. Unfiltered hate speech, conspiracy theories, overt lies and subtler misinformation can be crafted into clickbait that many find irresistible; those posts dictate what kinds of posts one will then see, further polluting their online information.

We have experienced that even the large, rich, free, and educated United States of America is not immune to amplified disinformation. The last few years have demonstrated that our public health (through COVID disinformation) and our democracy itself have been and are being undermined by mistakes, misinformation and lies on social media. How many of those who have died or been injured would not have been, save for the malignant effects of social media, is unknown.

When a person joins an extremist Facebook Group, sixty four percent of the time they do so because the platform recommended it. (32) Facebook acknowledges that at least 3 million persons have been members of pages and groups associated with QAnon extremism (33); arithmetic tells us that since Facebook helped radicalize some 64% of them, that's around 2 million people. The conglomeration of QAnon, MAGA, and the antivaxx movement has been facilitated by the platforms and policies of Facebook, YouTube, Instagram, and Twitter.

The platforms indicate that they do not want to be censors or be responsible for being arbiters of truth. But the amplification of lies, whether from the right or the left, from Trump or from the Russians, requires mitigation. So far the platforms continue to place a higher priority on their profits than they do on the health and safety of Americans. At this point the algorithms are continuing to injure people, and there is very little incentive for those who profit from that business model to address the harm they are doing. There should be incentive.

Chapter 14

Russians, Hoaxes, Climate Change... and "The Big Lie"

Trumpisms:

There is a lot of Fake information out there.

We need our country to be safe and secure.

We should all love our country.

His sell included:

Believe only me.

The Russians

There is no evidence that the Russians changed a single American vote in 2016 or in 2020. If you're a never-Trumper and you believe there is such evidence in the public domain, I'm sorry, but you're just wrong. No credible informed person is claiming such a thing. But that does not mean that the Russians did not influence the outcome of the election, and maybe influenced it a lot; we'll never know exactly how much, or whether their influence changed the outcome.

Apparently Vladimir Putin believes it is in his interest, as an autocratic dictator, to weaken the trans-Atlantic alliance of NATO, and to undermine Western democracies, especially that of the United States. The evidence for Russian intervention in the 2016 election is well-documented in the Mueller report (remember that?), by the testimony of Fiona Hill, and elsewhere.

If you're a Trump supporter and you believe the Mueller report either was all lies, or that it fully exonerated Trump, well, first, you're a bit conflicted there and you really should pick a horse, but aside from that, you may be willfully blind to evidence. It's easy enough to go online and read the indictments of the Russians who actuated the bots and trolls and committed crimes against our nation. The evidence is too voluminous to recapitulate here. Sometimes they paid in Russian rubles, which is pretty brazen; evidently they felt they could do so with impunity.

But in brief, the Mueller Report did say that "Russian intelligence officers who are part of the Russian military, launched a concerted attack on our political system.... The releases were designed and timed to interfere with our election and to damage a presidential candidate.... there were multiple, systemic efforts to interfere in our election. And that... deserves the attention of every American."

None of that by itself means that you are wrong to support Trump, were wrong to vote for Trump, or that Trump was not the legally elected President in 2016. He was. The fact that Russian state operatives were trying to influence the election, favoring Trump and damaging Clinton's chances, does not by itself mean that Trump did anything wrong or was/is a puppet of Putin.

Again from the Mueller Report: "The investigation established that the Russian government perceived it would benefit from a Trump presidency and worked to secure that outcome, and the [Trump] Campaign expected it would benefit electorally from information stolen and released through Russian efforts." But Trump doesn't control the actions of the GRU (and he could have just said as much while acknowledging and condemning what they were doing and saved himself a lot of grief), and while the buck should stop with him, we don't know what exactly he knew about what was going on with his campaign. You can understand why never-Trumpers see his behavior in Helsinki, note that he has insulted just about everyone except Putin, note all the contacts between Trump campaign personnel and Russians, and believe that where there's smoke there's fire, that there is some inappropriate reason for Trump to seem to be so beholden to Putin. If you're a Trump supporter, there are explanations for all that. I predict we won't be changing anyone's mind about any of that today.

But if you state unequivocally that the Russians did *not* influence the election, you may or may not be correct; but you cannot know that they didn't influence the outcome of the election. Lack of evidence for an effect is not the same as evidence for the lack of an effect. We know the Russians posted a lot of anti-Hillary material on social media that was shared and reposted millions of times. How many people that touched, how many were discouraged enough not to show up to vote for her in key districts, is not known, probably is not knowable, so we'll never know. But common sense tells us that the meddling did have some effect. That's why the Russians continued to do it. I think, it's my opinion, admittedly without adequate data to support it, that as a result of the Russian meddling, bots and trolls and fake ads etc., some Democrats and Hillary voters stayed home or voted third party or wrote in Bernie. And some voters who didn't want Trump went ahead and voted for him instead of her. Whether that was enough of the 120 million plus voters to change the 70,000 votes in three states that got Trump elected in 2016, we'll probably never know.

But one thing is perfectly clear: the government of Vladimir Putin is hostile to the democracy of the United States, and spreading disinformation that pits Americans against each other is in his playbook.

Hoaxes and conspiracy theories

During the run-up to the 2016 election, among the thousands of stories and posts, an article with this headline was shared on Facebook over half a million times: "FBI Agent Suspected In Hillary Email Leaks Found Dead In Apparent Murder-Suicide." The story was false, completely, never happened, no such FBI agent, nothing. Investigative reporters looked hard to learn how and why this story came about. They eventually found the man responsible for it, who dismissed them, but later agreed to be interviewed. He writes fake news stories (actually, he has a couple dozen writers working for him), and makes about ten to thirty thousand dollars a month from his advertisers by doing so. Regarding the dead FBI agent story, "The people wanted to hear this," he says. "So all it took was to write that story. Everything about it was fictional: the town, the people, the sheriff, the FBI guy. And then... our social media guys kind of go out and do a little dropping it throughout Trump groups and Trump forums and boy it spread like wildfire."

Asked if or when he noticed that fake news does best with Trump supporters, he replied: "Well, this isn't just a Trump-supporter problem. This is a right-wing issue. Sarah Palin's famous blasting of the lamestream media is kind of record and testament to the rise of these kinds of people. The post-fact era is what I would refer to it as. This isn't something that started with Trump. This is something that's been in the works for a while. His whole campaign was this thing of discrediting mainstream media sources, which is one of those dog whistles to his supporters. When we were coming up with headlines it's always kind of about the red meat. Trump really got into the red meat. He knew who his base was. He knew how to feed them a constant diet of this red meat.

"We've tried to do similar things to liberals. It just has never worked, it never takes off. You'll get debunked within the first two comments and then the whole thing just kind of fizzles out." (1)

Conspiracy theories abound. At times they are so readily disprovable that they seem to border on delusion, but most people who hold them are not at all psychotic; they are deluded, but not delusional.

There are conspiracy theories from all over the political spectrum, and many that are apolitical in American partisan terms, more anarchist. If you believe in chemtrails, or that the Moon landing was faked, or that 9/11 was an inside job by the Bush administration, or that there is no evidence that it was a plane that crashed into the Pentagon (there is conclusive evidence), you may or may not be on the left or the right.

But most conspiracy theories these days (at least most significant ones) have a distinctly partisan flavor, indeed, seem to be explicitly related to Trump in some way.

There are too many to count, but these are examples of what is out there:

"thousands Muslims on roofs in New Jersey" were cheering when the towers came down on 9/11; (2)

Hillary only won the popular vote because millions of illegal votes were cast; (3)

birtherism; Obama was born in Kenya, or Indonesia, but not Hawaii; (4)

hydroxyurea cures COVID-19;

Democrats are Satan worshippers drinking the blood of babies in a DC pizza parlor;

and so on, and on and on.

These have all been debunked, but live on, as their advocates double and triple down.

As we might learn from the comments of the fake news fellow quoted above, conspiracy theories or lies or bad spin on the left seem not to be as numerous nor so heartily held. For example, when then Senate candidate Jon Ossoff stated that Kelly Loeffler was campaigning with a member of the Ku Klux Klan, he was challenged by CNN's Jake Tapper, who correctly pointed out that while she had taken a picture with the former KKK fellow, it wasn't true that she was 'campaigning' with him. Ossoff did not double down; instead he deflected and made the point that the real concern was that such people were attracted to her and her campaign because of her racialized talking points etc. This moving of the goalposts can be exasperating but is different from an indissoluble attachment to a conspiracy theory, as at least he did not stick to the unsupportable notion that she was campaigning with a member of the Klan.

This is not to suggest that the left is populated exclusively by paragons of virtue, truth tellers free of dissembling. Charlie Sykes says that liberal spin and hyperbole have contributed to our current mess (albeit not as much as his own GOP's malfeasance) by having cried wolf. (5) He posits that by insisting in 2004 that George W. Bush was a racist and a warmonger, and in 2012 that Romney was a bigot, etc. liberals had expended their rhetorical ammunition, so that when they really needed to castigate the threat that was Trump, their adjectives and shrill warnings were met with a 'ho-hum' by many of the public who felt they'd heard it all before.

> Cry wolf often enough and everyone takes you for an imbecile or a knave, when after all there are wolves in this world. -
> - Russell Kirk to Robert Welch of the John Birch Society (6)

While the political conspiracy theories may have obvious impact upon political discourse, it may appear that many non-political tall tales serve no one, they're just wacky ideas being adopted by more or less wacky people. But there may yet be a through line, and to no surprise, it may travel through The Swamp.

For some decades now, a perspective that denies science and facts in general has grown in the US. Progressives see it as part of a coordinated effort to make people believe that the adverse changes in their lives are due to immigrants, minorities, growth of liberal values, etc., rather than to a systematic shift of economic and political power to the wealthiest. So, fossil fuels are OK because climate change is a hoax, the poor are responsible for their poverty because they're lazy cheating slackers, in-person voter fraud is rampant, government doesn't work and institutions are the enemy so you should be very angry, and those who champion liberals values are not trustworthy: Obama was born in Kenya, and Hillary is guilty of all manner of crimes. Progressives find that when you look under the hood, it's almost all nonsense, easily debunked, or innuendo and guilt by association (such as found in the book *Clinton Cash*). And unfortunately for the GOP and Fox news (not to mention the rest of us), this disregard for science and reality has created a Luddite monster in Trump, and he has escaped their control.

The Swamp doesn't need you to support their agenda. They just need you to be a bit conflicted about it, or to be confused enough not to know what action to take.

Money buys apathy. Money can buy confusion that leads to apathy; it has done so before, and it is doing so now. Because of our tribal nature, which has been exacerbated by the dynamics we've discussed, confusion in one area readily spreads into other areas. Policies that should have nothing to do with politics (like masks, and vaccines) have become intertwined with our values (such as *liberty* versus *oppression*) and identities. Tribal resistance that does not visibly help The Swamp, such as resistance to science-based public health measures, can readily bleed into resistance to other science-based measures to address, for instance, climate change; and that resistance does indeed help The Swamp.

Money can buy antagonism and enmity among kinsmen and countrymen, antagonism that saps the energies and ability of the electorate to come together to push back against The Swamp.

Climate change

We have an historical model that was employed by the tobacco industry. "The tobacco industry had a playbook, a script, that emphasized personal responsibility, paying scientists who delivered research that instilled doubt, criticizing the 'junk' science that found harms associated with smoking, making self-regulatory pledges, lobbying with massive resources to stifle government action, introducing 'safer' products, and simultaneously manipulating and denying both the addictive nature of their products and their marketing to children." (7)

As a former head of the FDA wrote, "Devised in the 1950s and '60s, the tobacco industry's strategy was embodied in a script written by the lawyers. Every tobacco company executive in the public eye was told to learn the script backwards and forwards, no deviation was allowed. The basic premise was simple—smoking had not been proved to cause cancer. Not proven, not proven, not proven—this would be stated insistently and repeatedly. Inject a thin wedge of doubt, create controversy, never deviate from the prepared line. It was a simple plan and it worked." (8)

And the tobacco industry had a point. You cannot perform a placebo controlled clinical trial, randomly assigning one group of people to smoke for years and another not to smoke. It would be unethical and impractical. So no one can show definitive conclusive 'proof' that a given case of lung cancer was caused by the patient smoking three packs a day for 30 years, or even that smoking causes lung cancer; yet these days no one disputes that connection. It is a scientific consensus based upon a preponderance of good evidence. And cherry-picking an article that might show a bunch of people smoking a lot and not getting lung cancer doesn't affect that consensus.

The same model, counterfeit science, the use of benign neutral sounding organizations (like *Americans for Puppies and Free Cable*) to beard for the industry, and hiding the money trail so that fossil fuel funding is not readily seen, has been employed to create doubt and confusion regarding climate change.

Drexel University's Robert Brulle, professor of sociology and environmental science, has documented that "Some of the same people and some of the same organizations that were involved in the tobacco issue are also involved in climate change." (9) The Koch brothers "poured almost $25 million into dozens of different organizations fighting climate reform." (10) Brulle reported that "140 foundations [made] grants totaling $558 million [not adjusted for inflation] to 91 organizations" effecting opposition to climate change science and action, between 2003 and 2010. (11)

At over half a billion dollars, the fossil fuel industry must have reason for such a huge investment. And they do; the Office of Management and Budget (OMB) determined the economic, social and health costs of carbon emissions at $45 (2015 dollars) per metric ton; 6.9 billion metric tons emitted per year means $310 billion in costs, or "negative externalities" that are passed on to us non-super-rich citizens each year. (12) The International Monetary Fund, accounting for other negative externalities, placed the costs at closer to $700 billion per year. (13) So the half a billion dollars doesn't seem so much to spend if the result is a subsidy of between $310 and $700 billion, about a thousand to one return on investment.

Attacks on climate science are coming ostensibly from people who do not like the policies that have been proposed to fight global warming. The 'scientific' arguments made by these groups (AKA, The Swamp) usually involve cherry-picking data, such as focusing on short-term blips in the temperature record or in sea ice, while ignoring the long-term trends. These attacks typically do not address either the policies or the science, but rather just try to subvert the persons and the processes of the science.

Selected climate deniers, including politicians, assert that climate scientists have conspired (thus, 'conspiracy theory') to deceive the public so that government can expand, control lives and deny liberty to the people. (14) This canard triggers the *Liberty* versus *Oppression* moral foundation.

If you are a never-Trumper, you probably favor measures to mitigate climate change, and you don't understand those who oppose you. Consider these points in understanding your Trump-supporting (and what you would call 'climate denying' countrymen): they believe that the science behind climate change is not to be trusted because they have been told so by trusted messengers, and they feel that their economic well-being and more important, their *liberty* is being threatened by those who want to address climate change.

The purpose of the misinformation is to allow those leaning toward the Red Team pro-Trump climate-change-is-a-hoax-or-at-least-unproven camp to ask themselves:

Must I believe that climate change is happening, and is caused by human activity, and can be successfully addressed by climate reform policies, or

Can I believe that any one of those points is in doubt, and thus relieve myself of any responsibility in dealing with it?

> Those who corrupt the public mind are just as evil as those who steal from the public purse. (15)
>
> - - Adlai Stevenson

Liberals and environmentalists have tons of information to support their perspective. The latest IPCC report just said 'red alert'. (16). But this is an uphill push. As I write this book there are people so embedded in their tribal interpretation of events that as they are dying of COVID, they maintain with literally their last breaths that they do not have COVID, that COVID is a hoax. Analogously, even though we see evidence of climate change happening today, it can be difficult to expect people to do something about climate change now, much less over the far time horizon, when you can't even get people to take a vaccine that saves lives today. Consider the following from a medical related post on social media.

> Climate change is like having a mole excised and it turns out to be a melanoma, and the margins aren't clear. Is it an emergency? Do you need a wide excision this afternoon? No. In fact, you could just sit tight and do nothing for a week or three and that delay would have no

effect. Indeed, a year or more from now, you may still feel fine; until you have your pathologic fracture or stroke from metastatic disease.

There is a window of opportunity to address the emissions fueling climate change. For some, that window may already be closed. CO2 levels are higher now than they've been in over a half million years. Some Pacific Islands, parts of the Sahara and Sub-Saharan Africa and Bangladesh, many coastal areas even in the US are forecast to be essentially uninhabitable in some couple or few decades. Even without foot-dragging and climate deniers, with the most robust efforts, it will take years to reduce emissions, and decades or more after that for climate effects to be mitigated. So, yes, for some people, and to a lesser or later degree for all the rest of us, the sky is indeed falling due to climate change.

But what do we Americans care about North Africans and Bangladeshis? Aside from the humanitarian aspects, if you care about national security you should note that some of the areas destined to be hardest hit have predominantly Muslim populations. Climate change and drought in Syria have already catalyzed civil war, creating ungoverned spaces, and terrorism. If you think Jihadism is a threat now, wait until tens to hundreds of millions of young, poor, angry, Muslim Bengalis and Nigerians etc. are displaced. So while someone may think his little mole is far from the most serious threat he faces, and the dramatic day-to-day headlines command his attention, ignoring the mole doesn't stop it from killing him. With every day's delay, if we don't act now, the actions required later will be more difficult, less effective, and more economically disruptive for our children and grandchildren.

Aside from the problem that it is not possible to determine a causal relationship between climate change writ large and a specific weather event (which is what we all experience after all, weather), there is the larger context of distrust of science and institutions. As per yet another social media post (pre-Trump) from a progressive to someone he identifies as a climate skeptic, these include conclusions that:

1) science doesn't work, the grant application and peer review processes that have given us so many advances for decades are good for pharmaceuticals (no money involved there) and everything else, but are corrupted for climate research, climate scientists are apparently able to falsify their data with no adverse consequences to their careers

(in which case, where would you turn to learn the truth? The fossil fuel industry? Politicians supported by PACs funded by the fossil fuel industry? Talk radio? Why would anyone trust them over scientists? I don't get it, unless it's just, 'whatever Obama is for, I'm against.') or

2) science does work, but there is no consensus, just as many scientists deny the risks of climate change as warn of it, which is demonstrably false, indicating that most scientists do not agree on the risks of catastrophic consequences, which is again demonstrably false.

Certain facts are known [quotes from the IPCC] and not in dispute:

1. Greenhouse gases (GHGs) raise temperature;

2. CO2 levels are higher than they've been in over half a million years;

3. We have already seen global higher temperatures;

4. "The current rise of atmospheric CO2 at a rate of near-three parts per million per year exceeds rates recorded in the history of the atmosphere for the last 55 million years, which retards the ability of species to adapt to environmental change in time,"

5. Multiple times in the remote past, "As the level of energy and temperature of the atmosphere increased, irreversible tipping points were reached where the synergy of feedback processes – ice melt, warming water, released methane, droughts and fires - combined to shift the climate from one state to the next;"

6. We are continuing to emit vast quantities of CO2 into the atmosphere, CO2 previously trapped underground in fossil fuels which will now stay in the atmosphere and oceans irreversibly, for centuries.

Now we come to the part about which there is indeed consensus but that has not yet been "demonstrated," the warnings that apparently you reject. Tell me if I'm wrong, but you seem to believe that despite those six points above, we are not at risk, not in 30 years, not in a 100 years, we do not have to worry about our progeny, no catastrophic changes will happen, these phenomena present no more danger than an age spot. Is that a fair recap of your opinion?

I don't understand which part of the climate change consensus is so objectionable. Are we humans not generating millions/billions of tons of greenhouse gases that go into the atmosphere? Are atmospheric CO2 levels not now higher than they have been in human history (by tens of thousands of years of Antarctic ice specimens)? Are those gases not known to trap infrared energy and cause a greenhouse effect? Have temperatures not risen? Have glaciers not retreated, sea levels not risen? Have oceans not become more acidic and warmer? Warmer water feeds stronger hurricanes; higher seas exacerbate storm surge, etc. How much more warming, how many more unprecedented extreme climate events must occur before you would recognize that the changes predicted by the climate science models are happening now? In science it is incumbent upon the critic to supply a better model; the question is not 'are we positive' or 'do we have proof,' but rather, what other competing hypothesis explains what we are experiencing? What is the evidence for that hypothesis? I don't hear any rational argument. What I do understand is that climate change and the threat it presents should be an issue championed by conservatives who believe that we humans should be responsible custodians of the world on which we live and which we will hand off to our descendants. Instead, the issue has become a surrogate for the tribal divisions that characterize our discourse. Big Oil and big donors have succeeded in obfuscating the issue using the same old tobacco industry playbook, and getting quite a few people to act against their own interests. If liberals favor something, even if the weight of evidence supports it, it must be resisted, and if some progressive snowflakes are discomfited, all the better.

A friend of mine recently seemed to get angry with me and my persistent questions and 'challenges,' I think he took them personally, like it's a competition on Facebook to win arguments. I don't need to "win;" nobody really cares what we write on Facebook, it's not going to affect anything one way or the other and if that were the point, it'd be a complete waste of time. I just want to understand points of view that are different from mine so I might learn something. The only way to do that is to ask and ask and ask reasonably intelligent people why they believe what they believe. I think the person who changes his mind after such a discourse is the one who 'wins,' so I'd love to be convinced. But it's perfectly legitimate to say, 'I'm happy with what I believe and I don't have the time or energy to do research to support my position and address all this stuff.' I think that's what most people do most of the time all their live-long days.

Progressives hear climate skeptics' arguments and it sounds like this:

Any information, any study, any review, any published research that affirms the consensus among climate scientists that climate change exists and that human activity is the major driver of it, must be false because it comes to our attention through the 'corrupt media'. So it is not possible to access any information generated through scientific methods executed by the experts in the field. And presumably if we could bypass the media and access such a consensus, the consensus cannot be trusted because the scientists also are corrupt (except the small minority, mostly non-climatologists, who assert that anthropogenic climate change is not real). Because national and international organizations such as the UN, NASA, NOAA, etc., and all the world's governments ranging from communists, liberal socialists, right wing nationalists, democracies both liberal and illiberal, representative or totalitarian, Islamic theocracies, from Norway to Iran to North Korea, all have adopted the 'left's worldwide agenda' to promote the false idea of climate change. Rather, unsupported blanket statements such as "It is an oversimplification to say that human activities are the main driving force behind global warming" are to be taken as Truth.

It should be no surprise that progressives don't buy those arguments.

So, as I wrote a couple pages ago, liberals and environmentalists have tons of information to support their perspective. There are websites dedicated to topics like "How to Talk to a Climate Skeptic" (17) There, criticisms of climate science, such as 'climate change existed before humans' and 'they named Greenland because it used to be green,' are addressed.

But once again, all this rational argument falls on deaf ears if the contrary party is operating from the perspective that interventions to address climate change limit his freedom or *liberty*; or, if he is just identified with his tribe. And once again to demonstrate the importance of tribal identification over the actual content of policy, consider this excerpt from a full page advertisement run in the *New York Times* in 2009, calling for action by the Obama administration:

> We support your effort to ensure meaningful and effective measures to control climate change, an immediate challenge facing the United States and the world today. Please don't postpone the Earth. If we fail to act now, it is scientifically irrefutable that there will be catastrophic and irreversible consequences for humanity and our planet. (18)

That advertisement was signed by Donald Trump (as well as Don Jr., Eric, and Ivanka). (19)

Again, The Swamp, as noted by Senator Whitehouse:

> The big polluters aren't just polluting our atmosphere and oceans, they're polluting our democracy, with misinformation and money. They're doing it purposely. The *Wall Street Journal* editorial page, and the whole denial apparatus, has been wrong every time they've gone down this road: wrong about tobacco, wrong about lead paint, wrong about acid rain, wrong about mercury, wrong about the ozone layer, and now wrong about climate change. Yet they keep going there. Being wrong over and over doesn't seem to bother them. If being right mattered to them, or to the corporate interests behind them, they'd reassess what they do. So you have to wonder if they don't mind being wrong. Maybe it's not their intention to be right. Maybe it's much more cynical than that. Maybe the point is simply to create doubt, buy time, and maximize profits. (20)

"The Big Lie"

Unless you've been living under a rock, you are aware that Trump claims, and a majority of Republicans believe, that Trump actually won the 2020 presidential election, and that Joe Biden is only president because of widespread voter fraud.

If you're progressive, consider the Trump supporters' position on this. They have been told for years that the mainstream media are liberal and are not to be trusted. They have been ripped off by The Swamp, they know it, they feel it, and they believe that the only person who has given voice to that reality is Donald Trump. He is the One they can believe. And, he was the duly elected President of the United States in 2016! And since then, to their minds he's done a great job so of course he would be re-elected.

When the President warns you about an existential threat to our nation, you sit up and take notice. When I grew up, there was no more trusted source of information than the President. When Trump warned for months in 2019 and 2020 that the upcoming election was going to be rife with fraud, and then he 'loses' the election and cries foul, he is only confirming that which he had previously predicted. That's enough to believe in The Steal; but that's not all.

Trump's contentions have also been echoed by conservative media, which, as we've analyzed, is often the only source of news for a large segment of society. Widely trusted figures in society (formerly trusted for many), such as Rudy Giuliani and Republican leaders, have contributed to these concerns, by either overtly supporting Trump's claims, or by obliquely acquiescing to them, or neglecting to refute them.

In any case, it becomes easy for Trump supporters to answer affirmatively to the question, '***can* I believe** Trump was cheated?'

And negatively to, '***must* I believe** the election was fair?'

Most of us have had the experience that there are some things we're just not good at, and so we work hard to get better at it, or, if we don't particularly care for it or need it, we just let it go. But we've all known people who were bad at something, but somehow, they didn't *know* they were bad at it. This is called the Dunning-Kruger Effect. Indeed, even though they're bad at it, they may think they're really good at something, just crushing it. If you want to see this in action, go to a karaoke bar. Psychologist David Dunning wrote: "The knowledge and intelligence that are required to be good at a task are often the same qualities needed to recognize that one is not good at that task — and if one lacks such knowledge and intelligence, one remains ignorant that one is not good at the task. This includes political judgment." (21) This is in part why some people are not just misinformed, but they don't know that they're misinformed, so they don't have the motivation to become informed because they think they're correct, period.

Neuroscientist Bobby Azarian lists three additional elements that contribute to strength of support for Trump and his positions. (22)

First is hypersensitivity to threat. We already noted back in chapter 3 that there is not just belief and bias involved in our politics, but biology. The amygdala, the part of the brain associated with perceiving threats, is larger in conservatives (new things are dangerous, stay away from them, don't change, keep what you've got). (23) Brain scans show that neural responses to disgusting images like mutilated bodies is highly predictive of political orientation. (24) Conservatives are more strongly affected, so rhetoric that evokes the image of Muslims or Mexicans (or Democrats!) as dangerous invaders or threats tends to trigger those underlying predispositions.

Second is "Terror Management Theory". The evocation of death (such as via invaders, vermin, 'American carnage', 'you walk down the street and get shot', etc.) has the effect of moving people to the right politically, increasing nationalism (25) and strengthening support for extreme military interventions (fire and fury, or Bush's Axis of Evil, or the Ayatollah's Great Satan, etc.) (26) and enhancing the tendency to vote for conservative candidates (27).

And third is "High Attentional Engagement". Not all of radio shock jock Howard Stern's listeners like him; many reported that even though they didn't like him, they listened, just to hear what he would say next. If you're a never-Trumper, admit it, you often can't help yourself when Trump is on TV. You find it a guilty pleasure to see him gesticulating foolishly, hear him mangle sentences and paragraphs and make misogynistic, racist, and divisive comments. You cry out to the television, 'Did you hear that? How stupid can he be?' And so forth. Biden is downright boring by comparison (which many find to be a blessing). Almost everyone finds Trump riveting, and his supporters are on the edge of their seats wanting more.

These phenomena: the Dunning-Kruger Effect, hypersensitivity to threat, Terror Management Theory, and high attentional engagement; are mechanisms that at least in part underlie the manifestation of our passions, making decisions that our reason then later justifies. So, many Trump supporters believe what Trump and others tell them about Democrats hating our country and wanting to destroy it.

If that stuff is true, then anything goes:

Storming of the Capitol by 'patriots', stopping the counting of the Electoral College votes, suppressing the votes of minorities; anything goes, everything is justified. According to the echo chamber of Trump supporting media, the insurrection was actually just Antifa, and voter suppression measures are actually 'voter integrity' measures. The ends justify the means. We are in crisis, and we need a Man On A Horse, to Save Us, and That Man is Trump.

QAnon is an extreme case of this same phenomenon, with more explicit cult-like features. On its surface it seems to be a semi-secret movement frantic about satanic rituals, drinking the blood of babies, rooting out the pedophilia and cannibalism being practiced by Democrats supported by the Deep State. It's so over the top it's laughable. But fundamentally it is a response to the message that there are evil forces and people, and they are to blame for why your life is not as good as it should be. And now you know, you have been let into the Secret, you are no longer among the sheeple but have joined the solution, you can make your life better and participate in saving the world from the malevolent forces at work. The purpose of socializing such ideas and mobilizing masses of people is not just to go after immigrants or minorities, that's small potatoes. The value is in having a cadre of people who can be directed anywhere, who will accept just about any premise if it comes from the Great Leader, and who are willing to do just about anything. As Voltaire noted in the epigraph beginning this chapter, such people can be so radicalized as to be willing to commit atrocities. In these ways it is like a religion, one gone awry.

Liberals often just cannot get their heads around QAnon and some MAGA folks. How can they believe this stuff? They may believe, or they may be uncertain, or they may not even be clear on what the specifics are that one needs to believe to be part of QAnon. But here's the kicker:

It doesn't matter.

QAnon, and the more outrageous cult-like aspects of Trump support, do indeed share a characteristic with religion:

It is more about belonging than belief.

I saw the acronym of the motto of QAnon on a bumper sticker recently:

WWG1WGA ; that is, Where We Go One, We Go All. If ever there was an explicit cry for solidarity in a community, that would be it.

A number of persons who have been arrested for crimes related to their participation in storming the Capitol on 6 January 2021 have experienced the sobering bucket of ice water that is associated with answering charges in federal court, and have come to recognize that they had been deceived. "'I kind of sound like an idiot now saying it, but my faith was in him,' defendant Anthony Antonio said, speaking of Trump. Antonio said he wasn't interested in politics before pandemic boredom led him to conservative cable news and right-wing social media. 'I think they did a great job of convincing people.'" (28) But that is the exception rather than the rule, even among those faced with the crisis of criminal charges. The vast majority of others appear to remain steadfast in their sense of belonging. Carl Sagan observed:

> One of the saddest lessons of history is this: If we've been bamboozled long enough, we tend to reject any evidence of the bamboozle. We're no longer interested in finding out the truth. The

> bamboozle has captured us. It's simply too painful to acknowledge, even to ourselves, that we've been taken. Once you give a charlatan power over you, you almost never get it back. (29)

Liberals then should be able to understand the thinking of Trump supporters. Many are genetically predisposed to react strongly and 'favorably' (that is, supportive of Trump) to his messaging, their fundamental moral imperatives are triggered, their elephants have determined their perspectives. As of March 2021, one poll showed that 75% of Republicans believe Trump won the 2020 election, and some 43% believe it was OK to storm the Capitol. (And 17% of Americans believed in vampires, so there's that....) But there is a difference between Trump supporters, and GOP elites and politicians, and we'll consider them in just a bit.

If you are a Trump supporter, you should have no problem understanding the perspective of those who do not believe that the election was stolen, **if** you care to... and I know that's a big "if." As with climate change, or voter fraud touched upon in the previous chapter, liberals have plenty of data to support their position.

The 'Stop the Steal' arguments are not new. The GOP has for years laid the groundwork by claiming without proof that Democrats cannot win without voter fraud. But voter fraud is rare (and in-person voter fraud vanishingly so). When Kris Kobach was Secretary of State of Kansas, he sought and received special powers to prosecute voter fraud cases, because he had claimed he knew of so many. He ended up with six prosecutions, of which four were successful. He later became the head of Trump's commission on voter fraud. He reported having found that, of 84 million votes cast in 22 states, there were 14 cases referred for prosecution. (30) With no retraction or recognition of the fundamental misinformation that inspired it, the commission faded away.

But let's get back to the progressive view of the 2020 election claims. There are a handful of non-claim claims such as, Trump must have won because Biden stayed in his basement, and Trump had bigger crowds, and Trump was leading early on so the shift in that lead must have been due to cheating, and mail-in ballots are inherently subject to fraud, because... and so forth. There is nothing to disprove because these phrases and statements don't really mean anything except to those who opt to give them meaning by inferring fraud.

The substantive claims are broadly that widespread voter fraud swayed the election away from Trump, that dead people and illegal aliens voted in numbers large enough to change the outcome, that Dominion voting machines had a glitch or a flaw or were hacked by China or by Venezuela or by Italy to change votes from Trump to Biden, that some states had more votes than they had registered voters, that pandemic related changes to voting procedures and mail-in voting were unconstitutional, and perhaps some other complaints.

This is so topical that you can easily investigate it all yourself, but the top line is that there has been no evidence of voter fraud widespread enough to affect the outcome of the presidential election of 2020. Per the US Constitution, state legislatures create the rules, change the rules, assign authority to election officials, as they see fit. (So when Ohio Congressman Jordan claims that states have acted unconstitutionally, he should know better... perhaps he's lying.) The Lieutenant Governor of Texas offered a reward of a million dollars to anyone who could find evidence of voter fraud. As of this writing, the only person who's claimed the reward was the Lieutenant Governor of Pennsylvania, who found a fellow who cast a vote for Trump on behalf of his dead mother. (He didn't collect the reward.)

At the back end of the process, state governors (like the Republican governors of Georgia and Arizona etc.) certify the results of their elections. In between, election officials of both parties across the nation run the elections and count the votes. If the numbers are close at all, they do recounts. Or, candidates can request recounts. Republican election officials who supported Trump have verified that their elections were correctly run and their results are accurate.

The final arbiter of election disputes becomes the courts. Over 60 Trump cases challenging the election results have failed in court due to having no evidence. Lawyers for the Stop the Steal folks admit in court, where they cannot deliberately misrepresent facts to the judge, that they do not have evidence of voter fraud. Some lawyers have been disciplined for bringing these frivolous cases.

In her decision in Michigan U.S. District Judge Linda Parker said, "This lawsuit represents a historic and profound abuse of the judicial process," and that the case "was never about fraud - it was about undermining the People's faith in our democracy and debasing the judicial process to do so." The judge said that the Trump lawyers "have scorned their oath, flouted the rules, and attempted to undermine the integrity of the judiciary along the way." (31)

Rudy Giuliani admitted in a deposition under oath that he didn't actually check to see if anything he was claiming was true, he didn't actually interview the witness he said had bombshell information (he said he didn't know if anyone had interviewed such a witness), got most of his information about the 'stolen election' and 'voter fraud' from social media, and essentially did not have a basis for the claims he made. (32)

The Cyber Ninja Arizona 'audit' ended up finding (assuming they actually knew what they were doing) slightly more votes for Biden than the original election results. Mike Lindell (the MyPillow CEO) claimed with no basis that there was voter fraud in Idaho; he claimed that *all* Idaho counties had experienced electronic computer manipulation that switched votes from Trump to Biden. Despite lawmakers noting that seven counties in Idaho *have **no** computerized electronic steps in their voting procedures,* they decided to spend taxpayer money investigating the claims. They found no significant discrepancy, just that Biden had a few more votes than he had had immediately after the election.

I am not trying to be divisive here. I hope that the chapters on The System is Rigged and Drain The Swamp presented plenty of reasons why anyone could support Trump, reasons that even liberals might appreciate. My point here is just that the reasons above, whether presented by Giuliani, the Trump lawyers, the MyPillow CEO, or Tucker Carlson, are not among those good reasons. My suggestion for Trump supporters is, respectfully: stick to good reasons for supporting him, not false ones.

Republican lawmakers are not (that I know of) particularly stupid, and they are (or should be) the consumers of the highest quality political information in the country. The short version is, reporting indicates that many if not most Republican members of Congress know better, they know that Joe Biden won, that 'Stop the Steal' is based on nonsense. How can we understand the shift of the GOP from the party of law and order, the party of Lincoln, to the party of Trump and misinformation?

Conservative Charles Sykes quotes Pulitzer prize winner Bret Stephens (33), formerly conservative columnist for the *Wall Street Journal,* now for the *New York Times*. Observes Sykes: "Stephens compared the Trumpian apologists to the postwar Polish communists described by Czeslaw Milosz in his book, *The Captive Mind*. Milosz's colleagues were not coerced into becoming Stalinists, but actually made the transition willingly."

Said Stephens:

> They wanted to believe. They wanted to adapt. They thought they could do more from the inside. They convinced

> themselves that their former principles didn't fit with the march of history, or that to hold fast to one's beliefs was a sign of pig-headedness. They felt that to reject the new order of things was to relegate themselves to irrelevance and oblivion. They mocked their former friends who refused to join the new order as morally vain reactionaries....
>
> I fear we are witnessing a similar process unfold among many conservative intellectuals on the right.... [The] mental pathways by which the new Trumpian conservatives have made their peace with their new political master aren't so different from Milosz's former colleagues....
>
> There's the same desperate desire for political influence; the same belief that Trump represents a historical force to which they ought to belong; the same willingness to bend or discard principles they once considered sacred; the same belief that you do more good by joining than by opposing; the same fear of seeming out of touch with the mood of the public; the same tendency to look the other way at comments or actions that they cannot possibly justify; the same Manichean belief that, if Hillary Clinton had been elected, the United States would have all-but ended as a country.

Progressives point out that, regarding the Big Lie, you may notice that the goal posts have moved. Jordan and Hawley and Cruz etc. are often no longer claiming election fraud. Rather, after months of upsetting and confusing people by spreading misinformation about it, they now say that people are upset and confused and don't trust the election processes, so we need investigations about that. (That is some impressive *chutzpah*.)

Republican senator Mitt Romney identified the remedy: "Tell them the truth!" Republican senator and Trump golf partner Lindsay Graham said "They claim tens of thousands of fraudulent ballots, but they can't produce even one. It's over." Even Trump's handpicked former Attorney General William Barr said there was "no evidence" of widespread voter fraud.

A never-Trumper proposed this thought experiment. 'If you are a Trump supporter, ask yourself: if the insurrectionists had stopped the presses, violated the Constitution and stopped the counting in Congress of electoral votes certified by the states, and/or if GOP Congressmen had their ten day emergency audit (which has already been done in and by the states), and the result was, yep, free and fair election, Biden won; would you accept that? Or is your mind closed to that possibility? What do you believe Trump would have said about such a result? Trump would say it was rigged, and you would believe him. Am I wrong?'

Umberto Eco was an Italian scholar and novelist who grew up as a fascist youth in the 1940s. In 1995 (when fascism wasn't anywhere so much a thing, and long before the rise of Trumpism) he wrote an article "Ur-Fascism" (or 'Eternal' or 'Proto-Fascism,') in which he identified 14 key elements of fascism. (34)

If you're a Trump supporter who just doesn't understand "Trump Derangement Syndrome", who doesn't get how never-Trumpers can be so opposed to Trump, it's worth a brief review. Trump supporters almost certainly won't agree with never-Trumpers but should be able to see how never-Trumpers view Trump shining through in each of the attributes of fascism, as noted below, and thus regard him as an existential threat to our democracy. Remember, this article is from the 1990s, not something that was dreamed up recently to make Trump look bad. Of course these points individually are not diagnostic of fascism (for instance, number six below has a sound basis in reality), but they can be exploited by those with fascist tendencies.

Whether or not you accept that they could be applied to Trump, **we should all be able to agree that, if these attributes accurately describe anyone now or in the future, that person should not be a candidate for high office** in the United States of America.

Quotes are from Eco's essay unless obviously otherwise, such as easily recognized quotes from Trump.

1. The cult of tradition. Never-Trumpers see this in Trump: We don't need any new stuff or new people. Make America Great *Again*. White Christians are the Real Americans.
2. The rejection of modernism. This includes a rejection of the Enlightenment, the Age of Reason, and science.
3. The cult of action for action's sake. Trump's rhetoric relied on simplicity; pointy headed analysts are not needed; complex problems are best dealt with swiftly and from the gut.
4. Disagreement is treason. Those who disagree with Trump must hate our country; they want to destroy America; they are socialists or members of the Deep State.

5. Fear of difference. "An appeal against the intruders;" Trump came out of the gate railing against Mexicans and one of his first acts as president was what he called his "Muslim ban."
6. Appeal to a frustrated middle class. As we've analyzed, The System is Rigged, so we must Drain the Swamp.
7. The obsession with a plot. Again, Trump repeatedly refers to plots such as the Deep State, the birther narrative, and lately the idea that the need for a COVID booster is just a pretext for Pfizer to make money; and winks and nods at conspiracy theorists.
8. Humiliation by enemies who are simultaneously strong and weak. The Democrats are weak and stupid, and yet simultaneously they are diabolical and are running a vast conspiracy; the left-wing is led by idiots, who are also so clever that they control everything and command the Deep State.
9. Pacifism is trafficking with the enemy, because life is permanent warfare. Everything is fodder for conflict with the Other Side. That is, if you're not upset, you should be; I mean just look at what the libs have done with Mr. Potato Head and Dr. Seuss. (You may note that 'permanent warfare' is not consistent with 'Keep America Great,' but this need not be logically coherent.)
10. Contempt for the weak, advocating for a popular elitism. Trump mocked a disabled reporter, called people dogs and labelled his opponents (low energy Jeb, little Marco, lyin' Ted, etc.), while telling his followers they are the elite. "I love the poorly educated."
11. Everybody is educated to become a hero. In mythology and history, heroes are exceptional. "But in Ur-Fascist ideology, heroism is the norm." Fascists are supposed to be like Klingons who crave death in combat. Or, as we heard on January 6th, "You must fight like hell or you're not going to have a country anymore."
12. Machismo, "...which implies both disdain for women and intolerance and condemnation of nonstandard sexual habits, from chastity to homosexuality." This can also involve weapons fetishes, an "ersatz phallic exercise," either overtly like Saddam Hussein firing his gun over the crowd, or in a surrogate manner, trying to get military parades in DC, or joking with police about not being so nice while putting a suspect in a patrol car.
13. Selective populism. "Individuals as individuals have no rights... the Leader pretends to be their interpreter.... The People is only a theatrical fiction. ...we no longer need Nuremberg Stadium. There is in our

future a TV or Internet populism, in which *the emotional response of a selected group of citizens can be presented and accepted as the Voice of the People.*” (italics added)

“Whenever a politician casts doubt on the legitimacy of a parliament because it no longer represents the Voice of the People, we can smell Ur-Fascism.”

14. Ur-Fascism speaks Newspeak. ‘Newspeak’ was the official language of English Socialism in Orwell’s *1984*. “All the Nazi or Fascist schoolbooks made use of an impoverished vocabulary, and an elementary syntax, in order to limit the instruments for complex and critical reasoning,”

“Ur-Fascism can come back in the most innocent of disguises. Our duty is to uncover it and point our finger at any of its new instances....”

> I venture the challenging statement that if American democracy ceases to move forward as a living force, seeking day and night by peaceful means to better the lot of our citizens, fascism will grow in strength in our land.
>
> - - Franklin Roosevelt, November 1938

Trump supporters say this ‘Trump as fascist’ bloviation is just more frantic liberal hyperbole; Trump is a true-blue American, he doesn’t believe in fascism. He was elected in 2016 fair and square and you libs just can’t get over that; he hugs the flag and loves America.

Progressives reply hey, he’s still here, now, it’s already happened. (It’s interesting to note that Umberto Eco wrote “Mussolini did not have any philosophy: he had only rhetoric.”) They point to Trump’s coup attempt of 6 January and his subsequent incessant attempts to overturn the election results as evidence.

Optimists can observe that we’re doing just fine; after all, what other country but the USA could have brushed off a coup attempt and that same night returned to count the Electoral College votes and then just kept moving forward?

Pessimists (or realists) warn that a coup attempt without consequences for the leaders of the coup is just a training exercise. The worst is yet to come. Republicans, the party of Trump, have demonstrated that they do not believe in the peaceful transition of power. They do not believe that any America-hating Democrats are legitimate; none of them should be allowed to be in power, regardless of election results. Trump Republicans do not believe that when you lose, you find a way to appeal to more voters than your opponents, no. Restriction of voting rights will assure minority GOP victory in 2022 and 2024, and once Trump enablers control again the levers of government, they will not be as incompetent as those of 2016, or as honest as many of them were in 2020. There will be no Brad Raffensperger to put the brakes on a coup, only a Marjorie Taylor Greene clone to execute it, and they will never surrender power.

Let's review again the reasons for having chewed through these last two chapters. Why all this?

Maybe you want to be better able to control the conversation and control what people think;

maybe just 'know thine enemy';

maybe understand each other better;

or maybe even change our own minds about something.

If you've changed your mind about something, bless you, as you must have been ready for change, open to new information. I don't believe I and my sublime verbiage can take credit for it. As Haidt pointed out about wagging a dog's tail for him, "You can't change people's minds by utterly refuting their arguments."

Or as Hume wrote in the 18th century:

> And as reasoning is not the source, whence either disputant derives his tenets; it is in vain to expect, that any logic, which speaks not to the affections, will ever engage him to embrace sounder principles.

I'm going to be optimistic and believe that you're not driven to control people, and that if you've read this far you haven't done so solely to prepare for Jedi psychological operations against political opponents or to drop the hammer on your least favorite relative at Thanksgiving dinner.

Rather, I choose to believe that if given the opportunity, Americans would prefer to 'speak to the affections' of their countrymen.

That is more about connection than it is about control.

Summary of Part 2

A lot of what Trump said was true, and more importantly to his supporters, he made them feel recognized, understood, and supported.

MAGA: our most prosperous era was characterized by plentiful employment; high marginal tax rates; robust government expenditure on infrastructure, education, and research and development; and modest corporate profits and executive salaries.

The system is rigged:

> The "Free Market" is more myth than reality.
>
> Corporations and the super-rich have outsized and malignant influence on our politics.

The Swamp is deep and wide: money in politics, revolving doors between government and business and media, the infiltration of the courts with pro-management activists; all serve to shift wealth from the masses to the rich.

To the degree Trumpism has an ideology beyond rhetoric, it is a populism closest to that of progressives; but that verity is opaque.

The Swamp runs pro-corporate ball carriers downfield behind blockers of wedge issues.

From guns to immigration, race relations to climate change, deficits to abortion, wedge issues distract and help to turn the interests of the middle class and working poor 180 degrees against themselves.

Liberals fuel wedge issues with 'political correctness' and readily misunderstood inflammatory mottos like "Defund the Police".

There is a wealthy industry of misinformation that supports and is coopted by the wealthiest of the donor class.

The Swamp has been successful in advancing the agenda of dividing the electorate by inflaming nationalism and blaming The Other.

But the rhetoric has slipped the leash of the donor class and morphed into authoritarianism that now threatens our democracy.

That doesn't mean we're helpless or hopeless. So now on to solutions.

Part III What We Can Do About It

Introduction to Part 3

We can connect with our relatives and friends, and our countrymen

We can connect with the best of our traditions.

We can improve ourselves as individuals, and commit ourselves to truth.

We can work to put in place measures to improve society, freeing ourselves from the unhealthy self-serving interests of The Swamp, taking steps to be sure that everyone's reputation is on the line and that people are accountable, and thus improving both our politics and our material and spiritual well-being.

We can execute policies that support our democracy and our Founders' vision.

Chapter 15

Connect Versus Control

Wouldn't the world be a better place if everyone would just agree with me? All of these dumb people running around with dumb ideas, it's so frustrating. I post brilliant arguments on Facebook, and they just don't seem to get it! If only I could get them to change their minds and see things correctly!

Well, spoiler alert; if you have such fantasies, dream on, but it isn't going to happen. In case you haven't learned by now:

You cannot ***control*** *others' beliefs.*

From this moment as you read these words through the day you take your last breath and even as your bones turn to dust, there will be people with different ideas in conflict with yours. So if your self-esteem is adversely impacted by the persistent existence of folks who disagree with you, you're out of luck.

Take heart, all is not lost. You can affect others' thinking. But that road travels through connection, not control.

If we want someone to listen to us, really hear us,

we must connect; control doesn't work.

I work with veterans with posttraumatic stress, but not medically, not anymore. I used to, in my practice, in the army, and in the Veterans Administration; but I often found that medical model frustrating and not as rewarding or effective as I'd want it to be.

I want to tell you some stories. Disclaimer: the presence of these men's stories does not mean that they agree with anything I'm saying in this book.

Three men

Ken Falke was a Master Chief Petty Officer, an explosive ordnance disposal (EOD) specialist in the U.S. Navy. (He is also the co-author with Josh Goldberg of *Struggle Well, Thriving in the Aftermath of Trauma*, and the author of *Lead Well.*) After retiring from the Navy Ken started his own company and had a very successful sale just eight years later. Soon after the onset of the war in Afghanistan, and more so in Iraq, casualties began to arrive at Walter Reed. The EOD community is small and tight, and Ken would go visit the casualties at Walter Reed. At that time there were limited accommodations for family members of injured servicemen in the expensive DC area. So he and his wife Julia would invite the family members of wounded servicemen to come and stay at their home nearby in Virginia. He thought there would be a handful of casualties and the wars would soon end. Of course it didn't turn out that way. And as the improvised explosive device (IED) became the weapon of choice for al Qaeda, EOD specialists were among those most affected. Their injuries tended to be devastating. If they survived, they often didn't survive with all their limbs intact.

Ken and Julia's house was constantly full of the family members of casualties and often the casualties themselves after they would be discharged from the hospital. As large and pleasant as their house was, the Falkes noted that their guests still felt like guests; they weren't comfortable sitting around in their underwear and breaking wind like they could at their own homes. So they decided to build a couple of cabins that family members could stay in with their kids and just be themselves. Eventually this turned into more cabins; the Falkes aimed at transforming the enterprise beyond the EOD community into a setting that would help returning warriors and their family members deal with the trauma they'd been through. Many facilities have various activities for veterans such as riding or communing with horses, canoeing, hiking, archery and regulatory practices such as some forms of meditation. Ken (and his co-author Josh Goldberg) investigated the state of the art of retreats and mental health services for posttraumatic stress in general, and found it wanting.

Science and medicine have recognized in the last decade that, despite the best intentions of dedicated people, the current trauma-focused treatments for posttraumatic stress have marked limitations. In 2017 the *Journal of the American Medical Association, Psychiatry* noted that "considerable room exists for improvement in treatment efficacy, and satisfaction appears bleak based on low treatment retention...we have probably come as far as we can with current dominant clinical approaches." Leaders in the field have called for "new innovative and engaging approaches for the treatment of PTSD." (1)

Enter Dusty Baxley. Dusty is a combat veteran of the 505th Parachute Infantry Regiment, 82nd Airborne Division; he jumped into Panama for Operation Just Cause in December 1989 and went to the Sandbox for the Gulf War. He retired from the army in July 1994 and left for Australia the day he signed out of uniform. While successful in business and powerlifting, all was not well. He met all the criteria for the diagnosis of post-traumatic stress, he had experienced a constellation of adverse childhood events (ACEs), he self-medicated with booze and sex and violence. He recalls that the only time he felt alive, felt anything, was when he was drinking a lot of whiskey and getting in bar fights (so that's the acronym soup of PTSD and ACE and SUD). Not surprisingly his life was a catalog of failed marriages and battered relationships. In technical terms, he was a hot mess. Like many veterans, he was unconnected, to himself, to his family, to his tribe.

In 2009 he came back to the states and met a woman he liked, Charlyn (spoiler alert, his future bride, happy ending). She practiced Transcendental Meditation (or "TM") and she told him that he seemed like a real nice guy, but he was a mess, and if he would learn TM she would be glad to keep seeing him; but if he didn't then he should lose her phone number. For a hard drinking airborne ranger combat veteran Southern boy, pursuing TM was about as likely as a trip to Mars. But, Dusty is a guy, like any other guy except maybe more so, and a guy who likes a girl is really the simplest of creatures. Long story short, he did as he was told, and much to his surprise he found TM not only tolerable, but worthwhile. His PTS symptoms and his excessive drinking began falling away and lo and behold, he found himself enjoying life.

In May 2011 he went to a reunion of his 82nd Airborne unit. He saw that a lot of his comrades were missing, many of them due to suicide, and a lot of those who remained were not thriving. Some asked, 'you look great, what have been doing?' Anticipating that if he told them he's practicing Transcendental Meditation they would think he's become a snowflake and chuck beer cans at him, he plunged ahead anyway. Once again to his surprise, they told him 'well whatever you're doing, you need to teach us how to do it.' And, Boom! Cue the picture with the giant lightbulb turning on over his head. Dusty had a new mission. He attended a TM teacher training course (not a trivial undertaking, essentially six months long in residence) and then began teaching TM to veterans and active duty at any venue he could find. The paths of Dusty, Josh, and Ken crossed in 2013; Dusty taught them TM and began teaching veterans at the facility that had grown from the cabins on Ken and Julia's property in northern Virginia (which has since become the Boulder Crest Foundation and the Boulder Crest Institute for Post Traumatic Growth (PTG)).

They were conducting weeklong 'retreats' (that term has since been abandoned in favor of 'training') on roughly a monthly basis. This led to a natural experiment. Dusty couldn't go to all of them as he sometimes had obligations elsewhere so about half the time there would be someone teaching another form of meditation. Ken and others noticed that there was a difference: the veterans did better when Dusty was there teaching them TM than when they learned something else. TM became *the* form of meditation to be used at this facility thenceforward. It is an integral part of the Warrior PATHH (Progressive and Alternative Training for Healing Heroes), the basic curriculum for enhancing PTG.

Let's back up a bit. I've been a TM teacher for decades. I think it's the best thing since sliced bread, that's my bias. There are hundreds of studies I could tell you about, but that's not this book. Still, I'll give you a couple of paragraphs just so you have some idea what I'm talking about.

TM is a mental technique, practiced for around 20 minutes twice a day sitting comfortably with eyes closed. It's easy to learn and effortless to practice. It's not a religion or a philosophy, it's compatible with any religion; it doesn't require any faith or belief or change in lifestyle (except that you actually need to do it to get the benefits). It takes about an hour and a half per day four or five days in a row to complete the basic course of training in TM. You must be trained by a certified teacher to be assured of quality control.

Here's the idea. Our minds have an active aspect, with which we're familiar as we experience it every day; often, it can seem to be too active, scattered, stressed, and intruded upon by regrets from the past and worries for the future. But our minds also have a quiet aspect, silent and peaceful. That silent aspect we don't experience so much; but we can, easily. It's already there, like the movie screen upon which the motion picture is projected. We don't have to work at it or try to conjure it up. Indeed, 'working' at it is counterproductive. (Have you ever been told just to 'empty your mind,' or 'clear your mind of all thoughts'? Good luck with that.)

TM uses the natural tendency of the mind to seek ever more charming experience. It allows for someone effortlessly to experience an inner silence that is beyond all the heretofore irreconcilable guilt and shame and conflict… in a word, an experience that is transcendental. This has beneficial effects on mind and body that have been well-documented.

There are hundreds of scientific papers about TM that have been published in peer reviewed journals. For these veterans, relief from stress, better sleep, improved relationships with family and friends and co-workers, decreased need for medicines or self-medication, all hit the spot and help open the door to the life they deserve. If you want to know more about the science, the benefits, the history, the origins, the stories of those who have practiced this technique, go to tm.org , or tmforveterans.org , or bouldercrest.org , or davidlynchfoundation.org, or read Bob Roth's book *Strength in Stillness*.

And now the third man, Ian Ricci. He's a combat veteran whose vehicle got smoked by an IED in Iraq; he was the sole survivor. He did what many infantrymen do after they have been traumatized: he drank, and he fought. Then, he was the victim of what has been described as a change in the 'operational environment'. Many of the traits he was trained to have, traits that made him an excellent soldier, did not translate perfectly when he got back to the World. Downrange he was looking out for the enemy, detail oriented making sure nobody made mistakes, speaking candidly and directly, with total emotional control on the battlefield; he was a super troop. But when he transitioned to civilian life, he was told he's broken, a mess. The very same previously positive attributes are now symptoms: he's hypervigilant, intolerant, too loud and angry and unfiltered, and when he's not those things, he's distant and unfeeling.

People who have been traumatized can tend to look at everything differently: themselves, other people, the whole world, even God. The world is not somewhere welcoming to be explored; it is a minefield, full of dangers. You can't count on other people, they will abuse you, rip you off, desert you, kick you to the curb, or just die. And the stuff I saw, the stuff that happened; what sort of a God can create a universe in which such things are allowed to happen? None of it makes any sense, it's just random, with no purpose or justice. And ultimately, I screwed up; I should have done this or not done that, or stopped this other thing from happening. It's my fault, and I keep screwing up, my kids are afraid of me, my wife is unhappy with me, I'm guilty, and I'm ashamed. Everyone would be better off without me. I don't have a place here anymore; I don't belong.

I met Ian at a PATHH in 2017 and taught him TM. Like most veteran course participants, he was a bit tentative at first but seemed to be doing fine. Toward the end of the weeklong initial program, we have an exercise wherein veterans make plans, set some short-term goals, work on how they're going to present themselves to their loved ones when they get home full of new ideas and experiences. Compared to other parts of the training, this block of training usually isn't very emotionally demanding. But in the midst of setting some goals for the next 30 days, Ian began to freeze up.

And then the true story emerged.

He'd been in a downward spiral. He'd applied for the PATHH not to get help, as he had felt too far gone for that. He'd applied in order to leave his home and have a hard goodbye, hug his spouse and daughters and tell them he loved them for the last time, and then commit suicide. He'd saved a sufficient quantity of drugs from the VA to do the job. He planned on taking them in a restroom at O'Hare in Chicago, but the place was too busy. So he'd been going through the motions at the PATHH, figuring the program would be of no help, as everything else had been of no help, planning on completing his suicide on his return trip. You could have picked my jaw up off the floor. I'd had no idea about all this; clueless.

This exercise of making 30-day plans had brought to his attention that he hadn't planned on having a life after that week. But over the course of just a few days, the practices he had learned had allowed a flicker of light into the very dark place in which he had been living. Only at that moment as he was going through the exercise did he realize that something had shifted, that he could indeed have a life, he could have something to look forward to, he could see his family again and not be overwhelmed by guilt and shame and loss. That was a good day.

About 18 months later I saw him, and he was one of the veterans guiding other veterans in the program. That was a good day too.

We work together now on a regular basis. Ian had experienced what is known as post traumatic growth (PTG).

Why am I recounting these biographies? What's the point?

For at least a couple of reasons; first, these are living examples of great men and women. They're warriors, and their stories should be told. And they're heroes: they've returned from their duty and service to teach us, and to continue to serve. They've been through the... bad stuff; some experienced Adverse Childhood Events (ACEs); were traumatized again in service to their country; were trained by the military to act and react in ways that often backfired when they got home; were cast aside and lost their tribes; were at the bottom; and managed to pass through it all not just to get by, but to thrive.

But second, I believe the lessons learned from their experiences can be generalized to the larger American population. Many of us have been traumatized; many overtly by beatings and sexual assaults, accidents or disasters, losses and illnesses; and many by upbringings that subjected people to an ongoing Death of a Thousand Invalidations rather than overt trauma.

Be Kind. Everyone around you is fighting
a battle you know nothing about.
- - Ian Maclaren

Even if they would have trouble articulating them, those who have been through trauma typically confront existential questions: what is the meaning of what happened to me? What am I supposed to do with this experience? How do I give it value? How do I emerge from it with dignity? How can I be worthy of those who sacrificed so much? What is the purpose of my existence? Why am I here?

That makes trauma both a curse and a blessing. The curse is obvious. The traumatized have been smacked in the face with these questions, and if they are not successful in finding some resolution to them, they can spiral into oblivion. But that smack in the face can be a blessing.

The unexamined life is not worth living.
- - Socrates

Most of us who have not been through significant trauma can muddle through life without ever really confronting these uncertainties, some of us reaching the end of our lives without ever having really lived. Many of those who have not been traumatized seem to be somewhat lost, unable to answer for themselves fundamental questions about their purpose in life, about what is important.

Happiness and connection

Much of this book has been about The Swamp, about material things, about how things are not fair and should be improved, about the distribution of wealth, about how moneyed special interests have used their wealth and power to further empower themselves, even at the cost of further disadvantaging the disadvantaged. Those things are important, and I'm not done talking about them. That's what a lot of government is about: regulating markets so people don't get ripped off, so we all get our fair share; taxing fairly; providing services fairly; assuring that work and productivity are incentivized; making sure that constituents get their proper piece of the pie.

But let's imagine that I had a magic wand and could make things fair: no one living in poverty, everyone with plenty of opportunity to excel, to advance themselves through education, and if higher education is not in the cards, then a living wage and adequate means, dignified work for anyone willing to work, sufficient to provide for a reasonable standard of living, with accommodations for those unable to work. Everyone lives in the Star Trek future free from want, from poverty, from the need to overcome barriers of race or geography or disability. Then what?

What is it that makes us happy? Ask many American undergraduates or working stiffs and it's about money. What kind of a job can I get that pays well? How much time must I trade to get how much money?

But, it isn't money. It's a cliché, 'money can't buy happiness,' but it's true. (That doesn't mean I'm opposed to being rich, Lord... just sayin.') Money and the material possessions we associate with having money, are like oxygen, or sex. If you're not getting any of it, it'll make you frantic. (Like the Taliban... story for another day.) But if you have "enough," you take it for granted, and getting more doesn't really make you happy either.

Researchers have found that, no surprise, being poor can be tough. It's harder to be resilient against stressors like divorce and ill health, etc. if you're broke. But getting rich isn't a cure. Emotional well-being varies directly with increases from very low incomes (that is, well-being goes up as income goes up) but it plateaus at about $75,000 (2010 dollars, so $93,750 in 2021 dollars) in income per year; people who make more than that, even up to two million dollars per year (about as high as they measured), demonstrated no improvement in emotional well-being. (2) We see this all the time, movie stars, children of rich people, seem to have not an unfulfilled want in the world, yet their lives are a mess and they're injecting heroin.

> It is pretty hard to tell what does bring happiness;
> poverty and wealth have both failed.
> - - Kin Hubbard

Among those of us who aren't making millions, whatever amount people make, there is a tendency to believe that we just need about another ten or twenty percent (or winning the lottery, that'd work), and then we'd be happy. But if you're rich and have virtually unlimited amounts of money, it's hard to believe that fiction, that just a little more money would do the trick... obviously, not. They can be faced with the fact that, despite tons of money, a big house and great food and fine wine and shiny vehicles, plenty of sex drugs and rock'n'roll, I'm not happy. And since I'm already rich, there is no realistic prospect of becoming happy if I could just get a *little bit* richer. Many of us non-rich folks experience "Sunday neurosis;" after getting over hump day, toiling all week, we Thank God It's Friday, but then on Sunday, when we should be at peak happiness, we're not, we're in an existential vacuum, and we feel unhappy about not feeling happy. (3)

We're missing something, our entire society is, not just veterans with posttraumatic stress. Suicide (over 1.6 million attempts in 2020) is high not only among veterans; and stress, anxiety, depression, insomnia, all are rampant among US civilians. Overdoses associated with the opioid epidemic have been termed "Deaths of Despair". Some of this is due to economic insecurity and the hollowing out of the middle class. But some is more existential.

> The richer we have become materially, the poorer we become morally and spiritually. We have learned to fly in the air like birds and swim in the sea like fish, but we have not learned the simple art of living together as brothers.
>
> – Martin Luther King Jr

A lot of what we know about drugs and the way they affect the brain and body comes from animal studies. Most of us are familiar with the idea that a rat will push a button or pull a lever to get heroin or cocaine rather than food, or will push a button that provides an electrical stimulation to the reward center of his brain, and will starve to death in the process. (4) And it's true; man, those drugs are powerful and can just take over your life. But there's more to the story.

If you've ever had your house or apartment building or alleyway infested with rats, the problem is, there are lots of them. They hang out together. This observation caused scientists to question the results of drug studies looking at the behavior of a single rat in a cage with a drug. So they gave rats another option. The rat could pull a lever and get methamphetamine or heroin, or it could pull a different lever, and get to hang out with another rat. Guess what: rats prefer social interaction to smack or meth. (5) This supports the idea that the opposite of addiction is not sobriety, but connection.

Of course people aren't rats. But data indicate that connection is key. The ongoing Harvard Study of Adult Development began following 268 men (including JFK by the way) since they were students in 1938 (the Grant Study). The study added 456 non-Harvard-student underprivileged Boston men in 1970 (the Glueck study). Over decades researchers have followed and evaluated these subjects extensively, looking at just about all aspects of their lives, through schools, wars, marriages, divorces, parenthood, illnesses, losses, crises, tragedies and successes of all sorts, old age, the approach of death. Their purpose was to discover through interviews, questionnaires, physical exams and physiological measures, what it is that provides for satisfaction in life, what if anything protects people from life's discontents, what helps to delay physical and mental decline, to add not just years to life but life to years.

Drumroll please: **close relationships** are better predictors of a long happy life than are social class, wealth, fame, IQ, even genetics. Strong relationships, connections with other people, are by far the most important factor in living a long and satisfied life. (6)

This is consistent with the insights expressed in psychiatrist and holocaust survivor Victor Frankl's classic book *Man's Search for Meaning*. He identified three avenues by which we arrive at meaning. Having been stripped of all his possessions and identity, having lost his wife and parents to the Nazis, having himself been starved and abused at Auschwitz and other camps, he had insight into suffering that likely is beyond what most of us ever experience. No surprise then that one of his three avenues involved making suffering ennobling rather than degrading.

But the other two are avenues we mundane humans can (or should, or perhaps even, must) employ routinely. They involve committing oneself to something, some work, some deed, greater than oneself; and most saliently, committing oneself to someone other than oneself; in a word: service, or love. (7)

To expand upon the point of this chapter: relationships and connection are paramount in our individual lives, and I believe in our national life as well. Unlike in crises past, our whole country is not connected. It is as if our entire nation has been traumatized and needs post traumatic growth.

The ability to disagree without being disagreeable, to have real connection and communication, all are facilitated in a safe and trusted environment. In today's United States, in our political discourse, in the way we treat each other, even the way we treat the people we love, a safe and trusted environment is not where we live.

Listen and learn

Guilty pleasure confession time: back in the 1980s and 90s when I had an 80-mile commute, I used to listen to Howard Stern (I know, but he's funny, and it made the commute fly by). And while he's a shock jock and outrageous and all that, he also is an excellent interviewer. He listens without judging. He's half-Jewish and his sidekick Robin Quivers is a black woman; but they would occasionally have guests by phone or in studio who no one else would have, because they're regarded by most of us as pretty vile, Nazis and Klan members and so forth. I've never met Howard Stern, but he seems like an insatiably curious man. It wasn't just shtick, he didn't argue with the Klansman; he seemed really to want to understand, to know everything about his Nazi guest, about what made him tick; it was fascinating.

There are some people with whom I really don't want to argue. My wife is at the top of the list. It took me some years, but eventually I learned that I never win an argument with my wife. Not because she's a great debater or is always factually correct, but because even if I 'win,' I lose. And that's not because she's mean or overbearing or unforgiving, not at all. It's because if I'm arguing, I'm losing. I'm not listening. I'm not hearing her. So I've already lost: because if the purpose of a conversation or an argument is to connect, to understand, to share a perspective, maybe even to bring someone else to my point of view so we can be of one mind, I'm doing the opposite. Rather than trying to connect, I was trying to control what she thinks, and that just Does. Not. Work.

That's in part why we Americans make ground rules for Thanksgiving about 'no religion or politics', because we've seen far too often that we don't seem to know how to listen, how to explore someone else's perspective without judgment or rebuttal. Then if we are invited or we stumble into an exchange, we don't know how to argue well. And if we end up disagreeing, we don't seem to know how to disagree without being disagreeable.

Part of the reason I participate in programs for veterans (and my entire military career really) is that, yes, it's my form of service, but also, I get to hang out with real heroes. My respect for such people is implicit. But that doesn't mean we don't disagree about things, including politics.

Bringing this back to our topic of listening rather than rebutting; I don't want to 'win' an argument with my fellow veterans. I respect them too much; it would be rude. I want to understand. I want to reach a common ground. I want to know how he or she came to hold the views s/he has; those views are real; I can't just deny them if it's his experience. I need to adapt my view of the world to accommodate his experience. What was it about the conditions in which he lived that allowed for what he saw? And how would what I think is best to do (in my idealized world) work, without recreating those conditions? I want to reach a point where we each go as far as we can with what we know, and say, "Hmm, I believe A. But if B were true, then I would believe C instead of A. But I don't know. I need to find out if B is true or not."

So there's one formula for connection: find someone heroic whom you respect deeply like these three men (and countless other men and women veterans and first responders I've been fortunate enough to know) and the respect you feel should allow you to restrain any impulse to be a jerk with them on social media. And guess what, it works; my team and I have some brisk disagreements, but we respect each other and follow one of the credos of the Warrior PATHH: "Mean what you say, say what you mean, but don't say it mean."

How do we connect with people with whom we disagree politically? After all, you may not get to work with heroes like I do. But it can't hurt to assume that, until proven otherwise, everyone you meet is a hero. Everyone is dealing with something. A default that presumes that everyone you meet has had some life experience that you haven't, that they know something you don't that can be informative, and that s/he has something worthwhile to say that might just help you grow a broader vision, is a good place to start. I'll admit that's easier said than done, and easier still if you're not particularly stressed.

If we want someone else to listen to us, it helps if we listen to them first. As a Marine PATHH Guide used to say, 'Never miss a golden opportunity to STFU' (shut up). But beware; as Kin Hubbard wrote, "A good listener is usually thinking about something else." As Mia Wallace pointed out to Vincent Vega, we all know that often, we appear to be listening, but we're not really listening, we're just waiting to get our turn to talk. We must listen, but listening isn't enough by itself. Indeed, exposure to the other side's perspectives can be seen as attacks, and can be likely to trigger rebuttal, not reflection. (8) We must value the other person enough to want to understand. We must really want to hear that person if we want to be heard. With your spouse or child, that's easy, or it should be easy.

Everyone wants to be seen, to be heard, to be valued. With just about anyone, it should be possible for you to say truthfully, "I want to hear you. I want to understand you. Tell me what you think, and how you came to think that."

Over a dozen years ago, I had occasion to be on a long car ride with Bob Roth. He's the CEO of the David Lynch Foundation which provides funding for courses in Transcendental Meditation for underserved populations such as students, inmates, abused teens, and others, including veterans and first responders. We were on our way to give a presentation. Bob and I had been acquainted for years and were always amiable, but I had never really had the chance to get to know him. He's a nice guy, and a good guy, and I was looking forward to this opportunity. I was interested in his story, and I had even recently stumbled upon some Dale Carnegie book or article, so I was ready to ask and to listen, a lot. I had a plan.

After some small talk, we started talking about our backgrounds a bit. Bob was asking me all about myself, and I was answering. Time was passing. He kept inquiring, and I kept talking and talking. After an hour or three or however long it was, we arrived. Bob knew all about me, I'd told all my favorite tall tales (many of them are true), but I had completely messed up my plan and I didn't know any more about Bob than I had when we started.

Listening is powerful. Being listened to, is intoxicating. We're all the heroes of our own stories. Believing that someone actually wants to hear your story and is interested in what you think is flattering. I had planned on listening and not talking, but Bob was a better listener than I; and it felt so good to be listened to, that evidently I couldn't stop talking.

Recounted by Princess Marie Louise, granddaughter of Queen Victoria:

> A young lady was taken to dinner one evening by Gladstone and the following evening by Disraeli. Asked what impres-

> sions these two celebrated men had made upon her, she replied, "When I left the dining room after sitting next to Mr. Gladstone I thought he was the cleverest man in England. But after sitting next to Mr. Disraeli I thought I was the cleverest woman in England." (9)

See how much you can learn about another person's ideas without ever volunteering your own. Don't worry, it is rare to sit with someone like Bob Roth, who was willing to hear me prattle on and who listened indefinitely. Almost everyone you meet will be glad to talk about themselves and their ideas without knowing that you are an expert listener. Ask for permission to ask questions, and ask questions honestly to learn what they think, not to trap them in some rhetorical 'gotcha.' Eventually, most people, after telling you about their ideas, want validation, want to know, what did you hear? And what do you think about it, about what I said? That's a start on connecting.

> There is nothing noble in being superior to your fellow man.
> The nobility is being superior to your former self.
>
> - - Ernest Hemingway

Candidly of course, some people have very closed minds, and very bad ideas; and some people are just not very smart and don't think clearly; and some people are just... obtuse, and not very charming. And some people have all of those flaws. So for all your willingness to be open and accepting, that may be a short conversation. You may not feel like you've connected; and with that particular person, you may not even want to bother to try to connect anymore. Some people seem to be dumb as a stump, and/or jerks, and you find you just don't value their ideas at all. But you don't know that until you've given it a try. (Aren't you a bit curious about how they got to where they are, when they started believing whatever it is they believe?) Even if you don't connect, you've modeled what it's like to be open to learning *something* about someone else's ideas. You didn't shame or castigate, you did what you could to create a safe and trusted environment, allowing him to say his piece. Maybe you're the one person that makes that other person consider later that, 'Well, maybe not *all* people on the other side are jerks, that guy seemed pretty reasonable.' And that ain't nothin'.

> We often refuse to accept an idea merely because the tone of voice in which it has been expressed is unsympathetic to us.
> -- Friedrich Nietzsche

Getting through to someone's rider, to their speaking press agent, to their voting persona, goes through their elephant. Connecting with someone's elephant generally is permissible only if that person has decided that you, the messenger, is trustworthy and safe, nonjudgmental and welcoming. The connection can happen in a couple of ways.

The simpler is through "social persuasion", wherein I am highly regarded as such a heckuva guy (I'm an old friend, or a celebrity, or a hero, whatever floats that person's boat; or, I have done such a great job listening that I have become trusted) that I can influence another person just by making my feelings or preferences known. The second is through "reasoned persuasion", wherein I first benefit from or use social persuasion to "convey respect, warmth, and an openness to dialogue before stating one's own case." (10) Spock and Data could convince people of things using logic and reason, but only because they had first shaped the discussion battlespace by social persuasion: they were honest brokers, never seemed to have a dog in the fight and they were never going to gloat if they 'won' the argument (as defined by having someone change his mind).

Whether you're a progressive never-Trumper or a Trump supporter, with an agenda of changing the others' minds, you can benefit from Haidt's insight:

> If you really want to change someone's mind on a moral or political matter, you'll need to see things from that person's angle as well as your own. And if you do truly see it the other person's way -- deeply and intuitively -- you might even find your own mind opening in response. Empathy is an antidote to righteousness, although it's very difficult to empathize across a moral divide. (11)

For what they're worth, here are a few tips for talking with your fellow Americans about potentially controversial topics, like Trump, or tracking chips in COVID vaccines, or anything else that has managed to be dragged into the gravitational sway of our polarization. Since this book is subtitled to "help liberals understand" I'll focus mostly on the perspective of liberals trying to understand Trump supporters, even conspiracy theorists. And if you're a Trump supporter, I hope that part 2 of this book brought to light a number of areas where you and never-Trumpers might even agree.

First, once again it's worthwhile to recall some examples of the difference between fact and opinion. It's a *fact* that unemployment went down during the first three years of the Trump administration and the market went up, so one could have the *opinion* that Trump was responsible for the greatest economy ever. It's a *fact* that there was economic growth for 77 straight months under Obama/Biden, and more jobs were created in the last three years under Obama than in the first three years under Trump; so one could have the *opinion* that Obama did better than Trump.

Occasionally I receive social media messages or emails from Trump-supporting friends. The following was in response to General Milley's comment before Congress that he was curious about 'white rage'.

1. I'm outraged that a duly elected President, the most effective President in my lifetime, was harassed, falsely accused of being a Russian agent, undermined, and lied about by "Deep State" career officials like yourself and a media that has become the mouthpiece of the Democrat Party; he was impeached and acquitted, not once but twice, during his entire 4-year term of office on clearly fraudulent charges.

2. I'm outraged that BLM, Antifa, and other Marxists rioted during the summer of 2020 in cities across the country, and "heels-up" Kamala Harris led an effort to bail those who were arrested, out of jail. Over 500 people, arrested for trespassing and vandalism at the Capitol on January 6th, remain in jail without bail and, in some cases, are held in solitary confinement. This is not a defense of vandalism, but, how does the damage from the riots of summer 2020 compare to that at the Capitol on January 6th?

3. I'm outraged that a president who accomplished more for the American people in 4 years than his three immediate predecessors did in 24 years, e.g. restored the US economy, cut taxes and regulations, made the US energy independent, brought unemployment rates down to their lowest level ever, destroyed ISIS, brokered peace deals between Israel and other Arab nations, defended our southern border, put America first, etc., etc., was fought every step of the way by Democrats and the Deep State.

4. I'm outraged that this same president, who received 11 million more votes than he did in 2016, was questionably defeated in an election in which election laws were unconstitutionally changed in the days, weeks, and months immediately preceding the election, supposedly because of a virus.

5. I'm outraged that a senile 78-year old career politician, who can't put a coherent sentence together, who accomplished nothing during his 36 years in the US Senate and 8 years as Vice President, who didn't campaign and seldom left his basement during the campaign for President, and who could never draw a crowd of more than 200 people at one time, was declared the winner over a President who drew tens of thousands of enthusiastic supporters at each of his multiple rallies, daily, during the campaign.

6. I'm outraged that Candidate Biden bragged about having put together "the most extensive and inclusive voter fraud organization in the history of American politics" (it's on video!) during an interview on October 24, 2020, with Crooked Media, a left-leaning media company founded in 2017 by former Obama staffers, and the media says that Trump lies when he claims the election was stolen!?

7. I'm outraged that on January 28, 2018, before the Council on Foreign Relations, Joe Biden bragged how he once threatened to withhold $1 billion in authorized military aid to Ukraine unless the former President of Ukraine "fired" the prosecutor who was investigating the corrupt energy conglomerate, Burisma, with whom Biden's son, Hunter, was being paid $84,000 per month to serve on the Board of Directors. Can you say, "quid pro quo?" But, when Trump congratulated the newly elected President of Ukraine, who campaigned on fighting corruption, and encouraged him to follow through on his campaign promise, Rep. Adam Schiff blatantly lied about what Trump said and Trump got impeached!

8. I'm outraged that the FBI was given Hunter Biden's abandoned laptop computer, the hard-drive of which contained emails reflecting the corrupt practices of the Biden family vis-a-vie Ukraine and China and the FBI did nothing with it since crazy old' Joe was running for President. Can you say: "Hillary Clinton and unauthorized servers containing top secret documents"? Do you see a pattern here?

9. I'm outraged that the "New Oligarchs" of high tech are censoring virologists of their right to voice their thoughts and opinions when those opinions are in conflict with the Democrat Party or the CDC.

10. I'm outraged that an agency for which I proudly worked for nearly 29 years was politicized and corrupted by James Comey who was accurately described as being "out of his mind" and a "crooked cop" by a former Deputy Director of the FBI.

11. I'm outraged that 13 US Marines were recently killed in Afghanistan by the Taliban just because our senile President was too arrogant to follow the blueprint put together by President Trump and his military advisers for the "conditioned" withdrawal of forces from Afghanistan. Perhaps, you and our incompetent Secretary of Defense objected but were either too cowardly or too busy promoting Critical Race Theory to push back and provide needed oversight of this withdrawal. You succumbed to "Trump Derangement Syndrome" and now, as a result, you have the blood of 13 dead Marines on your hands.

12. I'm outraged about how the precipitous withdrawal of US military personnel from Afghanistan was carried out "before" securing the removal of tens of thousands of US citizens, Afghani interpreters and others who assisted the US military over the past 20 years, leaving them and Afghani Christians to be tortured and killed by the Taliban. And, you didn't even give advance notice to our NATO allies!

13. I'm outraged that you and Lloyd Austin carried out the withdrawal of the US military without first securing the removal of $85 billion worth of military equipment, weapons, ammunition, Humvees and aircraft, which you left behind for the Taliban, al Qaeda, and a re-emerging ISIS to use. I agree with a retired British Colonel who recently publicly stated that President Biden shouldn't be impeached, but rather he should be court martialed. You should be, as well...for dereliction of duty and cowardice.

I could go on but I believe you get "my drift" as to why I and so many others - white, black, Hispanic, Asian, male and female, rich and poor, young and old - are experiencing flashes of "rage" and "anger" against this current administration. If you had any honor and decency, you would resign and retire.

These 13 arguments are difficult to respond to, primarily because the writer is at liberty to be outraged by anything that he chooses to be outraged by. He is at liberty to believe that the impeachment charges against Trump were 'fraudulent'; that belief may be poorly supported by fact, but that's his opinion. You could drill down into each paragraph and find errors of logic or fact (the Biden 'quid pro quo' for firing the Burisma prosecutor is fallacious, etc.), but as we've noted, generally you cannot change someone's mind by utterly refuting their arguments; arguing these points until the Second Coming is unlikely to change his opinions.

Pick your battles; and check your own biases. Some things really are conspiracy theories: COVID vaccines have killed thousands of Americans? Nope, false, wrong. The Green New Deal was responsible for the failure of Texas's power grid in February of 2021? No, that's not true either. But not every disagreement is a conspiracy theory.

Let's stipulate that many Trump supporters don't like Joe Biden and will find fault with him no matter what. If you're progressive, and a Trump supporter says that the way Biden managed our departure from Afghanistan was a terrible national tragedy, that's not a conspiracy theory, it's just an opinion, and he's entitled to his. You don't have to automatically disagree with him just because he likes Trump.

You might even agree in part, "Yes I felt that same way, it seemed like the biggest fiasco; but then they got 120 thousand people out, and that was pretty good."

"But what about losing thirteen service members?!?"

"I agree, that was tragic."

It *was* tragic, and agreeing with a Trump supporter about something is not a sign that you've lost your mind, so go ahead and agree with one sometime. You don't have to resort to 'whataboutism', as in, 'What about Trump setting the date for withdrawal, etc.' Look for any opportunity to find some smidgen of common ground, because that's a win, maybe a small win, but a win. Take the win.

Listening is a calm process. If you're raising your voice, you're not listening. If you're yelling, trust me, you're not convincing anyone of anything, except that you have lost control of yourself.

Psychologist Jovan Byford notes that conspiracy theories "...are not just about right and wrong, but [are] underpinned by feelings of resentment, anger and indignation over how the world works." They often have a strong emotional dimension. You can anticipate that the other person is firmly attached to their ideas and will defend them, even loudly. Getting loud back will block any hope of connection. Honest nonjudgmental inquiries leave that hope alive.

It may be irresistible, but it's rarely helpful to be dismissive. Remember, most people who believe in conspiracy theories do so because they have been dismissed, ridiculed, and shamed. They are angry and anxious because of it. Flaming them on Facebook or over a holiday meal may seem satisfying, but, aside from that temporary selfish glow of having been correct and oh-so-clever, it is rarely productive. Empathy and patience may lead to connection and even flexibility in thinking. Humiliation almost certainly will not.

Claire Wardle from First Draft, a not-for-profit which fights misinformation, says, "Listen to what they have to say with patience," and never publicly shame someone for their views, at least not someone with whom you care about ever connecting, as that's quite likely to backfire.

Conspiracy theorists got into conspiracy theories in part because of doubt, they doubted the usual sources of information. That doubt can be a good thing and can be a lifeline to reel some folks back toward reality. Jovan Byford notes that "Many people who believe in conspiracy theories see themselves as healthy sceptics and self-taught researchers into complex issues.... Present this as something that, in principle, you value and share.

"Your aim is not to make them less curious or skeptical, but to change what they are curious about, or skeptical of."

I know that the claim "I do my own research" can feel like fingernails on the blackboard. If you know about the scientific method, you may want to scream. This exasperation has been captured in a post credited to Linda Gamble Spadaro, a licensed mental health counselor in Florida:

> Please stop saying you researched it.
>
> You didn't research anything and it is highly probable you don't know how to do so.
>
> Did you compile a literature review and write abstracts on each article? Or better yet, did you collect a random sample of sources and perform independent probability statistics on the reported results? No?
>
> Did you at least take each article one by one and look into the source (that would be the author, publisher and funder), then critique the writing for logical fallacies, cognitive distortions and plain inaccuracies?
>
> Did you ask yourself why this source might publish these particular results? Did you follow the trail of references and apply the same source of scrutiny to them?
>
> No? Then you didn't...research anything. *You read or watched a video, most likely with little or no objectivity. You came across some-*

thing in your algorithm manipulated feed, something that jived with your implicit biases and served your confirmation bias, and subconsciously applied your emotional filters and called it proof." [italics added]

This doesn't even go into institutional review boards (IRBs), also known as independent ethics committees, ethical review boards, or touch on peer review, or meta-analyses.

To sum it up, a healthy dose of skepticism is/can be a good thing… as long as we are also applying it to those things we wish/think to be true, and not just those things we choose to be skeptical towards, or in denial of.

Most importantly, though, is to apply our best critical thinking skills to ensure we are doing our best to suss out the facts from the fiction, the myths, and outright BS in pseudoscience and politics.

Misinformation is being used as a tool of war and to undermine our public health, and it is up to each of us to fight against it.

I think you can hear her frustration; it's justified and worth putting out into the public sphere. But in dealing with someone one-on-one, pointing out that they sound silly and don't know what they're talking about when they say they 'do their own research', will likely not avail you. Better to use that doubt as a lever to provoke rational thought.

"Focus on those who are pushing these [false] ideas, and what they might be getting," says Claire Wardle. "For instance, financial gain by selling health supplements, or reputational gain in building a following."

So, encourage doubt and critical thinking.

Remember, you don't convince someone by completely refuting his arguments, so pump the brakes on fact checking. Rather, honest non-judgmental inquiries leave hope alive, so ask questions.

"Focusing on the tactics and techniques used by people pushing disinformation is a more effective way of addressing these conversations than trying to debunk the information," again from Claire Wardle.

Rather than just tell your uncle he's wrong, you can ask 'are you sure about that?' And if he is sure, 'hey, let's look it up.' A run through his favorite websites or other sources may open the door to observe that the source is saying something contradictory, or is selling something, or some other point that might trigger some suspicions in your uncle's mind about his source.

Questions can gently point out contradictions. “Wait, please help me understand what you’re saying, the people storming the Capitol were patriots, or they were Antifa?”

“Hmm... you said there’s no evidence of a plane having crashed into the Pentagon, but here are photos of engine parts. Do you really think someone was able to fake all that?” or “What good would it have done the Bush administration to bring down the Twin Towers? Or might your source be wrong?”

“What are chemtrails supposed to do? What about the pilots’ families, won’t they be affected too?”

You can ask questions either with a chip on your shoulder, or like someone who’s really trying to understand a friend. And if they start to question their own confidence in their source, or question their errant beliefs, don’t be a jerk and spike the football. You can smile, but smile because, “Thank you. I really enjoyed our conversation!” Because you really did.

But as psychologist Jovan Byford cautions us, “Be realistic about what you can achieve. Conspiracy theories instill in believers a sense of superiority. It's an important generator of self-esteem - which will make them resistant to change.”

So, don’t hold your breath.

Again from Claire Wardle, “Recognize that everyone has had their lives turned upside down, and is seeking explanations.... Conspiracy theories tend to be simple, powerful stories that explain the world. Reality is complex and messy, which is harder for our brains to process.”

Getting someone to abandon conspiracy theories and misinformation can be a long process. So don’t give up, but appreciate that getting invested in using *connection* in order to change someone’s mind is just *control* in another form. Connect because connection is good, in and of itself. Being attached to a particular outcome can be frustrating and unhealthy for you. If you’re a never-Trumper, no matter how passionately you wish Trumpers would just “Wake Up!”, remember, they feel the same way about you.

Further, recognize that some people are just so toxic it can be frustrating and unhealthy to persist in attempts to connect. Liberals can protect themselves by attending to the advice from forensic psychiatrist Bandy X. Lee:

> When the mind is hijacked for the benefit of the abuser, it becomes no longer a matter of presenting facts or appealing to logic. Removing Trump from power and influence will be healing in itself. But, I advise, first, not to confront [his supporters'] beliefs, for it will only rouse resistance. Second, persuasion should not be the goal but change of the circumstance that led to their faulty beliefs. Third, one should maintain one's own bearing and mental health, because people who harbor delusional narratives tend to bulldoze over reality in their attempt to deny that their own narrative is false. As for mini-Trumps, it is important, above all, to set firm boundaries, to limit contact or even to leave the relationship, if possible. (12)

You can't pour from an empty cup. If you're disconnected and stressed, it's less likely that someone will be open to connecting with you. If you're a liberal motivated to defeat Trumpism, you're likely to be more effective if you get your house in order first. Be honest in what you're trying to achieve, recognizing that controlling the thinking of Trump supporters is beyond you. Before attending to the errors of others, you may want to attend to the mote in your own eye. It'll be good for you, and good for what you're trying to do.

Truth alone triumphs.
-- The national motto of India

Chapter 16

We the People

That to secure these rights
[Life, Liberty, and the pursuit of Happiness],
Governments are instituted among Men,
deriving their just powers from the consent of the governed....

We are in the midst of a worldwide struggle, an ongoing determination of how we will govern ourselves. This book is concerned primarily with America, but we don't live in a vacuum.

In his book *The End of History and the Last Man,* Francis Fukuyama wrote not that history was literally over in the sense that nothing was ever going to happen again, not that there wouldn't be more fighting, but that the ongoing tension regarding which form of government was best, was... over. Liberal democracy had won. We could lose it, bad things could happen, but there would be no progress to an alternate system of government. Of course totalitarian regimes persisted, but they were on borrowed time, nobody really wanted them except the kleptocrats at the top. Communism as a form of government had demonstrated that it just didn't work. Marxist-Leninist state-controlled economies were not agile or responsive enough to keep up with the creativity of the people within them. The remaining examples like Cuba and miserable North Korea prove that conclusion to be true. Theocracies may work for some homogenous country that likes that sort of thing, but it's nothing anyone else wants.

And yet today, there is a genuine sentiment abroad in the world that maybe liberal democracy just isn't all it's cracked up to be. And that's our fault, because we're screwing it up. Of course this isn't the first time we've messed up. We enslaved Africans for centuries; we killed Native Americans for their land and then violated our own treaties and stole their land again; we ended slavery but replaced it with Jim Crow; we interned

American citizens because they were of Japanese descent; we abandoned the Kurds; we abandoned (some of) our Afghan allies. Et cetera. But this feels different now. We have had a system that was self-correcting, and we just needed to reach consensus on best policies… though for those on the short end of the stick, the 'self-correction' seemed to take forever. Now, we seem to be on the threshold of throwing that system into the trash.

What's wrong with us? We are heirs to such a great legacy; how are we snatching defeat from the jaws of victory?

China seems to be eating our lunch. They build miles of high-speed rail more quickly than we can fix a subway station. They build new cities while ours age, our roads deteriorate, our bridges fall down. And while their notion of self-government is a joke, *our* rhetoric about *our own* elections would lead anyone to conclude that their system is better. Our head of state and the leaders of one of the only two major American political parties announce to the world that our elections, the world's showcase of democracy, are rigged, corrupt, and fraudulent.

As we've seen, Russia has demonstrated that the cultural integrity, the spiritual health of America, is… not as strong as it could and should be. Putin and his intelligence services were able to penetrate our psyche and with small, often clumsy and blatant efforts, he was able to provoke us into turning on each other. Remember only twenty years ago, after 9/11, Republican and Democratic members of Congress stood together on the steps of the Capitol and sang in praise of our nation in a display of solidarity that is all but unimaginable today. We can't seem to agree on much of anything. We look like a marriage gone bad, a couple who dislike each other but neither can afford to move out; they occasionally reach an accord so that one or the other takes out the trash.

Trump supporters believe his approach was the winner, and if only the election hadn't been stolen he could have continued until we would all be tired of winning. The apparent discord is just due to Trump having frustrated the plans of socialists who hate America.

This leaves us wrestling with our same problem: we are divided, and we seem to have lost our connection to our common heritage.

Is there nothing we can agree upon?

Perhaps we can reach back to the mystic chords of our origins for inspiration, or at least clarity.

We the People
of the United States,
in Order to form a more perfect Union,
establish Justice,
insure domestic Tranquility,
provide for the common defence,
promote the general Welfare,
and secure the Blessings of Liberty
to ourselves and our Posterity,
do ordain and establish this Constitution
for the United States of America.

These six phrases are what the Founders had in mind for our purpose. These are the reasons we formed a government; for all of the Founders' flaws and our flaws, this is why we're Americans, and not just inhabitants of a changeable number of North American states. If you immigrate here and want to be an American, here in one sentence is the Cliff Notes version of our *raison d'etre*; here's the playbook. If you get this, you've got the 90% solution, you're in, you'll do fine. And if you were born here and you think being an American means beating the Other side no matter what, or higher profits or lower taxes (or higher taxes or no taxes, whatever), maybe it's time to take a knee, take a deep breath, and revisit what we're really all about.

....in Order to

1. form a more perfect Union,
2. establish Justice,
3. insure domestic Tranquility,
4. provide for the common defense,
5. promote the general Welfare, and
6. secure the Blessings of Liberty to ourselves and our Posterity,

"Form a more perfect Union" –

such a bold aspiration: a more perfect union. I'm not even sure what that is, but I'm sure we're not there yet.

This tickles our moral fundamentals, particularly *loyalty* vs *betrayal,* as we aspire to be a loyal part of a unified whole, and *sanctity* vs *degradation,* as perfection and unity are just about as close to the sacred as a secular covenant can get.

"Establish Justice," –

This was written at a time when enslaved persons were the property of many of the signers, so clearly the 'establishment of justice' was aspirational too. We should all be able to agree that justice should be for all, regardless of wealth, or race, or station. Anyone who does not agree, has, in my opinion, missed a lot of the point of being American.

Care vs *harm* and *fairness* vs *cheating* are addressed by the establishment of justice, as any of us can be harmed by injustice, and *fairness* and justice are almost synonymous.

"Insure domestic Tranquility," –

While at times it seems that this is the exception rather than the rule, most of us still get to go about our daily business in relative peace, we don't have to produce our papers, we often don't feel the need to protest injustice... most of us.

Tranquility can be seen as a surrogate marker for the successful employment of *liberty* vs *oppression*, and the perception thereof. A people who see themselves at liberty are tranquil; those who believe they are oppressed are not tranquil. I emphasize that this can be a function of perception; the unscrupulous can create discontent where it need not be. For instance, most people around the world do not see requirements to wear masks during a pandemic to be oppressive. As I write this I am in a mostly indigenous community in Ecuador; everyone (OK, *almost* everyone) wears a mask both indoors and outdoors, even in circumstances where it really isn't medically necessary; still, they just do, as a community, wear masks. But a significant number of Americans have become convinced that mask-wearing and vaccination mandates are signs of oppression. This is a manifestation of the polarization that has gripped us.

"Provide for the common defense," --

One would think that, of all our Founders' admonitions, this is the one we have embraced most whole-heartedly, as we spend more on our defense budget than the next ten highest spending countries in the world combined. But it's complicated. Providing for the common defense hits on a number of values, and some of them are in conflict.

For instance, we *care* for our countrymen, yet in the process of defending them, some of us will come to *harm*.

We must be willing to fight to preserve our *liberty*, and so we empower the federal government to raise an army; but until the recent all-volunteer force, we often relied upon conscription to fill the ranks, which some understandably regarded as *oppression*. The way we currently salute our service personnel, it would appear that all of us are 'all-in' regarding the need to defend our nation. But anti-vaxxers and anti-maskers reject completely the idea that one is defending the nation by embracing benign steps to stop the pandemic. Imagine what some of them would say about a government they have been conditioned not to trust, forcing them or their offspring into uniform to fight and possibly die in a far-off land.

The requirement or at least the moral obligation for all to serve in some way is only *fair*, and yet as recently as Vietnam, people (men) of means could get deferments or use influence to avoid the draft, which looks like *cheating*. Even now, military service *de facto* falls disproportionately on lower income Americans.

Failure to be *loyal* and serve to defend the nation could be seen as *betrayal*. Since so few Americans actually serve in the military, many conflate supporting defense with hugging the flag and becoming agitated when athletes don't stand for the national anthem: in such protest they see a rejection of *authority* and participation in *subversion*.

"Promote the general Welfare," --

My goodness, not only does the Constitution contain the word "regulated" in the second amendment, but it contains the word "welfare" in the preamble. I'm being facetious, but I believe that if the Constitution was being written today, our polarization would preclude those words being in there as they have become so emotionally loaded.

Progressives would argue that apparently the idea that we would establish a government in part to promote the general welfare of all was not so controversial an idea back in the late 18th century. Conservatives can point to the actions of the Founders, who certainly did not create a welfare state.

Care vs *harm* is activated here, and that being the primary concern of liberals, it is no surprise that government support for programs that help those in need are among the highest of progressive priorities. Liberals see that times have changed since the constitution was written, that we have greater means now, and that we are intolerant of the needy, especially children, living in poverty.

As we've discussed, all of us dislike free riders, but conservatives especially are intolerant as they embrace more strongly than do liberals the imperative of the *proportionality* dimension of *fairness* vs *cheating*. The smallest diversion of the wealth of the nation toward the undeserving is unacceptable.

Again, some of this passion is the result of the deliberate inflammation of biases that we discussed earlier. We've analyzed that emotional well-being has been shown not to improve with a growth in income from $94,000 per year up through two million dollars. But the idea that someone else is getting something they don't deserve can be bad for one's mental health, even if in reality you're actually doing OK financially. Data indicate that some of those on the right are suffering because of the bill of goods of resentment they have been sold by right wing media. Remember this data point from Chapter 10? "Republicans in the highest income quintile, those making more than $100,000 per year, were actually slightly less satisfied than Democrats in the lowest income quintile, those making less than $20,000 per year." (1)

Perception trumps reality, and the resulting resentment can make you sick.

"Secure the Blessings of Liberty to ourselves and our Posterity" --

Obviously, *liberty* vs *oppression* seems primary here. But there is conflict in securing the blessings of liberty for ourselves versus securing them for our posterity. Conservatives tend to view liberty as primary; we're here, we're Americans free to do whatever the heck we want, we're Christians who were told by God in the Book of Genesis that we were to have dominion over everything, animals and plants, the land and oceans and all the wealth to be found therein. So the idea of *not* exploiting nature is foreign. Tree hugging environmentalists who hold up progress to save an endangered snail are acting contrary to God's plan, or are at least just nuts.

Progressives on the other hand see *care* vs *harm* as primary. We are custodians of all with which nature has blessed us, and if we strip mine it to death we are not securing blessing to our posterity; rather we are just reiterating the Tragedy of the Commons, accruing the benefit to a wealthy few of ourselves in this time and the generations to follow will inherit the wind, they're on their own. If we pollute the oceans and ruin the climate for generations or even centuries to come, we are short-sighted and cruel, inattentive to the needs of our grandchildren.

This tension is not new. Teddy Roosevelt saw it and acted to establish National Parks immune from commercial exploitation. But it has a special salience in our generation as, with the possible exception of a global thermonuclear apocalypse, we as a human race have never been in position to have such adverse effects for such a catastrophic duration on such a global scale.

George Washington called our continent "a land designated by Providence for the display of human greatness." Still, at any moment, we can look at our behavior and wonder what we're doing now that will with hindsight so clearly have been a mistake. There are so many opportunities for things to go wrong even when we try to do everything right, that we certainly cannot afford the luxury of unforced errors.

Whether or not we can agree to embrace these six propositions specified in the preamble remains an open question. Assuming we can, then we are faced with what policies we should enact to support those objectives. It's OK to have different views on how we should behave, but if we can agree on the goals, perhaps all our elephants can lean in that direction, and we'll be able to agree that there should be rational reasons for the policies to support them. We have challenges in this area.

The Founders specified that "governments are established among men" in order to do certain things. We seem to have gotten stuck in a cycle of disparaging government. Ronald Reagan famously laid down the simplistic marker that 'government is the problem'. Many on the right seem to believe that government of any size is too big, that 'the government that governs least governs best', and if we would just stop interfering with capitalism and freedom, everything will work out for the best. Those on the left see, as we discussed in the chapter on 'the system is rigged', that we have had plenty of free market non-intervention for centuries, and it hasn't fixed things; indeed it led to a Gilded Age over a century ago and to awful inequality now.

Fareed Zakaria made the point that this perspective is becoming obsolete, that a number of well-governed states around the world, such as Singapore or Taiwan or in Scandinavia, demonstrate that the issue is not whether government should be big or little, but rather, it should just be *good* government. (2) There are some things that only government can do, like building an interstate freeway system or going to the moon. In other areas, too much centralized government just gets in the way, so if government is involved at all, it should just be local. The bottom line is, government should be tight and big when needed, loose and little when not, and whenever applied, it should be efficient and free of corruption and undue influence by special interests.

From the perspective of progressives, the 'big vs small' government argument has indeed become old news for Trump supporters. Now, for Trumpers, big government is OK, as long as it defeats the libs. Among the base, the traditional 'small government, low taxes, don't borrow' ideology just doesn't matter (although predictably, GOP members of Congress have found religion in limiting spending now that they are no longer in power). Government big or small is fine as long as the power of government can be wielded to keep liberals/ Demon-rats/ radicals/ antifa/ communists out of power. Politics has always been a contact sport, and often has been anti-democratic, such as big city political machines in Daley's Chicago or New York's Tammany Hall, or in the Jim Crow South. But it has been rare in the modern era for one of our two major political parties to be so overtly unwilling to recognize not just the desirability, but the legitimacy and the legality, of the other party coming to power.

In April of 2021 conservative columnist David Brooks reported on the results of surveys subsequent to Trump leaving office. When asked, 'Is politics for policies, or for national survival?' over 50% of Trump voters said politics was for national survival; only 19% said it was about policy. In a perhaps unintentional recapitulation of one of the salient effects of traumatic stress, surveyors asked, with which statement do you more agree: that 'the world is a big beautiful place that is full of people who are mostly good,' or that 'our lives are threatened by criminals, terrorists, and illegal immigrants.' Among Biden voters, 75% agreed with the 'beautiful world with good people,' while 66% of Trump voters believe that their lives are in threat. (3)

This degree of fear and pessimism is toxic in a democracy within which we must to some degree have faith in each other. We must believe that when the other guys win, they will govern as they see best; and then if the people decide to make a change, they will relinquish power so our team can take over. If Republicans, Trump supporters, believe in 'Stop the Steal', why should they ever agree to surrender power to Democrats? Democrats stole the election, they are not legitimate! Thus, politics is about survival, not policy; my team must win, or the radicals who hate America will destroy America.

And when Democrats see that Republicans are committed to gerrymandering districts and suppressing Democratic votes, are espousing the Big Lie that Trump won in 2020 and that our elections and institutions don't work and can't be trusted, they conclude that Republicans are no longer the 'loyal opposition'. Rather, they have drunk the Kool-Aid of authoritarianism and no longer support the rule of law and the peaceful transfer of power that undergird the great American experiment in democracy.

Liberals fear that *if Republicans win power, and especially if Trumpists (or Trump himself) regain power:*

They will continue to subvert our electoral processes so that they'll never lose again; and

Republican-led state legislatures will give themselves the power to overturn any election that doesn't go their way under the pretext of 'fraud' or 'irregularities'.

Our representative democracy is in peril as it has never been.

Well, that's a bummer. I can't leave you hanging like that. Let's get optimistic.

Chapter 17

How We Fix This: The Man in the Mirror

We've talked about a lot of problems, and of course I'll be glad to share what I see as solutions. They aren't original, but they will be from my perspective, my opinions about various policies and topics. I don't mean to preach, but... I might preach a little.

I see two axes along which to advance.

The first, this chapter, involves you, and me; us. Americans. What we are about, in and of ourselves.

The second axis, in the next chapter, involves a whole bunch of stuff, policies, goals, objectives.

The first axis: the person in the mirror

The task at hand is as Dusty Baxley articulated to Josh Goldberg soon after they first met. Josh wanted to find a way to be of service to the veteran community. And Dusty observed, 'You seem like a well-intentioned young man. But before you have anything to do with helping my brothers and sisters, you need to unf#*k yourself.'

What are we Americans all about? What is our purpose?

What do we want? What do we need?

As we discussed, it's not just money and possessions; it's connection, it's relationships. And, it's growth, as human beings. We need a group of three to five guys or gals that we hang out with. Most of us do have that. The trouble is that if your 'three-to-five' are drunks or dopers you're probably a jerk or a doper. If you're reading this book, I'm guessing that's probably not you. But if your three-to-five think and say that everything is a disaster and there's no point in anything, that our government is terrible and our leaders are awful, that we just need to tear everything down, there's good chance you're like that, wallowing in negativity, going nowhere and being of service to no one. And before you can contribute to a free and functional society in any meaningful way, you need to get yourself together.

> Only a virtuous people are capable of freedom. As nations become corrupt and vicious, they have more need of masters.
>
> -- Benjamin Franklin

We've discussed at length the phenomenon known as 'motivated reasoning'. As Haidt described it, "Once group loyalties are engaged, you can't change people's minds by utterly refuting their arguments. Thinking is mostly just rationalization, mostly just a search for supporting evidence." (1) We'll talk more about structural changes that can help overcome this fuel to disinformation on a societal level, but in the meantime, there must be something each of us can do with the person in the mirror, steps we can take to free ourselves from the thrall of group influences, steps that don't require funding sources or grand changes in society at large.

The tyranny of self-deception

> Lying to ourselves is more deeply ingrained than lying to others.
>
> -- Dostoyevsky

Ultimately you must want to be free of self-deception. You must want that freedom, and want it bad, because it does not come easily. There is a reason why 'former' Nazis and 'former' jihadists are the exception rather than the rule. As we quoted Carl Sagan, "If we've been bamboozled long enough, we tend to reject any evidence of the bamboozle."

One of the domains of Post Traumatic Growth is spiritual and existential change, which includes the 'exploration of beliefs and notions previously unconsidered'. We must be curious about the real truth and intolerant of lazy thinking that allows us to deceive ourselves. We must recognize that our passions and prejudices are structuring our reasoning and dictating our thinking, typically without our decision-making intellect even being aware of that fact.

More information isn't the answer by itself, because it is seen first through the prism of our passions, and often just helps us mislead ourselves. If you've ever gone deeply down the rabbit hole with a 9/11 denier, they know lots and lots of stuff; they can bury you with the melting points of steel, and testimony from engineer 9/11 deniers who say the buildings couldn't have fallen as they did, and on, and on, and on. Climate deniers have graphs and charts regarding climate change that can appear very convincing if you swallow the whole enchilada without parsing out the nonsense. Vaccine deniers and hydroxychloroquine or ivermectin advocates (hey, ivermectin or eye of newt may yet prove to be effective in treating COVID-19, but as of this writing, no) can produce very impressive looking articles that take a great deal of time and attention to evaluate before one can realize that they don't quite hold water.

> Avoid the precepts of those thinkers
> whose reasoning is not confirmed by experience.
> -- Leonardo da Vinci

The admonition to 'Do your own research' may be hard to obey. I'm a physician so the medical stuff is in my wheelhouse; even still I rely upon other scientists to comb through thousands of pages of data from vaccine trials. I can tell when interpretations of data and conclusions make sense and if/when they don't. But buildings falling down? I rely initially on common sense, as people saw and recorded the planes crashing into the Twin Towers, and also the Bush conspiracy angle doesn't make any sense to me; but for the physics of falling buildings, I must rely upon trusted experts. There is some work involved in finding honest and credible experts you can trust.

There is a delicate balance. Regarding a subject about which you know little but believe a lot, you must be wide open to dispassionately evaluating new and contrary information. It can be helpful to assume that you're wrong until you can prove yourself right, beyond whatever level of doubt works for you. But if you don't have emotionally invested beliefs yet you are quite knowledgeable, it can be exhausting keeping up with and debunking the never-ending absurdities. At some point, you do get to say, look, I've investigated this, and I'm not buying your wild unsupported ideas... but that's only after you've done quite a bit of work.

Further, embracing truth and giving up false beliefs can cost you. Yale law professor Dan Kahan and co-authors point out that we are subject to the influence of "identity protective cognition."

> Nothing any ordinary member of the public personally believes about the existence, causes, or likely consequences of

> global warming will affect the risk that climate change poses to her, or to anyone or anything she cares about. However, if she forms the wrong position on climate change relative to the one [held by] people with whom she has a close affinity -- and on whose high regard and support she depends on in myriad ways in her daily life -- she could suffer extremely unpleasant consequences, from shunning to the loss of employment....
>
> The cost to her of making a mistake on the science is zero, [but] the cost of being out of synch with her peers is potentially catastrophic. (2)

If even unconsciously then, we tend to allow the influences of our group to determine how we feel about complex issues such as climate change.

Ezra Klein notes that if anything, current pressures may well push us away from truth and away from credible sources of information. "One implication of an era where our political identities are becoming more sorted and more powerful is that it will bring a rise in identity-protective cognition, and that's particularly true if the relevant identity groups are able to construct sophisticated architectures of information that we can use to power our reasoning." (3) Overcoming this pressure, seeking information that informs, and not just information that 'powers our reasoning' to support our pre-existing ideas, requires a commitment to truth, and it requires work. Just as someone with substance use disorder should leave his 'friends' who enable his drinking or using, so we may need to extract ourselves from the influence of enablers of deception, even change our close 'three to five' if they sabotage our commitment to the pursuit of truth.

That may be easier said than done. If your family relationships or employment or political career depend upon staying in the good graces of conspiracy theorists, you are faced with tough choices. You may need to hide your true feelings and beliefs, and suffer as a result. (I almost feel compassion for many Republican politicians who no doubt find themselves in this position.) Boris Pasternak encapsulated this phenomenon in a paragraph in his novel *Doctor Zhivago*. Zhivago is describing his cardiac difficulties to an old friend:

> "It's a typical modern disease," Zhivago says, "I think its causes are of a moral order. The great majority of us are required to live a life of constant systematic duplicity. Your health is bound to

> be affected if day after day you say the opposite of what you feel, if you grovel before what you dislike and rejoice at what brings you nothing but misfortune. Our nervous system isn't just a fiction, it's a part of our physical body and our soul exists in space and is inside us like the teeth in our mouth. It can't be forever violated with impunity."

Perhaps this sense of living a life of duplicity is less today in the United States than in post-revolutionary Russia, but it is certainly not absent, and the health consequences are significant.

Aside from those above admonitions, there are indeed other ways to change your approach, change your feelings and thinking, and become a 'formerly deceived' (and a 'formerly self-deceived') person.

All the bad stuff we've talked about in this book is exacerbated by stress, so it'll probably help if you take a look at the ways you handle stress. I briefly alluded to TM (Transcendental Meditation) a couple of chapters ago. Meditation refers to deep thinking, and to 'transcend' means to go beyond, transcending superficial and even deep thinking, experiencing that unalloyed field of awareness that underlies and gives rise to thought.

That practice has been found to be very effective at removing stress; but if you think about its origins, reclusive seers living in caves in India thousands of years ago, 'relaxation' and 'stress management' were probably not high on their list of priorities. They were concerned with human growth, growth of awareness, experience of that innermost silence which is beyond conflict, beyond the apparently irreconcilable, and so beyond guilt, shame, and regret, and yes, beyond all lies and deception.

I cannot tell you that all practitioners of TM are beyond self-deception. I know quite a few who have screwball ideas. But you start where you are, and then get better.

Please indulge a moment of digression. I'll continue to make the case that for most people our reputations, the appearance of doing good, is more important than actually doing good; for most people; but not all.

Lawrence Kohlberg was the Director of Harvard's Center for Moral Education; he created the 'Kohlberg scale' of moral evolution which described the motivations of persons, based upon their moral development. At 'low' levels, people respond just to punishments and rewards; in intermediate states, they respond to group pressures and societal norms; but in advanced states they act on principle, and even on most abstract ethical considerations.

This recognition is taken to another level in a new book by Tony Nader MD PhD, *One Unbounded Ocean of Consciousness: Simple Answers to the Big Questions in Life*. This pulls together philosophy and quantum physics, good and evil, ethics and growth of human potential, in ways that make clear the understanding of humans as transcendent creatures who can identify themselves with the ultimate reality, far beyond considerations of reputation and political agendas. Glaucon was right in that we need to put people's reputations on the line to hold them accountable, but Socrates was right when he asserted that a truly happy person was just and harmonious on the inside; and Dr. Nader is right when he elucidates how any individual can align himself with universal truths and live in righteousness.

While this is open to all of us, I don't expect a universal enlightenment to be upon us before the midterms, so I'll continue with my exploration of how we deal with our countrymen and ourselves, we who are flawed and need to be held accountable. (But after you finish this book, if you'd like a breath of fresh air and some insights into the potential that life can hold, read Dr. Nader's book.)

From this same tradition comes wisdom about mindsets and attitudes that are healthy and helpful. I've described them in depth elsewhere. (4) Many religions and philosophies teach us the value of turning the other cheek. But back to the mundane and banal: many liberals find despicable and just can't stand Stephen Miller or Sean Hannity, not to mention Donald Trump himself.

Trust me, they don't care how you feel.

If you have hatred in your heart for Tucker Carlson (or if you're a Trump supporter who hates all Demonrats and hates Joe Biden because he's a demented pedophile), Carlson or Biden or Hannity or whoever, is not significantly impacted by your animosity... but you are.

You're stewing in it, marinating in a witch's brew of stress hormones and neurotransmitters that are noxious to your nervous system, poisoning your heart, toxic to your relationships, and generally are spreading venom throughout all aspects of your life, while the objects of your disgust are blissfully unaware of your existence. So... don't do that. It is perfectly possible to let go of all that misanthropy and still maintain your passion and action for social justice.

In order to change our politics, first we must work on ourselves; it is that work that effects the changes that improve our politics.

We are divided, but we have often been.

If you're a liberal, election night of 2020 was liberating, you felt like you'd been untied from the railroad tracks, right? But all the problems didn't go away, and now you feel faced with the dilemma of how to avoid Trump ever again.

We are divided, but we agree about a lot of things.

I hope that, if you're a liberal who has read this far, you have gotten past the need to insult and condescend; you have left behind the unhelpful bias that Trump supporters are stupid low information country bumpkins who don't know their own interests. Many of them had legitimate reasons to vote for Trump.

Barack Obama recalled that while running for statewide office in Illinois, he had to campaign not just in Chicago, but in rural parts of the state. He had to make his case to non-urban white voters, and he found that the people generally were intelligent, informed, and they listened attentively to him.

If you are so-called "elite", highly educated and well off financially, pay attention to the 'non-elite.' Knowledge is power; your relative wealth gives you privilege and power; and power corrupts. Don't let it.

Again I hope that, if you're a liberal who has read this far, you recognize that Trumpers actually had some good reasons to like Trump. That is part of the job description for all Americans, but especially liberals: accepting the fact that others get to have ideas in opposition to yours. It may not be an easy pill to swallow, but you need to do the work.

> Those who expect to reap the blessings of freedom
> must undergo like men the fatigue of supporting it.
> -- Thomas Paine

So go ahead and confront untruths, but there's nothing to be gained by being a jerk toward all Trump supporters, especially if you have not given understanding a fair attempt. It doesn't help win anyone over to your view. If you want results, you must do the work.

Our two political parties

The two parties have changed, and they're different.

I know that 'independents' make up a huge chunk of the electorate. But when they step into the ballot box, the choice typically is binary: for most offices most of the time, either a Democrat or a Republican will win.

An independent voter then functionally becomes either one or the other, or irrelevant. So back to 'our two parties'.

Thomas Mann and Norm Ornstein are notoriously 'balanced' journalists; Mann center left, and Ornstein frankly conservative. For decades they "embodied a fundamental assumption of American politics: the two parties were ideologically opposed but otherwise equivalent." (5) But by 2012, they had changed their perspective, writing:

> Today's Republican Party... is an insurgent outlier. It has become ideologically extreme; contemptuous of the inherited social and economic policy regime; scornful of compromise; unpersuaded by conventional understanding of facts, evidence, and science; and dismissive of the legitimacy of its political opposition, all but declaring war on government. The Democratic Party, while no paragon of virtue, is more ideologically centered and diverse, protective of the government's role as it developed over the course of the last century, open to incremental change in policy fashioned through bargaining with Republicans, and less disposed to or adept at take-no-prisoners conflict between the parties. This asymmetry between the parties, which journalists and scholars often brush aside or whitewash in a quest for "balance," constitutes a huge obstacle to effective governance. (6)

Ezra Klein wrote the following coda to their article, noting that the GOP was transforming itself into "vessels of revanchist rage", stating that "A few years later, Trump emerged like a golem summoned by Mann and Ornstein's words. He was their description of the GOP given a shock of orange hair, a cardiovascular system, and a Twitter account. In August 2015, when a Trump nomination... still sounded like a ridiculous prediction, Ornstein argued in *The Atlantic* that Trump really could win, that his candidacy and its triumph was predicted by a cycle of radicalization that was afflicting the Republican Party at every level:" (7)

> I have seen a GOP Congress in which the establishment, itself very conservative, has lost the battle to co-opt the Tea Party radicals, and itself has been largely co-opted, or at a minimum, cowed by them.
>
> As the congressional party has transformed, so has the activist component of the party outside Washington. In state leg-

> islatures, state party apparatuses, and state party platforms, there are regular statements or positions that make the most extreme lawmakers in Washington seem mild.
>
> Egged on by talk radio, cable news, right-wing blogs, and social media, the activist voters who make up the primary and caucus electorates have become angrier and angrier, not just at the Kenyan Socialist president but also at their own leaders. (8)

During the Obama administration, Republicans were willing to shut down the government and nearly throw the world into economic crisis by breaching the debt ceiling, and they shut down the government again during the Trump administration in a fight within themselves over not funding Trump's wall. As angry as Democrats felt toward Bush and then toward Trump, they never threatened to blow up the world economy or even refuse to fund what they saw as Bush's war. These dynamics, the willingness to discard norms and take extreme positions, have not lessened with Trump's departure from office. In September 2021, Republicans again threatened to breach the debt ceiling (not to mention tolerating the Big Lie, which I'll describe again soon).

Klein notes that many liberals view Democratic politicians' restraint as weakness. Frustration on the left is palpable as Democrats control the White House and both houses of Congress, and yet keep their own hands tied by allowing Republicans to filibuster their agenda. He observes:

> The polarizing forces I have described throughout this book have acted on both coalitions. So why has the Democratic Party weathered them in a way the Republican Party hasn't? Why are the two parties so different? The answer is two-fold: Democrats have an immune system of diversity and democracy. The Republican Party doesn't. This has not left the Democrats unaffected by the forces of polarization, to be sure. But if polarization has given the Democratic Party the flu, it has given the Republican Party pneumonia. (9)

This book has I hope argued successfully that our political system is sick, our political parties are sick, and our democracy is sick. One party is sick enough to make us miserable, but the other is so sick that the patient may die.

There are at least two essentials that our political parties must observe.

First, they must recognize that the other side can win; inevitably, the other side will win, and when it does, you shake hands and move on to improve your game and work to win next time.

Second, they must compromise. As the Rolling Stones noted, you can't always get what you want. The other guys live here too. Yes they can be dull and infuriating and not always behaving in good faith, but they're not going away. You make your best case, and then you compromise to get things done.

Our Republic will not survive if either party, and today it's the Republican Party, is unwilling to compromise, and unwilling to concede defeat. That brings us to The Big Lie.

The Big Lie

I must say to many of my Trump supporting friends: brothers and sisters I love you, and it saddens me to tell you, but you've been abused. Leaders whom you trusted have exploited your patriotism, your love of our flag and traditions, and they have deceived you. That shouldn't have happened to you. I'm sorry it happened, but it did. Lawyers like Rudy Giuliani, Lin Wood, Sidney Powell, and many others, non-lawyers including Donald Trump, have lied to you. Media sources have lied to you. Members of Congress like Gosar, Brooks, Biggs, Taylor-Greene, and many others, have lied to you. They shouldn't have done that, and it's not your fault that they did.

> He shirks the responsibility of pulling the house down, but he digs under it that it may fall of its own weight. (10)
>
> -- Abraham Lincoln, speaking of Stephen Douglas, 1858

Just because you've been lied to doesn't mean that there's something wrong with you. People who get their identities stolen or run afoul of con men or who are victimized by online scams often feel embarrassed and ashamed. But you don't need to feel that way. You're not alone in this. It's just something bad that happened to you, it doesn't have to last forever, you can promptly bring it to an end, and it doesn't mean that you're a bad person or that you don't have value.

Just because you've been lied to doesn't mean you have to become a detestable liberal. The Republican Party is suffering through a bizarre illness, an aberration that requires powerful treatment that will be a shock, but is necessary. A merciless look in the mirror will reveal that, for you to be congruent with reality, you must understand to be true some of the things that most liberals understand to be true. That may seem a bitter pill, agreeing with liberals about something. But that doesn't mean that liberals are better than you are, nor does it mean that you must leave your team. You don't have to change jerseys. You don't have to give up being a conservative. We can all agree that we are Americans, and that America should thrive. Liberals can agree with you and agree with Trump that The System Is Rigged against the common man and that we need to Drain The Swamp; you can agree with liberals that in fact the 2020 election wasn't stolen and that we have had a functioning democracy.

You may wonder why I am so adamant about the intolerability of The Big Lie. After all, there have been so many lies, and seemingly more dangerous ones at that. Believing the right-wing social media lies about COVID vaccines making women infertile or killing people, or injecting bleach or taking unapproved medications for COVID, can literally send you to an early grave. Acting on the lies about the debt ceiling can definitely lead to the economy tanking. So what's the big deal about The Big Lie?

As we've discussed, Trump supporters have often taken Trump seriously but not literally... in just one of thousands of possible examples, no there weren't thousands of Muslims in New Jersey cheering on 9/11 as the towers fell, but for his supporters, the spirit of what Trump said was OK. As inappropriate, as hurtful as those comments may have been to a young Muslim-American growing up in our country while feeling rejected by it, they weren't an existential threat to our democracy.

That has changed.

Now, Trump and some of his senior advisors have been explicit that The Big Lie is actually true, and many Trump supporters have adopted that position: the election was stolen, our electoral processes are not secure, Joe Biden is not the legitimate president, and we do not have a functioning democracy. Not only have those liars lied to you, but the insurrection persists, they continue to lie to you. And if you believe their lies, you will believe as they seem to, that it's OK, indeed, it's essential that Republican state lawmakers take over the electoral processes so that if Democrats win in the future, the results can be overturned. That is as dangerous as any threat to the survival of our republic has ever been in our history.

> "Woe to the shepherds who are destroying and scattering the sheep of my pasture!" declares the Lord....
>
> "They tell them and lead my people astray with their reckless lies, yet I did not send or appoint them. They do not benefit these people in the least," declares the Lord.
>
> - - Jeremiah 23:1, 32 NIV

Even while Trump and his campaign staffers were promulgating The Big Lie, the Trump campaign knew that The Big Lie was just that, a lie. (11) Despite knowing that the lie was a lie, they kept repeating it. Even the "cyber ninja" audit in Arizona found that there was no widespread fraud; they found some small change, 99 more votes for Biden, 261 fewer votes for Trump, but there was no stolen election.

A majority of Republicans believe that in order to be a Republican, one must believe The Big Lie. The Big Lie was the basis for January 6th, the attempt to overthrow the election. We've since learned that Trump himself met multiple times with members of the Department of Justice in order to overthrow the election. Those were his words, criticizing to his face his then acting Attorney General Jeffrey Rosen on January 3rd: "One thing we know is you, Rosen, aren't going to do anything to overturn the election."

If you are OK with this, you are only OK with it because you have been lied to. Think back just a few years or even months. Comments about the election being stolen or overthrowing an election would have sounded crazy to you. When Trump made his comments in 2016 that the election was going to be fraudulent, and then after he won he said, no, it wasn't fraudulent or fake after all, that was funny; because he was just being outrageous, and the libs were stupid for taking him literally. But now Trump supporters take him literally. You believe it mostly because you've been lied to, yes; but admit, for many Trump supporters it has become most important to own the libs, to return Trump to power, to have the Other team lose, in 2022, in 2024, no matter what.

Addicted to lies

In 2004 (long before the Trump rise in politics) a researcher looked at fMRI (functional magnetic resonance imaging, brain scans) in partisans (15 Republicans, 15 Democrats, all highly partisan). He showed them slide shows, demonstrating that their political heroes had done something hypocritical. This prompted a lot of brain activity in emotion-related areas, where misery and punishment are processed; the dorso-lateral prefrontal cortex (dlPFC), where sober reasoning takes place, was silent. The last slide though showed that actually, their hero did OK, he wasn't personally involved in the bad thing. This prompted activity in the reward center of the brain, just like the rats who push the button for stimulation, like cocaine and heroin. (12)

If you go on Facebook and see all those comments from treasonous socialist Demonrats, or watch your favorite channel and have described to you all the awful things the libtards are doing and have confirmed your suspicions that the election was stolen, the punishment/misery part of your brain fires up and you get distressed and angry. But when you learn of the progress Trump is making, and how his lawyers are winning in court (they're not) and how Trump is soon going to be reinstated as President (he isn't) and how true Americans are about to take our country back, you get a hit of dopamine in the ventral striatum and elsewhere, just like the partisans in the study, just like rats pushing the button, and you feel proud, vindicated; you feel gooood! But it's mostly lies, for someone else's agenda.

There are people who insist that COVID is a hoax, even with their last breaths as they are dying of it. As this deception morphs into self-deception, you can adapt your entire life around a fantastic delusion. It is difficult to imagine something more pathetic, and sad, and unnecessary.

If you're a Trump supporter, you may now be disappointed, having thought I was a reasonable guy, a veteran who was a bit ambiguous about my team but not a never-Trumper, and now I've revealed my true colors and I've probably been a leftie Democrat since the Ford administration. No, that's not the case. From 1972 even through the 2016 election I was never a Democrat, I was always Independent (except when I was in the Natural Law Party). I wasn't even a never-Trumper in that I thought he might be OK as a President, even though I had strong reservations about him and I never believed he would win.

After Trump's election in 2016, I wrote a long post on Facebook addressed to my liberal friends trying to talk them off the ledge, believing that now (then) that he had unexpectedly won the election, Trump was like the dog that caught the car, he would get sober, appreciate the weight of his sacred duty, abandon his crazy talk like Ali did after he beat Sonny

Liston, and be a reliably American President. Here it is, from mid-November 2016, what I thought Trump might do:

> My dear liberal and progressive friends,
> I know you are distressed, and with good reason. The prospect of a President Trump, the names being floated for his cabinet (Sarah Palin for Secretary of the Interior? Deliver us oh Lord)... you're feeling nauseated. I'm not going to list all the concerns and worries, there are almost literally too many to count. I get it. Our institutions and norms may be about to face unprecedented stress.
> But ever the optimist, I'd like to propose the possibility that, it just might not be that bad. It might be worse, but, it might not be. Anyway, let's go crazy glass-half-full, and consider the following, non-comprehensive list, in no particular order.
> Ideology and climate change: As his primary opponents often pointed out, he's neither a true Republican nor a true conservative. Thus, he may not be ideologically wedded to the most egregious elements of the right wing agenda, such as science denial, climate denial, trickle-down economics, etc. Yes he said he was, but that was the campaign, and he told so many falsehoods during the campaign that he melted the fact-checking industry; and now the campaign is over. So, if I were a Tea Party ideologue counting on his toeing the anti-progressive line, I'd be nervous. As the steel baron Frick said about Teddy Roosevelt, "We bought the son of a bitch, and then he didn't stay bought."
> Hyper-partisanship: I don't know the man, but he does seem to like to be active, and to build. I don't think he'll kowtow to the recent Republican dogma of obstructionism and doing nothing. He may want to govern, and may look for partners in governing. The Republican elite largely shunned him; he doesn't owe them anything and he may enjoy sticking his finger in their eye and working with Democrats to build infrastructure, etc. I don't believe the Democrats will adopt the posture of Mitch McConnell and oppose everything he tries just because he's Trump (an approach that I thought was profoundly un-American, prioritizing party and re-election over what was best for the country, rejecting policies previously supported by conservatives just to frustrate Obama).
> Economy and taxes: He said he would cut taxes, build the military, not cut entitlements, and not add to the national debt, while building infrastructure. Obviously, some of those are mutually exclusive. Something will have to give. I don't know what, but we might end up with some tax increases (better not be on working people or the middle class or he

may lose his base, so, the rich) and prudent borrowing at current bargain basement rates. Who knows.

Obamacare: Even the nuttiest of Republicans aren't going to take away insurance from 20 million people, restore the ability of insurance companies to kick people off for pre-existing conditions, etc. So after much gnashing of teeth and showboating, they'll repeal Obamacare, 'tear it out root and branch,' and replace it with… Obamacare. They'll call it TrumpCare, but it'll have all the elements of Obamacare, an individual mandate a la Romney, plus all the Republican governors will go along with Medicaid expansion, because unlike divisive Obama, Trump is such a great leader. Hooray.

Trade Deals: His trademark issue. Maybe his populism here will be a good thing, eschewing the interests of multinationals. I don't think he'll be able to get overt trade wars past the Republican Congress, and that's good. He may find it easier to align with Bernie's crowd than with Republicans.

Racism and Immigration: Only Nixon could go to China. The Great Wall will become a metaphor for border security, E-Verify will decrease supply of jobs, those here will gain some legal status (but for God's sake don't call it Amnesty!). It'll end up with the comprehensive immigration reform the senate already passed, but this time it'll go through because Trump Can Get Things Done. He'll find out that the vetting we're doing is actually quite thorough, but I doubt he'll adequately address the refugee crisis. Trump said plenty of racist things, and has done racist acts in the past. But he did act to open Mar-a-Lago to blacks and Jews. Is he really a racist in his heart? I don't know. If so, it wouldn't be the first time a racist has occupied the White House, historically that's probably been the rule rather than the exception. I fear he is racist… but maybe I'm wrong.

NATO and the military: Both Democrats and Republicans want NATO to remain intact. He will acquiesce to that consensus. He will not be able to do the awful things he said he would. Indiscriminate bombing, murder of the families of terrorists, torture; those are crimes, illegal orders, and the military would not follow them.

Supreme Court: Get ready for Scalia 2.0. That'll suck, but, elections have consequences, and we're stuck with this. We'll be no worse off than we were before he died.

Maybe he's just been a showman, and he will now etch-a-sketch away many of the other awful things we've heard and seen. Maybe now he'll be infused with the majesty of the office, and be uplifted by the collective consciousness of what I hope is fundamental goodness within the American body politic. Those of you practicing techniques that enhance

> coherence in national awareness will reaffirm your commitment to your practices. We won't hear any more bashing of Muslims or Hispanics, he doesn't need to do that anymore, and he'll distance himself from the Breitbart crowd. He has a couple months to witness up close the class and dignity of the sitting President, modeling the behavior I hope he'll adopt.
> I hope.
> But liberals should be praying for the health of Ruth Bader Ginsburg....

But I was mostly wrong, and a great opportunity was missed.

In 1787 Benjamin Franklin was walking out of the Constitutional Convention in Independence Hall in Philadelphia. A bystander asked, "What kind of government do we have?"

Franklin replied, "A republic, if you can keep it."

That "If" has never been a serious concern within my lifetime... until now.

Remember my story about my two favorite teams being the Lakers and whoever was playing the Celtics? There was a point to that... because it turned out not to be true.

In 1988, the Boston Celtics represented the NBA (and thus the USA) when they played in the preseason McDonald's Open tournament in Spain to open the 1988-89 season. Their first game was against Yugoslavia. I didn't know anything about basketball in Yugoslavia, but versus my nemeses Larry Bird and Kevin McHale and Robert Parish? C'mon man. The game began and to my shock, the Yugoslavians were not getting wiped out. What the hell is going on? You Celtics can torture my Lakers but you can't put away these tall bearded white guys with unpronounceable names? Only with time did I learn that Yugoslavia was loaded, Drazen Petrovic and Vlade Divac and Toni Kukoc, they all ended up in the NBA; those dudes could play.

At halftime the game was still close and I found myself yelling at the TV, telling the Celtics to get off their butts and start playing and beat these guys. Eventually the natural order of the universe was restored and the Celtics defeated the Yugoslavians, but there was no denying that the unthinkable had happened: I had been routing for the Celtics. My national pride trumped my Laker pride. (The following year Vlade Divac was drafted by the Lakers so I was routing for him... go figure.)

To hate like this is to be happy forever.
We must let that go.

There are some things that are more important than being a Laker fan; or being a liberal or a conservative; or being against Trump, or against Demonrats.

At this moment in America, our partisan polarized tribal identities are threatening our national survival. We must let them go, or at least, loosen our death grip on these identities.

And we must not tolerate politicians or media personalities who inflame these identities for their selfish interests. If we do tolerate them, we are just surrendering our autonomy and allowing ourselves to be manipulated by others. That is not freedom.

> Everything can be taken from a man but one thing: the last of the human freedoms -- to choose one's attitude in any given set of circumstances, to choose one's own way.
>
> -- Victor Frankl

In 1956 then Senator John F. Kennedy wrote *Profiles in Courage*. In it, he spelled out what was occasionally at stake for a politician. When faced with a tough issue or a tough vote, he (almost all 'he' back then) had to decide: do I make the politically expedient choice, do something that I know is not quite right but will allow me to remain in office so that I may do good things in the future? Or do I just do the right thing, knowing that it may cost me my seat? Unfortunately, these days most Republicans have wasted no time making the politically expedient, perhaps cowardly, choice. They have embraced The Big Lie.

Some, like Amash and Kinzinger and Cheney have passed the test, but they are now exiled within or from the party. Most Republicans have been tested and found wanting. They know better (or they should know better) but they have either embraced the lie, or they have adopted a posture of supine acquiescence, just remaining silent in the face of lies that threaten our electoral processes, the foundation of our democracy. They are afraid of a mean tweet or comment, or a primary challenge, or losing their job. Their silence is perhaps more cowardly than the cynicism of faux advocacy or the delusion of real belief.

It pains me to say it, but in my humble opinion, those are the predominant themes to be found in the political class of today's Republican Party: cowardice, cynicism, and delusion.

I say this not because I would choose to destroy the GOP, but rather I would choose to resurrect it.

> If you can't be a good example,
> you'll just have to be a horrible warning.
> -- Catherine Aird

For decades, polling has told us that more Americans call themselves conservative than call themselves liberal. It is only in recent years that even *half* of *Democrats* self-identify as liberal. (13) It turns out that recently, conservatism is more of an identity than an ideology, so the GOP, and Trump, have been able to lean into that identity and readily turn identity into votes. True conservatives who believe in limited government and the restraint of executive power should have been horrified by the Trump presidency (many were of course, like George Will, etc.); but instead, they embraced the things Trump said that enlivened their identities, and approved whatever he wanted to do, whether it was ideologically conservative or liberal. Ezra Klein noted, "This is what Trump understood about conservatives that so many of his critics missed: they were an identity group under threat, and so long as you promised them protection and victories, they would follow you to hell and back." (14)

> One would start with great confidence that he could convince any sane child that the simpler propositions of Euclid are true; but, nevertheless, he would fail, utterly, with one who should deny the definitions of axioms. (15)
> -- Abraham Lincoln

When identity is primary, the argument is not about fiscal policy or policing or the size of the defense budget, or even about rational beliefs; rather, it is a Manichaean struggle for existence. In a battle between good and evil, there is no room for compromise or seeing the other's point of view. Former Republican Congressman Justin Amash found this first-hand in dealing with his constituents during the Trump administration:

> A lot of Trump Republicans have this mindset that they have to fight this all out war against the left. And if they have to use big government to do it, they're perfectly fine with that. So when I go to Twitter and talk about overspending or the size of the government, I get a lot of reactions now from Trump supporters saying, "Who cares how big the government is," or "Who cares how much we're spending as long as we're fighting against illegal immigration and pushing back against the left." (16)

Democrats on the other hand are more ideologically diverse and require subtler handling by their politicians. That makes it more difficult for them to activate identity to win elections (or even win votes in Congress, as the September 2021 infrastructure bills negotiations show, as the distance between Joe Manchin and Bernie Sanders illustrates). The downside for Democrats is that their heterogeneity can seem to make them politically weak; it's said that Democrats bring a soup ladle to a gunfight. The upside: it protects them from demagogues who might lead them all over a cliff. While there is a liberal bias in mainstream media, we don't see the same overt embrace of falsehood; the diversity on the left disallows them from all getting in lockstep with a lie. Paradoxically, the demagoguery of Trump activated not just the GOP base, but Democrats, inspiring them to be willing to crawl over broken glass for a chance to vote against Trump.

Philosopher Bertrand Russell warned against the threats that too much influence from either the right or left might present, writing that "Every community is exposed to two opposite dangers: ossification through too much discipline and reverence for tradition, on the one hand; and on the other hand, dissolution, or subjection to foreign conquest, through the growth of an individualism and personal independence that makes cooperation impossible." (17)

It appears that today's Republican Party and right wing media have adopted the worst from right and left. It is uncompromising in its reactionary approach to liberal democracy, such as by constraining the voting rights of minorities; while promoting dissolution through unbalanced individualism, as we see in anti-vaccine and anti-mask rhetoric that has attenuated our ability to cooperate.

Liberals look back on the Trump administration with horror: such a waste of time, such a stain on the American character, such an embarrassment. But even if you believe that, maybe it was a good thing. We lanced a boil. If Clinton had been elected, we would have had a festering sore of right wing and Russian disinformation. We have a proclivity to look at our history and our politics through rose colored glasses: we are special and are destined for righteousness that will just inevitably come to pass. That perspective of American exceptionalism is harder to embrace now. We are special only if we do the work to be special. The Trump administration put all our flaws out in the open, including our assumptions that politicians' behavior would be constrained by shame, and our reliance upon norms rather than law; we can no longer ignore them.

I believe America needs a strong and intelligent conservative party. The GOP is the only logical candidate. But it has become untethered to its own conservatism, and has been joined at the hip with Donald Trump, allowing for utterly un-Republican and un-American positions, positions that whipsaw across the ideological spectrum and are defined by whatever Trump decides is in his own best interest. Trump attacks the pillars of our democracy: a free press (enemy of the people etc.), an independent judiciary (not fair, stupid judges, he's a Mexican, etc.), checks and balances through the separation of powers (disobeying Congressional subpoenas), the rule of law (obstruction of justice, interference in the justice department and FBI), and now the very essence of our democracy, the acceptance of the results of elections that don't go your way. And the vast majority of members of the Republican Party has either surrendered, or enthusiastically embraced the agenda of Trumpism.

> Fanaticism consists of redoubling your efforts
> when you have forgotten your aim.
> - - George Santayana

The GOP is sick, it is in crisis, in a delirium from which it must arise, or die. It is up to us Americans to awaken the GOP to its roots. And there is nothing quite so awakening as a thorough and complete butt-whipping.

We have divisions, but it could be worse. After the genocide in Rwanda in the 1990s within which Hutus massacred over 800,000 Tutsis, they managed to put together a National Unity and Reconciliation Commission. You could be forgiven for thinking that the task of reintegrating into society tens or hundreds of thousands of persons who had either hacked people to death with machetes or had enabled those murders, alongside the surviving family members of those murdered, may not be achievable. Their processes included such things as confessions by the perpetrators, and public apologies, and offering reparations. While outcomes there have not been perfect, if the Rwandans can do this, can't we Americans?

Mitt Romney touched upon the beginning of this process during the second impeachment when he called on his fellow Republicans to denounce The Big Lie and "Tell them the truth!"

Conservative commentator Charlie Sykes believes the following:

> Trumpism will only succeed if both the Right and the Left fail to understand the tenuous relationship between conservatism and the nativist authoritarianism with which it has become temporarily allied.
>
> What possible common ground could they find? We could start with a renewed appreciation for a reality-based politics, truth, ethics, checks and balances, civil liberties, and the constitutional limits on executive power. However tenuous, there should also be a mutual acknowledgement of the importance of diversity (of ideas as well as identity), tolerance (which needs to go both ways), and a commitment to America as an idea rather than a walled and isolated city. (18)

I would be glad to be wrong, but I think that the GOP is unlikely to come back to Earth and seek common ground if it can continue to inflame the base enough to turn out the vote but not so much that they vote to 'throw the bums out', continue to warrant the support of their wealthy donor base by delivering on the pro-corporate agenda, and continue to block meaningful and effective changes in government. I think the GOP will change only if it gets slaughtered. Like someone with substance use disorder who has been telling himself he's just a social drinker or lightweight user, finding himself in jail in a puddle of vomit can precipitate that 'rock bottom' experience that may catalyze change.

You may think it odd that I advocate for a conservative party, and yet I am about to suggest a bunch of interventions that ideally will bring the GOP to its knees. Maybe they'll all start TM and stop believing and spreading lies and stop sabotaging government so they can claim that government is the problem... but I doubt it. I believe the current iteration of the Republican Party must have a near-death experience before there is any chance of it really addressing its dysfunction and becoming a positive force in American life. Remember the title of this book, "... how reasonable Americans could support Trump... and whatever comes next." *Whatever comes next* is a scary prospect.

If you're a Trump supporter, you may remain unconcerned with all my worries expressed in this chapter. You may believe that giving GOP led state legislatures veto power over the votes of the people is a good idea, because you still believe the Big Lie about widespread voter fraud. You may be undisturbed by the undemocratic behaviors of Trump and elected Republicans, because you believe that defense of what you feel are true American values is more important than the obscure nuts and bolts of running elections. Those are your opinions.

In my opinion, The Big Lie, and the laws currently being passed allowing state legislatures to overturn the will of the people, are among the greatest dangers we have ever faced. The Big Lie is now a lie; but if election results really are overturned in 2022 or 2024, it will become a self-fulfilling prophecy. Democrats will see that, indeed, the election is being stolen, and that we have lost our democracy.

If, or when, both sides agree that we cannot express our national will through peaceful elections, what is the alternative?

In my opinion, the longer Trumpism draws breath, the more we risk our nation, because it is likely than sooner or later, "a savvier politician than Trump could focus on defending white privileges without constantly crossing into outright racism, and prove far more politically formidable."(19)

> It is to deny what the history of the world tells us is true, to suppose that men of ambition and talents will not continue to spring up amongst us. And when they do, they will as naturally seek the gratification of their ruling passion as others have done before them. The question then is, can that gratification be found in supporting and maintaining an edifice that has been erected by others? Most certainly it cannot.... Is it unreasonable, then, to expect that some man... with ambition sufficient to push... to its utmost stretch, will at some time spring up among us? And when such a one does, it will require the people to be united with each other, attached to the government and laws, and generally intelligent, to successfully frustrate his designs. Distinction will be his paramount object, and although he would as willingly, perhaps

> more so, acquire it by doing good as harm, yet, that opportunity being past, and nothing left to be done in the way of building up, he would set boldly to the task of pulling down.
>
> -- Abraham Lincoln, Lyceum Speech, 1838

We have had demagogues, men of ambition who would subvert our democracy; but we have never had the combination of such a man with a major political party so apparently willing to acquiesce to his malign desires.

Chapter 18

Truth or Consequences

Here's the second axis...a list of things to do. This is some of what things would look like if I could wave a magic wand.

I've already talked about immigration, guns, abortion, and a host of issues, but others remain.

I believe these first two are fundamental:

Enliven our commitment to truth through education and cultural change.

Reform our electoral structure.

And then here are others that can serve as examples, from a list that is not exhaustive, such as the Supreme Court, defunding the police, the Electoral College, adding states, national service, and more.

Truth, reputation, and accountability

We can just change our minds ourselves, but that is relatively rare. As we've analyzed from Haidt, the sequence usually goes like this: first, we make our intuitive judgment based on our elephant, our passions; then, we construct reasons to support the decision we've made. Occasionally, we can then sit down and rehash what we've decided, but generally, we're just awful at seeking out information in order to refute our own arguments; that would run contrary to our elephant.

Friends can help us change our minds. They can do something that we tend not to do ourselves: "they can challenge us, giving us reasons and arguments that sometimes trigger new intuitions, thereby making it possible for us to change our minds." (1)

When I was in high school, I am embarrassed to admit that I took my parents for granted. I was a nascent hippie, we weren't supposed to trust anyone over 30, and my parents were as 'square' as one would expect adults of that generation to be. I didn't dislike my parents, not at all, I loved them; but still, they were, you know, *parents*. One evening a close friend named Jay, senior to me in hippiedom, more experienced in the use of drugs and the ways of the world, was at my house. His reputation, in my eyes, was beyond reproach; without having given it conscious thought, I valued his opinions, far more than I valued those of my parents. My mother was in the kitchen preparing food or washing dishes or something, and she was singing. I remember as clearly as if it were yesterday, Jay commented: "Your mom is so mellow."

I was shocked. "Mellow" was the supreme compliment, and to hear it applied to an adult was extraordinary. It was a cattle prod to my elephant. This was an example of "social persuasion", one person's intuition-driven judgment (Jay's elephant's decision that my mother was mellow) affecting another person's intuition which in turn affects that person's judgment (my elephant ingesting and accepting that input from a dear and respected source and coming up with the judgment that, yes, my mother is mellow). Constructing the rationale (my rider, the reasoning to support my intuitive judgment) for concluding that my mother was mellow was easy, as data were abundant. She was a wonderful woman, infinitely patient, loving to her family and kind and respectful to everyone I ever saw her meet. It is mortifying to recall that I was so dull and weak-minded that I didn't see what was in front of my eyes, and it took the input of a friend to help me recognize not just that I loved my parents, but that it was OK for me to appreciate them as well.

Please note that while the term 'persuasion' denotes effort, Jay was making no effort to 'persuade' me of anything. Indeed, 'social persuasion' may be and often is effected simply by the power of one's example.

Fortunately for me, my 'three-to-five' included young men like Jay, who was a good man. Unfortunately for many, the social persuasion link (and/or the subsequent reasoned persuasion link) can be activated by malign actors. "Many of us believe that we follow an inner moral compass, but the history of social psychology richly demonstrates that other people exert a powerful force, able to make cruelty seem acceptable (2) and altruism seem embarrassing (3), without giving us any reasons." (4) We need ways to think better and make better decisions by ourselves (discussed in the previous chapter: TM, less stress, better thinking, etc.); and if we're going to be influenced, be influenced by good people (prune your three-to-five, add good influencers your life), and avoid being influenced by jerks. Avoiding jerks requires attending to their reputations, and tethering Truth to people's reputations.

You may recall back in chapter 3 I'd quoted Haidt regarding Plato's brother Glaucon indicating that "we need to make sure that everyone's *reputation* is on the line all the time," that reputation was important, and that we would deal with reputation later. Later is now. (5)

Philip Tetlock is a political science writer and expert in accountability, currently the Annenberg University Professor at the University of Pennsylvania. His research demonstrates that people behave differently if they know they're going to be held accountable than if they don't. When subjects are asked to decide guilt or innocence based upon some legal information they're given, if there's no accountability, if their reputations are not under scrutiny, their performance is lazy and logically flawed in many of the ways we have discussed. But if they know someone is going to review their work and ask them to explain their decision-making, they evaluate information critically, refrain from premature conclusions, and change their conclusions based upon new information if such is made available.

Tetlock found two kinds of rational thought: *exploratory* thought is an "evenhanded consideration of alternative points of view," whereas *confirmatory* thought is "a one-sided attempt to rationalize a particular point of view." (6) Clearly, our politics needs exploratory thought, but they are dominated by confirmatory thought. Tetlock explains:

> A central function of thought is making sure that one acts in ways *that can be persuasively justified or excused to others*. Indeed, the process of considering the justifiability of one's choices may be so prevalent that decision makers not only search for convincing reasons to make a choice when they must explain that choice to others, *they search for reasons to convince themselves* that they have made the "right" choice. (7)

Whether their thinking and decision making leads to true and reliable conclusions is less important to thinkers and decision makers than the *appearance* of their thinking being worthwhile. If they can appear to have made the right choice, their reputation remains intact.

Three conditions are required for *accountability* to lead to *exploratory thought*:

1) decision makers learn before forming any opinion that they will be held accountable to an audience,
2) the audience's views are unknown, and
3) the thinkers/decision makers believe the audience is well informed and interested in accuracy. (8)

Unfortunately, our current political and informational systems have failed epically and are still failing spectacularly in creating these three conditions. We are not putting people's reputations on the line in any coherent fashion.

1) Yes, politicians and media personalities know they will be held accountable to an audience, but the audiences demand confirmatory, not exploratory, thought. In the case of politicians the important audience is populated primarily by wealthy donors, and in today's GOP, often there is an audience of one: Donald Trump.

2) The audience's views are *not* unknown. In order to survive primaries in our gerrymandered world, politicians must cater to the extremes of their base; and for ratings and advertisers, Fox News and OAN commentators must fulfill the fevered expectations of their angriest viewers.

3) No; politicians, media personalities, and moneyed special interests (that is, The Swamp) spend tons of time and money making sure the audience is not well informed but misinformed, angry, and seeking confirmatory thought, not accuracy.

> No one lies so boldly as the man who is indignant.
>
> -- Friedrich Nietzsche

As a result, there is no, or certainly not enough, threat to the reputations of politicians or talking heads after they have lied or misled.

Confirmatory thought, confirmation bias, is only human, a built-in feature, not a bug. Overcoming it is a challenge, particularly when the unscrupulous exploit it for their economic or political gain.

For you and me as individuals dealing with our friends and relatives, I hope the tips in chapter 15 are helpful in effecting social persuasion, and in opening the door to reasoned persuasion. This isn't propaganda or exploitation of human nature; I believe that the connection required for you and me to enable social persuasion is a good unto itself.

But while connecting with each other and changing minds one at a time is important and worthwhile in the small circles within which we live, it may not do the job on a societal scale. We need to leverage our commitment to truth in order to effect change in the collective awareness of our fellow countrymen.

> We should not expect individuals to produce good, open-minded, truth-seeking reasoning, particularly when self-interest

> or reputational concerns are in play. But if you put individuals together in the right way, such that some individuals can use their reasoning powers to disconfirm the claims of others, and all individuals feel some common bond or shared fate that allows them to interact civilly, you can create a group that ends up producing good reasoning as an emergent property of the social system. That's why it's so important to have intellectual and ideological diversity within any group or institution whose goal is to find truth (such as an intelligence agency or a community of scientists) or to produce good public policy (such as a legislature or advisory board). (9)

In today's environment, with Truth under attack from so many directions, from Russia to the GOP to television and social media, I would add the electorate at large to the list of 'groups and institutions whose goal' should be to find truth. In addition to changing individual minds, to quote Haidt, we "can change the path that the elephant and rider find themselves traveling on. You can make minor and inexpensive tweaks to the environment, which can produce big increases in ethical behavior." (10)

Making real the threat to reputation has helped liberals with the truth; even if exposing even fairly moderate misbehavior (for example, that of comedian-turned-Senator Al Franken) seems to hurt the team in the short term, the perception of deceit or sexual impropriety on the part of Democratic politicians or liberal commentators has become disqualifying on the left. It can, but so far has not, seemed to help on the right. Trump is the personification of that phenomenon, sailing unscathed through sexual scandals and the defrauding of his customers or supporters. It may yet help, through the distaste of conservatives for free riders. At some point it may become recognized that people who stuff money into their own pockets through right-wing PACs or who make fortunes while telling lies, are free riders. Their castigation of the libs and embrace of Real Americans has so far protected their reputations from scrutiny and opprobrium; but it may not always be so.

Journalism, education and scientific truth-seeking

"Congress shall make no law... abridging the freedom of... the press...."

A free press is essential. To my mind, journalism is one of the professions (along with teaching) that are not accorded enough respect. Journalism done well by true professionals is worth its weight in gold. If free and fair elections are the skeleton and muscle of a democracy, journalism is the life-blood. But "journalism" as it is too widely practiced, without good editors; without basic corroboration from multiple sources; with a willingness to pass on misinformation in an attempt to be 'balanced'; with a weak-kneed acceptance of contrasting points of view without rigorous evaluation of the bases for those points of view; with its fascination with flash over substance; of horse-race over issues; is life-blood, yes, but blood full of toxic waste. And too much of what we consume as journalism is not journalism at all. As we've discussed, much of it is just half-truths and lies, designed to agitate people; it is poison. And in my opinion, it is not protected by the First Amendment.

Don't get me wrong, lies (with few exceptions) are protected speech. As I've said, liars can stand on the street corner and lie at the top of their lungs to their hearts' content, nobody will stop them. But if the limits to speech should be modest, there is certainly *no requirement to allow for the amplification of lies and disinformation that injure our democracy*.

> This Court has gone far toward accepting the doctrine that civil liberty means... that all local attempts to maintain order are impairments of the liberty of the citizen. The choice is not between order and liberty. It is between liberty with order and anarchy without either. There is danger that, if the Court does not temper its doctrine logic with a little practical wisdom, it will convert the constitutional Bill of Rights into a suicide pact.
>
> -- Justice Robert Jackson, *Terminiello v. Chicago* (1949)

The amplification of lies from Trump, from the Russians, from the left or the right, from news commentators who spread misinformation whether it's about vaccines or the insurrection, needs mitigation. The 'news' outlets themselves have failed. Mark Zuckerberg and Facebook and Instagram etc., have failed. Congress has failed. To their detriment of their legacies, they've all had their chances, and they've failed, utterly.

> No legacy is so rich as honesty.
>
> -- *All's well that ends well*, Act 3 scene iii

In the wake of lawsuits against many of those who had falsely claimed that Dominion and voting machines were hacked by the Chinese or Hugo Chavez's Venezuela, a number of right-wing news outlets have distanced themselves from those persons. In February of 2021, WABC played a disclaimer before Rudy Giuliani's radio program (11), indicating the radio station didn't stand by anything he said. The airwaves of radio and television, the bandwidth of the internet, belong to all of us. In addition to, for instance, consumer boycotts of sponsors of liars, there is a role for government. There is no right to have one's lies broadcasted. Congress could direct the FCC to re-enliven 'equal time' and fairness. If commentators are going to lie, their broadcasts could be fact checked in real-time. As the Voting Rights Act used to require special accommodations by states that had been guilty of racial discrimination in voting, so the FCC could set aside time in the broadcasts of liars to have rebuttal to their lies. Repeat offenders could face civil or even criminal penalties.

> In individuals, insanity is rare; but in groups,
> parties, nations and epochs, it is the rule.
> -- Friedrich Nietzsche

There are currently hearings in Congress, documenting that social media have been deliberately inattentive to the negative impact of their platforms, particularly upon teenage girls. In my opinion, it is past time for regulation of this industry. If they can't seem to figure out how to remove such offensive content, or even whether they should be in the business of removing lies; government can help with that. I know the argument that we don't want government censoring free speech. I don't buy it; no one is proposing government censorship. But these platforms are lacking in competition, in privacy, and in safety. Platforms and engineers, the people who create and implement the technology, are currently immune (Section 230 of the Communications Decency Act) from accountability for harms inflicted. We are poisoning ourselves, driving ourselves mad. We need to stop it. We are perfectly capable of regulating utilities. We have enough wise men and women who could populate apolitical regulatory agencies, who know lies from truth and can get rid of one without impacting the other.

Education

Unfortunately, while most of us would agree in the abstract that Truth is better than non-Truth, many if not most Americans know what they believe, but typically don't know why. Our education often does not usually include learning how to think about things.

Without going too deeply down the philosophical rabbit hole of intellectual virtues and epistemic responsibility, let's just hold on to the idea that Truth is good.

We should teach our young how it is that people discover the Truth. This includes learning about the scientific method, and journalism, social media, and fact checking. It should include obstacles to Truth, all the logical fallacies and cognitive biases that we've alluded to in this book. We've discussed how medical teams, juries, the best job you ever worked at, intelligence agencies, airplane crews, scientists, how we hope and expect and find that all these environments manage to overcome passion driven biases. Our young should know how that works, how we do that.

> A well-instructed people alone can be permanently a free people.
>
> -- James Madison

We should do a better job of teaching civics to our young.

Every American should be able to pass the test that every new American citizen must pass. Every American should learn our history; learn how we resolve tension between factions; what the pledge of allegiance means; how we balance between banning hate speech and tolerating unpopular speech; how we respect each other's values; what the values are that underlie our various positions; and what it means to love our country.

> A primary object... should be the education of our youth in the science of government. In a republic, what species of knowledge can be equally important? And what duty more pressing... than communicating it to those who are to be the future guardians of the liberty of the country?
>
> -- George Washington

Our electoral system

It's not broken as Trump would claim it is, but it is bent, and bending more at the moment. In my opinion, while taking certain steps may appear to be putting a thumb on the scale (actually lifting a thumb off) in favor of Democrats and killing off Republicans, in the medium to long term these actions paradoxically will restore the health of the Republican Party, and favorably impact the political health of the entire nation. That idea is, if Republicans see that the nasty unfair tactics they've been employing won't work, they'll give up the hateful nonsense and put their attention on issues and conservative policies that actually help people.

Political parties that can be given up for dead one year are only an election cycle away from recapturing the goodwill of the American voter through imagination and vision. As we learned in *The Princess Bride*, one can be just *mostly* dead and still emerge the hero. Here we go.

Voter suppression laws may be overcome by angering people enough to do whatever it takes to vote, but that is not sustainable. Voter suppression is terrible. Placing obstacles to voting, making people wait in line for multiple hours to vote, criminalizing giving them water while they wait in lines, inviting partisan 'poll watchers' to intimidate minority voters, requiring identification and then accepting a gun permit while rejecting a student ID, etc., etc., etc., are all un-American tactics and should be rejected. Voting rights bills now in Congress should be passed. Democrats should do so, immediately.

> We in America do not have government by the majority -- we have government by the majority who participate.... All tyranny needs to gain a foothold is for people of good conscience to remain silent.
>
> -- Thomas Jefferson

Apathy is enough of an impediment to our eternal vigilance against tyranny. Voter suppression laws are active steps toward tyranny and must be resisted.

The **revolving door** between government employees and lobbyists needs reform. The Swamp should indeed be drained.

Gerrymandering should be ended. Primaries should select for candidates with the broadest appeal who can win a general election when voted upon by people with diverse ideas and viewpoints. This will incentivize moderation and compromise and restore civility and function to our government.

We should resurrect and update the **Fairness Doctrine**.

We need **campaign finance reform**. We need to overturn *Citizens United* or pass legislation that renders the decision moot.

> The Supreme Court, is a series of rulings dating back to the '70s, has decided that political spending is constitutionally protected speech, so you can't regulate it out of politics. But that means that workable reforms tend to toss us between plans that would amplify the powers of small donors, which worsen the problems of polarization, or plans that permit institutional money to flood the system, with all the attendant corruption. So long as politics runs on private donations, you're left with the inescapable problem that the people who donate want something different from the people who don't. (12)

That leaves us with the option of publicly funded political campaigns. It won't be easy, but there are plenty of smart people with plenty of good ideas that could make this a reality.

> Now and then an innocent man is sent to the legislature.
> -- Kin Hubbard

With reform, it is likely that we'll attract a better class of people into the political sphere. Politicians are weird. They have a weird job, having to raise money all the time. Some politicians spend up to half their working hours, their entire political career, just raising money for their eternal campaigning. Who wants to do that?

Who thinks it's a good idea to have a system wherein our leaders, our decision makers, are selected from a population of people who are willing to spend so much of their lives groveling for money from people virtually all of whom have narrow self-serving interests? No wonder things are screwed up.

The **Electoral College** should be abandoned. Since it's in the Constitution, getting rid of it may be difficult (amending the Constitution is not a walk in the park), but making it functionally irrelevant is easier. The National Popular Vote Interstate Compact (NPVIC) would require states to award their electors to whomever wins the popular vote. Currently, states representing 195 electoral votes have signed on to the NPVIC; when it gets to 270, it goes into effect. The result would be that candidates would have to campaign all over the country and not be unduly influenced by a handful of swing states. Also, it would mean 'one-person, one-vote', that the person with the most votes would win the election (what an idea!).

Ranked voting would allow for people to vote first for whomever they really liked, including third party or write in candidates, without throwing their vote away if that person lost, and would disallow the election being thrown to the House of Representatives. It could also be applied to multiple congressional districts. If drawing fair lines for districts is too tough, combine three or four districts, and let all those people vote for their favorite candidates. After the ranking process works its way through, you're left with the top three or four as your representatives.

While we're waiting for the end of the Electoral College, Democrats could move the needle today. They could with a simple majority vote in Congress, either get rid of the filibuster, or carve out exceptions for voting rights legislation. They could vote for statehood for Puerto Rico (they're already US citizens) and the District of Columbia. Arguments that DC is too small are unpersuasive. Since when is size a criterion? Look at Rhode Island and Delaware. Arguments that it doesn't have enough people and should just be rolled into Maryland make no more sense than combining Wyoming and South Dakota; those two states combined have fewer people than does DC, but they have four senators representing them while DC has none (and forty million people in California have two).

You may think I must really hate the GOP, that since DC is mostly African-American and Puerto Rico is Latinx, that would add four Democratic senators, and I'm pitching for Democrats to take over forever. I disagree. Plenty of evidence indicates that African-American and Latinx Americans are intrinsically fairly religious and conservative. A GOP true to its roots should be able to reach those voters. But a GOP that remains tethered to policies that enrich already rich mostly white people and that relies on outraging non-rich white people, will not reach those voters. And it shouldn't reach them; it should waste away, until it figures out that it needs to reach them. It needs to represent them, and all the rest of us, and not just the donor class.

Also, we are looking toward a potentially very anti-democratic future. It is estimated that by 2040, 70% of the US population will live in just 15 states. So 70% of the population will have 30 senators, and 30% of the population will have 70 senators. With the appeal the GOP has now in rural areas, and the thrall in which the GOP is held by the super-rich, that could be dangerously unstable. We can help by freeing the GOP from its slavish service of money, and by breaking down these regional walls. More on that in the 'national service' section.

In order for corporations and moneyed special interests truly to 'behave themselves', we citizens through our elected representatives need to insist upon certain behaviors and proscribe others. Perhaps our greatest asset is a system that allows us to recognize and correct our mistakes (and avoid future ones) through free speech, a free press, and the vote. It is high time to exercise those rights, and with vigor.

And since we mentioned getting rid of **the filibuster**, we should get rid of the filibuster. Does anyone think that the filibuster as it currently exists adds civility and compromise to the senate? It's just an anti-democratic vestige that has outlived its usefulness. Some warn, look out what you wish for, imagine a Mitch McConnell unrestrained by the filibuster the next time the Republicans have the majority. I am unmoved. He already got rid of the filibuster for what was important to him, judges. I have no doubt that if something arose that he really wanted, he would carve out an exception for it. The fact is, Republicans don't need to end the filibuster: typically they don't pass legislation, they seem to want government to fail so they can point to what a mess it is, outrage people, and get pointy headed coastal elite globalists who believe in government tossed out. I say, if and when Republicans win, let them govern, unrestrained. If you want to end Obamacare, get rid of Medicare and gut social security, get rid of clean water and clean air, drill for oil in Yosemite, go ahead, do it. If that's what the people want, they'll re-elect you. No more hiding behind 'well we tried to do it, but the other party has that dang filibuster and they stopped us.' Let the party in charge, be in charge. Accountability is important, as we'll see soon.

I believe with all my heart that all these steps are in the best interest of the Republican Party and of conservative Americans (indeed, all Americans). Because what does America look like after its fundamental democratic processes have been debased? The GOP should abandon all efforts to limit the ability of any Americans to vote, should stop trying to choose their voters, and should embrace making an honest case for the voters to choose them.

> You can better succeed with the ballot. You can peaceably then redeem the government and preserve the liberties of mankind through your votes and voice and moral influence.... Let there be peace. Revolutionize through the ballot box and restore the government once more to the affections and hearts of men by

making it express, as it was intended to do, the highest spirit of justice and liberty. (13)

-- Abraham Lincoln

The Supreme Court

Expand it.

Democrats could do that tomorrow.

Much of the passionate interest in the Supreme Court and the selection of its Justices is fueled by wedge issues, such as abortion, as we've already discussed. It is in the interest of The Swamp to keep us peasants fighting each other about it. It is in the long-term interest of both political parties and of the American electorate to take this issue off the table.

There's nothing in the Constitution that says the Supreme Court (SCOTUS) is to have nine members. Respect for the court is diminishing. The idea that it is apolitical and just calls balls and strikes has taken a major hit in the last few years. This fantasy of a balanced court with four conservatives and four liberals, with a swing vote in the middle to go back and forth and keep things honest, is just that, a fantasy.

Let's back up. I understand the appeal of norms and traditions. We've had nine Supreme Court justices for a long time, since 1869. As recently as the Obama administration, the consensus was that 'elections had consequences'; whoever got elected President got to appoint federal judges, and even if you didn't like them, as long as they were competent and suitable, you confirmed them. Even Republican senators voted to confirm Obama SCOTUS appointees Sotomayor and Kagan. But then Senate Majority (Republican) Leader Mitch McConnell decided unilaterally to change the rules.

(The contrary-minded historians among you will point out that Democratic Senate Majority Leader Harry Reid ended the filibuster for non-Supreme Court nominees, so he started it. Well, he did that because the Republicans were filibustering all of Obama's appointments. We could go tit-for-tat back to Isaac and Ishmael, but let's just consider the matter at hand.)

Antonin Scalia died on 13 Feb 2016. Obama appointed Merrick Garland on 16 March 2016. The Constitution says the President nominates federal judges with the advice and consent of the senate. That always used to mean that the senate would hold hearings and have a vote. Occasionally the nominee was such a dog that even before any hearings, senators would tell the president that this guy's not going to get confirmed, so go find somebody else. Fine.

There's nothing in the Constitution that specifies *when* the senate should provide advice and consent. I figure that the Founders believed that mature adults would infer that since there's nothing that says it should be delayed, that the senate should act forthwith. That's the way it's always been. Hold hearings, then vote. If you don't like somebody, vote against him. But since they didn't anticipate the corruption of Mitch McConnell, and it doesn't say that the majority leader *can't* just blow it off and wait fourteen months (or two years, or four), it's 'constitutional' to wait, potentially, forever. I would defy anyone to say with a straight face that you believe that was the Founders' intent. Mitch McConnell's actions were hypocritical, but not unconstitutional, at least not in a strict sense.

McConnell knew Merrick Garland had nothing wrong with him, he was supported and respected by both parties, and there would be no rationale for Republican senators to vote against him. If brought to a vote, Garland would have been confirmed. So McConnell opted to protect his GOP senators from taking that vote (and either being a partisan hack by voting against a perfectly good nominee, or angering the base by voting for an Obama appointee) while still frustrating the nomination by making up the hypocrisy that 'we should wait for the upcoming election and let the people decide', which we now know was just pretextual nonsense. It was never about Garland, or about it being an election year; it was about Obama, denying him the appointment. (One may wonder what was so different, so unique, about Barack Obama....) McConnell stole the seat, and it worked. In so doing, he set a new standard: anything not proscribed by the Constitution is fair game. As the Athenians told the Melians: "The strong do as they will, and the weak suffer what they must."

We know that McConnell's actions were hypocritical, because we had a demonstration just four years later. Ruth Bader Ginsburg died on 18 September 2020. Remember Scalia had died in February of an election year, and McConnell said that was too close to an election to take action. But with a Republican in the White House, McConnell rushed, literally while people were voting for a new president, to consider Amy Coney Barrett, who replaced Ginsburg on 27 October 2020, less than six weeks after her death.

If you're a Trump supporter (or McConnell supporter, if there are such creatures) and that analysis sounds harsh or unfair, do the following thought experiment: pretend Trump had gotten re-elected, but Democrats controlled the senate so Chuck Schumer is the senate majority leader, and Clarence Thomas or Samuel Alito dropped dead tomorrow. Let's pretend RBG was still alive so it was a four-four court. Ask yourself if it would be OK for Schumer to say, 'Hey, there's a presidential election coming in 2024, so we're going to wait until then to give advice and consent regarding this nomination.'

McConnell exercised Raw Power; but what's good for the goose is good for the gander. Now that Biden is president with a Democratic Congress, if they decide to expand the court, they have the power to do so; if you had no problem with McConnell, you should have no problem with expansion.

I don't believe it would be a good idea for Democrats to expand the court just out of spite, just because they can, just because they were cheated out of one or even two seats. They should expand the court because it would be good for our politics, and good for the country.

There are a number of things wrong with our current Supreme Court. It is small and slow; it has become politicized; every time an octogenarian goes into the hospital, the country convulses; appointments are lifelong, enhancing the 'life-or-death' desperation of SCOTUS appointments. All this can and should be fixed.

Look at the Ninth Circuit Court of Appeals. It has 29 judges. Twenty-nine! There are arguments that it should be split, and pared down to 23 or 21 judges or such; whatever, it's a lot more than nine. If the Supreme Court had 21 Justices (or 17, or 19, whatever), that would have a number of good effects.

First, they can hear a lot more cases. (If you're like me, you read in the news about some urgent issue that's come up, requiring the Supreme Court's attention; and they'll hear the case... next year sometime? What is up with that? Jeez, get to work already.) Our whole judicial system is too damn slow. If I defied a subpoena, I don't think I would be able to piddle around literally for years running out the clock until the Friends of Brian Party takes power and makes my legal problems go away.

Second, they can have smaller panels of three to five Justices to hear cases, like lower courts do. The judges on the panels are rotated randomly. That way, 'issue lawyers' wouldn't shop for cases to put before the whole court as they do now, because they might get an unsympathetic panel of 3 or 5 and lose their case. If the panel makes a bad decision, the entire court can meet *en banc* to decide the case. With a large number of

Justices, even if death or disease leaves us with an even number now and again, tie decisions should be rare.

Supreme Court Justices should have term limits, say, eighteen years. Current Justices could be retired based upon how long they've been there. To avoid a nationwide freak-out that Biden is grabbing power and appointing radical socialists to take over the courts forever, the newest Justices would be seated for some shorter time period, from, whatever, three years to fifteen years. That way, every president to come is pretty well guaranteed to appoint a number of SCOTUS Justices. Between death and mandatory retirement, we would not see Justices entrenched there making questionable decisions for generations. Even if the Senate remains as polarized and politicized as it is now, if we get a stinker Justice, his or her malodorous effect would be diluted among the 16 or 24 other justices. I think this will take a lot of the tension and desperation out of the appointment and confirmation process, and we would get back to appointing judges based just upon legal competence rather than ideology.

> I am not an advocate for frequent changes in laws and constitutions, but laws and institutions must go hand in hand with the progress of the human mind. As that becomes more developed, more enlightened, as new discoveries are made, new truths discovered and manners and opinions change, with the change of circumstances, institutions must advance also to keep pace with the times. We might as well require a man to wear still the coat which fitted him when a boy as civilized society to remain ever under the regimen of their barbarous ancestors.
>
> -- Quoted on the wall of the Jefferson Memorial

The contest over the reform of the Supreme Court may be one of those occasions when Democrats bring a soup ladle to a gunfight, assuming they show up at all.

There are other proposals, such as that by a couple of law professors, Epps and Sitaraman. (14) They suggest starting over, with a Supreme Court with 15 justices, five selected by each party, and the last five appointed by seated upon unanimous agreement on the part of the first ten partisan selected justices. I don't see that happening, but I do believe we need some outside the box thinking. And again, Democrats could execute some variant of that almost immediately, it's just a matter of will.

And dear reader, I have a few more observations regarding some low hanging fruit that I believe can help move us forward. Thank you for indulging my *cri du coeur*.

Defund the police

Well, no; that's a terrible idea.

I understand the sentiment. White or black, old or young, I understand that some of you may feel like screaming, and some of you would be justified. But someone who may turn away from you as you scream in anger, may lean forward to hear you if you speak softly from the heart with the true benefit of all in mind.

Some police departments have been so awful, and the abuses may have been so egregious for so long, that it may seem worthwhile just to clean house, fire everybody, dissolve the organization, and start over. But almost certainly there are calm, helpful, compassionate officers in almost any department who would be kicked to the curb. And after you dissolve the department, you will need someone to do what it is that police are supposed to do. So you're going to have to fund someone; and even if you give them another name, those functioning as police, are police. It makes perfect sense though to fund mental health services and social support so that we're not asking those with badges and guns to be the first response to mental health and domestic crises. But when those encounters go sideways, and you need someone with the ability to employ force to establish order and security, you will learn very quickly that it was unwise to have 'defunded the police'.

More important than shrinking police departments is the connection between the community and the police. As we've seen, ragging on someone for their lousy ideas or behavior can tend to push them up on their hind legs and assume a defensive posture. This reinforces the culture of my group versus the world ('even the sheep are against us now'). It reinforces polarization and false dichotomies, you're either for the police or against the police, you're either for law and order or for lawlessness. That makes it that much harder for those within law enforcement who want change and reform to make it so.

And I think we do this best via connection, rather than control. Yes, elements of control must be effected. Law and order must be served: violations of the law must be addressed, and not just violations perpetrated by wolves, or by sheep, but also by police. Police Departments try to do this with their Internal Affairs, but ultimately the burden falls upon the rank and file. Structural changes can help this, and there is no lack of solutions. Best practices have been studied and published, such as having prosecutions of police be the responsibility of the state rather than the local prosecutors who have to work with those same police officers day by day. Connection and relationships between police and the communities they serve are paramount.

National service

How do you become an adult in a society that doesn't ask for sacrifice?
How do you become a man in a world that doesn't require courage?
-- Sebastian Junger, *Tribe*

The draft was in effect when I was a young man, and I was not thrilled. Older friends had been drafted and sent to Vietnam. My older cousin Pete was a helicopter pilot in Vietnam; he was killed in action. My parents and my aunt and uncle and cousins were traumatized by this, and their default toward patriotic support of our government's actions was torpedoed. Hundreds of young Americans were being killed daily, for reasons that were obscure. (Less than the thousands per day dying in this country during the pandemic, but still, plenty.)

The days of student deferments were gone. In the lottery, my draft number was 110; that's in the top third and put me at risk. I had never seen my father as impassioned as he was in opposition to one of my older brothers enlisting in the army. My parents did NOT want me to go to Vietnam, and I was none too enthusiastic myself. I turned 18 in 1972, and it so happened that the time of my highest risk for conscription coincided with the signing of the Paris Peace Accords in January of 1973. The draft fizzled out, as did the war in American awareness.

I mention all this just to indicate that, despite a military career of 38 years, I have no pie-in-the-sky naïve infatuation with conscription into the military. And yet conscription into national service, military or otherwise, is exactly that for which I shall advocate.

Junger describes growing up in a world with no demands upon him, no hardships, no expectations of contribution to the group. Neighbors were separated by hedges, and were not connected to one another. If something bad happened, the police or fire department or maintenance crews dealt with it.

> Humans don't mind hardship, in fact they thrive on it; what they mind is not feeling necessary. Modern society has perfected the art of making people not feel necessary.
>
> -- Junger, *Tribe*

We should all be able to appreciate this. Liberals should recognize that service to others is a function of *care* over *harm*. Conservatives should appreciate that service to the country demonstrates *loyalty* over *betrayal*, even if it's mandatory; indeed, mandatory service assures that slackers don't get a free ride, *fairness* over *cheating*. Yes, the libertarian I'm-a-free-American-and-the-damn-government-can't-tell-me-what-to-do streak in many of us values *liberty* over *oppression*, and there is no denying that a requirement for national service is an infringement upon liberty. But we've done it before without the Republic imploding, and I think we should do it again, forever.

I've already told you that I loved the army, because I loved the people in the army. As different as we all were and are, I felt connected with them; I still do. It's a feeling and an experience of immense value; it cannot be purchased; it cannot be delegated to one from elsewhere; it cannot be obtained except through the experience of shared values and shared sacrifice. The Greatest Generation benefitted from this shared experience. Whether in combat, or in support roles, or in working in factories or other venues at home, almost everyone was engaged in that national mission, and our nation was the better for it.

We do not have a sense of shared sacrifice today. Many if not most of us have not been required to make any sacrifices for our country. Many if not most of us associate with people like ourselves, racially, economically, politically, in just about every way. As we've discussed, we have either been sorted socio-economically into geographic enclaves, or we have sorted ourselves to be located primarily with people with whom we identify and agree, and have precious little experience with people from different regions (or even different parts of town) and with different perspectives. And when we do encounter such people, it typically is not in the context of a shared duty wherein we must find a way to work together and get along with one another.

All of these deficiencies can be met by a requirement for national service.

There are other benefits. The country benefits by having a source of labor not just for the military, but for any of a myriad number of forms of service, from old programs like Volunteers in Service to America (VISTA) or the Civilian Conservation Corps (CCC), fighting wildfires out west, improving parks or roads or trails, helping as teachers' aides in disadvantaged schools, almost ad infinitum. Each individual gets experience with a job, with having a boss, with working with people from different backgrounds. Some will find this taste of service intoxicating, and will choose it as a career.

Some will be miserable and will feel that the country has stolen their time from them. They'll get over it.

Jobs

It's not just that jobs are important, but good jobs, good-paying jobs, are important. Feeling challenged and needed is more difficult without meaningful employment. We've already discussed the need to strengthen unions and rebalance the relationship between capital and labor.

There are plenty of jobs in America that go unfilled. We should also be much better at shaping and coordinating the marketplace of jobs. Four years of college is great, but vocational training and apprenticeships are underutilized. The federal government should be able to do more to integrate visibility between employers and potential employees.

The Departments of Labor and Commerce and the business community should be able to communicate and create a database of available jobs. We should be able to have a clearinghouse of information specifying what jobs are located where, and what education and experience is required, that can help match up workers and jobs. If I can go online and find cat videos or have Hogwarts socks delivered to my door overnight, I should be able to enter my education and experience (or my prospective education and experience) and see what jobs are (or could be) available for me, anywhere in the country. Building relationships between employers and educational institutions so that trainees have a glideslope from the schoolhouse to the workplace is in the interest of all.

Barriers to unionization should be removed. Violations of labor laws should be prosecuted; not just with fines for faceless corporations, but real consequences for real people who make decisions causing illegal actions. Accountability is important.

Best practices worldwide should be studied and adopted. Mistreating workers may seem prudent in the short term. My bias is that treating employees as anyone would want to be treated, will be wise, and good business.

Taxes

We've already talked about welfare, and Universal Basic Income.

Taxes are complicated, right? Our tax codes are thousands of pages. Most Americans believe that our tax system is too complex, it's incomprehensible, and most importantly, it's unfair. (15)

In the best of all worlds, the vast majority of us would agree with the following. Taxes should be fair... more on that in a minute. Unless complexity is absolutely necessary, taxes should be simple. Taxes should be progressive, that is, the more you make, the more you have, the more you pay. This should not be so much that it discourages industry and hard work and productivity. But the burden should not fall disproportionately upon the poor. And, taxes should be necessary. If you want to argue that we shouldn't be spending all this money, then elect people who say they won't spend it. Oh yeah, that would be Republicans. They spend it anyway. Because apparently, Americans want the services that money buys.

Complexity is only of value to those who make money from the complexity; that includes tax preparers, or the "Tax Complexity Lobby." (16) Everyone needs to make a living, and we should accommodate the displacement of tax preparers. But we should not let the tail wag the dog. When I used to do my own taxes (yes, it was torture) I would occasionally get a letter from the IRS, saying 'hey you wrote $2312 on line 42, but it should be $2425, so we're changing your refund from X to Y.' When I bothered to look into it, the IRS was always right, so I stopped checking. But if the IRS already knows what my return should say, and they're going to check my work and correct it anyway, why do I need to go through all this agony of tax preparation? Well, I shouldn't, and neither should you. In many countries, tax preparation takes minutes. In Japan, you get a postcard from their version of the IRS that says, 'your tax is X, you had Y withheld, so you either owe or are owed Z.'

Still, the complexity benefits others: those who can hire experts to exploit the loopholes in the tax code so they pay less in tax. Generally, that is not you and I, it is disproportionately the wealthy. That brings us to fairness. There is an argument to be made for eliminating the entire code, getting rid of every deduction and credit and loophole, and starting all over with a simple code that has none of that stuff, because invariably, any loopholes will become corrupted into benefitting those who can pay for corruption. If the result was 'tax neutral' for the middle class, that is, I lose my mortgage deduction and everything else, but the rates go down so that I end up paying the same amount of tax overall, why not? Tax revenues would go up because those who can exploit the arcane loopholes will be deprived of them.

Having pitched for simplicity and getting rid of tax incentives, there is a case to be made for having taxes on employers vary with the wages they pay their employees. Those who pay wages commensurate with community needs and increasing them to match national economic growth would pay lower taxes; those who don't, would pay higher taxes. Similarly tax rates for corporate officers whose wages are, say, a hundred times that of their lowest paid employee would be higher than the tax rate for officers of corporations whose wages are only twenty five times that of their lowest paid employee.

Back to fairness; one simple criterion for determining whether something is fair or not is to ask: would you trade places? Most people are fair enough minded that they can understand when someone has worked hard for what they've earned, and if they were in that person's shoes, they would want to be amply rewarded for their efforts and not overly burdened by taxes. But if I won $100 million in the Powerball lottery (or in the genetic lottery, born into wealth), how much tax is fair? I didn't earn that wealth, in any meaningful way. I did get lucky though, and I believe I should be set up for life. But if the tax were 95%, I would still be set up for life. Having lots of untaxed, unearned income looks like free riding to me.

Social security tax: I don't see why the payroll tax cuts off at a certain level; that makes it regressive (like sales taxes, taking proportionately more from the poor). If you're blessed enough to make money beyond the cutoff level, count your blessings and appreciate your ability to help those less fortunate.

Means testing: I don't see any reason not to have means testing for all social security and other benefits.

Carbon tax: do it. It will raise revenues and reduce deficits, move development from fossil fuels to renewables, and help with climate change. Like social security or Medicare or tax-payer supported roads or police, it will not kill jobs or destroy the Republic.

The "death tax:" yeah, that's what they call the estate tax, so you'll believe that the government is coming after your family after you're dead. If you're one of the only 2000 American families that are exposed to the estate tax, passing on estates worth over 22 million dollars for a couple, then yes, Uncle Sam is coming. But if your heirs didn't hit the genetic lottery, if you're not passing on multiple millions of dollars, your family has nothing to worry about. Among the American wealthy, over 60% of wealth is inherited, unearned wealth. That's nice work if you can get it.

Wealth tax: we've already talked about how the wealthy can shield their wealth from taxes by arranging not to receive 'income', and borrowing spending money against their great wealth instead. A wealth tax of 2% on fortunes greater than $50 million (leaving you with $49 million) and 6% above one billion dollars (leaving you $940 million of your billion) (17) would raise between $2.6 and four trillion over ten years. (18) Is that unfair?

Fund stuff that saves money

Yes, fund stuff like the Internal Revenue Service. I get it, nobody likes the IRS. But if I must pay my taxes, I want everybody to pay their taxes just like I pay mine. Instead, budget cuts have weakened the ability of the IRS to find cheaters. The IRS pays for itself: every dollar spent funding the IRS adds over three dollars to the treasury. IRS audits of rich people have fallen, while audits of middle income taxpayers have stayed about the same. "In 2013, when the IRS agents conducted more than 6,000 audits on taxpayers who made more than $5 million, these audits resulted in $880 million of recommended additional taxes. This worked out to be $4,545 for every hour each agent spent on these cases." (19)

Also, we should invest in aggressively ferreting out as much fraud, waste and abuse as we can. Even if strictly speaking we might not get more than a dollar back for each dollar required for the effort, it'd still be money well spent. Conservatives can't stand the idea of free riders sitting on their backsides cheating and getting taxpayers' hard earned money. Paying to find cheaters and put them in jail is worth it. Liberals should support efforts to eliminate fraud because it is fraud, or the perception of fraud, that makes social spending less acceptable to many of your countrymen. If you want to catch tax cheats, then catch welfare cheats too.

The infrastructure packages are full of things that cost something, but save more.

> Cost-measurement analysis indicates that the annual aggregate cost of U.S. child poverty is $1.0298 trillion, representing 5.4% of the gross domestic product. These costs are clustered around the loss of economic productivity, increased health and crime costs, and increased costs as a result of child homelessness and maltreatment. In addition, it is estimated that for every dollar spent on reducing childhood poverty, the country would save at least seven dollars with respect to the economic costs of poverty. (20)

Investments in education leads to better jobs and more tax revenues; investments in health care, especially in kids, saves health care costs later; these savings range from four dollars saved per dollar invested to $25 saved per $1. Sometimes it's just the right thing to do, like raise children out of poverty. But when there is no net cost to do so, then it should be a lay-up; how much easier could a decision be? It just makes sense to spend money that will not just save you money, but will make you more money. That's a good investment, a win-win all the way around.

This list was not exhaustive, but you get the idea. There are plenty of actions we can take that make sense and are not partisan. There are websites that itemize more such ideas. (21)

Much, much more so now than in decades past, we tend first to evaluate any public policy such as those listed above through the lens of what one's team thinks of it, typically long before any consideration of whether or not it makes sense. If my team is against it, then my elephant is engaged, and I'm against it; and no matter how worthy and full of common sense the idea may be, nope, I'm still against it.

That is not wise.

Whichever team you're on, get past that.

And vote for people who are past that.

Epilogue

Let's suppose that all my fantasies in the previous chapter are adopted. The Rule of Unintended Consequences may jump up and bite us. My fears are mostly of Trump and Trumpism untethered to American values and norms; but we must consider what might happen if the GOP implodes and Democrats are ascendant for some time.

If the Left/ Democrats/ Liberals/ Progressives/ Whatever (LDLPW, my new acronym for this paragraph only) have been paying attention, and recognize the fears and anxieties that Trump tapped into, the real hollowing out of the middle class, the disrespect many in 'flyover' country feel from elites, the disgust with business-as-usual Swamp Creatures in Washington; and they get true with New Deal Democratic values of honesty and disallowing plutocrats to buy influence, championing the working man and woman and their families, then we'll be OK. If they (LDLPW) win midterms and Congress and sweep Trumpism away, but then get high and mighty and full of victory and crush the old William F Buckley / George Will Republican values (conservative but willing and able to govern while believing in fiscal responsibility and limited government, unlike today's sabotage-government-to-prove-it-can't-work GOP crowd who just anger and frighten people into voting for them and suppress the votes of others and borrow and spend money like they accuse Democrats of doing) as they extinguish Trumpism, and LDLPW abandon a rational intolerance for white supremacy and replace it with a holier-than-thou intolerance for any kind of non-leftist values, and make efforts to marginalize white working people, then we would be in trouble.

I believe we are at a tipping point in history. Lincoln said, "A house divided against itself cannot stand." To paraphrase, I believe our country cannot endure, permanently half-Trumpist, and half never-Trump. Said Lincoln:

> I do not expect the Union to be dissolved -- I do not expect the house to fall -- but I do expect it will cease to be divided. It will become all one thing, or all the other.

I fear that the struggle we face may become as intense and sanguinary as the one Lincoln endured. And I fear that if Trumpism prevails, our liberal democracy will end.

Dipping further into the bottomless well of Lincoln's wisdom, he anticipated our current situation:

> At what point shall we expect the approach of danger? By what means shall we fortify against it? Shall we expect some transatlantic military giant to step the ocean and crush us at a blow? Never! All the armies of Europe, Asia and Africa combined, with all the treasure of the earth (our own excepted) in their military chest, with a Bonaparte for a commander, could not by force take a drink from the Ohio or make a track on the Blue Ridge in a trial of a thousand years.
>
> At what point then is the approach of danger to be expected? I answer, if it ever reach us, it must spring from amongst us. It cannot come from abroad. If destruction be our lot, we must ourselves be its author and finisher. As a nation of freemen, we must live through all time or die by suicide.
>
> - - Lyceum Speech, 1838

We can hope that in such a moment as we find ourselves, the insight of Jefferson is accurate:

> The good sense of the people will always be found to be the best army. They may be led astray for a moment, but will soon correct themselves.
>
> -- Thomas Jefferson

The Sunk Cost Fallacy

I remember being a victim of that fallacy. My wife and I bought a timeshare, and while it seemed like a good idea when we signed up, after some time it became clear, it was a bad idea. But after you've put a bunch of money into it, it's hard to admit that you got talked into something. It's tempting just to ignore the bleeding. You feel like a fool. I know I did. But with each payment, it just felt worse.

Eventually I decided to look in the mirror (after finally listening to my wife, who always had reservations) and say, "I made a bad decision. The cost I've already sunk into it is not a good reason to continue throwing good money after bad. I need to cut my losses and get out."

You can get out; it can be easier than getting out of our timeshare. You can get out, let go, free yourself of the lies, today. It's just a decision. It's as easy as a thought.

My ask

Whether you are a Trump supporter whom I am asking to remove yourself from the influence of The Big Lie, or a never-Trumper whom I am asking to listen to your Trump-supporting countrymen and attend to their fears and concerns, I am asking that we all embrace the better angels of our nature.

In the Warrior PATHH we relate a story of an old Cherokee man teaching his grandson. 'There is a battle between two wolves inside all of us,' he instructs.

'One is evil. It is anger, envy, jealousy, sorrow, regret, greed, shame, arrogance, self-pity, guilt, resentment, inferiority, lies, false pride, superiority, and ego.

'The other is good. It is joy, peace, love, hope, serenity, humility, kindness, benevolence, empathy, generosity, truth, compassion, and faith.'

His grandson considered this for a minute and asked, 'Which wolf wins?'

The old Cherokee replied, 'The one you feed.'

Feed the good wolf.

Only you can decide whether or not to do so.

Feed the good wolf.

The time has come to hear the cries that have given rise to Trumpism. The time has come for a rebirth of our election processes, our taxation, our media, our relationships with information and knowledge and truth, our recognition that if government is to serve righteously, it must serve the many, not just the few.

> Stronger than an army is an idea whose time has come.
> -- Victor Hugo

Many times in my 38-year military career I swore to "support and defend the Constitution of the United States against all enemies, foreign and domestic." I believe that the flames of division, the behavior of those who fan those flames, the Big Lie, the rationalization and normalization of the insurrection by the Republican Party, the support of the GOP for, or at least their acquiescence to, efforts to overturn the 2020 election and to debase our electoral processes, are all domestic threats to our Constitution. I have written this book in partial fulfillment of my oath.

Since I have been so critical of the current Party of Lincoln, it is only fitting that I end by showing respect for its namesake. In his second inaugural address, in the midst of unprecedented, terrible, bloody national division, in anticipation of the end of the deadliest war in American history, with a view toward the Reconstruction to come, he left us with a charge that is as resonant today as it was then:

> With malice toward none; with charity for all; with firmness in the right, as God gives us to see the right, let us strive on to finish the work we are in; to bind up the nation's wounds; to care for him who shall have borne the battle, and for his widow, and his orphan--to do all which may achieve and cherish a just and lasting peace among ourselves, and with all nations.

Acknowledgments

My family and friends:

My wife Atsuko has retired, the kids are adults, and they didn't have much to do with this particular book. But Atsuko put up with me scurrying off to my computer to write while she did all the work I should have been helping with for a couple of years now. And my children, the big "why" in my life, are a never-ending source of new ideas and perspectives. You've taught me to listen and open my heart. Thank you all.

My siblings and cousins, thank you for enduring our texts and emails; yes, I've been doing research all this time.

Tom Williams thank you for all of your edits, they improved the text immensely; and Vince Morici, thanks for challenging my arguments.

And thanks to my editors David and Sarah, contracted via *upwork*.

Stubborn as I am, I did not adopt all the edits; the errors and malaprops are mine alone.

My veteran family:

I'll screw up and miss someone if I write a litany of names, but you know who you are. If we served together, or if we didn't, you're in this book. Those of you who have been through the Warrior PATHH, those who have become PATHH Guides, and those who have executed and supported the PATHH, you're in this book. I've learned so much listening to your wisdom, thank you.

My TM family:

Thank you for all your hard work making TM available to veterans and first responders, and to everyone else. Those of you at the David Lynch Foundation, and MFUSA, and MIU, keep doing the work. Without you, this book doesn't happen.

My political family:

All of you who responded to me in good faith, in emails, on social media, Trump supporters and never-Trumpers, all, thank you.

You've shown: we can do this.

Reading list

Klein, E. *Why we're polarized*. Avid Reader Press, New York. 2020.

Haidt, J. *The righteous mind: why good people are divided by politics and religion*. Vintage Books, New York. 2012.

Sykes, C. *How the right lost its mind*. Biteback Publishing, London. 2017.

Whitehouse, S. *Captured: the corporate infiltration of American democracy*. The New Press, New York. 2017.

Kendi, I. *How to be an antiracist*. One World, New York. 2019

McGhee, H. *The sum of us: what racism costs everyone and how we can prosper together*. One World, New York. 2021.

Reich, R. *Beyond outrage: what has gone wrong with our economy and our democracy, and how to fix it*. Vintage Books, New York. 2012

Reich, R *Saving capitalism: for the many, not the few*. Alfred A. Knopf, New York. 2015

Falke, K and Goldberg, J. *Struggle well: thriving in the aftermath of trauma*. Lioncrest Publishing, 2018.

Roth, B. *Strength in stillness: the power of Transcendental Meditation*. Simon & Schuster, New York. 2018

Nader, T. *One unbounded ocean of consciousness: simple answers to the big questions in life.* Penguin Random House, Buenos Aires. Digital edition. 2021.

Rees, B *Heal your self, heal your world: turn illness and suffering into health and peace through scientifically proven methods*. Manu Publishing, Pacific Palisades California. 1997.

Rees, B. *Detained: emails and musings from a spiritual journey through Abu Ghraib, Kandahar, and other garden spots*. Manu Publishing, San Luis Obispo California. 2015.

Zakaria, F. *Ten lessons for a post-pandemic world.* W.W. Norton & Company, New York. 2020.

Frankl, V. *Man's search for meaning*. Beacon Press, Boston. 1959, 2006.

Junger, S. *Tribe: on homecoming and belonging*. 4th Estate, London. 2016

Meacham, J. *The soul of America: the battle for our better angels*. Random House, New York. 2018.

Goodwin, DK. *Team of rivals: the political genius of Abraham Lincoln*. Simon & Schuster, New York. 2005.

References

All websites cited were accessed on or about 24 October 2021 unless otherwise specified.

Chapter One Trump supporters

1. Sykes, C. *How the right lost its mind.* Biteback Publishing, London. 2017. Page 217.

Chapter Two We are selfish, and we are groupish

1. Klein, E. *Why we're polarized.* Avid Reader Press, New York. 2020. p.58.
2. Haidt, J. *The righteous mind: why good people are divided by politics and religion.* Vintage Books, New York. 2012. p.221.
3. Blythe, W. *To hate like this is to be happy forever: a thoroughly obsessive, intermittently uplifting, and occasionally unbiased account of the Duke-North Carolina basketball rivalry.* HarperCollins, New York. 2006. As cited in Klein, p.57.
4. Klein op. cit., p.51.
5. Ibid., p.53, ref 5.
6. Ibid., p.55, ref 7.
7. Ibid., p.2.
8. Ibid., p.5, ref 5.
9. Ibid., p.6, ref 7.
10. Ibid., p.8.
11. Ibid., p.9.
12. Ibid., p.10.
13. Ibid., p.69.
14. Ibid., p.13.
15. Ibid., p.32-3.
16. Ibid., p.194.
17. Ibid., p.60-61, ref 13.
18. Ibid., p.62, ref 14.
19. Ibid., p.193.
20. Ibid., p.87, ref 14.
21. Ibid., p.74, ref 25.
22. Bryan Hood, often noted during Warrior PATHHs
23. Klein, op. cit. p.77, ref 27.
24. Ibid., p.4, ref 3.
25. Ibid., p.24 ref 7.
26. Ibid., p.24 ref 8.
27. Ibid., p.36, ref 18.
28. Ibid., p.30, ref 15.

29. Ibid., p.243.
30. https://m.facebook.com/RBReich/photos/pb.142474049098533.-2207520000.1456496520./1155789431100318/?type=3

Chapter Three It's really the way we are

1. Haidt, op. cit., p.29, ref 30.
2. Ibid., p.61
3. Ibid., p.39, ref 22
4. Ibid., p.54
5. Ibid., p.61 & 63.
6. Ibid., p.94 & 95, ref 21 & 22
7. Ibid., p.99
8. Ibid., p.112, ref 2
9. Ibid., p.112 ref 1
10. Ibid., p.146
11. Ibid., p.153
12. Ibid., p.238, ref 54
13. Ibid.
14. Ibid., p.242-3, ref 63
15. Ibid., p.250
16. Ibid., p.243, ref 65.
17. https://www.sciencedaily.com/releases/2012/03/120327124243.htm
18. Haidt op. cit., p244, ref 67.
19. Ibid., p245, ref 70
20. Ibid.
21. Ibid., p.298
22. Ibid., p.292, ref 14.
23. Rees, B *Heal your self, heal your world: turn illness and suffering into health and peace through scientifically proven methods*. Manu Publishing, Pacific Palisades California. 1997. p.145, ref 15
24. Haidt op. cit., p.298, ref 30.
25. Ibid., p.299, ref 32.
26. Ibid., p.310, ref 60.
27. Ibid., p.311
28. Ibid., p.303, ref 43
29. Rees op. cit., chapter 12; and Rees, B. *Detained: emails and musings from a spiritual journey through Abu Ghraib, Kandahar, and other garden spots*. Manu Publishing, San Luis Obispo California. 2015. Chapters 16, 17, 18.
30. Haidt op. cit., p.306, ref 46.
31. Whitehouse, S. *Captured: the corporate infiltration of American democracy*. The New Press, New York. 2017. p.89, ref 56.
32. Haidt op. cit., p.343, ref 44.
33. https://digitalcommons.unl.edu/cgi/viewcontent.cgi?article=1006&context=poliscifacpub as cited in Haidt, p.324, ref 15.

34. Haidt op. cit., p.324, ref 16.
35. Ibid., p.325, ref 17
36. Ibid., p.414, ref 53.
37. Ibid., p86.
38. Ibid., p.342-3
39. Ibid., p.335, ref 33

Part 2 The stuff Trump said that resonates with people

1. Ibid., p.57, ref 50

Chapter Four Make America great again

1. Jean LaCouture, *Le Souverain* (Editions de Seuil, Paris, 1989), pp. 364-365, https://historynewsnetwork.org/article/7886 accessed 9 Nov 2020
2. https://www.foreignaffairs.com/articles/united-states/2021-01-29/trump-gone-not-forgotten
3. Klein, op. cit., p.23, ref 4.
4. Reich, R *Saving capitalism: for the many, not the few*. Alfred A. Knopf, New York. 2015. p.119.
5. Ibid., p.120.

Chapter Five The system is rigged

1. Whitehouse, S. *Captured: the corporate infiltration of American democracy*. The New Press, New York. 2017. p8.
2. Ibid., p.6-7.
3. https://www.nytimes.com/roomfordebate/2015/04/16/what-are-corporations-obligations-to-shareholders/corporations-dont-have-to-maximize-profits
4. Whitehouse, op. cit., p.6.
5. Ibid., ref 19
6. Ibid., ref 20
7. Ibid., ref 21
8. Ibid., ref 23
9. Ibid., ref 24
10. Ibid., p.10, ref 38
11. Ibid., ref 39
12. Ibid., p.7.
13. Ibid., p.10, ref 37
14. https://www.science.org/doi/10.1126/science.162.3859.1243
15. Whitehouse, op. cit., p.8.
16. Ibid., p.13, ref 13.
17. Reich, op. cit., p.154.
18. Whitehouse, op. cit., p.64, ref 6

19. Reich, R. *Beyond outrage: what has gone wrong with our economy and our democracy, and how to fix it*. Vintage Books, New York. 2012. p.9.
20. Reich 2015, op. cit., p.103-4.
21. Ibid., p.104-5.
22. Ibid., p.137.
23. Whitehouse, op. cit., p.33, ref 45.
24. Ibid., ref 46.
25. http://a.msn.com/01/en-us/AAKORJv?ocid=se
26. Reich 2015, op. cit., p.131
27. https://centerforpolitics.org/crystalball/articles/just-how-many-obama-2012-trump-2016-voters-were-there/
28. Sykes op. cit., p.54, ref 1.

Chapter Six Drain the Swamp

1. https://www.washingtonpost.com/business/2021/02/23/mnuchin-investment-fund-gulf/
2. Whitehouse op. cit., p.124, ref 28.
3. Reich 2015, op. cit., p.186.
4. Whitehouse, op. cit. p.194, ref 12.
5. Ibid., p.18, ref 42
6. Ibid., p.60
7. Ibid., p.125, ref 43.
8. Ibid., ref 40.
9. Ibid., p.120, ref 13.
10. Ibid., p.116, ref 1.
11. Ibid., p.125, ref 47.
12. Ibid., p.123.
13. Ibid., p.123, ref 26.
14. Ibid., p.21, ref 58
15. Reich 2015, op. cit., p.159.
16. Whitehouse op. cit., p.22, ref 63.
17. Ibid., p.31, ref 43.
18. https://www.vox.com/polyarchy/2016/1/8/10736402/congress-fundraising-miserable
19. Lewis, C. *The buying of the Congress: How special interests have stolen your right to life liberty and the pursuit of happiness*. Avon Books, New York. 1998. p.xi.
20. Whitehouse op. cit., p.45, ref 117.
21. Ibid., p.44-45, ref 113.
22. Klein op. cit., p.179.
23. Ibid., p.190.
24. Whitehouse op. cit., p.85, ref 44.
25. https://www.nytimes.com/2018/08/27/us/north-carolina-congressional-districts.html Wines, Michael; Fausset, Richard (August 27, 2018).

"North Carolina Is Ordered to Redraw Its Gerrymandered Congressional Map. Again". The New York Times. Retrieved 23 March, 2021.
26. Reich 2015 op. cit., p.159.

Chapter Seven Conservative judges

1. Whitehouse op. cit., p.63
2. Ibid., p.64.
3. Ibid., p.66, ref 16.
4. Ibid., ref 19.
5. Ibid., p.91.
6. Ibid., p.77, ref 4.
7. Ibid., p.141-9.
8. Ibid., p.137.
9. Ibid., p.90, ref 61.
10. Ibid., p.78-9.
11. Ibid., p.88.
12. Ibid., p.97, ref 12.

Chapter Eight Political correctness

1. Klein, op. cit., p.125, ref 32.
2. Ibid.

Chapter Nine Stronger and safer America

1. Krugman, P. *End this depression now!* WW Norton & Company, New York. 2012. P130-149

Chapter Ten Do black lives really matter?

1. Accessed 2 May 2021 https://carolinacommentary.com/divide-and-conquer/
2. Klein op. cit. p.120, ref 27.
3. Ibid., p.115, ref 23.
4. Ibid., p.xiv, ref 5.

Chapter Eleven Wedge issues and bad arguments: the "Other"

1. Ibid., p.157, ref 8.
2. https://www.npr.org/2018/05/02/607652253/studies-say-illegal-immigration-does-not-increase-violent-crime
https://abcnews.go.com/Politics/fact-check-trumps-claims-illegal-immigrant-crime-rates/story?id=60311860
https://www.npr.org/.../studies-say-illegal-immigration
3. https://www.youtube.com/watch?v=XaR5kR8h4es (the relevant portion is 24 seconds of the video, from 2:56 to 3:20).

"Policing Immigrants: Local Law Enforcement on the Front Lines" (University of Chicago Press), particularly chapters 5 and 6. XX
4. Haidt op. cit. p.57.
5. https://www.pbs.org/wgbh/frontline/article/court-north-carolina-voter-id-law-targeted-black-voters/
6. https://www.washingtonpost.com/politics/courts_law/getting-a-photo-id-so-you-can-vote-is-easy-unless-youre-poor-black-latino-or-elderly/2016/05/23/8d5474ec-20f0-11e6-8690-f14ca9de2972_story.html?utm_term=.ff41cf603a12
https://www.brennancenter.org/analysis/debunking-voter-fraud-myth
https://www.theatlantic.com/politics/archive/2017/02/how-voter-id-laws-discriminate-study/517218/
http://www.aarp.org/politics-society/government-elections/info-01-2012/voter-id-laws-impact-older-americans.html
7. http://www.ca4.uscourts.gov/Opinions/Published/161468.P.pdf
8. https://www.youtube.com/watch?v=EuOT1bRYdK8
https://www.youtube.com/watch?v=CoYWgGY4ADY
9. https://lithub.com/how-fringe-christian-nationalists-made-abortion-a-central-political-issue/
https://www.youtube.com/watch?v=swbj_xGdbm4
10. https://www.politifact.com/truth-o-meter/statements/2019/jan/28/donald-trump/trump-wrongly-tweets-58000-noncitizens-voted-texas/
https://www.factcheck.org/2019/01/more-voter-fraud-misinformation-from-trump/

Chapter Twelve Big wedges: guns, welfare, and abortion

1. By The New York Times | Sources: Institute for Health Metrics and Evaluation at the University of Washington, Small Arms Survey, World Bank
2. Nicholas Kristof, the Times columnist, has written a good overview, called "How to Reduce Shootings."
3. Whitehouse op. cit., p.89.
4. https://abcnews.go.com/Politics/wireStory/background-checks-blocked-record-high-300000-gun-sales-78420709
5. https://mic.com/articles/142348/in-2016-toddlers-have-killed-more-people-in-the-us-than-muslim-terrorists-have
6. Junger, S. *Tribe: on homecoming and belonging*. 4th Estate, London. 2016. P.112.
7. https://www.lexingtonlaw.com/blog/finance/welfare-statistics.html
https://time.com/4711668/history-food-stamp-fraud/
8. https://datalab.usaspending.gov/americas-finance-guide/spending/
9. https://www.npr.org/2021/03/04/973653719/california-program-giving-500-no-strings-attached-stipends-pays-off-study-finds
10. https://www.asa3.org/ASA/PSCF/1970/JASA6-70Christian.html
11. https://www.christianitytoday.com/ct/1968/november-8/

12. 4190,05-May-1976.pdf (org.s3.amazonaws.com)
13. https://rewirenewsgroup.com/religion-dispatches/2019/09/27/when-the-biblical-view-for-evangelicals-was-that-life-begins-at-birth/
14. Balmer, R. *Thy kingdom come: How the religious right distorts the faith and threatens America. Basic Books, New York. 2006.*
15. https://www.npr.org/2019/06/20/734303135/throughline-traces-evangelicals-history-on-the-abortion-issue

Chapter Thirteen Fake news and social media

1. Sykes op. cit., p.13, ref 13.
2. Ibid., p.30, ref 15.
3. Ibid., p.36, ref 6.
4. Ibid., p.41, ref 16.
5. Ibid.
6. Ibid., p.45, ref 22.
7. Ibid.
8. https://donellameadows.org/archives/bring-back-the-fairness-doctrine/
9. https://casetext.com/case/syracuse-peace-council-v-fcc *In re Complaint of Syracuse Peach Council against Television Station WTVH Syracuse, New York*, 2 FCC Rcd 5043 (1987)
10. https://uh.edu/~englin/rephandout.html
11. Sykes op. cit., p.189, ref 17.
12. Ibid., p.134, ref 1.
13. http://mediaproject.wesleyan.edu/releases/jump-in-negativity- Accessed 18 July 2021
14. Alex Seitz-Wald, "Huckabee: Super PACs Are 'One of the Worst Things That Ever Happened in American Politics,'" *ThinkProgress*, January 3, 2012.
15. Sykes op. cit., p.134.
16. Ibid., p.83, ref 2.
17. Ibid., p.82, ref 1.
18. Klein op. cit., p.148-9, ref 4.
19. Ibid., p.151, ref 6.
20. Ibid., p.170.
21. Sykes op. cit., p.78, ref 26.
22. Klein op. cit., p.166.
23. Ibid., p.235-6, ref 11.
24. Sykes op. cit., p.84, ref 5.
25. Klein op. cit., p.294, ref 14.
26. Sykes op. cit., p.91, ref 6.
27. Ibid.
28. https://www.npr.org/2020/09/29/917747123/you-literally-cant-believe-the-facts-tucker-carlson-tells-you-so-say-fox-s-lawye
29. Whitehouse op. cit., p.198, refs 32 & 33.
30. Klein op. cit., p.187.

31. https://ngoeke.medium.com/how-to-stop-being-gullible-eb2ea502a34b 13Aug2021
32. https://www.wsj.com/articles/facebook-knows-it-encourages-division-top-executives-nixed-solutions-11590507499
33. https://www.latimes.com/opinion/story/2020-09-30/facebook-qanon-conspiracy-social-media-election

Chapter Fourteen Russians, hoaxes, climate change… and “The Big Lie”

1.https://www.npr.org/sections/alltechconsidered/2016/11/23/503146770/npr-finds-the-head-of-a-covert-fake-news-operation-in-the-suburbs?fbclid=IwAR39tgKt8PQFHXkRokeOmjn74N-p24M5armmJU82MCObpFMuFkbXYPqwhwQ
2. Sykes op. cit., p.91, & p.145, ref 22.
3. Ibid., p.98-99.
4. Ibid., p.122.
5. Ibid., p.157.
6. Ibid., p.43, ref 19.
7. https://www.ncbi.nlm.nih.gov/pmc/articles/PMC2879177/
8. Kessler DA. *A Question of Intent: A Great American Battle with a Deadly Industry*. New York: Public Affairs; 2001. p.xiii.
9. Whitehouse op. cit., p.153 ref 8.
10. Ibid., p.157, ref 33.
11. Ibid., ref 32.
12. Ibid., p.158, ref 36 & 37.
13. Ibid., ref 38.
14. https://www.amazon.com/The-Greatest-Hoax-Conspiracy-Threatens/dp/1936488493
15. Whitehouse op. cit., p.164, ref 66.
16. https://www.ipcc.ch/report/ar6/wg1/#SPM
17. http://grist.org/series/skeptics/
18. Whitehouse op. cit., p.200, ref 40.
19. Ibid.
20. Ibid., p.164.
21. https://www.politico.com/magazine/story/2016/05/donald-trump-supporters-dunning-kruger-effect-213904/
22. https://www.psychologytoday.com/us/blog/mind-in-the-machine/201609/the-psychology-behind-donald-trumps-unwavering-support
23. https://www.cell.com/current-biology/fulltext/S0960-9822(11)00289-2
24. https://www.cell.com/current-biology/fulltext/S0960-9822(14)01213-5
25. https://journals.sagepub.com/doi/abs/10.1177/0146167297238008
26. https://journals.sagepub.com/doi/abs/10.1177/0146167205282157
27. https://journals.sagepub.com/doi/abs/10.1177/0146167204267988
28. https://abcnews.go.com/Politics/wireStory/rioters-blame-actions-2020-election-misinformation-77977322

29. Sagan, C & Druyan, A. *The Demon-Haunted World: Science as a Candle in the Dark*. Random House, New York. 1995. P.144.
30. https://www.brennancenter.org/sites/default/files/analysis/Briefing_Memo_Debunking_Voter_Fraud_Myth.pdf
31. https://www.reuters.com/world/us/judge-sanctions-sidney-powell-other-pro-trump-lawyers-who-claimed-voter-fraud-2021-08-25/
32. https://lede-admin.coloradosun.com/wp-content/uploads/sites/15/2021/09/Giuliani-depo-in-Coomer-case.pdf
33. Sykes op. cit., p.209, ref 4.
34. http://www.pegc.us/archive/Articles/eco_ur-fascism.pdf

Chapter Fifteen Connect versus control

1. Steenkamp MM, et al. Psychotherapy for Military-Related PTSD: A Review of Randomized Clinical Trials. *JAMA* August 2015; 314 (5) 489-500
2. https://www.pnas.org/content/107/38/16489 Proceedings of the National Academy of Sciences of the United States of America. "High Income Improves Evaluation of Life but Not Emotional Well-Being." Accessed May 27, 2021.
3. Frankl, V. *Man's search for meaning*. Beacon Press, Boston. 1959, 2006. P.106-7.
4. Haidt op. cit., p.102, ref 44.
5. https://www.drugabuse.gov/news-events/nida-notes/2019/08/rats-prefer-social-interaction-to-heroin-or-methamphetamine
6. https://news.harvard.edu/gazette/story/2017/04/over-nearly-80-years-harvard-study-has-been-showing-how-to-live-a-healthy-and-happy-life/
   https://www.adultdevelopmentstudy.org/grantandglueckstudy
7. Frankl op. cit., p.145.
8. Klein op. cit., p.161.
9. Fadiman, C. Editor. *The Little, Brown book of anecdotes*. 1985. p.171.
10. Haidt op. cit., p.55-58.
11. Ibid., p.58.
12. https://www.scientificamerican.com/article/the-shared-psychosis-of-donald-trump-and-his-loyal-ists/?fbclid=IwAR01P0oqOuzqiHyQlHfeapGNN7FaS52iD025_FIqCGr-a8rPLiqQ9KH-b5c

Chapter Sixteen We the people

1. Klein op. cit., p.121, ref 27.
2. https://www.tvo.org/transcript/2660348/fareed-zakaria-is-this-the-worst-of-times
3. https://www.youtube.com/watch?v=dTu94t4LmUI starting at 9:50

Chapter Seventeen How we fix this: the man in the mirror

1. Klein op. cit., p.100, ref 29.
2. Ibid., p.96, ref 24.
3. Ibid., p.102.
4. Rees 1997 op. cit., chapter 10.
5. Klein op. cit., p.225.
6. Ibid., p.226, ref 1.
7. Ibid., p.227.
8. Ibid., ref 2.
9. Ibid., p.229.
10. *The Collected Works of Abraham Lincoln Vol 3* Edited by Roy P. Basler. The Abraham Lincoln Association, Springfield, Illinois and New Brunswick, New Jersey: Rutgers University Press. 1953-1955. p36, 1 Oct 1858.
11. https://www.youtube.com/watch?v=hmSinJo-fEo Start @ 1:40.
12. Haidt op. cit., p.101, ref 40.
13. Klein op. cit., p.231, ref 5.
14. Ibid., p.234.
15. Letter to HL Pierce and others, 6 April 1859. P.31. Cited in *Abraham Lincoln: His Speeches and Writings.* Edited by Roy P. Basler. Cleveland Ohio: World Pub. Co. 1946.
16. Klein op. cit., p.234, ref 9.
17. Haidt op. cit., p.344, ref 46.
18. Sykes op. cit., p.227.
19. Klein op cit., p.118.

Chapter Eighteen Truth or consequences

1. Haidt op. cit., p.55.
2. Ibid., p.56, ref45.
3. Ibid., ref 46.
4. Ibid.
5. Ibid., p.86.
6. Ibid., p.88, ref 13.
7. Ibid., p.89, ref 14.
8. Ibid., p.88.
9. Ibid., p.105.
10. Ibid., p.106, refs 54 & 55.
11. https://www.youtube.com/watch?v=y3tt4xi9aiA
12. Klein op. cit., p.191.
13. Speech to Springfield abolitionists, @ 1855. *Recollected Works of Abraham Lincoln.* Compiled & edited by Don E. and Virginia Fehrenbacher. Stanford, California: Stanford University Press. 1996.
14. Klein op. cit., p.259, ref 5.

15. https://www.pewresearch.org/politics/2017/04/14/top-frustrations-with-tax-system-sense-that-corporations-wealthy-dont-pay-fair-share/
16. https://www.nytimes.com/2017/04/14/opinion/filing-taxes-in-japan-is-a-breeze-why-not-here.html
17. https://elizabethwarren.com/plans/ultra-millionaire-tax Ref 38.
18. https://taxfoundation.org/wealth-tax/ Ref 39
19. https://budget.house.gov/publications/report/funding-irs
20. https://academic.oup.com/swr/article-abstract/42/2/73/4956930?redirectedFrom=fulltext
21. Haidt op. cit., p.363: www.civilpolitics.org

INDEX

Made in the USA
Monee, IL
25 July 2023